# THE SPELLCRAFTING COACH
## A Metaphysical Guide to Revamp your Life

B. Melusine Mihaltses, C.L.C., M.M., B.M.

Feminine Divine Works
Schertz, Texas, U.S.A.

ISBN#978-0-9851384-0-0

********

# THE SPELLCRAFTING COACH

## A Metaphysical Guide to Revamp your Life

## B. Melusine Mihaltses

**THE SPELLCRAFTING COACH**
A Metaphysical Guide to Revamp your Life
B. Melusine Mihaltses
ISBN#978-0-9851384-0-0
Feminine Divine Works

# THE SPELLCRAFTING COACH
## A Metaphysical Guide to Revamp your Life
### B. Melusine Mihaltses

ISBN#978-0-9851384-0-0
Publisher: Feminine Divine Works
Schertz, Texas 78154-0114, U.S.A
©B. Melusine Mihaltses
Year: 2014

The Spellcrafting Coach,
A Metaphysical Guide to Revamp your Life
© 2014 by B. Melusine Mihaltses

Published by:
Feminine Divine Works
P.O.Box 114
Schertz, Texas 78154-0114
Femininedivineworks@gmail.com

©B. Melusine Mihaltses  2014
B. Melusine Mihaltses asserts the moral right to be identified as the author of this work.

**Library of Congress Cataloging- in- Publication Data**
Mihaltses, B. Melusine, 1970-
      The Spellcrafting Coach, A Metaphysical Guide to Revamp your Life

     1. Metaphysical 2. Self-Improvement   3.Spirituality  4.Shamanism  5.Magick  I. title

Includes bibliographical references
ISBN: 978-0-9851384-0-0
Library of Congress Control Number: 2014953153

The Spellcrafting Coach, A Metaphysical Guide to Revamp your Life
© 2014 by B. Melusine Mihaltses
All rights reserved. No part of this book may be used, reproduced, nor transmitted in any form or by any means, electronically or mechanically, including photocopying, recording or by any information storage or retrieval system, whatsoever without written permission from Publisher; Feminine Divine Works, except in the case of brief quotations embodied in critical articles and reviews.

Although the author and publisher have made every effort to ensure accuracy and completeness of information contained in this book. We assume no responsibility for errors, inaccuracies, omissions, or any inconsistency herein. Any slights of people, places, or  organizations are Unintentional.

First edition
First printing, 2014
Cover Art: B. Melusine Mihaltses
Text, poetry and photographs all by:  B. Melusine Mihaltses
Interior Illustration and Original Art by: B. Melusine Mihaltses


Printed and bound in the U.S.A.                                                                  LCCN: 2014953153

# Other Books By B. Melusine Mihaltses

\*\*\*\*\*

Feminine Divine Works
Intuitive Oracle,
A Powerful Tool for Daily Insight and Inspiration
978-0-9851384-9-3

\*\*\*

Feminine Divine Works Intuitive 70x Oracle Deck

\*\*\*

Gathering for Goddess,
A Complete Manual for
Priestessing Women's Circles
978-0-9851384-4-8

\*\*\*

Living Goddess Spirituality,
A Feminine Divine Priestessing Handbook
978-0-9851384-7-9

\*\*\*

Goddess Grimoire Journal,
A Collection of
Simple Prose and Spells
978-0-9851384-3-1

*FEMININE DIVINE WORKS,
TEXAS, U.S.A.*

# Dedications

"Love is the Path Back to Self"

To All Who Seek And Walk The Path.....

\*\*\*\*

Dedicated to all beautiful birthed creations
That stem forth from
Our deepest longing to
Transform, enhance and manifest
a better world....

*To My Three Sons, With Love*

# THE SPELLCRAFTING COACH
## A Metaphysical Guide to Revamp your Life
### B. Melusine Mihaltses, C.L.C., M.M., B.M.

**Feminine Divine Works**
**Schertz, Texas, U.S.A.**

ISBN#978-0-9851384-0-0

# PREFACE

Author B. Melusine Mihaltses has created yet another instrumental guidebook, this time for those earnestly seeking to enhance their powers of manifestation. We've all heard of the Law of Attraction and there are numerous books on the market that shed much light on the basic tenets of this tradition. However, this is just one of many self-transformational tools that we can utilize to enrich our spiritual path. There are many Metaphysical tools from various traditions awaiting our deep exploration and this book introduces us to quite a few of them.

***"The Spellcrafting Coach, a Metaphysical Guide to Revamp Your Life***," is a wonderful compilation of Magick and Metaphysical wisdom. It introduces the various ways we can incorporate spell-crafting, magick and various spiritual tenets in our lives in order to create positive, transformational changes. It is a thoughtful compendium of, both modern and indigenous, spiritual customs, early metaphysical wisdom and helpful suggestions, on how to apply esoteric knowledge to our daily spiritual practice. In a very clear concise manner you will appreciate the wisdom and guidance offered within these pages.

In this highly ambitious manual of helpful spiritual traditions the author introduces ancient Metaphysical modalities like; Astrology, Numerology, Planetary days and hours and the important influence of the Moon's phase, on our spell workings. You will find much valuable esoteric knowledge on the Tarot, the meaning of each card and information related to the usage of sigils, amulets and talismans in spiritual practices. There is a plethora of information related to gemstones, sound healing, color magick and chakra work. Throughout the book there are hints of Shamanistic and Native American customs, like animal medicine, the exploration of trance and meditations, tree folklore and the importance of dreams awareness. There is an impressive list of animals offered to the reader for further exploration of animal attributes and their invaluable medicine. Numerous forms of magick are introduced like; Goddess spirituality, Candle magick, Invocations, Spell works, Angel connections, Faeries, Elemental and Sex Magick.

With great respect and reverence, this book explores the bounteous time-honored exercises and spiritual traditions from across the world that we can adopt today and utilize with much success in our own personal lives. The author explores various indigenous cultures and spiritual traditions, like Buddhism and Hinduism, and examines the ways they can positively influence our very own, contemporary way of living. In this book, the author introduces their potential contributions to our modern day spirituality, like the usage of Yoga, Mantras, Singing bowl, Mudras, Mandalas, Yantras, Prayers and Mala beads. As a certified life coach, B. Melusine Mihaltses also appears to introduce secular modern tools of magick like positive affirmations, visualization, dance and the usage of vision boards/soul-collages. This gem of a book essentially helps you awaken to the plethora of spiritual tools from various traditions, from across the globe, to facilitate spiritual growth and knowledge.

In this collection of esoteric tools, **"The Spellcrafting Coach, a Metaphysical Guide to Revamp Your Life,"** explores the art of magick, in all its myriad of beautiful forms and guises. Magick is known as the art of manifesting change in your life by working with both internal and external energies around you and it is one of the foundations for the Law of Attraction to work. It requires you to focus deeply and connect with your true desires, your powerful will, and the energies available to assist you. Any act of will that brings about change in a person's environment or selfhood is essentially classified as magick. It is the art of effecting change, within yourself and in your environment, by will and word, but there are numerous ways one can incorporate this essence in our daily lives, to effect positive changes. For some, this very act is indeed magick, for others, it is never classified or acknowledged as such. Naturally, one can surmise, that the approach to the practice of magick is going to vary from person to person. The premise of this book appears to be to help you, the reader, unearth and explore various ways to revamp your life, with the use of magick and Metaphysical wisdom.

Magick has been elaborately defined by numerous occultist and scholars throughout the ages. In the 1900's, Aleister Crowley is attributed for adding the "K" to the end of the word magic, to distinguish it from a word that had already a negative connotation. The word magic was so often maligned; meaning deception or a slight of hand and clearly, this was not the definition early spiritualist wanted connected with their art form. According to Dion Fortune, *"Magick is the art of changing consciousness at will."* I love best, the definition I found on the website, urban dictionary dotcom;

> *"True Magick is neither illusion, nor make believe,*
> *But an extension of imagination, Emotion and will,*
> *used for the Art of Transformation;*
> *whether material or spiritual..."* <sub>witchypo1975 from the urban dictionaries.com web site</sub>

However you personally define magick, it is my hope that you too will find here, a book that will serve as a stepping stone to kindle your curiosity about spiritual practices available to you. And through this process of Spiritual exploration, with the author, may you too find the inspiration to play, and experiment with various effective Metaphysical tools that can enhance your powers of manifestation and help you transform your life.

# THE SPELLCRAFTING COACH
A Metaphysical Guide to Revamp your Life
B. Melusine Mihaltses, C.L.C., M.M., B.M.

# TABLE OF CONTENTS

| | |
|---|---|
| DEDICATION | 6 |
| PREFACE | 8 |
| INTRODUCTION | 13 |

## I. EXPLORING TOOLS OF MAGICK — 14
1. Spell-Crafting Magick — 15
2. Candle Magick — 22
3. Color Magick — 26
4. Numerology Magick — 32
5. Moon Magick: — 36
6. Astrology Magick — 39
7. Planetary Hours and Days — 45
8. Herb & Flower Magick — 50
   - Poppets & Plackets — 57
   - **Scented Oil**; Aromatherapy — 60
9. Tree Magick — 61
10. Animal Magick — 68
11. Goddess Magick — 106
12. Allies in Magick — 140
    - Ancestors & Spirit Guides — 142
    - Archangels — 144
    - Faeries — 148
    - Elementals — 152
13. Natural Magick — 155

## II. HOLIDAYS & SABBATS — 158
1. Solstice/ Winter-December — 160
2. Imbolc-February — 162
3. Ostara/Spring-March — 164
4. Beltane-May — 166
5. Litha/Summer-June — 168
6. Lammas-August — 170
7. Mabon/ Fall-September — 172
8. Samhain-October — 174

## III. SOUND TOOLS OF MAGICK — 176
1. Magick of Sound — 178
2. The Power of the Word — 178
3. Music's Gift- Channeled Poem — 180
4. Power of Sound Frequencies — 181
5. Sound-Healing — 184
6. The Power of Singing Bowls — 187
7. Affirmations — 191
8. Mantras — 193
9. Prayers Beads — 196
10. Evocation /Drawing Down — 199
11. Channeling — 201
12. Meditations — 203

## IV. TASTE YOUR WORDS/INVOCATIONS — 212
### I. ROMANCE — 213
- Love
- Glamour
- Pleasure
- Fertility

### II. FAMILY — 219
- Clan Blessings
- Children Protection & Blessing
- Ancestral Honoring
- Animal Familiar Blessings

### III. WELLBEING & HEALING — 225
- Wellbeing & Health
- Dieting & Body work

### IV. PROTECTION — 228
- Reversals
- Banishing
- Poppet work
- Endings
- Forgiveness

### V. JOURNEYS — 235
- Travel wish
- Astral
- Shamanic Totem work

### VI. ABUNDANCE — 240
- Abundance
- Prosperity & Success
- Career & Employment Blessings

### VII. STUDIES & CREATIVITY — 245
- Studies
- Creativity
- Psychic Development

## V. VISUAL TOOLS OF MAGICK — 250
1. Talismans & Amulets — 251
2. Sigils & Symbols — 255
3. Vision Boards & Soul Collages — 256
4. Mandalas — 261
5. Yantras, Squares, Tablets — 263
6. Veve — 265
7. Dreams & Communication — 267
8. Oracles & Divination Tools — 276
9. Tarot- Major Arcana's Journey — 277 and Minor Arcana

## VI. PHYSICAL TOOLS OF MAGICK
### OUR ORACLE BODY — 284
1. Yoga — 286
2. Dance — 290
3. Sex Magick — 292
4. Mudras — 296
5. Gemstones — 297
6. Chakras — 310
7. Embodying Spirit — 317

## VII. LAW OF ATTRACTION — 321
1. Basic Tenets, The Vortex and Rampaging; "*what ifs*, Final thoughts…

| | |
|---|---|
| \*\*\*RESOURCES | 328 |
| \*\*\*BIBLIOGRAPHY | 331 |
| \*\*\*AUTHOR INFO | 336 |
| \*\*\*ORDER FORM | 338 |

*Most of the important things in the world
have been accomplished by people who have
kept on trying when there seemed to be no hope at all..."* Dale Carnegie

# INTRODUCTION

***"The Spellcrafting Coach, A Metaphysical Guide to Revamp Your Life,"*** is an extraordinary New Handbook for those seeking to learn and incorporate several effective techniques, from various Spiritual traditions, to enhance your powers of manifestation. This compendium of Metaphysical tools will help you to revamp your life through the use of several different spiritual practices, used by numerous traditions throughout the ages. We explore various ways of spell-crafting; astrology, numerology, candle magick, herbology, the Tarot, Gemstones, Animal magick, Healing Sounds and Mantras, and so much more.

I created this book when I realized I was successfully practicing magick, rituals and spell-crafting for a number of years in my own kind of style. In an effort to grow spiritually and expand my knowledge about esoteric subjects, I have always been very welcoming of information and diligent research. Throughout the years, I found myself slowly gathering and incorporating various traditions, from different cultures, into my own personal eclectic spirituality. What I discovered in the process was that there are many different ways to effect cathartic transformation, healing and magick.

**I define Magick as, the art or science, of effecting changes  
and shifting energies (both internally and externally)  
to desired outcomes, in alignment with our will and vision...**

The more I respectfully opened myself up to learning, the stronger my understanding and powers of manifestations were being enhanced. I found that I was able to shift internal and external energies, trance better and strengthen my concentration abilities. Today, I continue to grow exponentially and avail myself to more knowledge about various Metaphysic modalities, but I try to do this humbly, with much gratitude and reverence for the culture that is enlightening me with its wisdom.

In my work, as a priestess for the Sacred Feminine; coaching, facilitating women's circles and writing extensively about Goddess Spirituality, I was often consulted privately by friends and clients that were seeking deeper insight and advice about Metaphysical matters. They wanted the exact magickal formulary and detailed processes on how to help things come to fruition. My response was always sincerely generous and I was only too happy to share whatever knowledge I could. Even our monthly Goddess Gatherings and path days oftentimes included customized rituals and spell works to enhance our powers of manifestation. Over time, the idea of creating a guidebook with the helpful esoteric information I had garnered over the years, seemed like a logical idea that was very much encouraged by friends and clients.

Behold, this book is a collection of assorted, helpful Metaphysical tools that can be explored deeper at your own pace and, if you feel called, incorporated into your modern day spiritual practices. It is birthed with much love and offered in service to our collective growth as evolving spiritual beings. Blessed be! )o(

# I. EXPLORING TOOLS OF MAGICK

*"There is no absence of anything that you want
but there is a gestation period..."* Abraham Hicks

# 1. SPELL-CRAFTING MAGICK

Magick can be as simple or as elaborate as the witch, priestess, wizard or occultist wishes it to be. It can be as simple as whispering a wish upon the Full Moon, a breeze or upon a dandelion. It can be simply you connecting to your primal self and dancing ecstatically around a fire pit or in the midst of an orgasm. It can be as simple as lighting a candle with great focus and intention or as grand and elaborate, as a ceremonial rite before a bedecked altar, amongst a large group.

Presented in this extraordinary book are some of the most important components of a magick, spell works and traditional tools that if you choose to use, can further enhance your powers of manifestation and your spell workings. This is a self-transformational book, about magick, spell-crafting and all the various tools available to us to help shift our inner and outer lives. It is my intention to give you as much detailed information about manifesting and additional, oftentimes overlooked, facets to consider when crafting spells. It gives me great joy to get a chance to share one of my biggest passions with you and I am honored to be a part of your own journey, as we now embark on co-creation and opening ourselves up to leaning and applying different modalities of magick...let us just dive right in.

---

One of the first things we look at when crafting a spell, is the most essential and it is called, purpose. A concept, an aspect, something, someone, a situation or circumstance is very important to you and it is motivating you to act or at the very least, inspiring the need for some type of action. This now, is the very embryonic stage of a spell; it begins buried within a pulsing heart, with desire; a tiny seed of an idea. In the heart it is born and in the mind it develops and slowly unfolds as you begin to envision how to manifest or create a change.

**Purpose and Clear Intention is one of the most vital components of a Spell:**
Getting clear on your exact goals & purpose is crucial to the success of your spells. If you don't know what you want or you are ambivalent and wishy-washy about your desire, your spell can either run terribly amok or fizzle out. Many times, if we are unsure, confused or highly emotional about something, it can cloud our judgment on the validity of a spell, its execution, and its clear purpose and direction. For example; if we are highly angered, depressed or consumed by negative emotions, it's sometimes hard to clearly see and properly channel our energy for the most beneficial outcome. Being in a negative emotional state might not influence your spell work in the most positive way. You probably don't want to be in a sad, hopeless state of mind when doing a prosperity spell; it just won't turn out so prosperous. Magick and manifestation works on the principle of, *"like attracts like,"* therefore, you want to do some very important preliminary, preparatory energy work, before embarking on that spell. Examining

your emotions, your beliefs and your present state of mind is part of this important first step. I will add however, that powerful emotions like anger and frustration are not to be underestimated. When used correctly, they can be successfully harnessed and channeled towards other types of spells. Anger and frustration can be used to move us into physical action and are great for spells of courage, for example.

The outcome of what we truly want can become positively or negatively altered by our spell workings; depending on the preparatory work and the initial motivating factors. Therefore, once we unearth and state our desire there must be an initial assessment of our inner realm (our beliefs and emotions).

## I. The First Step Is To Get Clear On The Purpose Of The Spell

Step #1. Getting clear and focus in a fast paced world, that is always shifting and changing, offerings a plethora of distractions, might prove tricky. Attaining this clarity, however, is ultimately the secret to quintessentially manifesting our heart's desire. Therefore, it behooves us to consider what can provide us with this much needed clarity and how do we shift our mind to effectively engage in the art of manifestation?

Most of the tools and exercises offered throughout this book aim to positively contribute to your powers of manifestation. Some tools that help in this process are; trance work, prayer or meditation, journaling, nocturnal dream work, visiting with the nature folks through a walk. Sometimes even rampaging, which is talking aloud uncensored solely with self, can deliver quick, positive results. You can even record your ranting and brainstorming for better insight into your psyche. Simple quietude, or what some call mindful prayer, can help. Taking the time to consciously reflect on the situation, can help bring more focus to your intention and allow greater clarity to come in regarding your situation and the best approach for your spell.

## II. Connecting with our Spiritual Allies, Committing To our Work

Step #2. What usually transpires after genuinely going through step number one is that, images and ideas begin to flow and sometimes you will be greatly astounded at what the Universe begins to reveals to you even at this early stage in the process of creating a spell. This is the time when you'll want to make note of any special dreams, any strange coincidences, words or names that keep appearing to you or anything really that appears to be speaking to your higher consciousness. Make note of what is being expressed to you by Spirit now. Any hunches or inspirations resurfacing can be viewed as direct communication from your Spiritual allies.

This would be a perfect time to also look at what Goddesses are endearing you to them and what deity would be most appropriate for the type of spell you are considering. Deities, ancestors, animal totems, faeries, elementals, angels and various spirits can become wonderful important allies to your spell work. And simply by your awareness & willingness to connect with them, your allies will make themselves known. The first thing to do is to consider what deity you feel drawn to, as you go deeper to consider your situation. For example; a court or Justice spell working falls in line with the Greek Goddesses of Justice; Themis, Athena, the Roman

Goddess Justicia or the Egyptian Goddess Ma'at. A Glamour spell or a spell related to Love and Beauty would logically fall under Aphrodite's domain, as well as Erzulie-Freda, Hathor and Isis. A spell working having to do with developing your intuition and psychic powers might benefit from calling upon; Aradia, Inanna or Hekate. A prosperity spell would be greatly enhanced by Goddesses like Hambodia, Gaia, the Hindu Goddess, Lakshmi, or the Roman Goddess Fortuna. A fertility spell can only be blessed even more when Gaia is invoked, or the Mayan Goddess, IxChel. These are just a few, tiny examples of ways our spell working can be enhanced with the input and invocation of our spiritual allies, like Goddesses, and clearly calling upon our ancestors, the elements or angels would be as helpful too. You might be inspired to look up more information on a particular Goddess to learn about, not only how she can empower your spell, but also to learn how she can be an asset to your own spiritual growth at this time. Sometimes, through subtle or very obvious blatant coincidences in your life, Goddesses will make themselves known to you but you need to be open, aware and welcoming of this type of spiritual connection. **Thus, the 2nd step is the importance of alertness and awareness of the different ways Spirit will communicate with you; both before and after a working.**

### III. Prose and Incantations, Your Unique Call and Imprint

*"Your own words are the bricks and mortar of the dreams you want to realize, your words are the greatest power you have. The words you choose and their use establish the life you experience..."* Sonya Choquette.

Step #3. There is an old Occult tradition that suggests the advantage of a repetitive, handcrafted, short rhyming prose or incantation for successful spell rites. It is believed this repetitive chant or incantation will more likely be well received and aided by the Universe, when making our petitions and magickal request. The very act of creating your own incantation has the great power of initiating your spell's success. Quite frankly, this becomes a natural next step in the process and preparation for a spell working rite. You've cleared your mind in the first step, attained a clearer image of what you wish and have solicited the interest and assistant from your guides (deities, animals, ancestors, spirits etc..) The natural progression now is to create a short incantation that you can easily incorporate into your spell. This prose can be as elaborate or as simple as you'd like and you may even chose to simply use a positive affirmation statement. The important thing at this stage is to recognize the great value and power found in your own unique voice. Chapter III and IV in this book explores this invaluable tool and offers helpful suggestions that can be applied to your personal spell rites.

### IV. Surrendering and How To Cap Your Spells

Step #4. Before getting into more precise details on spell-crafting, I also want to talk about how to cap your spell at the end, with your words. Magick and manifesting is abetted best when we visualize its fruition, accept its reality and truly embrace that it is done. Usually at the end of any spell working it is customary to declare, **"it is done"** and traditionally, commonly state, **"Blessed Be"** or **"So mote it be."** Typically, however, I like to add a statement of karmic protection, such as, **"An it harm none, so mote it be..."** or **"I manifest these things or better, so mote it be"** or **"Herein, this spell is complete, I manifest that which is for my** highest good, so mote it be..."or **"This spell bound round and it shall be, these things or better, so mote it be..."** It is only wise to be protect yourself, even from your own strong, passionate will. For we are humans with naturally bias thoughts, beliefs and desires and not always equipped with the capacity to see the full impact of our wish manifested. Let's be honest, we don't always desire the best things for us and sometimes our desire for something or someone could be so strong that it clouds our judgment and brings upon, more harm than good. Adding a simple karmic protective statement will assure that you don't inadvertently, negatively affect anyone's free-will and karma, including your own. It is a statement of trust and surrenderment to Spirit that you invite only the best outcome for your highest good. This is by far one, of the most important components of spell-crafting, because in the end; after all of your preparation, visualization, invocations, passionate will, focus and intention, you will need to simply surrender...surrender to the Universe and trust that all will manifest as it is meant to. Sometimes what we hope for ourselves is smaller than what the Universe has actually planned for us, so you don't want to close off the potential for something greater to come into your life. You might have this great job in mind or a great person that you are just adamant about linking up with but in your stubbornness you might be blinded to some other factors and the Universe might just have something far better in mind for you, that in your humanness, you can't possibly comprehend or even accept just yet. Trust!!! Once your spell is crafted, surrender it to the Universe and put it out of your mind. It is done, deemed as already manifested and there is nothing else to do. That is why most occultists also suggest not talking about your spells, vowing secrecy, while they are in the process of being manifested. You don't want to cast any doubt or dilute your work. Thus, the last step in the process of spell-crafting is quietude, capping the spell, simply trusting and releasing your wish out into the Universe.

## **V. Now for the Knitty-Gritty Details of a Successful Spell**

Step #5. Up till this point, you have created your incantation and now you are ready to do your spell... Aw, but we have only just begun.... The next juicy step awaits us now. Traditional Occultist and those that practice various forms of Magick have always, since the beginning of time, placed emphasis and particular significance to the lunar phases, astrological placements, the season, the time and days of the week and the planetary hours when crafting a spell or Ceremonial Rite. All these intricate consideration guaranteed that a spell or ceremony would be successful and not a complete waste of time, money and energy. They were time proven traditions passed down from generation to generation and thus; the imprint of their power and validity was established long ago, but also here, ancestral sanctions assured and validated the magician in his/her work. A great deal of time and energy is expected in the realization of our most cherished wish and every effort is made to assure its fruition. When you consider how much energy, money and time you would put into a spell now, you would not risk its failure by discounting the importance of the details. Consider a gathering or social party you have wanted to host....you approach this endeavor making every concerted effort to assure its success. Many times the success of such an event is pendent on how much commitment, time and effort, you as a host, have put into your pre-planning and the details of it. The same can be said when preparing for a spell working. When you really think about it, a spell, much like a prayer, is a special intimate gathering between you and the Divine Universal forces. In our highly fast paced modern times, some might not see the value in all the tiny minutiae and preparation for one spell working but I must add that the very arduous, sometimes painstaking process in the preparation, already begins the magick of your spell.

## **VI. Let Us Begin Exploring**

There are numerous types of approaches to spells and documented in numerous ancient manuscripts, Grimoires and treatise throughout history, we are left with a collection of ancient views on ceremonial magick. Studying the works by Cornelius Agrippa, who worte-"*Fourth Book Of Occult Philosophy*," and Francis Barrett, who wrote a Treatise Titled, "*The Magus; The Celestial Intelligencer,*" Macgregors Mathers, who wrote, "*The Sacred Magic Of Abramelin The Mage*" and the most famous one, the Clavicle known as "*The Key of Solomon.*" We have evidence of the many different ways our ancestors practiced magick and ceremonial rites. The more we learn about our ancestor's beliefs, spiritual and Metaphysical practices, the more we can tap into that reservoir of unlimited wisdom about the cosmic laws of the Universe. This ancient knowledge is passed down to us and given new life in our hands and we are then able to add our generational imprint for future generations to come. This book encourages you to explore the many ways of magick and learn from ancient traditions, while co-creating and experimenting with new ones.

## The Ways of Magick

Candle Spells are probably by far, one of the most popular forms of magick. Their value can be seen throughout numerous religious and spiritual traditions. The art of candle magick offers many exciting nuances and possibilities and thus, it requires its own special category. However, there are many other forms of magick to consider like:

- **Witch Bottles to protect your home**. A bottle containing an assortment of items and liquids, charged with a specific intention; like protection of your home. There are many ancient recipes for witch bottles as they have been consistently used throughout the ages. Some require red wine, oils, vinegar or body fluids. It depends on your exact intention but as usual, you are encouraged to be as creative as you'd like with your spell-crafting.
- **Herbal plackets, voodoo dolls and Poppets.** A sewn and hand-crafted form that will contain a collection of charged items and herbs for your specific intention.
- **Cords and Knot spells.** A rope made of any material of your choosing (usually yarn, hemp, satin or cotton) where a number of knots are made as a wish is declared upon it. Typically the lunar charged rope will hold nine knots for nine specific wishes or one wish uttered upon each knot, nine times.
- **Gemstones and wanga bags**. A specially crafted small bag with sacred items you place inside of it, for the manifestation of a specific intention or wish.
- **Creation of talisman and amulets**. See Chapter V for more information
- **Music spells- via singing or chanting your wish.** See Chapter III for more information
- **Tarot Spells, using Tarot card Grids with your Candles.** Using oracle cards or your Tarot deck as a visual aid to lend its energy towards your spell working. You can surround your candles or sit your candle upon a symbolic card. See Chapter V
- **Mini travel altars or shrine boxes.** A small box dedicated and decorated with sacred items that have significant meaning to you and your specific spell.
- **Kitchen Witchery-Magick with our food creations**. Charging your kitchen tools and baking and cooking while holding a specific intention.
- **Hearth and Fire spells like burning a petition.** Writing out your wish or affirmation on a piece of paper and torching it within a hearth fire as you declare it into reality.
- **Air spells**. Releasing your wish to the winds with a wind chime or enchanted grains
- **Earth spells**. Burying your wish upon the land.
- **Water spells**. Dissolving the ink of your written petition upon a designated body of water in nature or a chalice of water.
- **Animal magick**. Incorporating your familiars or totems and their fur, teeth, nails, bones or other items into your spell workings. Exploring our personal connections to specific animals. Welcoming animals and their attributes as sacred teachers and allies to our workings and spiritual path.
- **Creating a soul collage or vision board.** With your wish. See Chapter V
- **Crafting Sigils.** Drawing, painting and designing esoteric symbols like Voodoo Veve, Hindu Yantra or Mandalas. See Chapter V

- **Sympathetic Magick**. Recreating a miniature form of what you wish to attain. *"Like attracts like,"* therefore recreating, in miniature form, a symbol of your spell manifested influences its fruition.

These are just some of the more traditional spells and tools that immediately come to mind for spell-crafting but unquestionably there are numerous other ways to craft a spell and we are only limited by our minds. Dig deeper and do not be afraid to explore and create your own form of special magick. I hope these, at the very least, get you to begin thinking creatively about magick.

# 2. CANDLE MAGICK

## EXPLORING CANDLE MAGICK

There are many Types of Candles, besides Pillar & Glass Pull-Out Candles, that we can use in our spell-crafting.

- **Image Candles and Adam and Eve candles;** (woman/ man) Nude figurine images of wax. Used for love spells, wellbeing and healing spells as well as prosperity works. Used to attract new love.
- **Knob candles/wishing candles-** usually 7 knobs, each one burned daily for anything you wish.
- **Wedded Couples** to bond/intertwined couples, usually burned to unite or separate a couple.
- **Separated Couples Candle-** two people facing opposite direction-burned to separate a couple.
- **Genitals Candles;** (Penis and Yoni) usually burned for healing, fertility, pleasure and sex magick.
- **Skull candles**: traditionally used for ancestral worship & healing spells, also used for intellectual pursuits; helps with addiction or mind controlling works.
- **Devil candle-** if your tradition acknowledges the image of the devil, these candles can be used for exorcisms, hexing and banishing spells.
- **Cat Candles-** Depending on your view of cats. They are perfect for honoring Goddesses like Bast, Freya, Aradia. Great for healing spells for your cat, or to draw in a new familiar. I have seen them being used to end gossip, to reverse your luck as well as for glamour spells.
- **Pyramid Candles-** used in spells related to court or Justice but also perfect for high spiritual request, special rites, psychic and occult studies.
- **Mummy candles-** I have heard of these being used for success. Personally I would use them to bind or put something to rest.
- **Snake candles-** great to bring about change, honor Serpent Deities like, Lilith. These are good for healing and spells of a regenerative nature.
- **Witch Candles-** traditionally used for love spells, I find them good to use for students of the craft and enhancing occult studies.
- **Cross Candles-** if your tradition honors the image of the cross, these candles can be used for Memorial rites, to acquire balance and as altar candles.
- **Glass enclosed 7 day Novena-** the premise is that once lit it will burn, safely for 7 days. These candles can be blessed on the top and the glass can be decorated as well.
- **Votive Candles-** small candles that can be used with travel altars and great to burn daily when time is of concern
- **Double action or reversing candle-** usually two colors, black and another color (red, green or white ) and used to reverse or send back an unwanted energy.

You can inscribe candle with names, initials, zodiac sign, unique sigils, planetary squares, Hindu Yantras and Mandalas, Collages and Vision boards to enhance your spell working. These can help focus and hold your intention while being created and they can be placed under or near your working candles, once lit.

# WORKING WITH CANDLE MAGICK

**PREPARING YOUR CANDLE:** Whether you are making your own candles or preparing store bought Candles, the process is still the same...

    1. First we physically clean them from any actual physical debris. Take a cloth and wipe down any grime or dirt.

    2. Then using the four elements, we psychically clean them from any negative vibration from its previous owners and bless them; using consecrated salt, herbs, incense, and water you begin the blessing process.

    3. Next we carve unto them a pentacle to seal them. We can also carve any other symbols relevant to our spell as we continue to bless them. There are many books out there on the subject of sigils & symbols and their powerful usage in all forms of magick. I highly recommend some further research in this area if you can't intuitively come up with a personal symbol to carve into your candle. Remember you can carve out anything that is personally meaningful to you, even initials work just fine.

4. Next we begin to dress and charge the candle by rubbing our chosen consecrated, scented oil upon the wax, while visualizing the goal and the exact purpose of your candle. Herman Slater instructed his clients to rub from center to the end to banish and rub from end to center to attract and manifest. As you rub the oil concentrate on your wish. I also like to breathe into my working candle and whisper into it, my intended purpose.

5. When your candle is covered in oil, this is a perfect time to dust your carved candle with what I call faerie dust aka some sparkle/glitter. You can also use crushed herbs or special powders related to your specific spell. These will embed themselves into the carved portion of your candle, enhancing its potency. Make note that some suggest feeding your candle daily with iron fillings which are magnetic to help draw in and attract your desire. If you are burning a bit of your candle every day you can smear a bit of Honey offering on its edge as well. Lastly, I would wrap the charged candle in paper or a cloth and put it away until the appropriate planetary day and hour to light it.

6. One final note about preparing your candles; Depending on the type of candle you select to work with, you may place a written petition or a corresponding gemstone or herb or flower inside your candle. If, for example, you are working with a large pillar candle or a pyramid or a skull candle you may dig out a little bit of wax from the bottom, gently creating a small cavern at the base. With this created small opening in your candle you can insert a little piece of paper with your written petition or prayer. It's great in particular for healing candle spells, when we might wish to specify the name of the person the candle is for or the affliction we want to heal. This piece of paper may have also been consecrated and blessed by you with oil and it serves to enhance the magick of your candle even more. Obviously, it depends on how much space your own candle allows and your petition might only be written on a tiny paper but its impact will be of great value to your work. Feel free to experiment with your candle spell workings and intuit what feel best.

*These are home-crafted candles I made with the help of my metal molds, colored crayons and wax paraffin.*

## 3. COLOR MAGICK

## COLOR MAGICK

By far one of the most important and widely accepted components of magick is color. Color carries vibrational energy that communicates both to spirit and to our subconscious mind. Each color not only has a planetary correlation but also a seasonal one as well… for example we can't help but associate green and pastel colors with the spring, while autumn might connote deeper hues like reds and oranges, which reflect the scattered autumnal leaves typically found at this time of year. The season of winter might have us thinking about white, if we live in an area that gets a lot of snow. If you are living close to the land and all appears dead and barren at winter time, you might associate this season with the color black. I will discuss in general, traditional metaphysical views on colors, but ultimately whatever feels right for you will work best.

- **BROWN:** A color associated with the earth, it is often used for spells related to animals or anything related to the land and the earth itself. It can be used for grounding, fidelity, commitment spells and concretizing anything in your life. Sometimes used for prosperity and abundance.

- **RED:** Red is the color often associated with our blood, life, great passion and sexual energy. It is a very Mars like color and correlates to strength, aggression, retribution, war, revenge, conquering, the charioteer's unstoppable ambition, stamina, drive and great energy. Any workings having to do with these themes, along with courage, radiant health and assertion of power, would benefit from the use of the color Red. It is also the color of our blood and carries the potent vibration of vitality and our important life force. I find it interesting that both in China and in India a new bride is traditionally expected to wear red, quite the contrast to the white dress so often donned by brides in the U.S.A.

- **PINK:** The Vibration of the color pink tends to be very soft, subtle, affectionate, bringing harmony, joy and peace and speaks of deep spiritual love and friendship. It is the remover of disruption, melancholy and negativity. It is a color associated with nostalgia and youthful energy and because of its hue can be linked to feminine sensuality. It is often used in love spells where one is seeking their soul-mate.

- **BLUE:** This color is often associated with the serenity, tranquility and Peace. A color well suited for workings to bring blessing in the home or resolve disputes. It is a color associated with the law and constabularies and helps bring about resolutions. It is a color associated with truth, psychic studies, faithfulness and in relationships- fidelity.

- **GREEN:** This color speaks volume on the powers of creation, fertility, artistry, growth and wellbeing. It is a color often associated with the Heart Chakra, Spring season and its powers of fecundity. The maiden is exalted in green and it is a color used for love, beauty, youthfulness, rebirth, abundance and prosperity workings.

- **YELLOW/GOLD:** Considered a Solar color, its vibration speaks of excellent health, cosmic knowledge, fame, recognition, persuasion, success, prosperity, the performing arts, intellectual growth and scholastic pursuits, joy and wellbeing. It also relates to children and their natural enthusiasm and it dispels melancholy and negativity. It provides clarity and insight, illuminating anything hidden. This color is great when one is seeking success or completion in any endeavor.

- **ORANGE:** It is a color associated with our Sacral/second chakra, a color often linked to the sun, Summer time, vitality, good health, concentration, Harvest & attracting attention. It is also a youthful color full of energy and vitality and its vibration exalts the champion, promising success.

- **PURPLE:** This is the color of sovereignty and royalty. It has an unquestionable high vibration and is most effective in protective workings, spiritual growth, priestess initiations, and anything having to do with Spiritual or psychic healing. It is a great color for new undertaking and also, when seeking spiritual strength and power.

- **GREY:** Considered a neutral color in magickal workings, for those who are hesitant to light a black candle, a grey candle can be used in its place. It is a color associated with the Tarot card of Justice and any court dealings and can help neutralize and remove negative influences.

- **SILVER:** Considered the color of the Moon, this is a great candle color to honor the Feminine aspect of the Divine, the Goddess, and anything related to Priestess work. It logically is also a good color for psychic development and intuitive workings.

- **WHITE:** A color often symbolizing newborns, newness, protection, elevated spirits, purity, truth, virginity, angels, ether and the highest virtues. It is a color that can substitute for any other color missing and lends its strong positive peaceful vibration to any spell working.

- **BLACK:** Probably by far, one of the most controversial colors due to its numerous views throughout the ages and its many considerations in various cultures, Black is unquestionably a very powerful color to work with. Black is the absence or the void of any color or some might say, it is the inclusivity of ALL colors, amalgamated together. It is a color linked to the occult, to the unknown, to the shadow, the mysteries, the night and thus, darkness. It is a color that can either lend you anonymity or make you stand out in its overpowering presence. Throughout the ages it has always been linked to witchcraft and magick. Some cultures still view it as a color to use only for black magick or anything related to curses, bindings and banishing. However, it is unquestionably a color of power and one that, quite possible had its early association with women, the Goddess and early Pagan rites. Naturally, as all things initially connected with the Goddess were eventually warped, it would be a color maligned and given a bad rap to discourage it usage. It is however a color used today for endings, releasing anything you wish (whether good or bad) and it can help with healing and restorative spells. Its vibration is also very protective and it can be used to either veil or unveil occult knowledge. This is a color you will personally need to consult with your own inner intuition to decide how to best apply it in your workings.

## **COLOR MEDITATION**

## **OFFERING OUR BODIES COLOR MEDICINE MEDITATION**
    To begin this meditation, I invite you to sit comfortably or lie down and simply rest. Let go of your stressors and feel every cell in your body surrender to this moment in time. Take a breath and allow your body to sink into this moment with each inhalation. Breathe deeply and exhale. Exhale all the stressors from your day or week or even from the last month. Take another nice deep breath, letting your lungs expand fully and allowing your expanded lungs to fully take over the space of your chest cavity and your whole body. Release your breath and with it, release any toxins or negativity. Breathe gently, effortlessly and now exhale. Survey your body at

this moment for any signs of stress or tension as you easily breathe in and out. Continue to breathe as we begin to look more closely, with our inner eye, for any signs of physical tension or stress upon the body.

I invite you to scan and survey your whole body now with your inner eye. We will do this together, more methodically, as we experiment with color energy and its magickal usage. We will place colors to the different parts of our sacred body and offer color medicine to alter and heal those parts that need it most. We begin this meditation by first bringing our attention to the lower part of the body. Let us first examine the part of our body that holds the entire weight of our existence and is responsible for our physical journeys, our **feet**. How do they feel at this very moment? Connect with your feet and toes and scan them for any tension? What color do they exude at this very moment? **See if you can offer your feet a different experience now and change the color. How does that now, make you feel in this feet region? (pause)**

Now we will bring our attention to our **knees.** Consider for a moment how you are often called to utilize your knees in the mundane world. How they bend at our request and support our physical form. How do they feel at this very moment? Can you associate a color to your knees? At this moment are your knees; red, brown white, pink, blue, green, orange or purple? Pick any color that initially comes to mind and do not worry of its accuracy. Trust your instincts and allow yourself to experiment. There is no wrong or right answer here. This is your own personal imagery and everyone will come up with their own personal assessment. **Now take a moment to see if you can alter the color in your knee region and see how it effects your sensation in this area. (pause)**

Next, I invite you to take a deep breath and connect now with your **pelvic region**, your hips. These are your majestic, womanly curves! They rumble and sway and have their own rhythmic dance at various intersections of your daily life. Notice how they feel at this very moment. Is there any tension in this area? What color would you assign to your hip region? Is this a color you feel happy maintaining or would you like to experiment by switching the color? **Take this moment to offer your hips this color therapy. Focus on a color in your pelvic region and make note of how it changes now the sensation in your physical body. (pause)**

Now let us visit with the **belly region**, a consecrated area that is so often neglected and yet so revealing to us as women. Again please make note of how you are physically feeling in this part of your body and please, associate a color with your belly. How does it feel? Can you detect any subtle sensations in this region? Are you holding any tension or are you totally relax in this area around your stomach? **If you care to experiment with this sacred region, ask yourself what color can you offer your belly now to bring further healing to this area? Notice how this color offering changes the sensation of your belly region. (pause)**

Now I invite you to bring your attention to the middle of your chest, your **heart centered area.** Carefully and with reverence come to this region, inspect its present state and quietly search for a color you can link your heart with at this moment. Is it pink, or blue? Is it a fertile green or a dark hue like black? Is it a brilliant orange or a Queenly purple? See the color appear in your heart region and now consider how vastly different it might feel to you if you changed its present color. **Experiment and take this moment now to change the color** association with your heart region. **How does that make you feel? How does this color change alter and heal the physical sensations in this region? (pause)**

Now I invite you to visit with your neck, the **throat area.** Place your attention in this region and make note how your throat physically feels. Is it fatigued or energized? Is it dry and raspy or well hydrated? Take this time to search for a color you would like to assign to this region. Consider how vastly different your throat would feel now if we changed the color association. **If you will, please choose a different color to offer your throat region now and study the effects of this change. How does that make your throat region feel now? (pause)**

We have arrived to the last area of this Color therapy exercise. I invite you now to bring your attention to your **cranium,** your head or crown region. Take this moment to inspect how your head physically feels at this very moment. Is it heavy or lightweight? Is it holding any tension at this moment? Ask yourself what color do you see associated to your head region. Do you see blues, yellows or maybe black? Is it white or red? Or maybe you prefer to detect another fancier color linked with your cranium. Take this time to associate a color with your head region and all its physical attributes connected with this hue. See this color vividly and if you will, offer it now a different color. **What color therapy can you offer your head region now to alter and heal it further? How does that effect the physical sensations around your crown region? (pause)**

We have traveled through seven important regions of our body to offer healing and color energy medicine to these areas. In the future you may wish to experiment further and offer this therapeutic exercise, in color magick, to other parts of your body as you see fit but for now we will end our special journey here. As we began with our breath we end this mediation in the same way by breathing deeply and connecting to our breath. Take a deep breath now and again, exhale. I invite you to scan your body one last time to release any lingering tension. Breathe and with your breath offer yourself infinite healing and continue to breathe in your favorite colors as we transition back to this time and place. Follow my voice as it guides you back to this room. I will count backwards from seven to one and on the count of one, please open your eyes and join us back in this room for a final check-in. ***Seven, six, five…continue to breathe and exhale. Four, three, two, one…Welcome back!

## 4. NUMEROLOGY MAGICK

## NUMEROLOGY

Numerology is a Metaphysical science that uses numbers as a form of Divination and it is considered a tool for better insight into a situation or persona. It places numeric value on everything; including names and words, as each letter corresponds to a number. It is based on the theory that everything in the universe has a vibratory connection to numbers and if we can determine the number or frequency, we can gain invaluable understanding of a situation or a person's destiny, strengths and challenges.

Since the earliest of times, the *science of symbols and numbers*, as an effective tool of magick has been consistently practiced by many. Its origins can be traced back to early Babylonian and Egyptian times but often it is connected to Pythagoras (590 BC). Pythagoras was a beloved, well known Greek philosopher, teacher and mathematician, to name just a few of his significant titles. His contribution to our modern day beliefs on various sciences is still palpable today. He was a teacher and founder of a secret school/society that taught the sciences of Astronomy, Music and Mathematics and related these interconnected forms to vibrational frequencies. He was one of the first to develop numerous theories and principles regarding numbers; connecting them to the early laws of Metaphysics, and he believed that everything in the Universe could be expressed with numbers.

It is not difficult to see the enormous relevance and impact numbers have in our daily existence and the ancients shared in our curiosity about this theme. Influenced by the Hebrews, the Chaldean believed everything in the world had a pulse and vibrational frequency that could be linked back to numbers. Consider for a moment what our world would be without the prevalence of numbers. It is the last thing we might see and the first thing we awaken to; numbers connected to our alarm clocks, our monetary currency, our computers, phones, and now in particular our cell phones, are constant reminders of the importance of numbers. Every item on a store shelf has a numeric value attached to it, not to mention its barcode, and from the day we are first born, a number is attached to our existence, via our social security number and an assigned serial number placed on our Birth certificates. Every single thing in our world is connected with numbers, I need not present every single proof of this, but the powerful frequency associated with numbers and their patterns cannot be overlooked. It is almost impossible to imagine a world without numbers and it goes without saying we are consciously and unconsciously submersed and influenced by its vibration powers.

Every number has a vibrational frequency and they are a symbol of bigger vibrational patterns in our Universe. The next page will briefly introduce the meaning and vibration behind every number. Numerology uses the *"Fadic system,"* known also as *"natural addition,"* in which you must keep adding integers until you narrow it down to a single digit. With the exception of the spiritually high vibrating numbers of 11 and 22, every number should be reduced to a single digit. This final number is thus interpreted, based on its known vibrational frequency. Therefore, there are technically only nine digits that infinitely repeat. We can use this technique for greater insight into the particular vibration of a specific day, our date of birth, an upcoming event, a specific year and even our names. The chart below will help your understanding of how letters correspond to numbers and then how numbers reveal vibrational energy and specific attributes related to a larger cyclical pattern in the cosmos.

To exemplify this best, if you have a first name like Dee and you want to determine the number frequency of this first name only, you would add for example, 4+5+5=14 then 1+4=5. Her first name reveals a number frequency of 5. Typically, when you endeavor to determine the number frequency of your name, you would use your full birth name and add the numbers in the same way the example elucidated. Using the *"Fadic system"* you can also do this for almost anything; a date of birth, a month, year in the past or forthcoming and also if you wish to know the numeric frequency of a particular day.

## PYTHAGOREAN CHART

| 1 | 2 | 3 | 4 | 5 | 6 | 7 | 8 | 9 |
|---|---|---|---|---|---|---|---|---|
| A | B | C | D | E | F | G | H | I |
| J | K | L | M | N | O | P | Q | R |
| S | T | U | V | W | X | Y | Z |   |

It may surprise many of us to know that the term Numerology first appeared in a published book in 1937, long after the initial theories of numbers were first formulated. It is not a term attributed to the great mathematician Pythagoras, but rather to Dr. Julia Stenton. She was the first to coin the term Numerology and defined it, as the science of numbers.

Similar to astrology, Numerology acts as a Metaphysical tool that uses number as the vehicle for deeper understandings of any situation, person's character and temperament and deeper insight into one's destiny. For example if we wish to start a new project and succeed, we might choose a starting date vibrating with the energy of the number one. When we consider a new partner or employee we might add up his/her number to determine compatibility. These are just a few simple ways we can personally use numbers to enhance our Metaphysical lives. Numbers help to reveal the natural patterns and cycles within the Universe, and their effects in our personal lives. When we consider the meaning of each number in relation to a cycle, we can gain deeper understanding of our lives & the patterns that govern them.

## 1 ONE
The number one has the energy of the initiator, beginnings, innovations, new visions and conceptions. There's a strong drive to succeed and lead. The energy of the Sun is often linked with the number one. This number reveals the start of a new cycle and the energy of the leader.

## 2 TWO
Two is the number of partnership; of duality and balance. It is a number closely linked with the energy of the Moon. It is a harmonious number that speaks of relationships and cooperation.

## 3 THREE
Three is a very fertile number, representing growth and expansion. It is the curious explorer seeking advancement and growth. It naturally beholds the energy of the planet of generosity and expansion, Jupiter.

## 4 FOUR
Four is the number of structures and foundation. It is a number that gives life and form to ideas and concepts. It makes tangible, etheric ideas and sculpts them into physical reality. Four is the hard worker and thus it has the energy of Saturn, the task master.

## 5 FIVE
Five is the number of change, chaos and imbalances. It has the energy of the trickster God, Hermes and thus, it is ruled by Mercury. There is uncertainty and flux, which gives birth to change and thus, we have the archetype of the student, who gathers scattered knowledge and eventually fuses it into wisdom.

## 6 SIX
Six is a number of harmony and the peace seeker. It is a number related to re-balancing and re-connections. It also has the energy of beauty and appreciation, thus, not surprising it is traditionally linked with the planet of Love and prosperity, Venus.

## 7 SEVEN
Seven is the number of our spiritual awareness, collective consciousness, and rebelliousness. It sometimes shares similarities with the fluctuating energy of the number five. It can be chaotic because it bring revolutions and awakens us to new growth. It is not surprising to learn this number is traditionally linked to Uranus, the planet of powerful transformations and revolutionary changes on a humanitarian scale. Sometimes related to the planet Neptune, seven helps shift the status quo and brings global awareness.

## 8 EIGHT
Eight is the number of manifestation, power and the entrepreneur. It is linked with the energy of the red planet, Mars, thus it is ambitious by its very nature. It has exceptional organizational skills and seeks to enterprise itself. Fast moving and determined, it creates, invents, executes and exudes power.

## 9 NINE
Nine can often be seen as a number of completions and of endings. It is the realm of the psychic, intuitive Spiritualist and traditionally has been linked with the planet, Neptune. Although we often think of ten as a number of finality, nine is, in reality, the last number before the start of double digits. In traditional numerology, nine is indeed the final number before the cycle of numbers repeats itself again. The number nine can also be seen as a number of transition, as it often leads back to the number 10, which is really the number one in numerology because 10, when converted to a single digit, become one again. Nine is thus a number of completion, wisdom, retrospection, reviews and transitions. In the end, it is also a number related to service and deeper insight. It is not surprising to learn that this number has deep connection to the mystical planet of illusion, Neptune.

## 10 Ten
If we were to really take a look at the number 10, especially in relation to the study of Tarot, it is considered the number of endings and completions. It is also a number related to death, rebirth, regeneration and transformation. In numerology however, ten does not really exist, for if we add these two digits using the *"Fadic system,"* in an effort to narrow it down, we arrive, yet again at the number One. Thus, ten shares the same characteristic of the number one. Here, much like the number nine, we are reborn again and thus, it is not surprising that the planet of rebirth and transformations, Pluto, is associated with the number ten.

## 11 ELEVEN
The number eleven is considered a spiritual number. It is a highly vibrational number often associated with Spirits, Angelic energy and Ascension. It does not need to be narrowed down.

## 22 TWENTY-TWO
The number twenty-two is also a highly vibrational number, often linked to spiritual blessings. It is a number that reflects humanitarian & global matters. It does not need to be narrowed down.

# 5. MOON MAGICK

*"When I admire the wonders of a sunset or the beauty of the moon,
My soul expands in the worship of the creator..."* Mahatma Gandhi

# MOON MAGICK ASTROLOGY
## TIMING YOUR SPELLS: WHEN IS THE BEST TIME TO LIGHT YOUR CANDLES?

*Considering the Moon Phase*
*Full Moon, Waning, Dark of the Moon, New Moon, Waxing*

When the moon is **waxing**, that is, going from New to Full, this is the best time to draw things to you, expand and manifest your wishes. For example, the night before a Full moon is a most powerful time to draw and attract your most precious wish. Prosperity, Luck with a New Job search or even a new Love spell, would benefit greatly from this auspicious time period.

However, when the moon is **waning**, that is, going from Full towards the approaching Dark New Moon, this is the best time to release, surrender and diminish things in your life. For example, a few nights before the New Moon would be an ideal time to release negativity in your life, debt, banishment or even craft a healing spell.

**We Release and Banish with the Waning moon,**
**Begin new Projects upon the New Moon.**

**Work on Manifesting spells upon a waxing moon and**
**celebrate achievements upon a Full Moon. (3day)**

*"...Our great symbol of the Goddess is the moon, whose aspects reflect the Three stages in women's lives and whose cycles of waxing and waning Coincides with woman's menstrual cycles..."* Carol P. Christ

## ASTROLOGICAL ATTRIBUTES OF THE MOON

The moon's presence in an astrological sign can help your spell workings. It changes signs every 2-3 days; therefore it is wise to become familiar with its transit. It also helps to be aware of the larger Astro transits of other planets, like Venus and Mercury.

### 1. ARIES
Moon in Aries is good for new goals, ambitions, has warrior energy, sexually aggressive, protective, energetic, volatile and passionate.

### 2. PISCES
Moon in Pisces is watery, intuitive, psychic, boundless, and conducive for dreaming, wishes, pleasure seeking, music and occult studies.

### 3. TAURUS
Taurus Moon rules Earthly pleasures, sensual delights, determinations, tenacity & growth.

### 4. GEMINI
Gemini Moon rules communications, commerce, skills, intellect, entertainment & fun.

### 5. CANCER
Moon in Cancer rules the Mother, home, domesticity, emotions, lunar energy & water.

### 6. LEO
Leo Moon is showmanship, attraction, sun power, confidence, popularity, beauty & roar.

### 7. VIRGO
Virgo Moon rules over health, wellbeing, fertility, organization, cleaning, growth, details.

### 8. LIBRA
Moon in Libra rules over balance, relationships, partnerships, beauty, harmony & peace.

### 9. SCORPIO
Scorpio Moon rules the occult, spiritual matters, revenge, retribution, sexuality, passion, deaths, esoteric knowledge, transformation, mysteries, drive and desire.

### 10. SAGITTARIUS
Moon in Sagittarius is the Archer, with aim & focus, expansion, social, confidence, jovial, athletic pursuit, the traveler, higher education and the gift of generosity.

### 11. CAPRICORN
Capricorn Moon rules hard work, responsibility, career, commitment, justice, the father, Money-maker, industrious, moral and the law.

### 12. AQUARIUS
This Moon rules change, courage, the radical rebel, innovator, liberator & uniqueness.

# 6. ASTROLOGY MAGICK

## ASTROLOGY

The Metaphysical science of Astrology is the study of the stars, the moon and the planets and their configurations and pertinent influence in our lives. When we are born, there is an encapsulated, frozen picture of the heavens, which reveals the placement of all the stars, moon and planets at the exact moment of our birth. This unique picture of the cosmos at the time of our birth can reveal our inherited strengths, weaknesses and our inevitable destiny but we can extrapolate this type of helpful information for any date we wish to understand further. Some use Astrology as a form of divination and some use it as a form of self-awareness and transformation. No matter how you personally incorporate Astrology, learning as much as we can about this ancient practice, can help us become more aware of the sacred patterns of life and our capacity to utilize the planetary energies to augment our powers of manifestation.

# ASTROLOGY

The dance of the Universe and the consistent journey of each heavenly body has its own distinct energies that can influence our day to day human existence. The study of Astrology can unquestionably heighten our understanding and appreciation of the patterns in our personal lives and those of our loved ones. We gain deeper insight about the supportive or conflicting energies in our auric field and eventually learn to make the best use of this information to enhance our lives. Below is a helpful chart to encapsulate the zodiac and their respective symbols and houses.

| First | The Self | Aries | The Ram | Mars |
|---|---|---|---|---|

**ARIES: Cardinal/Fire/Masculine**
This is the Initiator, the fiery drive of the Go-Getter, the Ambitious one and the fire starter.

| Second | Values, Self-worth | Taurus | The Bull | Venus |
|---|---|---|---|---|

**TAURUS: Fixed/Earth/Feminine**
Stubborn slow bull that delights in the pedantic luxuries of life and prioritizes the senses.

| Third | Communications | Gemini | The Twins | Mercury |
|---|---|---|---|---|

**GEMINI: Mutable/Air/Masculine**
The Communicator, the fast talking, multi-tasker, who is constantly seeking the next best thrill. The Twin with vastly different interest, multiple skills executed at once & multi-talented.

| Fourth | Home & Family | Cancer | The Crab | Moon |
|---|---|---|---|---|

**CANCER: Cardinal/Water/Feminine**
The Moody Crab, emotional, heart-centered. Feeling everything to the tenth degree. Lover of her pets, her home and family. Queen of domesticity and the Divine nurturer.

| Fifth | Pleasure & Inner child | Leo | The Lion | Sun |
|---|---|---|---|---|

**LEO: Fixed/Fire/Masculine**
Lion's roar, always the center of attention, dramatic, commanding admiration & accolades. In touch with the inner-child, exploring her creative gifts & her dramatic flair, primal & energetic.

| Sixth | Routine & Health | Virgo | The Virgin | Mercury |
|---|---|---|---|---|

**VIRGO: Mutable/Earth/Feminine**
The Virgin, highly detailed, knit picking Earth sign, analytically dissecting that which needs to be deeply examined, compartmentalizing with ease, manifest organization. Humanitarian servant.

| Seventh | Relationships | Libra | The Scales | Venus |
|---|---|---|---|---|

**LIBRA: Cardinal/Air/Masculine**
The peace-maker, she who sees all sides to every situation and want to deliver peace and harmony. Compassionate one, typically takes into consideration all parties in every situation in her quest for peace for the greater community.

| Eighth | Others Finances | Scorpio | The Scorpion | Pluto/Mar |

**SCORPIO: Fixed/Water/Feminine**

Scorpio is the deep, esoteric intuitive knowledge, the sign of mysteries, shadows and death. She rules over transformation, regeneration, sex, power and rebirth, delivers an intense message wrapped in sometimes painful crisis and upheavals. Symbol of the phoenix rising and brings about massive transformations. Uncovers secrets & deep exploration of all things taboo. She is not bashful when it comes to entering and exploring the shadows & deep dark abyss of our soul.

| Ninth | Foreign travels & Education | Sagittarius | The Archer | Jupiter |

**SAGITTARIUS: Mutable/Fire/Masculine**

Embodiment of benevolence, generosity and joy. The celestial archer that successfully focuses her will to achieve her aim. She is the philosopher, the writer, the teacher, the maiden celebrating herself. Seeker of higher knowledge, ascension, spirituality and great travel adventures. She is the power of expansion, social graces, proliferation and the enjoyment of the flight of the arrow.

| Tenth | Vocation/Career | Capricorn | The Goat | Saturn |

**CAPRICORN: Cardinal/Earth/Feminine**

This is the image of the old strict Father figure. The dogmatic, rule setting, disciplinarian and goal affirming guru; he carefully and methodically executes plans to fit his bigger picture ideal. This is the stubborn mountain goat, the one who will not let go and will tenaciously hold on to his vision. Living very carefully and methodically, the goat is loving, hardworking and determined to attain some measure of success in the world.

| Eleventh | Friends & Groups | Aquarius | Water Bearer | Uranus |

**AQUARIUS: Fixed/Air/Masculine**

This is the radical rebel. She is the one who considers the world at large and introduces world revolutions and global change. She knows about taking care of herself and her community at large with regards to laws, amendments, leadership and general politics are part of her gifts. She protects and awakens & incites new ways of thinking and being. Behold the Revolutionist soul.

| Twelfth | Solitude, Psychic/Esoteric | Pisces | The Fishes | Neptune |

**PISCES: Mutable/Water/Feminine**

This is the watery realm that knows no boundaries. It melds, and like its element of water, it takes the shape of its container. Intuitive Pisces takes us deep into the murky, vast ocean realm, into a vastly altered world with different requirements of us and a sense of surrendering to spirit with eyes fully shut. It heightens our psychic & intuitive gifts and it also rules our creativity; painting, decorating, designing, dancing, guitar playing, piano, singing… It feels deeply the emotions of others and lives amidst dreams and vapors.

## THE ASTROLOGICAL HOUSES

In Astrology there are twelve houses which are often viewed as individual rooms in a large house. Each room or astrological house has a different hue or personality on its walls. Each house governs a particular area in our lives; like the house of Relationships, 7th house or the house of Communication, in the 3rd or the Career house in the 10th etc... In every respective house we can consider the influence of a planet(s) that visits and transits that house. Learning the corresponding theme of each house helps us understand the Metaphysical science of Astrology better and we begin to understand the natural patterns & transits influencing our day to day activities. We can apply this knowledge to our natal charts to see the influence upon each house.

## THE FIRST HOUSE
First house also known as the ascendant or rising sign. It represents the self, the first impression you make to the outside world. It describes the way you're seen. It is the representation of you and how you appear and present yourself to the world. This is your symbolic front door, it is the picture of who you are and how you present yourself.

## THE SECOND HOUSE
The second house is the house of value, possessions and often connected to our self-worth. It is a money house and unlike the eighth house, it is money that is directly related to you. It shows how you make money and how you value yourself and your possessions.

## THE THIRD HOUSE
The Third house is a house related to communication, your community, and your neighbors. It also reflects your siblings and your day to day short travels. This is the house that represents learning and teaching but on a very day to day, practical level; learning things that are necessary and applicable to your lives. Unlike the corresponding ninth house, where it's more higher education, philosophy, higher spiritual learning, this is more about acquiring skills and learning relate to your vocation. It is also the house of networking and marketing and technological learning such as computers Internet and social media. And it is a house related to our short trips unlike the ninth house which is related to long distant travels. Again it is a house that relates to our neighbors, our siblings and our community.

## THE FOURTH HOUSE
This is the realm of domesticity. It relates to our childhood home, our family, our birth parents and those that nurtured us. It is where we find the place of comfort, our sanctuary and abode. This is the house that also relates to real estate matters, our family home and our physical home.

## THE FIFTH HOUSE
Here is the house of romance, pleasure, creativity, children and our inner child. This is the house that represents your hobbies and your special interest and great passions. It can also relate to gambling and speculations. This is the house of proclivities and it sheds a deeper light into what

brings you joy and how you personally manifest pleasure in your life. It is also related to romance and thus, the process of courtship.

## THE SIXTH HOUSE
This house is often viewed as your day to day routines. It is a house related to your overall health and well-being. It can also relate to your work environment since your work is something that you do every day. Interesting to note the sixth house also relates to our pets and how we tend to them, for this too is something we engage in on a daily basis. The best description of this house is the realm of your daily routine.

## THE SEVENTH HOUSE
This is the house of relationships; marriages, partnerships, including business alliances and partnerships. All types of relationships are represented in this house. It is a house that reflects how we deal with others, how we interact with others. On an astrological chart the seventh house, which deals with relationships, is directly across from the first house, which deals with the self. Therefore the seventh house reflects how the self now interacts and melds with the other. Who are you when you are partnered with someone else? This is revealed in the seventh house.

## THE EIGHTH HOUSE
The eight house is considered a money house, but unlike the second house, which also has to do with money, we now encounter other people's money. This house reflects how we deal with other people's resources. This may include a spouse or a business partner or someone we share resources with. This house also rules over monumental issues related to taboos such as; sex, death, taxes, rebirth, regeneration, endings and transformational changes. It is a house that will reflect how we handle crisis and how we rejuvenate ourselves after a loss or a big change. There are some that also call this the shadow house, revealing those things we are not conscious about. Typically, this is a money house that relates to other people's finances, like our spouses/partners. When we look at an astrological chart, the eighth house is found right across from the second house, which is where we are learning how to handle our own resources, money and self-worth. Here in the eighth house we're learning how to handle other people's resources and how to handle ourselves in connection with other people's money.

## THE NINTH HOUSE
The ninth house, on an astrological chart, can be found right across from the third house, therefore, you will quickly realize the ninth house has to do with communication, Higher education and more expansive travels. This is not the type of local travel that the 3rd house speaks of, but rather it concerns itself with long distant, foreign travels abroad. The ninth house seeks explorations and adventures and wants to expand its knowledge about life and larger philosophical issues. This house also relates to legal matters, advertising, politics and not surprising, publishing. This is the house of higher learning, of acquiring esoteric knowledge, spiritual growth and expansion.

## THE TENTH HOUSE
The tenth house can be found in the placement known as the mid heaven. This is the place reflecting our grand purpose or calling in the world. Most commonly, the 10th house is known as the career house, your vocation and your public persona indicator. It is the house that reflects our reputation and social status and how we exist in the presence of authority figures. On an astrological chart the 10th house is directly across from the fourth house and while we embrace our family life and our cherished sanctuaries in the fourth house, the tenth house leads us into sanctuaries found in our workplace and our careers. This house rules our career and destiny in the work force.

## THE ELEVENTH HOUSE
The eleventh house is the social house. Here is where we find our tribe of true friends, our kindred spirits, peer groups and organizations that reflect us the best. This house reflects how we exist within our chosen groups of kindred folks. This is also the house of your deepest wish, your most cherished aspirations. On the astrological wheel, the 11th house falls directly across the fifth house of pleasure, romance, children and creativity. It is thus not surprising that the 11th house would also carry a similar essence of enjoyment. Our friends and our involvement in groups and organizations oftentimes, bring us pleasure and enjoyment. Thus, this house, across from the creative and pleasurable fifth house, makes perfect sense when we view it in this context. The eleventh house reflects our social involvement with groups, friends and our alliances.

## THE TWELFTH HOUSE
Astrologers hold many different views on the true nature of the Twelfth house and thus, it lives up to its name by being considered the house of mystery. It is the house that reflects the secret side of you, where hidden parts of you are revealed. The twelfth house is often closely linked with fantasy, illusions, hidden enemies, spiritual matters and the occult. It is the house of solitude and inner wisdom. It is the place where we retreat and reflect and examine the you that exists in moments of solitude and retrieval. The twelfth house on the astrological wheel sits across from the sixth house of daily routines. It is a house sometimes connected with hospitals, prisons, asylums, monasteries & places that typically contribute to our Spiritual evolution and growth.

## 7. PLANETARY HOURS AND DAYS

**Planetary Days & Hours:** Ancient Occultist believed every day was ruled by a planet and every hour had a corresponding planetary energy. The first hour of the day began at sunrise and the first hour of night began at sunset and these were particularly powerful times for magick. In the darker winter season there are shorter daylight hours and in the spring your nights or dark hours begin to become shorter. Therefore, hours have various lengths, depending on the season. There are many books on the subject, like the King of Solomon, which sheds light on planetary hours, special formulary for its configuration and easy charts one can attain via the internet. Below is a simple chart that may prove helpful as you begin your exploration of this deeply insightful subject. You will find this ancient Metaphysical knowledge can greatly enhance your spell-workings and powers of manifestation in remarkable ways. *(See References on page 330 for The Planetary chart)*

**PLANETARY DAYS & HOURS:** These are based on an ancient astrological system and the use of the Chaldean order to divide time. Your daily planetary hours can be easily attained through a google search and you'll also want to know the exact time of sunrise, which begins the planetary hour of the day. This information can be used to better plan your spell-workings and even to set up special dates.

| Day & Planet it Rules | Zodiac Influence | Corresponding Colors |
|---|---|---|
| **MONDAY/MOON** | Ruled by Cancer | Silver, Grey, White |

*Feminine, emotions, water, occult, mysteries, intuition, the mother.

| | | |
|---|---|---|
| **TUESDAY/MARS** | Ruled by Aries | Red |

*Energy, passion, sex, aggression, retribution, revenge, competition, stamina, determination.

| | | |
|---|---|---|
| **WEDNESDAY/MERCURY** | Ruled by Gemini and Virgo | Yellow |

*Studies, intellectual & scholastic pursuits, communications, short travel, siblings, neighbors, science and education.

| | | |
|---|---|---|
| **THURSDAY/JUPITER** | Ruled by Sagittarius | Blue |

*Benevolence, charity, generosity, increase, growth, expansion, education, abundance, foreign travel, good luck, socializing.

| | | |
|---|---|---|
| **FRIDAY/VENUS** | Ruled by Libra | Green/Pink |

*Love, beauty, attraction, glamour, enchantment, luxury, prosperity, pleasure, creativity.

| | | |
|---|---|---|
| **SATURDAY/SATURN** | Ruled by Capricorn | Purple |

*Discipline, karma, the elder, authority, father, contracts, institutions.

| | | |
|---|---|---|
| **SUNDAY/SUN** | Ruled by Leo | Gold, Yellow |

*Success, completion, exposure, recognition, happiness, accomplishment, health, happiness, wellbeing, leadership.

# THE PLANETS

Every known planet in our Solar System has a list of attributes; both positive and negative influences to our astrological charts. Depending on their placement in our Natal (birth) charts, planets can reveal a great deal about our personality, challenges, strengths and our life's journey. Unequivocally, they can also shed insight into the influence of astrological transits occurring more frequently in our present, day to day lives. We have all heard of the dreaded influence of Mercury going retrograde (backwards), which is **only** the appearance of the planet going backwards from our Earth's vantage point. As the exalted planet of communication and short distant travels, when Mercury goes retrograde (usually for 3 weeks, several times a year) it is reputed to turn our world topsy-turvy with miscommunications, snafus and delays. Often, astrologers will discourage any signing of important documents or embarking on any important voyages in anticipation of annoying obstructions. The direct transit and placement of the planet Venus, on the contrary, makes us aware of where the planet of love and prosperity is shining her enchanting gifts. While knowing the placement of the planet of aggression and energy, Mars, can reveal where we might need to temper our impulses or channel them to best suit our personal lives. Having this information surely can help us avert potential problems or at the very least, make us conscientious and aware of the energies that are available to us, if we choose to use them. Our understanding of Astrology is enhanced when we learn the significance of each planet and closely observe its various transits throughout the year. Their distinct characteristics and influences, once learned, becomes palpable and an invaluable tool in our lives.

## **SUN**

The Sun, ever brilliant; our source of life and vitality, is one of the most important orbs in our lives. It is soo essential for us as a species, that it is the center of our Solar System. The very name of our Solar System reflects the importance of this orb. All other orbs and planets surround the sun; exalts it really, as they partake in this infinite dance, around it. We fail to thrive without the presence of the sun and life cannot exist. It is thus, associated with wellbeing, happiness, growth, children and energy. As a powerful symbol of vitality and our life-force, the sun, represents, "The Self," in astrology. It is a representation of our true identity and how we exist in the world at large. When light is cast and all is visible, what do we see? This is the physical area of your life, where you are truly seen and exposed. The Sun reflects your outer being. Considered a masculine-like energy, it also represents the Father aspect. It is the mask you wear for the world to see, to identify you.

## **MOON**

The Moon is our inner compass and speaks of our private self. That brilliant orb that hangs in the night sky, with its unique 28 day cycle, whose beauty has been venerated since the beginning of time, is our Moon. She is the Sacred Feminine, the Mother aspect, connected with nurturance and inner guidance. She reflects how we nurture ourselves and others. The moon is simply feeling based, it waxes and wanes, much like the ocean's ebb and flow. This is the realm of emotions, ever flowing mysteriously to and from. The Moon seems most content in the darken night sky. Make note, it is only in darkness that she appears. In astrology, this is where we too make ourselves known in dark, private realms. This is our concealed inner self. It is where we feel safe enough to let out another aspect of ourselves. As a caretaker of the self, the moon is involved with what we do to make ourselves feel safe. It is solely related to how you feel and how you exist in the night sky. It is entwined with "Her" watery, intuitive, psychic realm and thus, it also reveals how connected we are to this illusive source.  The Moon is where we use our senses and hunches to walk our path.  Here, when no one is watching, is where we reveal who we truly are and where we soothe ourselves. This is where we form our inner light for guidance.

## MERCURY

Mercury is named after the trickster Greek God of Science and Knowledge, also known as Hermes, in Roman Mythology.  The planet shares many of his known attributes, as an intriguing important figure in mythology. When we look closely at the God Hermes/Mercury, we begin to better understand the qualities of the planet Mercury.  In Greek mythology, Mercury was the lightning speed messenger of the Gods and thus, had to travel a great deal to perform this task. He was also known as the trickster God, who delighted in creating a bit of intrigue and chaos to any situation. Known as the God of Science, one can only surmise the importance of studies, new discoveries, language and knowledge. It is not surprising the planet Mercury, in astrology, is considered the communication planet. This is where we attain and process information and rules over all forms of personal expression. Mercury thus reflects how we speak, write and convey our thoughts. It shows how we explore languages and how we gain knowledge and mentally process it.  It would come as no surprise that it rules over education and the manner in which we learn best. This is where we also network and connect with our immediate environment; our neighbors and also our siblings.  These days, it would likewise include how we interact with the internet (a global network) and our social media environment.  Known as the Merchant, Mercury also reflects where our marketing, inner salesmen and entrepreneur spirit, flourishes. He's got the gift of gab and is able to charm you with his words and persuade you to believe and buy almost anything. This is the planetary influence of Mercury.  Lastly, we cannot forget, Mercury rules over short distant travels, the type possibly related to our daily commute to our workplace.  This is the area in our lives where we are traveling, learning, communicating and interacting with our immediate environment.

## VENUS

The planet Venus is named after the Roman Goddess of Love and Beauty, also known as Aphrodite, in Greek Mythology.   Its energy is deeply intertwined with the attributes of this beloved ancient Goddess. In mythology, Aphrodite and Venus were known as the Goddesses of beauty, attraction, romance and love.  Being such a widely known and desired state of existence, the Goddess of Love is universally understood and embraced by all. Her gifts are apparent in the planetary influence of Venus. In astrology, Venus rules over our social interactions with others. It can reveal how we express and receive affection and love. It speaks of what we value and what we are most attracted to. Venus points to our self-love, love for others and our physical beauty as well. It is the realm of attraction but also the realm of prosperity, joy and wellbeing, for all is made perfect and right in her Venusian light. She brings abundance, prosperity and our heart's deepest desire. Wherever your Venus is placed, reveals how you love, what you value, and how you express yourself creatively.

## MARS

The red planet Mars, has garnered a reputation for being aggressive, fierce, loud, impulsive, determined and sometimes volatile. It is also associated with great passion and sexual voracity. While, at face value, its energy can be frightful and intimidating to some, to others it can be just what the Doctor ordered. Mar's deep expressive fires can bring healing and melt the cold, frigid soul. Mars can lend itself to be quite necessary in the lives of those that seek courage, energy and direction. And while Mars is often associated with the masculine, men are not the only ones that can benefit from working with this energy. Women can explore their inner male with the help of Mars and bring much needed healing to themselves and their relationships. It can help bring balance between the genders and a restoring and awakening to our inner strengths. I must admit, if you are already well gifted in the art of expressing your anger, speaking your mind and getting things done, then perhaps you'll never feel the need to work with this energy. But to the shy and unmotivated; the energy of Mars can be an invaluable gift that opens up a whole new way of existing in the world. Mars gets us motivated and sparks our internal fires. It moves us to action and helps us put aside fears of the *"what ifs."* It thrives on just moving, executing and getting things done. Mars does not care about right or wrong, nor sentimentalities entangled with things. It simply wants to fulfill itself, conquer and feel its bulging, sweaty muscles at work. Yes, the energy of the planet Mars can get you into some hot waters but it can also provide just the right momentum to get you moving into the right direction. In astrology, wherever your Mars is, reflect your place of aggression, ambition and sexual appetite.

## JUPITER

The planet Jupiter is one of the most beneficent planets in the zodiac. Considered the planet of expansion and generosity, its energy is jovial, magnetic and gregarious all at once. It is bigger than life, expressing infinite joy, deriving great pleasure in its ability to expand and multiply itself. Jupiter is also known as the higher expression of Venus and therefore it shares in its gifts of beauty and great abundance. Whatever it touched, it expands voluminously and after familiarizing yourself with this great energy you will quickly learn, both the joys and dangers in this gift. Jupiter is a wonderful energy to work with when we are seeking prosperity but much care needs to be asserted when inviting its energy. It is expansive and will only amplify what is already present. Therefore, make sure your wallets have some currency before calling in Jupiter's assistance. You may also want to be extra careful not to invoke her blessing on your physical body, less your waist lines may see an unwelcomed expansion as well. Wherever Jupiter sits in your astrological chart points to the need to always grow, learn and expand. It reveals where you are prosperous, lucky and divinely blessed.

## SATURN

The planet Saturn often gets a bad reputation. Considered patriarchal, strict dominant, authoritative, and demanding; it is the planet that sets the rules in your life. It is often associated with the father archetype in astrology but I know a few mothers that can easily fall under this description as well. It is not that Saturn is all that bad. It is just that Saturn, much like many parents, sees, demands and expects the best from us. We can either struggle with its cautious, limiting energy or learn to harness it to make our life lessons more palatable. It's not an easy task at hand but with Saturn you could not expect anything less. You try your very best, stay diligent and become highly aware of karma and your responsibilities in this life time. Personally, I have learned to appreciate this energy, as it can help you overcome self-limiting thoughts, patterns and unconscious habits, to reach liberating, newer levels of existence. Wherever Saturn sits in your astrological chart you will feel restricted and overworked. But you will also eventually understand where Saturn is trying to elevate, train and sculpt you, all in its pious effort to help you grow up and transform.

## URANUS
The planet Uranus is the humanitarian rebel that seeks to shock, shift, and change status quo, by igniting certain volcanoes along the way. It relishes in the upheaval and knows that scabbed skin (once removed and done with) can bring about cathartic, effective changes. It is unconventional and unique in its energy and needs to be free. Wherever it sits in your astrological chart, it wants to shake things up and liberate itself from societal and self-imposed penitentiaries. Uranus seeks to emancipate us from that which is not in alignment with our highest humanitarian good. It wants to free us from tyranny and oppression, both inner and outer, and will go to great lengths to emancipate us for our highest good.   Uranus brings transformation, sometimes through painful severing and monumental unexpected changes.

## NEPTUNE
The planet Neptune represents the amorphous, encompassing powers of the ocean and its deep connection to mysticism. It is an energy often associated with illusion, fantasy and getting lost in the deep cavernous labyrinth of the soul.  It is compassionate, spiritual, and nebulous at times; and it is challenged by boundaries. It has the ability to empathize and lose itself, while feeling the weight of the world and its emotions. Wherever Neptune's influence is felt, we need to be careful to cultivate our gifts and use them balanced and wisely, without misplacing our true authentic self.

## PLUTO
The now dwarf planet, Pluto, rules over Hades realm, the underworld. And thus, it rules over the intense themes of death, sex, rebirth and transformation.  All that is hidden in our subconscious, all that is percolating in darkness, under the surface, is the planetary influence of the distant planet, Pluto. Ironically, for such a seemingly small, dwarf planet, it packs a big, powerful punch, when we feel its influences in our respective natal chart. Wherever Pluto sits in your astrological chart it wants to transform through the experience of death and rebirth.

## 8. HERBS & FLOWERS

Every Herb has a corresponding planetary influence and can be made into special infusions, teas and elixirs for your intended purpose. They can be charged under the light of the Full Moon and petition for specific needs. We can also include them in our herbal plackets, dream pillows, poppets, bath rituals and sachets. We can also use herbs to make anointing oils for ourselves or for our working spell candles, to help charge and bless them.

# HERB MAGICK

**ALLSPICE-Mars**
To attract healing, money luck and friendships.

**ALOE-Moon**
Protection and healing. Keep as a plant in the house to repel evil according to folklore.

**ANGELICA-Sun**
Protection, purification, Biblical, healing exorcism, removes curses.

**ASAFOETIDA-Mars**
For exorcism and protection. Warning it has a putrid smell but burning small amounts helps repel negative entities.

**ANISE-Jupiter**
Protection, Purification, Repels negativity Averts the evil eye.

**ASH-Sun**
Wellbeing, Love & Prosperity. For Love carry the leaves. Place under your pillow for Prophetic dreams.

**BALM OF GILEAD-Venus**
Heal a Broken Heart and help attract new love.

**BARLEY-Venus**
Love & protection herb. When scattered on floor, it helps keep negativity away.

**BASIL-Mars**
For Love, wealth and friendships. Blesses New Homes. Rubbed on the body to attract love with its scent. For Businesses, used to attract customers when carried in the pocket.

**BAY LEAF-Sun**
For Psychic powers, protection and manifestations. Traditionally you can write your wish on a bay leaf and burn it to make it come true.

**BLACK/BLUE COHOSH-Moon**
For strength and protection against evil and jinxes. Also known as Black snake root. Known as Papoose root to Native Americans.

**CARAWAY SEEDS-Mercury**
Placed in love charms to attract a partner and keep your mate faithful. It can also strengthen memory and protect children from illness.

**CARNATION-Sun**
For healing, protection and an herb for strengthening. Often you find carnations are the preferred flowers in hospitals and cemeteries.

**CHAMOMILE-Sun**
Prosperity, love, restful sleep & dreams. Sedative. Drinking the herbal tea is reputed to help calm nerves.

**CINNAMON-Sun**
Prosperity, ambition, incite passion, spirituality, success, love and psychic development.

**CLOVE-Jupiter**
For wealth, love, friendship and to raise spiritual vibration. When burned as an incense it cleanses and removes negativity. Also burned to halt gossip. A scent often smelled during Yule.

### COPAL-Sun
Traditionally for purification and love.

### CYCLAMEN-Venus
For happiness and love. Used to awaken lust and encourage fertility. Keep a plant of Cyclamen by your bedside for additional blessings and protection.

### DAMIANA-Mars
For lust, passion, vision and sexual awakenings. It is ingested as an aphrodisiac.

### DEER TONGUE- Mars
Also known as Vanilla leaf/Wild Vanilla it is used for eloquence in speech, love spells to attract men, psychic powers and extra help with the judicial system.

### FRANKINCENSE-Sun
An herb of purification, consecration, spirituality and protection, it is mentioned in the Bible and numerous other sacred scriptures from other cultures. It is used as a powerful purifier to remove evil and negativity and raise the vibration of a space. It is also burned to induce visions.

### GALANGAL-Mars
Protection & purification, assist in psychic development. Worn or carried on the physical body to protect and draw in good fortune. The root is made into a powder to burn for clearing jinxes, hex-breaking and removal of negativity. It can also stir lust and passion.

### GARDENIA-Moon
For Beauty, Love, Healing. It helps to induce a more peaceful, harmonious environment when it's scattered across a room. A blossom of these flowers helps heal the sick.

### GARLIC-Mars
Protection, healing, exorcism, and repelling negative entities. Sacred to the Goddess of the crossroad, Hekate. It is used in offerings to the beloved crone. When digested, it can induce lust. Homes and businesses are often protected and blessed by a string of garlic bulbs near the entrance. It is reputed to absorbs diseases when left in a room where the sick are.

### GINGER-Mars
Money, Prosperity, ambition, passion, Love and power. Whole ginger roots are often used in Money attraction plackets and they can be blessed as effigy & poppets due to their shape. When made into a powder you can sprinkle and consecrate your wallet and checkbooks to bring in more money.

### HIGH JOHN CONQUEROR-Mars
An herb for success, happiness, prosperity, it is known to protect against all hexes or negativity. It has a longstanding tradition of being a powerful tool of magick. You can include it in your sachet or herbal plackets. You can also create special anointing oil with it, by leaving it to soak for weeks in mineral, olive or vegetable oil. It is a very auspicious herb to work with.

### HONEYSUCKLE-Jupiter
Psychic powers, protection, love and wealth. Candles can be anointed by

rubbing these flowers on the wax before lighting with your spiritual requests.

## HYSSOP-Jupiter

For purification & blessings. It is mention in early scriptures. Since early times, Hyssop has been known as a traditional purifying herb to purge the space of any negativity or evil entities. It is reputed to elevate the vibrations of any space where it is used, either as burnt incense or as a spray infusion.

## IVY-Saturn

For luck, love and fidelity. Ivy is a traditional herb for Brides to carry in their wedding bouquet. It can be used for a number of working to promote fidelity.

## JASMINE- Moon

For beauty, money, love and romance. An herb sacred to the Hindu matriarchal Goddess, Saraswati, it bring all types of blessings and good fortune to those who carry this herb. It is reputed to help in attracting a powerful, spiritual love, when included in love workings. The scent can induce prophetic dreams.

## LAVENDAR-Mercury

Chastity, longevity and peace. Lavendar is also known to calm nerves and induce peaceful, deep sleep. It dispels depression and is used for protection, purifications and Love spells. It attracts assistance and blessings from the faerie's realm.

## LICORICE STICKS-Venus

Commanding rites and used for love spells

## MANDRAKE-Mercury

Love, Fertility, Prosperity, Protection, Health and all forms of Manifestations

## MARIGOLD-Sun

Protection, wealth, psychic development and helps with any legal issues. A bath made of marigold is reputed to help raise your popularity and win respect and admiration from those you encounter. It blesses any court dealings and it helps stop negativity from rooting itself in your home, by stringing a garland at the entrance of your home.

## MINT- Mercury

Prosperity, travels, healing and protection. To invite more abundance in your life rub your wallet with this herb.

## MISTLETOE- Sun

Protection, healing, love, fertility, exorcism. This herb was highly revered by the druids and there are countless of documented ways they incorporated its magickal use. It is carried for good luck and worn for protection. Of course, everyone knows of the widely practiced tradition of kissing whoever you meet under the mistletoe during the holidays for extra good luck.

## MUGWORT-Venus

Strength, scrying and psychic powers with this herb. Mugwort is sacred to the Greek Goddess, Artemis, it is used to heighten psychic abilities. You may sleep with it under your pillow for prophetic dreams or to help with astral travels. You can make an infusion of it to trance and awaken psychic abilities. It is also reputed to help with menses.

**MUSTARD SEED-Mars**
Fertility, protection and it is known to awaken mental capacity. Women ingested it to help with fertility.

**MYRRH-Moon**
Purification, protection, healing and repelling negativity. Usually it is burned in conjunction with another sacred herb, like Frankincense or Sandalwood. It is often used to purge, cleanse and consecrate places, ritual tools, objects and altars. It is also an effective trance inducer when burned as incense. It raises the spiritual vibration of any room where it is used.

**Nettle-Mars**
Protection, healing, lust, purification. Often used to remove curses and to keep evil away. It is sprinkled around the home or business to cleanse it of any negativity. It is also used for purification baths by Shamans. It can help restore health to your hair and when used as an infusion, it can also be made to induce lust.

**ONION-Mars**
Protection, healing, absorb illness and repel negativity. Placed under your pillow for prophetic dreams.

**ORANGE BLOSSOM-Sun**
For Love, Beauty, Marriage Commitment, Divination, Luck, Harmony, Prosperity. Traditionally added to Love sachets and wedding bouquets. The blossoms added to a bath water can make one more attractive. They can also be used in a prosperity spells or added to incense.

**ROSES-Venus**
Traditionally related to Love, beauty, divination, luck, good fortune and protection. Since ancient times, Roses have long been linked with all things connected to love and romance. Priestesses and women would bathe in rose water to induce love and their own powers of attraction. Altars dedicated to the Goddesses of love were, and still are, often bedecked with roses as offerings to the Goddess. Roses are one of the most beautiful symbols of the Sacred Feminine. It is clear to see the connection between roses and any desire for beauty and romance. A tea made of rose buds has the ability to induce prophetic dreams about our future spouse and rose petals are often used in love poppets, sachets and herbal plackets. It is also believed that a bouquet of roses or rose petals scattered across a room has the ability to shift the vibration of that room and call in the blessings of the faeries.

**ROSEMARY-Sun**
An herb for purification, healing, mental powers and protection, it is one of the oldest herbs used in purification rites. Kept under your pillow, it protects you as you sleep. It helps with remembrance and can be used in an infusion or a bath. It reputed to attract elves and assistance from faeries. It is known to stimulate the mind and improve our memory.

## RUE- Mars

Consecration, healing, love, mental powers, exorcism and blessing. Rue has long been reputed as an overall effective herb of purification. It helps one repel negativity and the evil eye. The leaves placed on the body can help with ailments. A special bath of Rue cleanses and purifies one from hexes. Add to healing poppets to promote better health.

## SAGE- Jupiter

Purification, consecrations, protection, wisdom herb. Wearing sage averts the evil eye and repels negativity. Sage is also carried to attain wisdom and it can be used for prosperity and healing spells.

## SANDALWOOD-Moon

Purification and consecrations. It has been used since ancient time to purify and consecrate, it is made into a powder and scattered across a space to clear it of any negativity. It becomes even more potent as an incense, when combined with frankincense. This herb is reputed to help conjure spirits and elevate the vibration in a room.

## SARSAPARILLA-Jupiter

Love and prosperity blessings. Combining it with sandalwood powder and cinnamon, it can be sprinkled around a business or home to promote abundance and prosperity. It can also be used in love plackets and puppets

## SLIPPERY ELM-Saturn

Halts Gossip. Used as an incense or in an herbal poppet, it can help dispel rumors gossip and improve reputation.

## TOBACCO-Mars

Used for healing, purification rites, ancestral & spirit offerings. For Native Americans and numerous other indigenous cultures, the tobacco has long been considered and used in sacred rites. It is used in Voodoo, Santeria and Hoodoo rites and it is presented as offerings to spirits, ancestors, deities and orishas. Shamans in training are expected to drink an infusion to induced trance and visions, as part of their training. Tobacco is burned or sprayed as an infusion to purify the space of any negativity.

## VALERIAN-Venus

For Love, purification, protection and to induce sleep. Valerian root can be added to love spells or protective plackets. It is reputed to bring peace and harmony to a home and calm an argumentative couple. Placed under the pillow it helps induce peaceful sleep.

## VERVAIN-Venus

Healing, love, protection, purification, youthfulness, consecration, prosperity, harmony, peace, these are just some of the many attributes this sacred herb can assist us with. Vervain has many known magickal usages throughout the ages. It is used for love and beauty spells. Worn close to the skin, it is believed to keep your skin looking youthful and beautiful. For craftsman and wizards, it was an important protective herb to have on hand when involved in magick or ceremonial rites. In ancient Rome, Vervain was used to purify altars. It is known to banish negativity. It is also an herb used in money spells but also to bring peace and harmony to a home. As you can tell by now, this herb has a multitude of important usage and becomes an almost vital component to a magician's tool box.

## **WOLF'S BANE- Saturn**
Protection, exorcism, courage. It has a very strong, putrid scent and it is indeed known to be poisonous but it is most effective for protection rights and invisibility workings. It can also be incorporated to works requiring courage or other desired characteristic of the sacred Wolf.

## **YARROW-Venus**
For Love, Protection, courage and psychic development. Yarrow protects the wearer and blesses them with love, courage and prosperity. It helps to attract friends and is reputed to elevate one's popularity. A tea infusion can be made to induce psychic powers. Yarrow is also used to exorcise evil and any negative entities from a space.

## **Poppets**

The word poppet is linked to the word puppet and comes from the Middle English word, poppet. Its meaning is connected to a child or a small doll and also used by the British as a term of endearment for young girls. It is similar to voodoo doll, as it is a tool of magick and healing. Shaped and sewn into the likes of a human being, it is blessed, consecrated and named after the person it is meant for and typically it is filled with herbs. It may also be filled with other personal objects related to the nature of the working. It is based on Sympathetic Magick and whatever is done to the doll will be, essentially, done unto the person the doll represents. Poppets are an excellent tool for self-healing and personal self-work.

## POPPETS

Poppets are a type of effigy that can be made of any material. Typically they are made of felt fabric and stuffed with consecrated herbs and flowers but in earlier times they have been made of wax, clay, potatoes, roots, paper, corn and tree branches.

**HERBAL PLACKETS** are similar to a poppet, it is a pouch made of a material like felt and it is stuffed with special consecrated herbs that correspond to your desire.

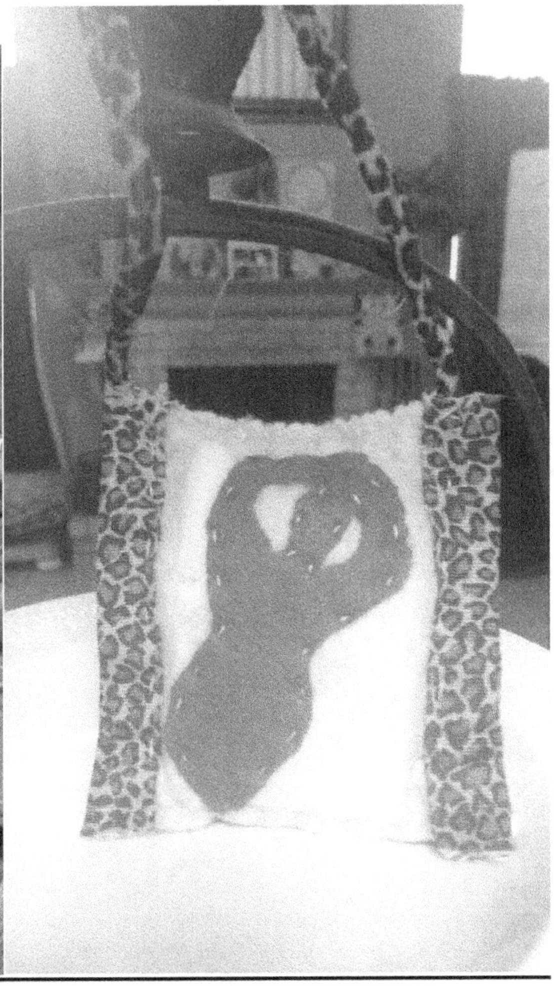

*Tools of Magick: Herbal plackets, Poppets and Witch Bottles*

**WITCH BOTTLES** *are typically made to protect your property. They are created with different consecrated herbs, wine or vinegar (sometimes urine), shattered mirror pieces, thorns, pins and rusted nails. They can include an assortment of objects and throughout the ages there have been many varying recipes for their creations. Once made, they are buried near your home for protection.*

# AROMATHERAPY & OIL RECIPES TO EXPLORE

## SEXY HATHOR LOVE OIL
Gardenia Oil
Jasmine Oil
Rose Oil
Orange Oil
Cinnamon Oil

## AMBITION & FOCUS OIL
Pennyroyal (minty) Oil
Sandalwood Oil
Vanilla Oil
Lavendar Oil
Lilac Oil
Pinch of Cinnamon

## GET IT DONE/COURAGE OIL
Rosemary Oil
Lotus Oil
Lily Oil
Lilac Oil
Hyancinth oil
Tangerine Oil
A pinch of Frankincense powder

## HEKATE OIL
Pine needle Oil
Myrrh Oil
Patchouli Oil
Patchouli herbs
Nutmeg Oil
Garlic herb powder
Vervain herbs

## ENCHANTRESS OIL
Gardenia Oil
Coconut Oil
Lemon grass Oil
Ylang-Ylang Oil

## SABBAT OIL
Lavender Oil
Jasmine Oil
Cinnamon Oil
Hyancinth Oil
Lilac Oil

## MAIDEN GIFTS DEDICATION OIL
Honeysuckle Oil
Lotus Oil
Hyacinth Oil
Cinnamon Oil
Gardenia Blossom Oil
Damiana Leaves
White/Silver sparkles

## DWELLING BLESSING
Carnation oil
Hyssop oil
Rosemary Oil
Pennyroyal oil
Black Cohosh herb

## POSITIVITY & GRATITUDE
Jasmine Oil
Cinnamon Oil
Patchouli Oil
Yarrow herbs
Sparkle, a pearl, Peach coloring

## SHIELD & PROTECT ME
Rosemary Oil
Myrrh Oil
Hyssop Oil
Sandalwood Oil
Vanilla Oil
Patchouli Oil

## TRUTH REVEALER
Myrrh Oil
Lilac Oil
Hyssop Oil

## CLARITY (dispel confusion)
Myrrh Oil
Lilac Oil
Cinnamon Oil
Tangerine Oil
Clove powder
Frankincense Granules
Blue/green color

## SUCCESS OIL
Pennyroyal Oil
Hyssop Oil
Frankincense Oil
Myrrh Oil

## SUN OIL
Frankincense Oil
Myrrh Oil
Sandalwood Oil

## FIRE GODDESS OIL
Myrrh Oil
Orange/Tangerine Oil
Patchouli Oil
Nutmeg Oil
Cinnamon Oil
Ylang-Ylang Oil
Honeysuckle Oil

## PRIESTESS OIL
Frankincense Oil
Ylang-Ylang Oil
Palmorosa Oil
Patchouli Oil
Tuber rose Oil

## 9. TREE MAGICK

## VENERATED TREES IN FOLKLORES

Since ancient time, trees have always been considered sacred and commonly worshipped by early Christians, Muslims, Buddhist and many other Spiritual faiths. Throughout Europe, West Asia, Indian culture, Druids and for today's modern Pagans, trees continue to be venerated for their numerous spiritual attributes. Trees exemplify the sacredness of the Divine, as they reside in all three realms; living on the earth, as it reaches up to the sky, yet its roots are deep down within the Earth, touching upon the underworld. They link and unify all three sacred realms. Trees can also be seen as feminine in her ability to nurture; birth and sustain life. They are the embodiment of the Sacred Feminine, while also a sometimes phallic masculine symbol with its tall standing, erect trunk.

### BELOW ARE SOME TREES OF SIGNIFICANCE TO PAGANS

### Oak Tree
A tree of great strength and symbol of endurance, the Oak tree, has been highly venerated throughout the years. It was believed that Druid priest and priestess would quietly listen to the rustling of the leaves of the Oak Tree to receive Divine insight. The Oak tree was considered King of all Trees. Most sacred to the Celts, it was revered by various cultures namely for its size, longevity and its reputed magickal qualities. Magickal wands made from Oak Tree were considered very powerful. It was also used in spells of protection, success and stability. Some would burn Oak leaves to purify rooms and it was believed that Acorns, gathered by women in the evening hour were valued for their powers of fertility.

## Birch Tree
Known also as the Lady of the Wood and associated with the Goddess Cerridwen, this tree provided gifts for spell workings of love and romance. Considered an ornamental tree, it grows thin and very tall, giving the appearance of a graceful dancer. The sap can provide syrup, perfect for candy making and Birch beer.

## Hazel Tree
Wands made of this tree were often noted for their protective attributes. They were traditionally used to gain poetic inspiration, knowledge and wisdom.

## Elder Tree
The Elder was also known as Elderberry and Lady Elder and it is linked with the Pagan sabbat of Midsummer/Summer Solstice. It was sometimes used to drive out evil spirits. Special wands were made of this tree, but also reeds, musical panpipes and flutes.

## Apple Tree
A Druid tree, the Apple tree, is highly connected to healing Magick and often utilized in spells related to love and romance.

## Ash Tree
Another sacred tree for the Druids was the Ash tree. It has a straight grain which made it excellent for making magickal wands and rods. The leaves were known to provide prophetic dreams when placed underneath your pillow. It is associated with Solar Magick and the realm of Faeries.

## Elm Tree
Beloved Elm tree is associated with the Mother archetype, earth magick and the Goddess of the earth. It was believed to house faeries and it's admired for it stability and grounding qualities. Often described as being fibrous, having tan colored wood, with a high sheen, it was valued for its resistance to splitting.

## Pine Tree
Sweetest of woods, it is a tree of the Druids and was often utilize for fertility spells. One of the Chieftain trees of the Irish, it is believed to purify the home, and was successfully employed in cleansing baths.

## Alder tree
A Druid Tree known for its connection to the elemental powers of Air. Found in shades of oranges, reds and browns, it is a softer wood than many others and was used to make broom handles, cabinets and toys, like whistles. It is believed to reduce anxiety and gifts us with courage to face what we've tried to avoid.

## Fir Tree
Often described as a very tall, slender tree, that grows high in mountainous terrain. It is believed to gift us with excellent views and long distant vision. For this reason it is a tree associated with clarity and insight. It is also a tree whose cones respond to water/rain by closing and then opening with the light of the sun.

## Fir Silver Tree
Known also as Birth tree because of its reputed blessings and connection with Mothers and Child birthing, the Fir Silver tree shares many similarities to the Yew tree. Their foliage is almost identical.

## Blackthorn Tree
It was known as a winter tree, with white flowers. Some ancient text reveal its sharp piercing thorns were often used in spells requiring piercing waxen images.

## Hawthorn Tree
Wands made from this tree were considered very powerful. It was reputed to have erotic attributes for men. Often employed in love and marriage spells, it was also known to have protective qualities. This beloved tree became associated with Beltane and May Day, a licentious celebratory Pagan holiday.

## Juniper Tree
A Druid Tree reputed to give vision and insight. It is also a tree associated with protective qualities.

## Cedar Tree
Cedar tree is considered the tree of life and a grounding tree often associated with the elemental powers of the Earth.

## Willow Tree
Known as the Tree of Enchantments, it is a special tree for priestesses and witches. It is a tree associated with the Moon and therefore the Divine Feminine. One of the most sacred trees to the Irish, it was rumored to give eloquence & inspiration. It is associated with ease of childbirth, thus, connected with the Goddess Artemis. It also has a connection to the maiden Goddess, Persephone. Beloved as a wish granter, many would sit under the tree to receive its gifts and prophetic insight.

## Holly Tree
It appears as white wood with invisible grain and sometimes used for sleep spells. As the name Holly is closely linked with the word "holy," this tree often was associated with holiness, consecrations, spirit and beauty. It is also often connected with death and rebirth and thus, became a powerful symbol for Yule and the Winter Solstice.

## Mistletoe Tree
A Tree that grants protection, it is one of the most sacred trees for the Druids. It is known as the great healer and was oftentimes used in love spells and incenses. It was also sacred to the Norse and considered the tree of the Norse Goddess Freya. She is a highly venerated deity of love, beauty, fertility and sexual potency which makes the correlation easy to understand. Today it is a tree often associated with peace and harmonious energy and exalted most during Yule and the Winter Solstice holidays.

## Yew Tree
Believed to be one of the oldest of trees, it is smooth, with wavy grain, a beautiful gold colored wood. Known to enhance magickal and psychic skills, it induced visions. It is a tree that represents the attributes of death and rebirth and naturally has a connection with the crone Goddesses, like Hekate. It also became associated with the Winter Solstice holiday. It is reputed to be the original Worlds tree, in Scandinavian Myths. All parts of the tree are believed to be poisonous. It was commonly used in dagger handles, bows, barrels and placed on cemetery plots to comfort the dead.

## Rowan Tree
A Druid, Sacred Tree, also known as Mountain Ash, Witchwood, Sorbid Apple. It was a protective tree with the ability to help in locating water, metals and knowledge. Used to make rods, wands, amulets, it was considered protective against any type of enchantment. The Rowan Tree was sacred to the ancient Celtic Goddess, Brigit.

## ASHERAH TREE MEDITATION

    Find a comfortable spot to sit or lay down upon.... Close your eyes and let your body sink into this moment and time. Take your first deep breath and let it fill your lungs. (pause) Then release this breath and inhale one more time, realizing that with each inhalation you are clearing and regenerating your lungs. Exhale, breathe again and with each exhalation you are releasing stress and the mundane. (pause) Deep inhalation, one more time, feeling your breath coming from deep below, clearing your body of any toxins or stress as you let your breath go. Now breathe and exhale once more. Allow your body to relax and sink a little deeper with each breath. (pause)

    Now I want you to imagine yourself standing before a large open field. Let your mind's eye guide you to this open, vast, expansive landscape. There is nothing in sight for miles on end. It is bright and sunny but the vast, open field before you appears empty, nothing has grown on it in a few months. Continue to study this expansive landscape, letting your mind's eye take in the picturesque sight. (pause)

    Look deeply past this landscape to search for a sign of life somewhere. There seems to be nothing before you. Take a look all around you, make note of how this open, vastness makes you feel. Then take a breath and exhaled. Feel now, the weight of your feet pressing against the cold ground. Feel yourself fully alive and present on the earth. There is clearly a palpable energy surrounding you now. See if you can detect its source and simply be a witness to this electric energy. (pause) Feel the weight of the soles of your feet upon the dark soil and notice how they begin to sink a little deeper into the earth beneath you. Take a deep breath and with your breath feel your feet sinking, going deeper into the earth. Breathe. (pause) You sense the beginning of this journey now and you are ready to surrender to the earth and its gift.

Let yourself go deeper into the earth with each inhalation. Exhale, breathe and notice your whole body sinking deeper and deeper into the earth now. (pause) Breathe, surrender and exhale. Feel your body submersed fully into the earth with each breath.

Notice how the lower part of your body has already descended and disappeared into the earth's soil. With your next exhalation let the rest of your body follow through and descend even further into the earth. Breathe... (pause) With this next inhalation let your head also go within. Breathe as your head follows the rest of your body, disappearing under the soil. Continue to breathe deeply, comfortably and then exhale. (pause)

Your body is resting now in the moist, rich soil of the earth. Let your body rest quietly, peacefully relaxed, as you close your eyes and feel a mother's embrace surrounding you now. Feel the warmth of her womb surrounded by this dark soil. Feel her embracing you, nurturing you now. Allow yourself to sink ever deeper into the earth. Allow yourself to be lulled and cradled in her loving, warm embrace. Allow yourself to be held by her magick in this special moment.

The season of Spring has arrived. This is a sacred time of birth and rejuvenations, of all things renewed, of all things sprouting and seedlings latching onto their source of nurturance, in Mother Earth. You are one of her seedlings, now underneath the rich soil, held and nurtured by all of her rich elements and minerals. You lay deep in the earth, dormant, corpse-like but very much alive, awaiting for your debut and re-emergence into this world. Breathe, sinking into this moment, resting in the knowledge that you are safe. Breathe and sink ever deeper, nuzzled up comfortably against mother earth. No concerns, nor worries. You are safe in this vast, boundless dark void. You are consoled by her warmth, secure and supported by her strong presence. Breathe; resting like an embryo in her womb, you are a seed. Breathe and exhale in comfort (pause...) All of your needs are serenely met now through your mother, the earth. All your thirst is quenched and all your hunger is tended to. Breathe and release all concerns with your exhalation. (pause)

Now, see if you can begin to wiggle your toes and feel how they are starting to slowly aspire to stretch out and extend beyond where they were initially. Feel your toes now slowly elongate, like snakes, they are stretching out further, becoming like roots. And as your toes begin to stretch and dig deeper down into the earth, feel your body simultaneously begin to stretch upward. Sense your own body's need to slowly begin to stretch further upward, up towards a glimmer of light above your head, through the soil now. Feel your hands reaching upwards too, as they begin to stretch up, above your head, while you feel your toes continue to stretch downward, slithering, entangled roots, amidst the critters of the deep earth. Allow your feet to stretch further, going deeper into the earth. Your arms and your torso now begin to push through the soil up above, as you continue moving upward, piercing right through the earth, your torso moving from darkness to the light. (pause)

Breathe and with this exhalation feel your arms and torso stretch further upward, above the soil, as if it was reaching for the light of the sun. Notice your toes, which are now tree roots, firmly, intertwined, planted solidly in the earth. While your toes have tenaciously attached themselves to the core of mother earth, your torso and limbs reach up in a state of ecstasy trying to behold the light of the sun above. Your hands are still growing outward, stretching in every direction and you see your fingers becoming extended, sturdy branches, as they stretch towards the sky. Your torso continues to stand tall reaching for the sky and above your head you feel the hair on your scalp, also stretching upward, becoming tree branches and filling itself with bright, abundantly, fertile green leaves, sprouting from your scalp.

Breathe and exhale, make note of how you feel at this very moment. Make note of how your toes feel, deeply rooted in mother earth. (pause) Make note of how your torso feels as it stands solidly, straight, covered in the dark bark of this sacred tree. Make note of how your fingers and your outstretched hands and arms feel, while embodying tree branches. (pause) Make note of how the crown of your scalp feels, as verdant, fertile green leaves are sprouting abundantly from your head. (pause) Breathe, exhale and make note of how your body takes in this breath and how it feels when you exhale now as this magnificent tree. Make note of how you feel as you stand as the tree, as you stand upon mother earth, firmly planted, strong and rooted as a tree. Breathe and exhale. (pause)

Down below, your toes are the roots, enmeshed in the soil that is Mother Earth. Your outstretched arms and elongated phalanges are your branches and your crown is adorned with the most beautiful fertile collection of verdant leaves. Make note of how you feel now as you stand as a tree. This is no ordinary tree; this is you, the **sacred aspect** of you, embodying a tree, embodying **Asherah**.

You stand tall and strong as you are her offspring. You are her divine conduit, you are her creation. You are her magick! You are Goddess!!! Listen as they speak of you...

*"Oh Great and powerful Asherah,*
*immortal and ancient Goddess,*
*we stand to honor, exalt and embody you today.*
*May we know you from deep within in our shared roots.*
*May we know you as our elevated branches reach outwardly*
*in exaltation of you. May we feel your fertile presence within our bark*
*and solid tree trunk.... In the Spring and throughout the seasons,*
*may we honor you, all the days of our lives"*

Hold this image of yourself as Asherah in your mind's eye for as long as you can. Then breathe and exhale. (pause) It is Springtime, there are many fertile things growing amidst nature at this time of the year. You have grown from a seedling, nestled within mother earth, to this grand, majestic divine tree, the sacred Asherah.

Bring your attention now to the crown of your head, overflowing with verdant leaves. Breathe and exhale now...Consider at this moment, what you wish to grow and give birth to in your life (pause). Take this moment to contemplate and envision what you hope to grow in this season of growth and rebirth. (pause)

When you're ready, hold out your branches and whisper this wish into the gentle passing breeze. Let your outstretched limbs sway back and forth, as you send your wish towards the sky. And then, let this wish reach down through your solid tree trunk and down through your feeding, fertile roots. (pause)

Let your wish rest there, upon the bountiful roots and then move your energy towards the center of your torso, the Asherah tree trunk. Feel this as the place where your heart begins to beat. Listen carefully as it faintly begins to make itself known. (pause) Detect now the faint, subtle heartbeat. You begin to hear the thump of your human heart now against your tree trunk torso as it corresponds to the tree's pulse and heat beat. Listen carefully to the rhythm and pulse of your heart coming from the torso of the tree trunk.... (pause) Listen to your heart beat as it gets stronger and you begin to remember your human form. Your heartbeat will serve to remind you of your human form and how this journey began. Feel your heart beat, hear it pulsating with hers and remember how this journey began.

Let your human limbs, that are branches now, revert back to being arms and fingertips and tender hands to hold your heart chakra. Feel your human legs, which were the strong roots of this Asherah, now become your two legs and human feet, once more. Feel your torso revert back to the way it was when we commenced this journey. (pause) Feel your head, adorned with the gifts of verdant leaves, now return to your own natural hair and the one you had at the start of this journey. Continue to hear the sound of your heart beat and connect with your human form once more. Return to your human body and spirit, and follow my voice as we begin to return home.

Breathe and exhale. (pause) With your inhalation feel your body once more as human. Feel your feet and your toes, now standing upon Mother Earth. Feel your legs relaxed and comfortably supporting and holding your body up. Become aware of the sensations upon your human flesh now. With each breath expand your belly over your pelvic bones. Exhale, releasing and leaving behind the memories of your tree form. Breathe, feel your breath expand your lungs now, then exhale ready to return. Feel each inhalation pass through your nose, your mouth and throat, then exhale. Breathe… feel yourself present once more as you… magically, simply you, still her offspring; whether as a tree or as a human being. You are a child of the Goddess, a child of mother earth, an extension of her Divine powers.

Breathe now and with this exhalation begin to step back into this time and place, the portal from which this journey had commenced. Follow my voice as I count from ten to one backwards and slowly help you return to this room, fully back into your body, back to this time and space. *Ten, nine, eight*, continue to breathe and release any tension as you exhale. *Seven, six, five*, become more aware of my voice and follow it. Prepare to join us once again. *Four, three*, breathe and gently sense your own body now. *Two, one*, be here now. You are welcomed back.

When you are ready, open your eyes and gently stretch out your body. If you need further assistance grounding, place the palms of your hand flat on the ground and be still for a moment. Give yourself time to readjust to your physical body, this space, this room, the lights and your surroundings and when you are ready, please feel free to gently raise yourself up. If you feel called to share your experience from this meditation, feel free to write or speak about it, if you are working within a group. It is always wise to document your meditation experiences especially one involving the Goddess.

# 10. ANIMAL MAGICK

By far, one of our greatest spiritual teachers can be found in the animal Queendom and Kingdom. While our beloved domesticated house pets; like dogs and cats, are unquestionably influencing our lives and spiritual paths, in both subtle and obvious ways, our teachers are not limited to them. The animal realm is quite vast and its teachers are numerous. Whether we have access to a snake, a tiger or a ginormous elephant; makes no difference, our spiritual path can only be enhanced by connecting with these allies. If an animal is tugging at your soul, you would be wise to listen up and find whichever way is most appropriate to you to personally connect with this animal and its medicine. Animals have much wisdom to share with us; from the tiniest bug, to the most ferocious looking beast. Ancient indigenous cultures, Shamans and many spiritual traditions throughout the ages recognize this fact and highly venerated the spirit of animals. They can appear to us in recurring dreams, coincidental images and conversations, and slowly necessitate our deeper inquiry as to their recurring visitations. They are teachers. Make no mistake about it; animals and their gifts to us, known as animal medicine, are an invaluable aspect to anyone on a spiritual path of growth and transformation.

# ANIMAL MAGICK & MEDICINE

## EARTH
### 1. Cow/Bovine                                                Hathor

Cows are generally calm, have a tender nature and are considered the providers to humanity's sustenance, for centuries. They are slow to move, have incredible stamina and thus, help us with grounding our energy to the earth. They are linked with maternal instincts; nurturance, caring and there is an element of sacrifice to their energy, due in part, to the way they have been depended upon for food. They awaken us to the gifts of belonging, strength, fertility, wealth and Goddess energy. The Egyptian Goddess of love, Hathor, was considered the Great Divine Bovine. Hathor was the great Mother Goddess of joy, pleasure and nurturance. For Egyptians, she was the Mother of the Cosmos that lovingly nourished humanity. She was often represented as a cow or as a woman with the head of a cow. Lakshmi, the Hindu, matriarchal Goddess of abundance, was also connected with the Cow and our very Milky Way Galaxy was perceived as the milk that flowed from the cow's sacred udders. It is clear; Cows are considered sacred and deeply connected with the Sacred Feminine. Look to cow medicine to help with maternal characteristics; strength, nurturance and grounding to earth energy.

### 2. Buffalo/Bison                                                Oya

Buffalo is a powerful symbol of strength, community, generosity, sacrifice, protection, courage and survival. They connect us with the gift of gratitude for our ancestry and the recognition of the sacrifices offered for the greater good of all. They are a powerful symbol of survival, as they were on the brink of extinction and struggled collectively to survive. Buffalo is a stable teacher of valuing the traditions and riches from the past and the service to the prosperity of our community. They are deeply connected with the earth, powers of manifestation and courage. Native Americans would offer prayers of gratitude before and after a buffalo is killed, to honor the spirit of the animal that provided them with meat, shelter and clothing. Indeed every part of the Buffalo was valued and utilize. For the Native Americans, the buffalo/bison was one of the most important, revered, sacred animals. According to indigenous tribes, buffalo can show us how we store and release our burdens. The shoulders were considered a sacred power point on our physical bodies and this particular animal carried a large hump around his shoulder. It is thus, a symbol of the responsibility it shoulders for its community, an attribute we can study and learn from. We can learn to be more mindful of the sacrifices of life that have allowed us to survive. The buffalo is a symbol of community and the sacrifices necessary for the protection and nurturance of the whole. Interesting to note, when provoked, buffaloes can be unpredictably dangerous and when they feel threatened, they are known to form circles of protection. In an effort to protect themselves, the Female buffaloes, will form circles around other smaller animals, like calves. The male buffaloes will form circles around the cows. These unusual act of encircling, exemplifies the buffaloes' attributes of respect for all in the community. Their natural instinct is to protect and honor all life and in this manner they are invaluable teachers to humanity.

### 3. Rabbit                                                                 Ostara/Persephone

Rabbits are one of the most ancient symbols of fertility, cleverness, luck and playfulness. They bring to mind a multitude of memorable characters and images throughout history that sustain this warm vision of our fuzzy friend. The old animation character of our clever, beloved "Bugs' Bunny," in the USA, immediately comes to mind, as does the rabbits in the story of, *"Alice and Wonderland,"* and *"The Rabbit and the Hare."* We are reminded of their lightning speed cleverness, beauty and their connection to good humor.
The Goddess Freya and the Norse Germanic Goddess, Holda, were both linked with an entourage of rabbits. The Greek Goddess of Love, Aphrodite, was also linked with the attributes of the rabbit. Teutonic legend explains the hare's intricate connection with spring. It conveys the story of the rabbit, once actually being a bird. One day when it was in danger of perishing, the Maiden, Goddess of spring, Ostara, rescued it by transforming it into its present day form, the rabbit. Since then, the hare and its eggs are offered as gratitude to the Goddess Ostara, every April, at the annual spring festival to the Goddess. Rabbits are not only associated with the season of spring but also with the faerie portals and the moon. Lunar deities like the Mayan Goddess, Ix Chel was often depicted near or holding a rabbit and the Greek Maiden Goddess, Artemis, was fiercely protective of these creatures.

These beautiful, furry beings have long been associated with sexuality and fertility. Think of the sexy animation character of, Jessica Rabbit and Hugh Hefner's billion dollar empire, built on the image of the "Playboy Bunny." Rabbits are endearing and closely linked with the enchanting allure of the maiden. Their exceptional powers of fecundity are apparent when we realize they can have two to five litters of young per year, with three to six baby bunnies in every litter. This definitely contributes to their survival but it's interesting to note, the young ones are expected to quickly move out of the nest and survive on their own, in order to make room for new offspring. This push for independence is also akin to maiden energy. Rabbits have long been connected with good fortune and luck; hence the old surviving superstition that carrying a rabbit's foot will bring good fortune. More specifically, a rabbit's foot held in the left hand is believed to be particularly auspicious.

The rabbit triumphs over her adversaries and predators not by brute strength but by her own strong wits. They are considered prey animals and thus their skills to survive are notable for us to look at. When they detect danger, they have this ability to stay motionless and wait patiently until the coast is clear, to move swiftly out of sight. It is a gift that most prey animals, like the deer, behold. It is also an invaluable gift we can benefit from, if incorporated into our own lives. Awareness of our surroundings and knowing when to take action for our own protection and survival are important Rabbit medicine gifts. Rabbit connects us to our powers of attraction, speediness, fecundity and our own playfulness. It is a worthy energy to explore and incorporate in our magick.

### 4. Pig                                                                                         Demeter

The pig is probably one of the most misunderstood animals in our culture. We only have to review the number of negative aphorisms and colloquialism related to pigs, to understand how deep the prejudice is against them- at least in our modern times, in the USA. Pigs are actual clean animals, yet we often hear the term, *"Dirty as a Pig"* or *"Your house is as dirty as a pigsty."* Though they are found in messy pigpens, in farms, and sometimes are fed a diet of left-overs, when domesticated as house pets, they are actually one of the cleanest, most intelligent animals. It is important to examine pigs as they are known across cultures and throughout history, to really understand their value. In the Chinese culture, for example, pigs are still revered today as symbols of prosperity, good luck and abundance. Shops and entrepreneurs in China, embrace the energy of the pig, to assure the success of their businesses. They are considered self-reliant, confident, independent, tenacious and rather auspicious. Observe a pig and you will see they move swiftly and with purpose; appearing highly determined and intelligent.

In ancient times, pigs were actually used as currency. They were also connected with ancient deities like, the Greek Goddess, Demeter and the Celtic Goddess, Cerridwen. Demeter was often depicted holding her beloved pig as a symbol of her harvest & fruitfulness. Pigs were also known to be sacrificed as Temple offerings to appeal to ancient deities. Across numerous cultures and traditions, it becomes obvious; the pig is a sign of prosperity and abundance.

The popular term, *"Greedy as a Pig,"* alludes to the presence of abundance and riches that are not shared. We are holding on tight to something of value, this is the interpretation of the *"Four of Pentacles"* in the Tarot but it also reflects the energy of the Pig. Children receive piggy banks to begin learning the value of saving their money and this too, is a symbol of one of Pig's attributes. Traditionally Pig medicine speaks of great abundance and good fortune at hand but it also warns about hoarding too much, being too stingy and stubbornly refusing to allow change to occur.

### 5. Tiger                                                                                         Durga

The Tiger is respected as one of the most fierce, ferocious animals in the animal kingdom. They are popularly linked with courage, willpower, great passion, sovereignty, and inner strength. Greatly revered in China, Africa, India and numerous other cultures, throughout history, tigers are attributed with the primal energy of the invincible warrior, the passionate fighter and the unstoppable victor. They are linked with the gift of leadership, courage, protection, tenacity, ambition, and confidence. For indigenous people and shamans, tigers are known as the walkers of the ancient path. They are the fearless, diviners of personal truths, beauty, grace and power; holding on to their strength and personal conviction. They are nocturnal beings that relish in their solitary freedom and unencumbered explorations. Their night vision is known to be six times better than any human. With their exceptionally keen sense of smell, hearing and sight, they are effective, silent hunters in the night, deliberately weighting carefully their strategy before an attack. Study a Tigers' approach to their prey and it will send shivers down your spine. They are invincible in combat and their powerful energy is unmatched.

Rests assure, when you are called by tiger's medicine, it will awaken your fiery courage and creativity, your inner and physical strength, and your ability to express your deepest feelings, with great passion. You will feel things at a heightened level. Tiger medicine is known as the awakener of our sensitivity. Because tigers are sensual beings; carrying themselves majestically in these sleek muscular bodies, they can awaken us to our own physicality and sensuality. We become more physically in tuned with our bodies and discover deeper levels to our senses. Tiger's natural nocturnal tendency may find you being most productive and creative at night. And... suddenly all those things that you have been avoiding, due to fear or intimidation, become a welcomed challenge to exercise your new found courage.

Tiger medicine offers a plethora of attributes worthy of further exploration. It offers us, willpower, in the face of adversity. It offers us passion, to pursue exactly what we desire, and a fierce sense of focus, that is able to clear the mind of all distractions, and help us tap into the power of now.

The tiger loves to travel and roam the earth freely and typically alone. It has a curiosity and appetite for life that leads him to unexpected adventures and new terrains. For the most part, they are solitary beings that only come together with partners when they are ready to mate. Tigers will have a litter of cubs once, every three to four years, and their litter will vary, anywhere from a single birth, to six offspring. Mama tigers are known to be fiercely devoted mothers. Their baby cubs are born blind and thus, need to stay with their mother until around the age of two. It is not surprising that mothers keep a vigilant watch on their little ones for such a long time. Tigers also remind us of the value of our sanctuary to repose and gather our strength. After extraneous activities like hunting, fighting, birthing etc... a tiger will require a period of rest and recuperation. It often has a den hidden in plain sight which no one will dare penetrate due to her ferocious protective nature. She is, after all, known to be very territorial and she knows her capacity to rest and recuperate will directly influence her success and survival in the wild. Among the numerous attributes already discussed here, Tiger medicine also encourages you to spend time in complete solitude, in your personal lair or sanctuary, to luxuriate in your alone time and fully recharge yourself. Great courage and strength awaits you with this animal medicine.

## 6. Deer/Stag                                                                 Artemis

The deer is one of the gentlest creatures in the forest. A beloved being of the Maiden Greek, Goddess, Artemis, deer exemplifies beauty, grace and gentleness. She is a prey animal and thus, lives most of her life in an alert, defensive mode; acutely aware of her surroundings. She is able to camouflage with her environment and remain motionless when confronted with a threat, before swiftly running away. She teaches us the art of being unseen and knowing when to stand still and when to act, to protect ourselves from predators. In the wild, there is clearly a need to quiet down and trust your intuition; it is the only way to survive. Deer reminds us of this gift. Considered one of the most docile, kind and compassionate animals, just look into her big, brown eyes and you will feel her gentle energy, tug at your heart. She is not the aggressor, nor the initiator of an attack; she approaches life with empathy and benevolence. She serves to remind you to be gentle with yourself and others.

Often times, the unexpected discovery of a deer amidst my early morning, nature walks, have stopped me right in my tracks, leaving me transfixed and enchanted. I usually take that opportunity to quietly watch her beauty in awe. She helps you discover your inner child and explore the world through innocent, wide-eyes.

Their horns or antlers are used to defend and protect themselves from predators but, interestingly enough, they have a remarkable regenerative quality about them. When they fall off or break, they are able to grow back, much like the skin of a snake. The antlers, reaching up towards the sky from the crown chakra are a symbol of psychic powers. They help us connect to spirit and our higher knowledge. We are connected to our intuition with deer energy and may even traverse into her beloved faery realm, in the forest.

Deer medicine awakens beauty, compassion and also an affinity to the arts, poetry and music. It is important to note a deer survives best with her clan. They are typically social animals that find comfort and safety among the herd; an attribute we can explore further if deer medicine is calling out to you.

## 7. Bear                                                                         Artemis

One of the most revered totem animals for Native Americans, and many other cultures, is the Bear. With its large size and its menacing growl, the bear commands our reverence and respect. In the north, the Vikings were known to wear Bear skin, during times of war, to purposefully scare off their enemies and avoid battles.

Bear is often associated with protection, courage and stamina. They are tree climbers and slow to anger. Because they are active, both, during the day and night, they are connected to both, Lunar and Solar energy. One of the most fascinating information regarded bears is their ability to go into a deep state of sleep, known as hibernation, during the winter months. This means that the Bear really exist; awake and interactive upon the earth, in the spring and summer months. In the winter, it enters another world, the dream realm; a magickal place for shamans and Native Americans. The more food and fats the bear is able to store in her body, the deeper her hibernation can be experienced in the winter months. For Native Americans, bear is a highly revered Warrior spirit and spirit guide, connected with fearlessness, power, hidden strengths and protective mama bear assets. *"Mama Bear,"* is a term used for a super protective human mother, it is a perfect aphorism for her.

Bears are best known for their fierce protective nature with regards to their cubs. They are known as the sole responsible parent for teaching, feeding, protecting and guiding their cubs and they are relentless in their devotion to their offspring. Bear medicine connects us to her primal energy, and puts us in the honored role of the guardian and protector. Interesting to note, in Siberia the word for a woman shaman is the same word used in North America for Bear. Therefore, a woman shaman, a spirit-woman, beholds the spirit of Bear.

Bear medicine helps us to stand up against adversity; we are strong enough to face the seemingly unsurmountable. Discernment and discrimination are awakened in us and we learn how to make the right decisions, considering all aspects. Bear medicine reveals knowledge through introspection and emphasizes the importance of solitude to recharge and recuperate ourselves. It also connects us to the importance of sleep and dreamtime, where we are able to channel spirit and receive much valuable guidance. Spring and summer are the bear's power cycle and during the winter it sleeps. If Bear medicine is calling us, we need to be mindful of this unique productivity cycle and use it to our advantage.

Bear connects us to our deep courage and our inner strength. This animal is both feared and revered throughout numerous cultures and it can serve as a catalyst for us, to embrace a new leadership role. It can also help us unearth a powerful, more primal, side to ourselves that we perhaps never knew existed. I often equate this to some new mothers that all of a sudden, upon becoming moms, discover that they would do anything for their child's happiness and wellbeing. Some mothers really do take on the form and spirit of the *Sacred Bear*; physically, mentally and emotionally. Bear medicine also serves as a reminder of the importance of introspection and solitude in order to regroup and re-strengthen ourselves on all levels.

## 8. Horse                                    Rhiannon

One of the biggest contributors to humanities' evolution and advancement is the horse. Prior to the use of horses, people were stuck in their birth place or resigned to either, taking long journeys by foot or by water. The horse, across all cultures, is highly respected and well regarded. It allowed for travel and thus, discovery of new terrains, new cultures and new ways of life. It expanded our world exponentially and radicalized our primitive way of living. Our land could be tilled easier and it had a positive effect on our agricultural advancement. Horses allowed for transporting items and inaugurated commerce. They were so valuable, that horses were also seen as currency and their existence in our household was just as treasured as another member in our family and our workforce. Horses, as you can see, have always been a trustworthy, welcomed ally to humanity.

Throughout the ages, they have tirelessly helped us, human, by carrying our burdens and even fighting our wars. They are known for their great speed, stamina, strength, devotion and their cooperative spirit. They are deeply loved by their owners' today, as they have been since the beginning of time. They are freedom lovers, wild and untamable but also work well within the herd to help advance their owners lot. Horses are adventuresome, extremely tenacious and hardworking. Ever heard the saying, *"they are working him like a horse…?"* Horses are known to get things done and their spirit can be relentless once they have a goal set in motion. Horse medicine, therefore is invaluable for overcoming obstacles. It can help us better direct our energy. As a powerful spirit guide they can help us with all types of travels; physical or spiritual. Shamans believed horse to be a Spirit guide that could travel through different realms; helping the soul travel from life to death. Horse medicine therefore can be used for astral travels and other shamanic spiritual journeys.

For Native Americans, horses were connected to the element of air, due to the fact that it literally felt like you were flying in the air, when speedily riding a horse. The introduction of horses to Native Americans was reputed to have come from the Spaniards, when they came to the new land.

Horses have long been associated with various deities in numerous cultures, like the Norse God, Odin and the Greek Goddess of the Hunt, Artemis. The Middle Eastern Goddess, Anahit rode a chariot of Horses and the Greek Sun God, Apollo was also depicted riding a chariot of horses. Kwan Yin, the Buddhist Goddess of Compassion, was sometimes symbolized as a white horse, as was the Welsh Goddess, Rhiannon. The Hindu deity, Vishnu, was purported to one day incarnate as a white horse and in India, the Sun God, Surya, was also connected with horses. Roman and Celtic myths connected the horse with the Godesses; Epona, Macha, Edain and Rigatonia.

Horses have incredible stamina, yet need very little sleep, making them ideal workers. They were easy to domesticate in the new land and are mostly herbivores. They are known for their physical prowess and their immeasurable energy. Their personality tends to be compassionate, forgiving, kind-hearted, and socially oriented. For shamans, a horse was an excellent ally to travel through the realms because of its swift movement. It is often associated with the element of air but also with the element of the earth, as it is solely responsible for advancing our agrarian society. Horse medicine connects us to the energy of faithfulness, loyalty and trustworthiness. It is an industrious, hard-working energy that can be harnessed to help us grow and prosper in our lives. It can help us unearth the physical prowess and powerful energy to get things done. Horse medicine helps us attract the right friends and group alliances. It is considered both solar and lunar and it represents completed life cycles; birth death and rebirth. Horse has always been an ally, unconditionally offering itself in service to humanity's prosperous growth. Among the numerous attributes it offers, it will awaken the spirit of servitude and charity. Horse medicine is an invaluable spirit for us to explore and connect with.

## 9. Wolf                                                                     Skadhi

Wolf medicine is related to strength, cunningness, endurance, courage and freedom. It awakens our self-confidence, self-reliance and alerts us to the importance of our family. Wolf is also a staunch lover of his freedom to roam the earth and find new adventures. Wolf is a Great Spirit teacher that awakens our intuition and our primal senses. Known as a path finder, it will help us locate the right path to our true destiny. They have a strong connection with the Moon and are known as shape-shifters; adapting and melding into the environment. Wolves are teachers that show us when we need to be more resourceful and how to find the right resources when we need to. Wolf medicine encourages us to move forward; assessing and adapting to each situation individually, helping you find what you are searching for. As a pathfinder, wolf is important when you feel lost. It will guide you in the right direction. Loyal, protector of the family, they help us face our deepest fears and in shamanic trance journeys, they will offer themselves as invaluable spirit guides.

> *"Only the mountains has lived long enough*
> *to listen objectively to the howl of a wolf..."* **Aldo Leopold**

Wolves have inhabited almost every continent (except extreme dry desert planes) and their inevitable paths, crossings with human beings, have allowed us to learn from them. Wolves are part of the canine family known as *"Cani Lupus."* They are highly intelligent, freedom loving, wanderers of the earth. They are also devoted tribe members, seen traveling with other wolves in small to medium packs. They display a strong sense of allegiance to their wolf family and are fiercely protective of them. They are travelers that move about in search for food and new adventures but they are never far from their tribe. Known as "Howlers of the Moon," they use their distinct howling to communicate at great distance with their clan. Much scientific research has been done regarding this phenomenon, but there has been no concrete proven evidence that wolves actually howl at the moon. There are however, a number of observations and logical conclusions to this intriguing phenomenon.

Wolves are always howling. This is how they communicate with one another. They are nocturnal creatures and thus, you will naturally find them awake, active and communicative at night. The presence of the Moon can only be spied in the dark of night; therefore it would make sense to connect wolves with the moon. The fact that, since Neolithic times, wolves have always been connected with the moon is evident in early cave drawing and documents of the time. This only anchored further this association between the two. Wolves howl for many different reasons and as mentioned before, it is their most effective form of long distance communication. Wolf Medicine should then be viewed as an awakener to more effective communication skills, as well. Wolves howl to assemble the pack and warn them of impending danger. Wolves howl to alert the tribe of his whereabouts, to scare off their enemies and to signal an alarm. Funnily enough, wolves are known to howl when they simply get together as a way to reaffirming their bonds to one another. They also howl to mark their territory and attract their mates.

During a time of courtship, usually peaking in the winter months, from about December to January, you will hear many wolves howling as a mating call. Perhaps this is one reason why the month of January has a Full Moon that was given the name, "Wolf Moon." For indigenous cultures that lived so intensely aware of nature and its cycles, they would have noticed the increase in the wolves' nightly song. It is easy to see how the wolf and his distinct howl would've been linked to the Full Moon, especially at this time.

There is also an ancient belief that a wolf could hear and communicate with the spirits of the dead. And because a Full Moon has esoteric links with spirits and the deities from the underworld, it is very easy to fuse the two together. The Full Moon was believed to open the gates of the underworld for the pervasive presence of spirits and wolves howling were simply seen as communicating with the dead. For the Native Americans, more specifically the Seneca tribe, there is a belief that the wolf's song or howl helped to manifest the Moon into existence. The wolf was associated with numerous deities like Apollo, Aries, Mars and Silvanus. Descendants of the Trickster God, Loki, in Norse mythology, are believed to be wolves. The God Cernunnos, was often depicted with a wolf and in Ireland, the King Cormac, was pictured accompanied by wolves. The Egyptian God, Wepwawet, whose image was revered and publicized openly during celebratory processionals among the pharaohs, was often depicted as a wolf or with a wolf head. In Norse mythology, the Moon and the Sun are chased by two wolves. They are known as Skoll (repulsion) and Hati (hatred) and they are purported to beckon the night and day to arrive daily. When there was an eclipse, in ancient times, it was alleged the wolves had temporarily swallowed the sun. There is an ancient view that one day they will devour the sun and the moon and fulfill the doomsday prophesy. The God Odin was believed to enjoy the loyal companionship of two wolves, known as Geri and Freki. They may have been the offspring of Hel's mother. Wolves were sacrificed and sometimes eaten at the Temple of Arcadia, where there existed a well-known Wolf cult that worshipped Zeus Lycaeus. Here the initiates would call themselves, Lukoi. The Goddess in early Rome was known as Lupa or Feronia, meaning the great *"she wolf."* Here she was worshipped and honored in the legendary Lupercalia festivals, known as the festival of the *"she wolf."* In this aspect, the Great Goddess was celebrated as the mother of Roman ancestors.

Indigenous cultures consider wolf to be an invaluable teacher. Highly revered by shamans for their strength and confidence, they can help you come to conclusive decisions. They help you trust your instincts and your inner voice. Wolf medicine helps you balance friends, family and find time for yourself. They are able to maintain autonomy and individuality, while still being a part of a tribe and we can extract much wisdom from this gift. Wolf medicine is connected with intelligence, outwitting those who want to harm us and invisibility, or being able to avoid enemies. For Native Americans, wolf is a powerful spirit teacher that offers us wisdom, introspection, strong protection and spiritual guidance in dreams, meditation and trance journeys. They are invaluable as we learn to balance our own autonomy and our friends and family obligations.

**10. Dog                                                                                       Hekate**

Dogs, as modern day pets, have become revered in our homes as our beloved trustworthy partners. They offer us companionship, unconditional love, loyalty, protection and for many, they are deemed as extension of our family. Throughout the ages, in various cultures, dogs, which are descendant of the wolf, and have always been prized as our trusted, loyal friend and protector. They have this huge capacity to love, forgive, and alert us, when trouble is sensed nearby.
Respected and valued throughout numerous cultures, the Dog has a long history of being in service to humanity. The Egyptian God, Anubis, for example, was purported to faithfully meet you in the afterlife as a guide. He assured your transition from the physical world into the spiritual and he indeed wore the head of a jackal or a dog. Here again, the symbol of the dog is one of service, protection and loyalty, as the soul's final journey would be guided into the afterlife, by the Jackal-headed God. In Greek Mythology, Cerberus, is the three-headed dog that guards the gates of Hade and here too we see a dog being employed as a guardian and protector. Also important to note, the Greek Crone Goddess of the witches, Hekate, was sometimes referred to as the *"black bitch,"* meaning the black female dog. She protected and guided those who could not guard or protect themselves. At this point in ancient history that included; women, children, elders and the ones that had been marginalized out of accepted society. It was believed she would often shape-shift into black hounds.

Consequently, dogs were the preferred choice for altar offering to this Goddess of the Crossroads and beloved Crone.

In Celtic mythology, dogs were trained to assist in battles, as they were also believed to be invaluable companions and protectors during hunting excursions. In the Chinese tradition, dogs are harbingers of friendship. Fu Dog, for the Chinese, is the guardian of sacred spaces and a symbol of good luck, loyalty, prosperity and protection.

Dog medicine touches upon these admirable attributes already mentioned but it also connects us to our primal instincts, our ability to cooperate and serve humanity and our loyalty and commitment to those we recognize in our tribe.

## 11. Elephant                                                                      Lakshmi

Elephants are often associated with ancient wisdom and have been strongly revered in various cultures for numerous years. Most notably, we find the worship of elephants prevalent in India, where they are connected with the Goddess, Lakshmi and the God, Ganesh. Lakshmi, is known as the Hindu Goddess of Beauty, Love, Abundance and Prosperity. She is the beautiful wife and the celestial matriarch of the family. Elephants are often depicted showering her abundantly with water as a symbol of her fecundity and her sovereignty. Most importantly, the veneration of elephants is best exemplified in the existence of Ganesh. Ganesh is the beloved Hindu God, represented as a multi-armed elephant and sometimes, as a multi-headed elephant. His energy is quite loving, generous and cheerful. He is the celestial obstacle remover and his worship extends far beyond the borders of India.

As one of the largest mammals walking our earth today they represent, sovereign power, strength and stamina. They convey the energy of abundance, temperance, dignity and longevity. In ancient India, the elephant was a powerful weapon of war that was utilized to crush and stampede over the enemy. They were often associated with royalty, as Kings were required to parade upon elephants to show their massive dominance and sovereignty.

Elephants are very interesting mammals and, as intimidating as their size makes them out to appear, they are actually quite tenderhearted and family oriented. Mama elephants are particular, highly revered and are known to lead the pact with much gentleness and inclusivity. According to animal studies, elephants display great affection towards their tribe and are often willing to risk their own safety to protect the family as a whole. Elephants tend to live in separate groups, determined by their gender and it might be quite surprising to learn that they actually have a very strong sex drive.

Among the numerous attributes already mentioned, Elephant medicine helps us to let go of repressed memories by bringing them to light and then consciously letting them go. Elephants also offer us the gift of discernment and discrimination. With their long trunks, they have an extraordinary sense of smell, which helps them discriminate between positive and negative environments. They are also known to communicate telepathically. Ever heard of the saying, *"something doesn't smell right here?"* This alludes to the elephant's medicine of discrimination. Elephants are known to have poor vision but their hearing, sense of smell, touch and taste are highly developed. They live a long time and they exhibit the traits of patience, contentment and temperance. Naturally, fragrances and the study of Aromatherapy are connected with elephant medicine due to its dominating nose. Most importantly, Elephant medicine reminds us of the importance of family, love, patience, using all of our senses and embracing our majestic selves. It is a wonderful animal medicine to work with, especially when seeking to develop a better sense of self-worth and enhance our ability to ground.

## 12. Coyote                                                                         Loki

For Native Americans, Coyote is the cunning energy of the trickster. He is the joker and the fool; learning lessons from his silly follies. He is the perpetual prankster, child-like and adaptive to any situation. Navajo tribe believed the coyote is sacred because it accompanied the first man and woman into the actual entrance of our physical world.

Coyote medicine introduces us to playfulness and resourcefulness. He is reputed to be a shape-shifter, clever and purely instinctual. His energy can seem a bit chaotic but he offers us a unique gift that can inaugurate a new, much needed, adventure on our spiritual journey.

## 13. Snake/Serpent                                                    Lilith/IxChel

The subject of snakes would be a vast, ambitious undertaking for me to take on in this book and while I am quite passionate about my love and reverence for snakes, I will try to keep this chapter as concise as possible.

There are over 2,700 different species of snakes around the world today. Apart from dinosaurs, I don't know of any other animal more ancient in stature than the snake. Scriptures and early writings, document the existence of snakes, present at the inception of the earth, possibly even before mankind. Myths and folklores from across the globe, throughout the ages reflect different tales about the snake and its importance in our cosmology. It helps us to understand a little better this slithering ancestor.

Snakes are cold-blooded, reptiles. They cannot regulate their own body temperature and thus, require an external source of heat to keep them active and alive. They enjoy a diet of mammals; mostly rodents. Of course, in the wild, they will consume just about anything that can fit into their unhinged jaw. They can be found in different lengths and different colors and for the most part, they are covered with small scales and the most intriguing patterns across their bodies. Many of them have lethal venom that makes them poisonous, others are known as powerful constrictors that will choke their prey to death before consuming. Today, much like in ancient times, some snake species are enjoyed as household pets. I myself have had a corn snake from the time she could fit snuggly in the palm of my hands, at 3 months of age. She has been a wonderful teacher and companion.

Since the earliest of times snakes have, almost exclusively, been associated with the sacred feminine. They are a symbol of the earth but also of healing and balancing of polarities. The snake's ability to shed its skin and re-grow new one on a consistent level, makes her relatable to women. Its regenerative skills mimics those found in a woman's reproductive system. As a woman bleeds and sheds her uterine lining approximately every 28-30 days, when it has not been fertilized, so too is the snake able to shed its skin lining and start anew. It is a physical reflection of a more monumental, ethereal concept in mysticism.

The snake is a symbol of transformation, reincarnation and immortality. It has always, for the most part, been linked with the Goddess and for humanity it serves as an intermediary between the worlds, being both a spiritual and an earth creature. It represents deep ancient wisdom and mystical knowledge.

Snakes were embraced and exalted in Mediterranean and European myths much more than in the near-eastern and Indo-European region. The snake in Roman, Greek and Cretan households was well regarded. Here they were linked with the present day cults, like the Mystery cults and deities associated with healing. The Greek God of the Sun, Apollo had two offspring, Hygeia, the Goddess of woman's healing and Aesclepius /Asclepius, the God of Medicine. They were both often depicted holding snakes and their worshipping temples often maintained snakes for rites. The two intertwining snakes on a rod, often associated with Aesclepius/Asclepius is known as the Caduceus; a healing symbol that continues to be recognized today.

Before the Sun God, Apollo, took over the Delphic Oracle, we must remember it was first maintained and founded by the Greek Goddess of the Earth, Gaia. Gaia at that time was referred to as "Gaea Pelope," which means, "female serpent." Interesting to note the priestesses that served at this temple were known as serpent priestesses, named, Pythonesses. In Greek mythology, the Goddess Hera was reputed to have had a gigantic snake named, Ladon, which protected the apple tree of life. A snake guarded the temple for the beloved Goddess of Wisdom, Athena, in Athens and of course we cannot forget the foreboding image of the serpent headed Goddess, Medusa, so often linked with the myths of the Goddess, Athena.

In Northern India, a rainbow is called, *"Budhi Nagin,"* which, interestingly enough means, "old female snake." The Sanskrit word for snake is "Naga." In India the Nagas are a special group of female, rain deities with the body of a snake and the head of a human or simply depicted as a full snake. They were guardians of the riches of the world, namely material and spiritual riches. They resided in the underworld with all the rich minerals of the earth, surrounded by extravagance and they symbolized Shakti and cosmic power. They had dominion over rainclouds and rainbows and they were keepers of the ancient mysteries. The mother of the Nagas is the Indian serpent Goddess; Kadru. The Nagas appear reminiscent of the Mayan Goddess of the Moon, Ix Chel, as she too had dominion over rainclouds and rainbows. She is also linked with a multitude of serpents adorning her skull. This correlation between serpent deities, water, rain, the moon and women seems to be compulsory throughout history.

For most Native Americans, they believed snakes had great power and was a potent teacher. For the Celts, snake is connected with the healing Goddess, Brigit. According to Celtic mythology there was an Imbolc tradition that involves the search for the Goddess, embodied as a slithering snake, coming down from the mountains to announce the early arrival of spring on Imbolc. This is a rite reminiscent of our U.S.A. Ground hog day. Nordic tradition spoke of the Midgard serpent, also known as the World serpent that swallows its tail to create a whole circle and reflect the infinity of life. In Greece this serpent was known as Oceanos. In Japan the Oceanic God of turbulence, Susano-O, was sometimes depicted as a snake and although modern Chinese view serpents as destructive and deceitful, ancient Chinese tradition did not. The Goddess of Creation, Nu-Kua and her mate/brother Fu-Xi are both depicted as half human and half serpent. In ancient Chinese tradition, this half serpent Goddess is recognized as the Creatrix, responsible for birthing humanity upon the earth.

Unquestionably, one of the most powerful symbols of transformation and regeneration is the reptile of the snake. Often associated with healing and esoteric knowledge it is the earliest animal mentioned and documented as existing upon the inception of humanity. It is one of the oldest beings mentioned in early scriptures and well documented in the earliest of folklores and mythologies. Snake medicine connects us to ancient wisdom, the sacred feminine, birth, rebirth, transformation and regeneration. It is spiral energy, related to healing waters, the moon, and infinity. It connects us to Kundalini Energy, varying levels of consciousness and esoteric knowledge. It is death and rebirth, shedding and surrendering our skin to let new growth take place. Snake connects us to the Goddess, our feminine intuition and our gifts of transformation. We are reminded that we are descendants of the Sacred Feminine, embodying snake energy.

## 14. Skunk

It's funny to think how a small animal can command such high respect and provoke such heart-racing terror from just about every being it encounters on this planet. Skunks are about the size of a cat but the threat and the terror they elicit make you think they are the size of tigers. They are most recognized by their black and white coloring. Most notably, they can be identified by the double stripe that runs from its head to its tail.

Peaceful, friendly, slow and deliberate in their movement, it is only when they feel threatened that they will emit a revolting smelling essence that can be detected from miles away. Skunks are considered predators but you wouldn't know it from looking at one. They humbly go about their business, walking self-assuredly, moving at their own pace, and appearing quite self-confident. They do not need to aggressively pursue or physically threaten anyone. They are not flexing muscles or attacking their prey the way one would expect. Skunk's method of attack is sheer sophistication. They simply get into position, lift up their tail and from twelve to fifteen feet away, they are able to deliver a most noxious fume, sprayed right at their target. Rest assure, it is an attack, but while other predators will use their claws, teeth and physical strength to bring down their prey, skunks simply sprays them and renders them helpless; attacking their senses.

Skunk medicine teaches us a thing or two about the importance of boundaries. As a passive, non-aggressive mammal, skunk gives plenty of warnings before executing her lethal sprayer. It is as if she really doesn't want to engage in combat and she gives you a chance to reconsider your plan. As a spirit guide and animal medicine, Skunk is invaluable for those of us who have boundary and confrontation issues. With skunk medicine we explore how we set boundaries and how we can defend ourselves when those boundaries are compromised. We learn that brute force is not the only way to fight and sometimes it's not the biggest or loudest that can deliver the most lethal punch. Skunk medicine helps us explore defense magick that does not include physical harm. Skunk medicine offers the gift of self-respect, self-awareness, independence and the value of a well-earned reputation.

Skunks have a life span of about ten years and they are indeed susceptible to having rabies. Skunks can have one litter of young per year, with about ten baby skunks per litter. From the moment these baby skunks open their eyes, they have the gift of using their sprayer. At twenty weeks of age, they are able to separate from their mama and stand on their own. They are carnivorous and they will eat almost anything, including insects, fruits and berries. Most of their hunting occurs at night, typical of a nocturnal animal, and you won't find them in large groups, as they are solitary creatures. With its distinctive black and white appearance, its medicine offers us a chance to also look at things either black or white; in other words, with acute clarity.

It might surprise some of you to know that skunks are highly sexual beings. Immediately, I can't help but see, in my mind's eye, the memorable, Warner Brothers' animation character named, "*Pepe Le Pew.*" He was the overly romantic French skunk, with a thick French accent that was determined to *make-looooove* to the neighborhood cat; which he mistaken as one of his own, due to a fake white strip on her black fur, acquired with a can of paint.... Long, long, story, but I digress! This animation character perfectly depicts the skunk as a charismatic, overly affectionate, sexualized being. Indeed the skunk is considered a very sensual being and because it uses an attack on our sense of smell as its mode of protection, it behooves us to explore Aphrodisiacs and Aromatherapy.

Aphrodisiac, scents and the study of fragrances are deeply connected with this totem. As we know through scientific research, there are some scents and foods that have a direct influence on our sexual organs. Skunk medicine will often awaken an interest in this subject matter and connect us to our body language, attraction and sexual energy. Some believe the stripe on a skunk's body relates to Kundalini Energy and when we have skunk medicine it will, no doubt, activate and amplify our sexuality.

With skunk medicine there is a belief that the strong odor of the skunk not only has the capacity to repel our enemies but to attract like-minded people in our lives. Therefore, it offers the gift of discernment and being able to sort through who our real friends are, and uncover who are our hidden enemies. It will ask you to observe whether or not you are repelling others because of envy, jealousy or a projection of **their** own, low self-esteem. *"Something stinks around here..."* is a phrase we use when we sense that something's not right but we can't quite put our finger on it. With skunk energy we may find the help to unearth the source of that stench.

The skunk walks with confidence, knowing it can protect itself, from even the largest beast, by simply lifting up its tail and spraying its offensive essence. Therefore, among the numerous other attributes already discussed, there is also great inner strength to tap into, when you behold skunk energy. Known throughout Europe and the United States as Mephitis, skunks have garnered quite a reputation among the animal kingdom for their impressive method of self-defense. Skunk medicine will awaken courage, willpower, self-defense and the ability to raise a stink wherever and whenever it is needed.

## **<u>AIR</u>**
### **<u>15. Dove                                                                                       Aphrodite</u>**

Doves are quintessential the most popularly embraced symbol of peace. It is perhaps one reason why they are so often incorporated in wedding rites, military and religious services. For many cultures, throughout history, the dove was often seen as the peaceful soul in flight to its celestial home. It is intrinsically linked with prophecy, serenity and maternal blessing.

The dove is recognized as a member of the pigeon family. Its sweet cooing voice can best be detected at dawn and dusk, which is so often considered a magickal time of transcendence. Perhaps due to the fact that doves built their nest near populated areas, they were readily observed by humans in their habitats. They were seen as gentle and non-aggressive and their incessant sweet cooing made them even more endearing. As humans we quickly learned they were ground feeders, mostly consumers of seeds, and not carcass. Unlike other birds; like the falcons, eagles and vultures, doves were closely observed by humans as being non-threatening, affectionate and attentive to their family. They quickly became embraced as a symbol of love, affection, purity, gentleness, hopefulness and grace. Throughout numerous cultures there appears to be a consensus regarding doves. They are viewed as the Divine messengers, linked with spiritual ascension.

Early scriptures mention the dove in a positive light and for Christians; it is linked to the Holy Spirit. For Slavs, they believed when someone died, their soul would return to its dove form. In the Mediterranean, the Goddess of Wisdom, Sophia, was alleged to have descended upon the earth by shape-shifting into a dove, and thus, we often associate divinity and the Holy Spirit with the symbol of the dove. Here she is deemed as the Goddess herself. For Egyptians, the dove was perceived as a symbol of innocence. In Greek mythology, the white dove was often associated with the golden Goddess of Love, Aphrodite. Its characteristics of beauty, love, affection and grace were well represented with the beloved Cypriot Goddess of Love. Early Pagans associated the dove with female sexuality, maternity and the Goddesses, Astarte and Isis. In ancient times it was also believed that doves would carry ambrosia to the Gods, to keep them immortal.

It is clear; the dove is a symbol of peace, love and harmony. Its medicine can help us better connect with stillness, spiritual messages and attracting true-love. The dove is also a symbol of letting go what does not serve our highest purpose. It teaches us to surrender, in order to tap into the power of our wings and effortlessly ascend to higher consciousness.

## 16. Owl                                              Blodeuwedd/Athena/Lilith

Snowy Owl, Great Horned Owl, Barn Owl, Western Screech Owls, Spotted Owl, Long-Eared Owl, Hoot Owl, Burrowing Owl, Eurasian eagle Owl, Elf Owl, etc... Across the globe it might surprise you to know that there are at least two hundred sixteen different types of owls that exist today. They are all absolutely gorgeous and might have various subtle differences, too many for us to discuss here. For now we will discuss their common similarities, learning about the owl and its medicine.

Owls are nocturnal, birds of prey. They are best distinguished by their large piercing eyes and their impeccable night vision. They have the capacity to nearly rotate their heads all the way around, which only supports the concept of the owl as an all seeing predator.

Owl medicine helps us to see and extract hidden secrets. It facilitates our own ability to discern the truth in all situations. They are known as, *"Guardians of Wisdom,"* and can awaken in us Clairvoyant and Clairaudience gifts.

Owls have the proclivity for adventures and absolute freedom. Owls are solitary beings and you won't find them in groups but rather alone in their sanctuaries, perched, high up on tree tops. They are keen observers of their environment and natural silent fliers in the night. They are able to quietly swoop down on their prey, virtually unnoticed. Their distinguishable hoot heard across the night sky, however, is received as an omen of change and those studying spirituality, would not dismiss its call.

Due to their nocturnal nature, they are naturally affiliated with shadow work and the Moon. Their nocturnal vision characteristic helps us see beyond the veil of deception and illusion. Owl medicine warns us of impending change and offers deep insight and spiritual guidance. They are an ally to those committed to esoteric studies and spiritual growth.

Across numerous European traditions and folktales, the owl appears to have been the preferred animal for witches to shape-shift into and partake in nocturnal journeys. They served as eyes and spirit teachers to those seeking ethereal wisdom. In Celtic mythology, the owl was a guide for the soul traveling into the underworld. Owl in this tradition became known as the, "*Gatekeeper to the Akashic realm.*" The Romans believed Owls helped to ward off evil. In some Native American traditions, Owl is seen as a harbinger of death, whether it was an actual, physical death of someone we knew, or a visit from a deceased loved one. Owl was connected with the dead. There was a strong correlation between the underworld and the presence of an owl, in particular the sound of his haunting hoot, which signals a change. Owl medicine allows us to connect with our deceased loved ones and here we see a strong link between our beloved wide-eye creature and the underworld. For ancient Sumerians, the screeching owl was linked to the Goddess Lilith, who was believed to have owl talons as feet. The piercing high pitched sound of a screeching owl announced her presence nearby. For most indigenous cultures, the owl is known as the "*night eagle,*" a nocturnal version of the highly revered eagle seen in the light of day. The owl is closely linked with the Athenian Goddess of Wisdom, Athena. In Greek mythology the Goddess of Wisdom and War, was purported to carry an owl on her shoulder as a symbol of her infinite wisdom and foresight.

As an animal connected to the Goddess of wisdom, Owl medicine awakens in us a desire to acquire knowledge and commune with our spirit guides. It can also stir our hunger for freedom and travel adventures, including astral travel capabilities. We become more aware of our surrounding and all the many ways the Universe is speaking to us; via omens, oracles and animal sounds. We learn to value more our sanctuaries and our solitary moments, especially our evening hours. As a "*Guardian of the Underworld,*" Owl medicine connects us to change that is often linked with a death of some sort. Whether we are physically parting with a loved one or psychically saying goodbye to an "energy," owl medicine helps us connect to the truth of all matters and strengthens our ability to fly forward, with greater wisdom.

*"In the beginning of all things, Wisdom and Knowledge were with the animals;
for Tirawa, the One Above, did not speak directly to man.
He sent certain animals to tell men that he showed himself through the beasts,
and that from them, and from the stars,
and the moon, man should learn.
Tirawa spoke to man through his work..."* Chief Letakots-Lesa, Pawnee Tribe

## 17. Peacock — Hera/Juno/Saraswati

Peacocks are often associated with great beauty, vanity and self-confidence. Observe a peacock how it struts about, with its elaborate plumes fanned out and you will clearly understand why. They are gorgeous and they are awakeners of our self-esteem, inner and outer beauty, refinement and royalty. They are also symbols of rejuvenation, glory and immortality. Interesting to note their voices lack the same beauty and is considered quite a loud, penetrating shrill.

In Greek mythology, the peacock was the sacred bird to the beautiful Goddess of matrimony, Hera. The collection of a multitude of peacock feathers gave the appearance of a million watchful eyes. There are a number of myths that connect the manifestation of the peacock, to Hera's personal watchman, Argus. He was alleged to have many eyes due to his esteemed position as the personal watchman to the Goddess. Other folklores connect the peacock's unique, beautiful feathers to the myriads of stars in the night sky. The Peacock is the guardian and mascot to the different monarchs in both Persia and Babylonia. Ancient throne remnants and engravings attest to the importance and veneration of the peacock. Several sculptures and artistic images depict the peacock accompanying Hindu Goddesses. The Hindu Goddess of Beauty, Love and Prosperity, Lakshmi, is often shown with a peacock nearby. Here it represents benevolence, kindness, good fortune and patience. Saraswati, who is the Hindu matriarchal Goddess of truth and wisdom, was also depicted with the peacock by her feet. In this case it serves as a warning to be mindful of our vanity.

Peacock medicine helps us unearth and embrace our regal beauty. We learn that our beauty shines best when we let ourselves be seen by the world. This medicine endeavors to help us attain wholeness and understanding, regarding past lives and our karmic connections. We are able to explore our past, present and future to bring further integration into our life. The appearance of a million eyes on the Peacock's extravagant feathers, speaks to us about awareness and divine knowledge.

## 18. Ostrich — Ma'at

One of the largest living birds in the animal Queendom, that does not fly, Ostrich is a symbol of purity and truth. Ostriches can stand as tall as 8 feet and weigh as much as 300 pounds. The head and neck of this majestic bird have short feathers but their bare legs and thighs do not. It will eat just about anything and with its super speed capabilities; it can outrace its enemies.

Ostrich, as a totem animal, is not recognized by Native American traditions but it is still a worthy animal to explore and work with. As one of the tallest birds, with its long, outstretched neck reaching for the heavens, it is often connected with Divine knowledge, more specifically, the desire to attain ethereal esoteric insight. It is also strongly connected with the earth and grounding our energy to its fertile life source. An ostrich's feet are flanked, big and rooted on the earth; therefore we can call on ostrich when we are in need of grounding ourselves to mother earth. It becomes clear that ostrich medicine has an affinity to the elements of both earth and air and it speaks to us about taking ethereal knowledge and applying it to our earthly, everyday life. With ostrich medicine we can stand tall and proud. We can also connect with its protective powers that can help us sort out what is no longer needed and what must be surrendered in our lives. It is therefore connected with exorcism, psychic protection and truth.

The ostrich was linked with the dark Goddess in Semitic and Babylonian cultures, known as Tiamat. Here her animal energy might have been viewed differently than in other cultures. However, we can probably learn most about Ostrich and its prized attributes through Egyptian scriptures and mythologies.

In Egypt, the Ostrich was intimately connected with the Goddess of Truth and Justice, Ma'at. She is the Goddess who meets you in the underworld to judge the whole of your life against her divine virtues and tenets of morality. Upon her golden sacred scales she takes your heart and weights it against the light Ostrich feather. If your heart is heavy, it will outweigh the feather, and you will be judged harshly. A heavy heart revealed a life that did not measure up to the ideals represented by that ostrich feather and thus, the heart would meet its fate, devoured by the awaiting jackal-headed deity, Annubis.

If your heart weights lighter than the feather then you have lived a good life and are welcomed into her graces. It is a most revealing example of how important the Ostrich, more specifically her feather, was deemed in ancient Egyptian culture. Some of the writings of the time even go as far as to name the ostrich feather as the Goddess herself. Clearly the ostrich was considered a symbol of truth and thus, her feathers were a sacred symbol of the Goddess of Justice.

Ostrich energy can be invaluable to explore. It is a powerful symbol of truth and integrity. It is also a protector against harmful psychic or spiritual invasions. It can tell you when to stand tall and be seen or when to lay low and become invisible. It is an energy that allows us to seek spiritual knowledge and ascension, while also remaining rooted upon the earth. Interesting to note, the ostrich creates a huge egg, which can be interpreted as the gift of fertility as well, and this can be another added attribute one can explore with this gigantic, stately bird.

## 19. Raven                                                                      Morrighan

The Raven is known as one of the largest song birds in North America. Donning black regal plumage in shades of iridescent purples and midnight blues, it is a bird associated with magick, the occult, the cycles of death and rebirth and spirit messages from across the veil. Often mistaken for crows, another beautiful black feathered being, ravens are much larger in stature. These birds are highly intelligent food scavengers that are even good at mimicking the sounds of other animals and thus, are considered good communicators. They can help us explore our own ability to be eloquent and expressive. They are good at camouflaging themselves against the background of the night and their brooding silence can make them appear even more intimidating but these beautiful creatures can be allies to those submersed in mysticism and spiritual studies. Though they spend an inordinate amount of time silently observing their surroundings, they can be loud squawkers when they need to be. They exemplify for us the value of recycling, as they tend to reuse their nest over and over again, rebuilding and fortified it as needed. Usually they choose the sides of cliffs as ideal locations for their nest and interesting to note; they will only choose one partner at a time to mate with.

Ravens are known as excellent food scavengers and again, here we see yet another example of their connection to the spirit message of, recycling. They are the ones that clean up, retrieve and devour dead carcasses. Their diet of mainly dead animals links them to the underworld and they are thus, excellent creature, to work with spirits and ancestral magick. Raven medicine connects us to the power of death and rebirth so perfectly illustrated in their recycling practices. They are also considered the divine messenger between the realms and have the ability to move through time and space. Their medicine can facilitate our own study and practice of astral-travel. Ravens are known as spirit guides, protectors and guardian of secrets. They are teachers of courage, creativity, transitions, self-awareness and intuition.

For indigenous cultures, the Raven was seen as keeper of secrets and teacher of mysticism, due to its black feathers and its association with night. It was the Raven who brought fire and light to the darkness, according to the natives of the Pacific Northwest. The warrior Goddess, Morrighan, was often depicted with the raven on her shoulders as a symbol of life and death. Raven was believed to be the protector and creator of mankind for many cultures. In Germanic mythology, Odin, the God of Magic was associated with ravens. More specifically he was connected to raven energy that served as his eyes and ears. According to Norse mythology his two beloved ravens were known as Huginn (thought) and Muninn (memory). In Welsh mythology the birds associated with the Goddess Rhiannon are three black birds, more than likely they were ravens. These black birds were attributed to putting their listeners into an enchanted trance or deep sleep, which enabled them to travel through the other worlds. Their singing would impart mystical knowledge as they trance deeper.

Ravens are believed to be obstacle removers that help us take long, frightful journeys into the night, whether physically or metaphorically. We can enter and explore unknown frightful terrains with raven's support of courage and insight. In some indigenous tribes, raven is also a trickster, who feeds and steals from humanity and from other spirits. He can be playful and yet ominous. In this manner he is a juxtaposition of opposites; a provider and a thief, a hero and yet, a fool. Raven is light and darkness, a symbol of death and rebirth.

In the occult tradition, Ravens are known as shape-shifters, harbinger of magick, spiritual forces and mystical energies. Sometimes they were believed to alert you of impending deaths. Since the earliest of times they are embraced as the patron totem animal for magicians, witches, shamans, sorcerers and students of the craft. Ravens are also connected to the sacred archetype of the wise crone, witchcraft and the art of divination. They are excellent guides in trance work due to their connection with the underworld. Raven medicine can be an invaluable partner in our spiritual growth and evolution. There are a plethora of fascinating tales and information connected to this most esteemed totem animal and our spiritual journey can only be enhanced by working with it.

## **20. Eagle**                                                                                                      **Eagle Woman**

The eagle is a majestic bird in the sky and by far, one of the most highly revered animal totems for Native Americans. They are connected with the Great Spirit and are a powerful totem for all forms of spiritual work and manifestation. The eagle is the Spirit keeper of the Eastern direction or Air quadrant, in the Native American medicine wheel. They are teachers of vision, discernment and clarity. Ever heard of the aphorism, *"He has an eagle's eye"*? From extraordinary distances the eagle is able to spot his prey and at great velocity, fly to attain it. It is a study, for us, on the effectiveness of great vision and laser beam focus. It serves to remind us to connect with the power of now and learn to get clear on what we truly desire most. The eagle is a strong medicine that offers us keen insight, visionary gifts, clairvoyant abilities and spiritual growth. The eagle becomes an invaluable guide to those learning how to harness their powers in alignment with the law of attraction.

    With their impressive, expansive huge, wing span they are rulers of the sky. The eagle can fly to great heights, higher than any other creature and thus, they are intimately linked with the element of air. They are also connected with the element of earth in their ability to feed off the land. Eagle medicine teaches us to be able to live in the spirit realm and still maintain connection and balance with Mother Earth. Eagles are typically connected to freedom and new explorations. Its medicine is able to take you to new journeys, whether physical or metamorphically, to offer new insight and new vistas of perception.

    The eagle's long talons and its ability to effortlessly grab what it needs, is yet another exemplary gift it offers us. Eagle medicine carefully advises us to grab opportunities while we can, while they are within our grasp, for they can slip away from us, just as quickly as they came. Eagle medicine also teaches us to harness our courage to soar above the mundane levels of life and engage our inner vision to truly see the truth in all situations.

    The bald eagle is a symbol of truth and justice, and has been embraced by the United States of America to represent our devotion to freedom, honor, respect and dignity. These are all commendable attributes connected to the eagle and thus, exalted by the United States of America. Eagle's spiritual message is to be victorious, proud and strong but also to show humility in the process. Eagle encourages us to use our gift of sight to discern the truth in all situations and to courageously fly to new heights of awareness.

## 21. Bat                                                                    Camazotz

One of the only mammals with the ability to fly, due to its unique webbed wings, the Bat is a most intriguing teacher. It is associated with initiations, psychic abilities, wisdom, journeying, and transformation of the ego. It is highly valued in shamanistic traditions for its ability to help us explore past lives and the concept of death and rebirth and reincarnation. Bat medicine helps us see through illusions, and enhances our discriminating gifts and the ability to discern truth.

Bats are nocturnal beings with an extraordinary heighten sense of smell to help them navigate themselves in the world. They behold special sonars in their noses that help them circumnavigate their way even through the darkest of caves. The bat uses sound waves to find what it desires. Bat medicine thus, can help us develop other ways of seeing; other ways of knowing, by incorporating our sense of smell and auditory gifts. One of its medicines is clairaudience, the ability to hear spirits. We are also invited to explore unknown terrains and other levels of consciousness through our senses. Within the bat's dark cavernous caves we find ourselves introspective, quieting down, entering the psychic realm; a more meditative, receptive state of being where we can hear spirit. It is only then that we can understand our true calling, only within her sacred wombs.

Bats are known to live in the tropics, the rainforest and in deep dark caves. Their cave habitats are reminiscent of the womb and yoni, thus, bats are often connected with the symbol of rebirth, death and transformation. When we examine the fact that bats spend most of their time upside down, in a rather, traditional fetus-like position, it supports even more this correlation. Bats are also considered highly sexual beings and are quite social. You will rarely find them alone but rather in small to medium flocks.

Contrary to popular fanatical beliefs, bats do not live off of human blood nor do they seek to live entangled in our tresses. They have no factual connections with vampires or the character Count Dracula, either. They are mainly insectivores and for the most part, fruit eaters. There are numerous classifications of bats. The two that I will mention here are megabats, which feed off of fruits and the smaller, microbats, which feeds off of insects. They are invaluable in the management of mosquitoes in our ecosystem and also seem to help with pollination. There are other classifications of bats that eat smaller mammals like; frogs and fishes, but again they are not consumers of human blood. And unlike early Christian beliefs, bats are not the devil incarnated; they are however highly revered in a number of cultures.

In the Chinese culture, bats are a symbol of long life and happiness. More specifically, they are connected to the five levels of happiness; *long life, wealth, health, comforting to morals and the carrying out heaven's will.* "*Fu*" is the name given to bats in China and this name means happiness. It is clear that for the Chinese, the bat is a bringer of good fortune and happiness. In Japan, however, the bat symbolizes unrest and chaos. In the practice of Feng Shui, bats are connected to good fortune. In Babylonia and South Africa bats are thought to carry souls. In some Native American tribes, like the Apache Cherokee, the bat is recognized as a trickster spirit. It is believed his energy can help enhance your psychic visions, when you are in darkness. To the Toltec, Mayan, Aztec and Tolucans, the bat is considered a powerful totem symbol. The ancient Mayan revered a bat deity (Camazotz) which they considered to be very powerful. There is even a city in Mexico named after the bat, called, *"Yzinacent Lan"* (Bat City). For practitioners of shamanism, bat medicine is called upon to help with initiation rite and shamanistic death rituals, where a part of the initiate must essentially die. The initiate must release an old part of him/herself to be reborn, re-rooted and blessed on his/her new spiritual walk. This process would entail a long period of time in darkness, like the bat, probably within a dark cave or buried under ground -in utter silence and stillness. The initiate would have to confront his/her ego and at some point surrender it, thus creating an emblematic, ritualistic death. Bat medicine helps us trust our intuition and unearth the ability to navigate in the darkest of realms; whether physically, psychically or symbolically. Bat medicine blesses all of our spiritual journeys and helps us become more aware of our surroundings by using our senses. It also helps us avoid obstacles and troublesome people. For indigenous cultures there is a belief that whatever you do will affect the next seven generations and thus, tribal teachings make us aware of our responsibility to future generations, for we are indeed the ancestors of the future. Bat medicine helps us explore our karma and past life and our contribution to the next generation.

## **BUGS**
### **22. Dragonfly                                                                              Ix Chel**
Dragonflies represent beauty, change, adaptability and transformation. They are closely linked with the Mayan Goddess of the Moon, Ix Chel. In Mayan mythology they are attributed for resurrecting the Goddess back to life, after a period of death. They are beautiful winged creatures that resemble actual faeries. It is not surprising they are so often connected with magick and the faery realm. They are born in or near water and when they develop their magickal gossamer wings, they ascend to the ethers. This makes them connected with the elements of water and air. Because they grow in water and then move into the air, to fly, they are related to the spiritual gifts of metamorphosis, evolution and ascension. There is a lightness and benevolence to Dragonfly energy. Their connection with Faeries, often inspire visions and help us to skillfully maneuver all terrains with swift precision.

Dragonfly medicine helps us embrace our ability to bring light into the world and unearth our inner child. They invoke joy, imagination and help us express our very true colors. Dragonfly is an ally that can help you discern the true motives of others. They teach us to go beyond illusion and self-limiting beliefs and see right through deceptions. Interesting to note, the dragonfly is Japan's national emblem, which exalts the tenet of truth.

Another interesting point is that there is also a connection to spinning forms of meditations with Dragonfly medicine, due to their similar movements. Spinning forms of trance meditations include, walking labyrinths and Sufi Sama; a spinning into ecstasy, type of meditation, practiced by the Sufis. Dragonfly medicine holds the magic of joy, truth, ecstasy, lightness, inner child, playfulness, and bridging worlds together; from the aquatic to the etheric.

## 23. Spider                               Grandmother Spider/Iktomi

One of the first things we need to address when speaking about spiders is that they are not insects. Their body consists of two sections, unlike the three parts of an insect, and they have eight legs, unlike the typical six of most bugs. The fact that they have eight legs, (some species even have eight eyes too) and their body seems to form, what looks like the number eight, speaks to us about the symbolism of this number. When we look at the number eight, it forms the symbol of infinity, a highly regard metaphysical emblem that represents the never ending energy of life. It is related to spiral energy which connects everything in the cosmos. The past is always interwoven with the future and we are intrinsically linked with our ancestors and one another. As we walk our individual path, all things are connected and we are all one. Knowledge and wisdom travels to us through these sacred silk-pun threads.

Spiders are connected with the wheel of life. They are emblematic of our power as weavers and keepers of our own destiny. We weave our lives with our daily thoughts, feelings and actions. For indigenous cultures there was a belief that we are all born with these sacred threads coming out of our crown chakra and when these threads fuse themselves with others, we are creating a powerful tapestry, the web of life. There is magick in our creative life force. The Spider is an ancient symbol reflecting this belief. Just study a spider's web long enough and you will understand what I mean. They are exquisite, and yet here, in this beautifully created work of art, is where life and death takes place. The spider traps, ensnares and eats its prey on this intricate web labyrinth. Life and death are held in this special place. It is also where she will lay her numerous eggs and nurture new life. The creation of such an intricate master piece can sometimes also exhaust a spider to the point of death. Clearly, life and death are represented in her creative domain. It is not hard to see how a spider's web becomes a powerful symbol of our world and she; an invaluable teacher and guide.

Spider medicine awakens our creativity but also our awareness of how influential we all are to one another. We are awakened to our part in the circle of life. We become aware of ourselves in the small center of this ever expanding web and we see how far reaching its effects can be felt.

Most spiders are poisonous and most weave and spin their intricate silk webs to catch their prey. The tarantula, one of the biggest types of spiders, is the only exception. It catches its prey by digging itself under sand, hiding there, and attacking its victim when it senses it nearby. Its mouth is located under her belly and she does not weave webs but spins.

Spiders are a symbol of strong feminine power and assertiveness. The black widow spider, for example, is reputed to kill her male partner after copulating and rendering him weak. Spider medicine represents beauty, strength, unity, balance, gentleness and creativity. It is industrious, loquacious and wise.

Spiders and their important lore have long existed throughout history in numerous cultures. In the Lakota tradition, she is known as Iktomi, the trickster and shape shifter, teaching moral lessons to humanity. In Greece, she was associated with the three Fates, the celestial weavers of our lives. She was also known as Arachne, the woman who dared challenge the Greek Goddess, Athena, in a weaving contest. She lost her human form to become a spider, after boasting that her skills were comparable to the Goddess. In India she was known as Maya, the Goddess of illusion. For most Native Americans, she was known as Grandmother and sometimes just as Spiderwoman.

For ancient cultures, Spider was attributed for creating our alphabet and thus our language. Through the intricate patterns of a spider's web, early humans detected letters and shapes that would later become our language. Thus, Spider medicine is highly linked with the magick of words and the power of our language. She is the teacher of invocations and spells. She blesses the orator, the poet, the writer and all those that endeavor to weave words in creative ways that can magically affect others. Spider is mother, grandmother, sister energy that inspires us to create and tap into our feminine creative life force. She is a most powerful totem to work with, especially for those in the creative arts.

## 24. Ladybug

Who doesn't smile at the sight of a teeny, little lady bug? They have a very cheerful appearance due to their bright colored exterior and the sight of one might sweep you away into the scene of a happy memory from your childhood. Lady Bugs are small beetles, sometimes referred to as *"lady bird beetle."* They are red with tiny black polka dots and the females normally have about seven spots. Adult Lady Bugs live from 9 months to about a year, a time frame that can be utilized in your spiritual life, when divining how long her blessings will be felt. She is always considered a fortunate omen. And when Lady Bugs arrive, it is usually with a message of cheer and good fortune.

Throughout the ages and numerous cultures, I fail to find one, that doesn't have something positive to say about Lady Bugs. Lady bugs present to us the blessing of fertility, abundance, beauty, wellbeing and love. They announce the inauguration of positive shifts, forthcoming into our life. Lady bugs help with pollination. They hibernate in the fall and by the spring begin to lay eggs. Their breeding cycle last for four weeks and thus, in one summer they can create a multitude of generations. As a testament to her great power of fecundity, an adult Lady Bug, as tiny as she is, will lay as much as eight hundred eggs. She is unquestionably a powerful source to connect with our own powers of fertility and abundance.

Lady bug's energy initiates change where it is most needed and it offers us a chance to restore our faith and get out of our own way. They are nurturing, protective and highly resourceful. It might also surprise you to know they have a voracious appetite and their outer hard shell, is reflective of the protection she brings with her medicine.

Lady bug medicine offers growth, renewal and metamorphosis. This medicine blesses any endeavor you begin to pursue. When Lady Bugs appear in dreams, it is a sign that you are divinely protected and you are encouraged to share the joys of your creativity. Lady bugs are a sign of a wish to be fulfilled through perseverance and charm, and due to their universal admiration, they speak of social skills, popularity and accolades. She uplifts our spirits and is a harbinger of good things to come.

## **WATER**
### **25. Frog**                                                                                                **Heket**

Frogs have a longstanding reputation of being connected with sorcerers and witches. They are shrouded in a sort of mystery that will either repulse you or intrigue you. Known as amphibians, these bulging eye creatures can be found in an array of colors and sizes, but their most popular color appears to be a mossy olive green. Their unique ability to live and travel through multiple realms makes them particularly interesting, especially to those of us entrenched in spiritual studies. They live under water and yet they spend a lot of time on lily pads, above water. This intimate connection with the sacred element of water links them with the attributes of healing and transformation. It might surprise many of us to learn that the frog is also deeply connected with cleanliness and the banishing of negativity. Frog medicine reminds us of the power of being reborn, after periods of paralysis and inactivity. It speaks to us of resurrections and the gifts of the womb. When you really think about it, every child that comes out of the womb greets the world appearing like a frog. Their arms and legs are bent in a frog-like formation due to the limited space it became accustomed to while inside the cramped womb. And after spending 9 1/2 months swimming in its mother's amniotic fluids, newborns come out wet, slippery and still covered in an array of fluids; from mucus, to blood, to that white creamy substance known as, *vernix-caseosa.* Yes, newborns remind us of frogs and thus, frogs are closely linked with the magic of births, rebirths, transformation, women and the cycles of life.

Since Neolithic times, the frog was seen as a symbol of rebirth and the Sacred Feminine. Their connection with water made them an obvious choice when performing rain rites and rain charms. The shamans, in Aztec and Mayan cultures, hold the vision of the Frog in their mind as they spray water onto those that are seeking purification and healing, through special cleansing rites.

In the ancient Hindu, sacred texts of the Rig Veda, frogs were invoked as deities, in their own rights. For Egyptians, the Frog is a symbol of the fetus and thus, connected with death and rebirth. Mummies were sent to the afterlife with a piece of a frog's skeletal, as an amulet. Etched on the amulet were the words, "*I am the resurrection*," a phrase later allegedly copied by early Christians. In the Egyptian pantheon there exists the Goddess Heket. She is an Egyptian deity who was considered the midwife of the world. She protects mothers and newborns and was often portrayed as a frog herself or as a woman with the head of a frog. The frog was also a symbol of the great Mother Isis and Hathor in the Egyptian tradition. For Romans, frogs were believed to bring good fortune and therefore were used as lucky mascots. In China, the frog is worshipped as a healer and it is purported to bring about prosperity, especially for businesses. Frog is also considered a lunar symbol. Not all frogs are nocturnal but camouflage frogs tend to be, and this connection to the night would understandably link it with the moon and thus, with the Goddess.

Frog medicine is related to water energy; our tears, our womb, our ability to refresh and purify our souls. It connects us to the necessity to clear out negativity and start anew. Frog medicine teaches us to be adaptive to our environment, and allow ourselves to connect to the gift of transformation. It invites you to wholeness, to come into your power and tap into your voice. Frogs are notoriously known for their singing/croaking abilities. It is believed their collective nightly croaks can invoke the blessings of rain unto dry, parched land. This again connects Frogs to fertility and the ripe womb setting for new births, found in the newly wet soil. It is also a symbol of fertility due to the many number of eggs, frogs lay, at once. "*Look before you leap*," is a popular saying we've often heard before. It hints to one of Frog's medicine, which encourages you to follow your dreams but to do it in a practical, down to earth manner. Frog encourages you to pursue your goals and connect to the power of your voice to attract what you most desire. It inspires us to explore our creative expressions through music, singing, and other artistic gifts. We explore our vocal gifts, prosperity and the powers of transformation and rebirth with Frog medicine.

## 26. Turtle                                                                 Nu-kua

Turtles are one of the oldest symbols of the planet and this very fact intimately links them to the Sacred Feminine and our Mother Earth. Turtles are reptiles that breathe air and live, both on land and in water, thus, earth and water are the elements connected with this medicine. Sea turtles, in particular, can successfully navigate under, really deep waters through vibrations and sound waves. It serves to remind us to also connect with vibrations and learn to use, this higher dimensional, mode of communication. Everything around us is vibrating at varying levels and learning this form of communication is simply a matter of practice and awareness.

Unquestionably, turtles have an extraordinary heightened sense of smell and hearing. They also have strong jaws but by far their most interesting physical characteristic is the hard shell that covers most of their body. It is essentially their home, carried upon their back. Most importantly, it is their protective hard shield from predators which has kept them from extinction throughout the centuries. Turtles walk slowly upon the earth never needing to fear predators, for they are securely shielded within their hard shell. It is one of the most vital elements that has helped them survive all these years. Clearly, the turtle is a powerful symbol of longevity and survival, as one of the oldest living creatures on the earth. They can live to be hundreds of years old and they survive not by being the biggest, strongest, loudest or most aggressive, but by being cautious and slow. Turtle medicine thus, speaks to us about the value of slowing down, being cautious of our surroundings and learning when it is in our best interest to retreat within our shells.

When turtles reproduce, they deposits a multitude of eggs within the earth, letting the sun hatch them naturally into being. Their survival is assured, due also to the sheer volume of eggs they bury within the earth. Turtles eat plants, insects, and fish, and on occasions, even small mammals; making them omnivorous. It's important to note they also have very slow metabolism.

For indigenous people, turtle is a most powerful teacher and Spirit guide. She is a symbol of mother earth, who is infinitely seen as a provider to humanity. In ancient Chinese and Hindu folklore, it is the tortoise that supports and carries the world on its back. Here turtle is the nurturer and the protective celestial Mother of the earth. In Japanese mythology, the mountains were believed to be supported by a divine tortoise. In Greek and Roman mythology, turtle was often linked with the Goddesses of love and beauty, respectively, Venus and Aphrodite. The messenger deities, Hermes and Mercury were also linked with the turtle. In West Africa, the turtle symbolized fertility and was directly connected to female energy. For Native Americans the turtle has always been a symbol of the Sacred Feminine and was closely linked with the element of earth and water.

Turtle is a healer that helps us cultivate a respectful relationship with mother earth. It is considered a powerful spirit guide that will help you to acquire ancient wisdom. The energy of turtle is not one of aggression or force, but rather one of peace and defense. When turtle rattles are produced and used in indigenous rites, it is emblematic of the peace and harmony that is strived for among the tribe.

Turtle medicine is a symbol of peace, patience, self-reliance, nurturance and protection. Its energy is slow but it assures steady progress toward reaching our goals. It teaches us to honor the creative source within us and thrive to attain goals through patience and perseverance. It also warns us to beware of our surroundings. We are encourage to retreat into our shell, and go within, when we feel unsafe and perceive a threat.

Turtle teaches us to develop our ideas before bringing them out into the light, much like a turtle buries its precious eggs in the sand and allows the sun to slowly hatch the little ones into being. Our creative ideas sometimes need time to be anchored and formed quietly, hidden away from the critical eyes of others. Turtles are connected with self-paced journeys, strength and the wisdom of our foremothers. When we find ourselves in need of guidance, connecting quietly with turtle can open us up to her infinite wisdom and counsel.

## 27. Swan                                                                                           Saraswati

Swans are connected with elegance, beauty, grace and longevity, as they tend to live a long time. They are teachers of patience, empathy and altered states of awareness. They are also linked with magick portals and faery realms. Because the swan is often seen emerging annually in the spring, when the sun is growing in light, they were believed to usher in the spring.

Study a Swan in her habitat and you will be immediately entranced by her exceptional beauty and flowing grace. They are typically white, although in Australia they are black, and they have these long elegant necks that demand our admiration. When they are in the water, they appear to glide seamlessly as if they are on ice. They invoke a feeling of peace and serenity, and speak to us of the importance of grace through movement. Swans are beautiful, powerful birds. They can cause much harm to a perceived enemy with the beat of their strong wings and it must be noted they can execute a gnarly bite.

As an aquatic bird, they do not like the heat and prefer cool wetlands or land surrounded by water. They are very territorial and protective of their offspring. Swans usually reach maturity within two to three years and they breed at three to four years of age. Mother swans tend to stay with their young for a long period of time. They are fiercely protective, devoted parents and can live up to twenty years in the wild and fifty years in captivity. Interesting to note, they are known to mate for life and thus, become a powerful message of love, truth, fidelity and honoring our commitments. White swans, in particular, predict happiness and enduring love. They are seen as harbingers of blessings on our most romantic relationships.

Swans are very social living beings. During migration, swans fly together in a V formation at great heights. Their wings beat slowly and steady; this gives them the endurance needed to reach their destination quickly without tiring. Pacing yourself, therefore, is one of the many gifts swan medicine offers us.

Swan medicine also teaches us that there is beauty in all things, even those things we initially don't consider beautiful. Just think back to our beloved childhood fairytale, by Hans Christian Andersen, titled, *"The Ugly Duckling."* It is a message about transformation, inner strength and patience. It is an apropos, sweet message for children transitioning into their teen years and those going from awkward adolescence into adulthood. It serves to remind us that no matter what ugly phase in life you find yourself in, powerful transformation will always begin with the discomfort of an ugly phase before birthing itself into something quite beautiful and remarkable. We are encouraged to unearth and embrace our own inner beauty with Swan Medicine.

Swans also help us work with our inner child and throughout folklores we see swans being connected with the sacred archetype of the maiden. Swans are considered solar beings, connected with the direction of the north and have an affinity to the elements of air, earth, and water. In mythologies from across the globe, they were often perceived as a sacred bridge between the worlds and awakeners of intuitive gifts. Because they have always been connected to music, poetry and the mysteries of songs, they have a strong connection to the bard. The skin and feathers of swans were often incorporated into Bardic rites and ceremonial cloaks were decorated with the swan's feathers for added swan blessings.

Working with the swans can facilitate travels to other realms, according to ancient Druid beliefs. They related this sacred bird with the festival of Samhain due to its mystical nature. For the Celts, Swan is associated with water deities, healing and the sun. Swans were believed to be shape-shifters that can take the form of humans and they were often associated with music, love and poetry.

For nearly all Native American traditions, the Swan is associated with the gift of grace. Because it is able to fly even higher than the revered eagle, the Elders believed the swan is a great shamaness, who is able to see, not only this world, but into the next. Here, she is connected to divination and the ability to see into the future. Swan feathers were also used in smudging and healing ceremonies, a practice that still takes place today. In Greek mythology the Swan was the bird associated with the Sun God, Apollo, who one should remember is linked with music and songs. The swan is purported to sing a melody of haunting beauty just before its death, according to Greek legends. She was also known as an emblem for the muses. The Greek Goddess of beauty and love, Aphrodite, was often represented riding on a swan or a goose. Both of these creatures are represented, at times, interchangeably. According to one Greek myth, the God Zeus was alleged to have turned himself into a swan, in order to facilitate sexual relations with Leda. In Hindu mythology there are swan Maidens known as the heavenly nymphs, called Apsaras. The Hindu God, Krishna, became a swan knight in order to copulate with these beautiful swan maidens. We often see the swan with various Hindu deities. She represents breath and spirit in Hindu mythology and is often the sacred vehicle for the beloved matriarchal Goddess of Wisdom, Saraswati. Swan is clearly an invaluable animal medicine to explore for those in the artistic expression and musical field but also most importantly for those studying mysticism and metaphysics.

## 28. Crocodile                                                                  Sobek

Crocodiles are powerful prehistoric predators, closely linked with ancient wisdom and the power of Mother Earth. They are courageous, cunning, patient and relentless with their prey. One of the most feared creatures; they are highly regarded across numerous cultures, throughout the ages, for their great strength and fearlessness. Their existence, much of it unchanged, is believed to be millions of years old and thus, like the turtle, they offer us the gift of survival and longevity. These reptiles are quite fascinating to get to know and if Crocodile medicine is tugging at your soul, it is important to explore this ancient teacher.

At five to ten years of age crocodiles begin to breed and the mother chooses to dig a big ditch to lay her eggs in, much like a turtle. The female crocodile can lay up to ninety eggs. In four months, the eggs are expected to hatch and the fiercely protective mother crocodile will tenderly take each of her offspring into her mouth and carry them down into the water, where they can be sheltered by her. Her protective nature as a mother cannot be underestimated. Crocodile medicine speaks to us of the fiercely protective gifts of the mother archetype.

Interesting to note the word crocodile derives from the Greek word, *"Kroko deilos"* which is interpreted to mean, *"Pebble man,"* perhaps a reference to its outer shell and its slow movement in the water. They emit a low sounding vibration within the waters when they are ready to attract a mate and they are known to live comfortably both in and out of water. The temperature of their environment is of extreme importance and if it gets too hot or too cold, they will move to where it is more comfortable. Their medicine serves to remind us to be wary of our own environment and not hesitate to move and make adjustments as needed in our own respective lives. Their heightened primal instincts and extraordinary sense of sight translates as an invaluable spiritual gift for us to explore. Crocodile helps to enhance our intuition and primal instincts. Their pupils widen, giving them extraordinary nocturnal vision and allowing them to see under water. Crocodile medicine will quite often alert you to develop keener eyesight and care for your eyes. It will also help you to be more observant of your environment and remain out of sight and hidden, until just the right moment. Crocodiles' ability to see under water speaks to us of our own ability to acquire discernment and extrasensory sight, amidst emotional terrains that are so often represented by the element of water. Crocodile speaks to us about maintaining our cool and being patient amidst other people's chaos. Because the crocodile lives comfortably upon the earth and in water, its medicine speaks to us about the proper balance between these two sacred elements. It is also a symbol of destruction and creation, life and death; attributes connected to the primordial sacred feminine.

Crocodiles are descendants of Archosaurian reptiles. There is a belief that Crocodiles and Alligators are closely linked with ancient dinosaurs, due to the fact that their existence can be traced back to the end of the Paleozoic era, which was approximately, 250 million years ago. Oftentimes, we can easily confused crocodiles and alligators and while they both share similar spiritual attributes for the student of magick, it is important to note their physical differences; especially if they appear to you in a vision or a dream. Both beings are similar in color and both have almost impermeable tough skin and regenerative teeth. Differences can be noted upon closer inspection however, as you will see that alligators have u-shaped snouts and wider jaws, which gives them exceedingly powerful teeth crushing abilities. Crocodiles have longer, more pointed v-shaped snouts and four of their teeth in their lower jaw, protrude, coming up over their upper lips. Their crushing ability, while still powerful, is not as strong as the alligator, when it comes to penetrating turtle shells and larger mammals for a meal. Crocodiles are more commonly found in Africa, Australia and India, while Alligators are more often found in America and China. Alligators prefer to inhabit freshwaters, while Crocodiles behold a special gland in their tongues that allows them to filter the salt from their salt water habitat.

For Native Americans the crocodile is deemed as extremely powerful and fearless. The Mayans revered the crocodile so much that they included him in their astrological system. Here it is known for its superiority and sensitivity to criticism. In Egyptian mythology there is a city named after crocodiles and in their pantheon they venerate a highly regarded crocodile deity who greets every soul in the underworld. For Egyptians, the Crocodile God, Sobek, is believed to have authoritative gifts and omnipotent powers to help determine the fate of a soul in the afterlife.

Crocodile is a powerful animal to work with. It awakens our strength, intellect, patience and fearlessness. We are more alert of our environment and tap into the ability to hide, while safely assessing our surroundings. Our primal instincts & intuition are enhanced with crocodile medicine and we learn when to wait for just the right moment to execute our strategies. It may also indicate a need for us to be more aware of deceptive, hypocritical or untrustworthy people in our lives and a warning to look deeply under the surface of all things. Crocodile is a protective ally when traversing dark marshy or murky, unstable situations and we learn to adapt, to clearly see through emotionally charged circumstances. These reptiles evoke our strength and inner knowing.

## **ANIMAL FRIEND MEDITATION**

    We begin by taking a deep breath in, hold (1-2-3) and release (1-2-3). Breathe in again, hold for three counts (1-2-3) and then release (1-2-3). Release all tension with that exhalation. Again breathe in and audibly sigh with you exhalation. On this next inhalation feel yourself slowly fill your lungs with brand new air. Feel this air revitalize and regenerate your lungs and your internal cells. On the count of three now, release this breath (1-2-3). With each breath being release now, you sink deeper and deeper into relaxation. Slowly breathe in, hold for three (1-2-3) and exhale. Continue to breathe in this manner as your attention now shifts to my voice. Listen to my voice as it gently guides you on this meditation. Remember that you are in full control of your journey and you will go only as far as you wish to go. Throughout our time together, rest assure, that you will be safe and you will only go as deep as you choose to. My voice will simply serve as a guide; where it ultimately leads you is up to you. Breathe and relax deeper, deeper into your subconscious. Breathe, as each breath will anchor you deeper into this journey now. Today we will journey through the elements and meet our personal animal guides through the process.

    Take a brand new breath now to begin and exhale. With each breath, notice its effect on your physical body; notice how relax and limber your body is now and how it loses its weight. Weightless, it drops all stress and concerns and just falls relaxed, weightless. As you breathe in and out, notice the lightness of this air now and how it rises and falls gently. See how your chest rises and falls gently with each breath cycle. As you continue to breathe in and out, become acutely aware of the journey your breath is taking. In and out, it journeys, light as a feather. It flows effortlessly. In your mind's eye see this breath not only within you but all around you. **This is the sacred element of air.** (pause) Follow your breath. As it exhales, it joins the breeze that is surrounding your flesh, this room, and everything around you. It can only be felt and seen with your third eye. Follow this breeze as it swirls and dances lighter and lighter, ascending higher and higher to the ethers. You are ascending higher and higher to the ethers. (pause)

With your mind's eye, survey the area now, see yourself floating, suspended in the air. There are tree-tops that you hang over and mountaintops nearby. Look around you, what do you see? (pause) You can even gauge how close you are to the celestial, white feathery clouds. Take this moment to breathe into this new environment. Breathe into this airy new space and survey how light and bright this area is. Use your senses to fully recognize the winged creature trying to hold your attention with its sound. Listen closely. (pause) This special winged creature has made the long journey to greet you today and it has a special message just for you. Take this moment now to connect with this animal. Study its shape, size, color, feathers and physical form. Gaze deeply into its eyes. It will deliver its message to you, if you quiet down your mind enough to hear it with your crown chakra. (pause)

Delighting in the gentle breeze, your beloved new friend flaps its wings and invites you to fly with him to experience the ecstasy of this element. His message has been delivered to you and now it's time to bid him adieu. When the message has been received you will feel your winged animal friend transport you back to the ground. Thank your friend for his presence in this meditation today then sincerely bid him adieu.

As you stand now on the ground, feel the earth beneath your feet. (pause) Make note of how the ground is supporting your weight and let your gaze stretch over, across the landscape of this vast, fertile, rich earth. The earth is old and wise, with much to share with you. Take a moment to connect with **this sacred element of Earth**, beneath you and let yourself relax into its rich, dark soil. Breathe in and with your exhalation let your eyes rest upon all the beautiful reflections of Mother Earth; the dark patch of soil under your feet, the blades of green grass surrounding the area, the tree trunks and their mangled roots. (Pause) All appears lush and fertile in this realm and it draws you into a deeper, relaxed trance. The various hues of greens and browns all around you shape-shift and takes on a form. Look deeply into this form to make out who or what wants to be known. (Pause) An animal of the earth steps forward shyly, unsure if you are ready for its visit. Let her know you are ready to fully see and receive her now. (pause) Be still and silent, as you study this beloved earth creature. She greets you with her familiar animal sound and begins to speak in a language you can strangely comprehend. She has traveled a long way to get this special message to you. Welcome her and open yourself to receive the message from your new animal friend. What message does it have for you? (pause) After it delivers its message, your earth animal friend asks you to follow her even further down a verdant, dark winding pathway. You agree to follow, putting aside any fears of the unknown, trusting your totem animal will not lead you astray. Breathe as you begin to walk and walk, until you are led to a nearby body of water. Here you will give your thanks and bid her adieu. She encircles you and rubs her body gently against your flesh as she affectionately says her goodbyes. Take this moment to connect with the animal of the earth and thank it for its message. (pause)

Seeing the body of water thrills you and you run to be near it. It has been quite a journey thus far, with much to process from your previous animal friends but now you are ready to relax into this serene scene. Greet **the sacred element of water** with reverence and gratitude. You are invited to sit by this water and drink of her pool of compassion and love. If you feel called to, you may even swim in this water and relax. (Pause) You begin to detect the faint sound of a splash in the distance and you sense you are no longer alone. Quietly you wait in the water as the splashing sound appears to draw closer to you. Within minutes there, before your eyes, appears an animal of the sea. As it stands before you in the water, you now can fully recognize and embrace your aquatic new animal friend. Greet it with reverence and wait patiently for its ensuing spiritual message to you. (Pause) It giggles effervescently and begins to speak through its bubbly nature. You strangely understand its language. (Pause) When her message has been well received by you, show your gratitude and respect to your new aquatic friend and lovingly bid her adieu. (pause)

You have met your three personal animals in this meditation. Each one traveled to you through the sacred elements of; Air, Earth and Water. They came via this meditation with a unique personal message just for you. We're reaching the end of our meditation and the last realm we will visit is the element of Fire. Breathe and as you exhale you are invited to take a moment now to feel the heat that your own physical body is generating. Breathe and exhale. Notice that your very breath is emblematic of the fire that you hold within you. **The element of fire** is visited now but it is reached by simply connecting with your own internal fires. You too are a primal being and at this moment you are invited to connect with your inner animal of fire. Continue to breathe and feel as your hot breath leads you within the furnace of your heart. Listen to its consistent thump, as it pulsates and carries blood to and from. Quietly dig deep and connect within your own inner flames and make note of any particular messages that are coming through at this moment (Pause). Continue to breathe and exhale. Our journey is now coming to an end. The sacred elements of Earth, Air, Water and Fire thank you, for your presence in this meditation here today. Your personal animal totems also thank you for partaking in this journey. (pause)

We end this spiritual expedition the way we began it, through our breath. Continue to breathe and listen to my voice as it leads you out of the elemental labyrinth and back into your present consciousness. Feel yourself approach my voice, closer and closer, with each breath. You will hear me count from seven to one, backwards and by the count of one, you will find yourself fully conscious and awake, in your body, returned to this time and space. We begin, **seven six, five,** breathe and exhale, **four, three, two and one...**

Welcome back and when you're ready, please open your eyes and bring your consciousness back into this space. If you have a journal you are encouraged to make note of any particular observations and any special messages that were given to you during this meditation. Documenting your experience here can prove to be invaluable in your spiritual growth. Blessed be!!!!

# 11. GODDESS MAGICK

*"The simplest and most basic meaning of the symbol of the Goddess is the acknowledgement of the legitimacy of female power as a beneficent and independent power..."* Carol P. Christ

# GODDESS MAGICK

## Reclaiming Goddess Mythologies
*"I Found God in Myself and I Loved her Fiercely..." Ntozake Shange*

    One of the first questions that comes to mind is; Why Goddess, why should we embrace her collective mythologies? Why is it so important for women to connect with this type of work? The short answer to this question is, because if we don't reclaim our stories, who will? Because Goddess Mythologies are **our** lineage and her-story...because they are indeed OUR stories, that have been hidden, altered or forgotten, \*\*And if we don't reclaim our own stories, we leave it for patriarchy to continually distort, butcher and falsifying them, as has been done throughout the years. Unearthing, reclaiming and embracing our numerous Goddess mythologies is important and valuable for modern day women, especially those that have been maligned, disempowered, oppressed, violated, and entrenched in false ideologies from society and patriarchal religions. It becomes more and more important for women (in particular) to seek and embrace a more empowering vision of themselves and unearth the Divine, as a mirrored reflection of herself - a vision that has been blocked and tainted by patriarchy and one that many scholars believed, existed before the rise of monotheistic religions. It is up to us to reclaim our stories, our Goddess myths and heritage and in so doing, unearth our direct connection to source.

    To embrace the unquestionable existence of the Sacred Feminine, with all of its proof found in the plethora of archeological finds, opens us up to an awareness of our own divinity and suppressed lineage. And when we scrutinize the scattered collection of

Goddess myths and tales found from around the world and consider for a brief moment how many of them survived despite the obvious negative alterations to their original fiber, it stirs our curiosity and inaugurates the journey to find ourselves, through "hers" myths.

Part of my passion has been researching and connecting the relevance of these Goddesses of ancient cultures, and giving them new life; to be appreciated by new audiences, through modern day women. I love myths and storytelling and have a great appreciation for the role and value they have towards a person's psyche and wellbeing. What I have personally found, however, is that some stories and images offered to us by patriarchal religions have done very little to break us free from tyranny and oppression but instead have been the deep rooted subconscious glue to blindly anchor us into slavery, complacency and subordination...that is... until we as women awaken. If we go to our grave asleep; never questioning those limiting images of our gender and accepting false half tales regarding the Divine, we miss an essential part to our inherent strength and power.

For far too long we have blindly accepted stories and doctrines about women and the Divine that appear to have deemed women as a deformed second sex, an inferior gender, requiring rulership and dominion. It does not serve us well to embrace and adopt images about us that are false, limiting, incomplete and clearly altered by men with less than honorable, ulterior motives. When the stories we are hearing (the popular stories being documented and pass down to us from generation to generation in scriptures) fail to authentically reveal our true nature, it is time to excavate the truth. . . The truth is; in Ancient times it was not a threat in our society to accept, respect and embrace the Sacred Feminine. The Goddesses was revered and sometimes even stood side by side, right along male gods in her worship. The obvious consequences of such an inclusive view on the Divine effected societal views on humanity as a whole and unquestionably, greatly influenced women's role in ancient religious rites, as well as in her communities.

\* This quote by Goddess Scholar and beloved bard and poet, Patricia Monaghan, who was always an inspiration to my work, says it best....

*The most important fact about Goddesses, it seems to me,*
*is that they are invariably connected to Polytheism.*
*Put another way; there is no monotheistic religion*
*based on Goddess. Not a single Goddess appears*
*without friends, companions, lovers, children.*
*The presence of the Goddess demands other Goddesses*
*and Gods, as well. This is comforting to me,*
*for in my vision of the world redeemed, the world made whole,*
*I yearn for connection, not separation.*
*Throughout human history, gods have banished the Goddess,*
*demanding that we hold no other gods before them.*
*But the Goddess did not respond in kind.*
*In the religion that honors her,*
*"She" had welcomed –even embraced – the other... Patricia Monaghan*

This equally exalted, Feminine view of the Divine amidst other gods within a community, and in important religious rites, **only** became a problem and a threat, when the need to dominate and suppress one group over another, became necessary for the rising warrior monotheistic religions. Since the beginning of time, however, man had witnessed and embraced the gifts of the Great Mother via nature and her daughters. Women and our astounding powers of fecundity, our powers of nurturance in our production of milk via our breast, powers of **life** giving in birth and creations via our lotus-opening yoni and our clear powers of survival & transformation, via our monthly flowing blood, were all perceptible to early man, as worthy of veneration. Clearly something changed drastically in our civilization, when "She," who all along had been revered as the Great Mother (and had been so exalted) was now being completely hidden, disregarded, silenced and relegated to the back.

Part of my personal mission has been to expose the plethora of forgotten faces of the Sacred Feminine, the divine images and stories of those who were once so prominently worshipped and revered, and those whose stories were later strategically altered to demote her and in so doing, slowly erased our her-story; deliberately altering our gender's status in civilization and religious practices. For as patriarchy began to assert itself, new monotheistic religions and societal structures needed to be created to support those who sought to oppress and elevate themselves to higher religious and political powers. New systems and structures implemented by patriarchy required edited, censored, reconstructed tales, re-interpretation of our oral history, new rules for our gender and a new belief system that would slowly make the memories of "Her" greatness, regressed to the forgotten recesses of our minds. But, take heart....for in the metaphysical world, nothing is ever really forgotten and the truth cannot be askew or suppressed for long periods of time; eventually all resurfaces to its proper place.

It is in the heart of every woman, deeply lodged in her DNA that the memory of ages past still exist, when she was honored and revered....when she was Goddess. In every woman lives and auric cellular memory of her lineage, her ancestry, her inherent powers as a woman. In every woman lives a tiny grain of deep remembrance that occasionally reveals itself and women are slowly awakening now to this memory. Often the first thing I hear, from women discovering Goddess Spirituality, is a sense of coming home, a rare sense of familiarity, even though they might have only known (and been indoctrinated from an early age) into a patriarchal religion. There is a sense of familiarity, a sense that we as women and our collective experiences are not so distant from those found in ancient Goddess mythologies. She does not reside far up, away, in the sky, apart from us; she dwells among us, in our hearts, in our souls, in the wheat fields (Demeter), in the storms (Oya), in the downpours (Ix Chel), in the embers of your hearth fires (Hestia) and the brilliance of the Moon (Hina/ Selene), in the oceans (Yemaya), and the breeze (Nike), in Tree Groves (Asherah), in volcanoes (Pele), in a fellow Sister's gaze, in our Mother's embrace, amidst the earth and all of nature. We already recognized her because she was always there....I love this quote by the creator of the 13Moon Mystery, Ariel Spilsbury, says;

> *"The number of expressions of the feminine in a patriarchal world is limited, has been limited for many years but when we embrace the full spectrum of women/ feminine archetypes, we begin to tap into a larger energy field... a fuller spectrum of the Divine becomes available to us... within us...."* Ariel Spilsbury

Indisputably, patriarchy appears to only strategically show women in very constricting images of; either the immaculate virgin or the dangerous whore. Along with these limiting views are the negative implications of our gender's capacity, enough to alter our gender's standing in society and consequently our collective self-esteem. We need to embrace more positive imagery of women and the Divine and view all dimensions of women as sacred; *from the maiden, the chaste one, the fertile one, nurturing mother, the warrior, the huntress, the sacrificial one, the priestess, the executor, the queen, the shaman, the midwife, the medicine woman, the wise crone, the magic woman, the sexual one, the hermit, the sovereign one, the competitive athlete, the political activist, the fiery volcanic one, the Amazon and fighter, the orator and peacemaker, the Creatrix, the glamour one, the mermaid, the seer, the teacher, our mother, our daughters, sisters, grandmother etc...* We need to excavate and hear all of her stories and behold in awe, the multitude of images, of the Sacred Feminine, via womankind. And, not pit them against each other or place them in a hierarchical system; which would only delight those who know and fear the great power of women actually uniting. From Kali to Kwan Yin, to Aphrodite to Athena, From Oya to Bridget from Pele to Lilith, from Hestia to Asherah, from Hathor to Ma'at....etc Their myths & stories are ours, for they are our ancestresses and there is great value, not in fragmenting their stories, as patriarchy has done, but in embracing all of them within us.

Embracing the full spectrum of women, via the Goddess, connects us to the most potent divine source within ourselves. When we dive in, to research further and come to the realization that there were others, like us, who were called Goddess... that the Divine does not just hold the male species as sacred but long before this one male God came to be, there were many others and they looked like you and me.... we uncover a deep blocked part of our soul. And there we find "Her." *

- We find her, like the Japanese Sun Goddess, Amaterasu, still honored and worshipped today in Shintoism, who encourages us not to dim our radiance.
- We find her, like the Love Goddesses, Aphrodite and the Egyptian Goddess, Hathor, who remind us of the value of pleasure, beauty and enjoyment of life
- We find her, like the Chinese matriarchal Goddess, Nu-Kua, who is attributed with creating humanity and helps us tap into our inner savioress and creatress.

- We find her, like the primordial earth Goddess, Gaia, who gave birth to everything upon the earth and connects us to our powers of fertility, procreation and abundance.
- We find her, like the Hindu Goddess Durga, still worshipped today in India, who awakens the multi-armed warrior within and compels us to fight for our freedom and autonomy.
- We find her, like the Ukrainian Crone Goddess, BabaYaga, who beckons us deep into her dark, scary forest to face and transform our biggest fears.
- We find her, like the Goddesses of the Americas; Corn Mother, Selu, Iyatiku, who feed us and teach us the gift of food and the power of sacrifice; revealing the secrets of life, death, rebirth and our own resurrections.
- We find her, like the Yoruban Goddess Oya, still honored and worshipped today in some parts of Africa and the Americas. She who fiercely controls the storms and tornadoes of life and catapults us into unimaginable, life altering changes.
- We find her, like the beautiful Welsh Flower Goddess, Blodeuwedd, who awakens us to these dark, hidden parts of our subconscious and guides us into balancing and exploring our light & dark aspects
- We find her, like the ancient Norse Goddess, the Jotunheim Giantess Skadi, who teaches us to demand what is just and right in our lives and bravely set our own life standards
- We find her, like the Crone Goddess, Hekate, who meets us at the crossroads with her illuminating lantern to light our path into the next realm.
- We find her, like the Polynesian Goddesses Pele, still honored and worshipped today in Hawaii's volcanoes, she who lends us her fierce, hot fires to relentless pursue our deepest desires and awaken our inner roar and passion.
- We find her, like the voodoo Goddess Maman Brigitte, still honored in parts of Haiti and the Americas, the keeper of our bones, our death mother who awaits our arrival in her cemetery and is our honored midwife, as we go through powerful transformative journeys into the afterlife.
- We find her, like the Sumerian Goddess, Lilith, Adam's hidden first wife in Judaic scriptures, who demands her equality and emancipation from oppression and refuses to subordinate herself by lying beneath man.
- We find her, like the Greek Maiden Goddess Artemis, who reminds us to value our inner maiden, defy conventional stereotypes and refuse to be tamed or domesticated.
- We find her, like The Egyptian Goddess, Ma'at, who teaches us to value the content of our heart…for it is the only thing you take with you into the afterlife.

These are **only** some of the many Goddesses I have personally lived with, researched and, in great detail, written about in my published books and I can attest to their powerful, transformative influence in my life.

*There is something that reaches deep within my soul; a comforting memory when I learn about Goddesses and my Spiritual lineage. The many faces of the sacred feminine and the diverse ways in which she appears in various cultures (revealing her relevance, immortality and infinite presence) even still today. Speaks volume to me... It is as if I am learning about my own sisters, mothers, great-grandmothers, my teachers, my ancestresses, my clan. It is **this** way because it is so and in learning of them I get a glimpse into a portal... a sweet sacred doorway, where the thread of my empowered matriarchal lineage exists. I'm able to follow this moon-spun silver thread into a crystalline lucid pool of water, that when I reach it, and look deeply upon it, reveals to me my own reflection... my own powers... my own sacred Divinity -**that is Goddess Spirituality**. That is the "*coming home*" sentiment so often expressed by women who are radiantly catapulted and transformed, when they first encounter the Goddess. It is this recognition, this resonance with Her numerous diverse myths that draws her in to us, as a long lost relative and thus, her myths become **our** myths, reminiscent of the same tales you might tell today around a holiday dining table or a family gathering. These are the same stories that one can easily hear our children or grandchildren tell one another, of days long past, still ripe in its vibrating relevance.

Goddess mythologies are our tales being passed down to us; re-collected, re-membered, re-claimed by us and for our future generation. Consider the gift we give to ourselves and to young girls upon learning that the Divine looks just like us -that the Sacred long ago was accepted as Goddess, that **"God was/is a Woman and She has many Names**..." And we are her descendants, called upon now to keep her infinite legacy alive today.

Goddess myths are the collection of diverse examples of our beautiful, powerful gender via the Divine Feminine. These are our lyrical, textual, photo albums capturing the essence of who we are... who we have been... and who we will continue to be. Thus, in reclaiming Goddess Mythology we are inspired, encouraged, empowered and awakened. These are the stories that are not meant to silence, kill or oppress us, as patriarchal propaganda would hope it would, but these Goddess myths we reclaim now, are meant to serve the continual strong evolution of our gender...as empowered, valued and solidly anchored in this world and the next.

**RITUAL ACTIVITY:** We're going to document our story and add it to the collective consciousness & the Goddess mythos. On a sheet of paper or your personal journal, you are invited to write your birth name or take this opportunity to give yourself a Goddess name, a name that quite possibly will live on, long after your body and flesh are no more....Write the name that your future heirs can call you by, when they light a candle in your honor. Give yourself the name you want to be called by, the name you'll respond to, when you're called in prayer or invocation.

**I.** I am _____

**II.** Describe maybe three or more prominent **physical attributes** you are known for ....

_____

_____

_____

**III.** On this next line, You are invited to contemplate 3-5 of your most cherished gifts and talents. Think about those things that you're known for by your family and friends. What gifts have you inherited from your family and what gifts have you yourself developed? Think about those gifts and talents that you proudly embrace within.

1. _____
2. _____
3. _____
4. _____
5. _____

**IV.** Now if you can, I want you to take this moment to consider what has been your greatest achievement in your life up to this point. What are you most proud of having achieved? What do you want to be remembered for?

_____

**V.** Let us take a moment now and Listen to what invocations may be uttered in whispers to you, as part of the immortal, assembly of Goddesses.... Take this moment to pen a short invocation to yourself as part of the Collective consciousness of the infinite Sacred Feminine that you are now a part of...

**Ex: Invocation Template:**

*I invoke you Goddess, _____ (your name).*
*You, who shall always be remembered for your _____,*
*_____, _____(Describe Physical attributes here)*
*Beloved Sister, Magick woman and ancestress,*
*I honor you and your gifts of _____ and _____*
*Thy talents of _____ and _____and _____*
*I will forever remember to exalt your name, these gifts you shared and your memory. When I find myself in need of inspiration, courage and support I will remember my lineage so deeply connecting me back to you. Oh Goddess _____ (name). You, who's tales of triumph still echoes in the infinite chambers of our lineage and history when you successfully,*

*_____*
*_____*

*Beloved Goddess and ancestress.... I seek now to connect with your gifts of*
*_____(which gifts do you want to connect with now?)*
*For_____ (state your wish/spell-working )*
*May I touch upon your gifts and honor you in this remembrance and appreciation of your existence... Blessed Be!!!!*

# SAY YES TO YOUR INNER GODDESS, THREE WAYS TO UNEARTH, EMBRACE & EMPLOY GODDESS TO REVAMP YOURSELF AND YOUR LIFE!!!!

How many of you have long standing goals and big dreams that you wish you could accomplish? And how many of you are actively pursuing those goals and those dreams? How many of you are in the paralysis stage; where you're not sure how to go about pursuing your dreams or you're not sure if it's a dream worthy of pursuit. Then I'm giving a great shot out of gratitude to the Universe for bringing you to the right place at the right time because it is no coincidence that this book has found you. Our meeting here today is no coincidence. The universe has a way of always orchestrating important meetings and events long before we can possibly comprehend their fated purpose and it is my hope to inspire you to live the life you desire.

The name of this chapter is called, **"Say YES to your Inner Goddess, Three ways to Unearth, Embrace & Employ the Goddess to Revamp Yourself and Your Life."** What I hope to offer you is a chance to meet someone very powerful and instrumental to your success…**you.** What I hope to offer you is a chance to say **YES, to your inner Goddess and as a result of that, help you; unearth, embrace and employ her to revamp yourself and your life.**

Now I know the term Goddess might take some of you off guard and that perhaps my goal here might sound a tad ambitious, but what I'd like to do is introduce you to some pretty important information and share with you, who I am, the work that I do, the significance of this work and how it can better serve you.

I am the founder of **"Feminine Divine Works"** and CEO and head life coach at **"Goddess Empowerment Life Coaching."** I am a professional certified life coach, specializing in the empowerment of women and a published author of five books, presently working on my sixth. I am an intuitive artist and a classically trained singer, holding both a Bachelor's of Music in Vocal Pedagogy and a Master's of Music in Voice Performance and I am woman's group facilitator. For the last six years I have been facilitating & priestessing for, **"Grove of the Feminine Divine"** (an all-women's Goddess Group that meet monthly to explore Goddesses, Feminine Archetypes and their positive impact on modern day women.) I have also been traveling to various Goddess Conferences across the USA; speaking and presenting workshops on this subject, as well. Clearly, I am a passionate advocate and researcher of the Goddess and a writer of books on Women spirituality, Goddess mythologies and their positive influence on women's psyche, growth and transformational development. Two of my Books; **"Gathering for Goddess, A Complete Manual For Priestessing Woman Circles" And "Living Goddess Spirituality, a Feminine Divine Priestessing Handbook"** both Illustrate beautifully the kind of work I do, in regards to empowering women, and creating workshops and sacred spaces for women to meet their inner Goddess. Collectively in both of these books, you will find a plethora of scholarly research, rituals and writings for over 35 different Goddesses from across the globe. In reading these two comprehensive books you enter a realm where women are affirmed and you, as the reader, are welcomed into a sisterhood; where women gather together monthly to create community and explore the Divine Feminine. We not only explore and celebrate the Goddesses of ancient times, but we also look at how impactful and relevant this type of work is to a modern day women, when she begins to embraces her inner Goddess.

My third book is a collection of prose, poems and Goddess invocations titled; **"Goddess Grimoire Journal, a Collection of Simple Prose and Spells."** It is a lovely companion workbook that also allows the reader to notate their own thoughts and document their development and spiritual practice. I have also created a very special, 70x cards Oracle Deck with my own illustrated unique art work and my fourth book is the companion, colored guide book, for this oracle deck. It is titled; **"Feminine Divine Works Intuitive Oracle, A Powerful Tool For Daily Insight and Inspiration."** The Oracle Deck is a perfect tool to use when you are seeking guidance, deeper insight on a subject matter or plagued with indecisions. For one thing, just holding the cards forces you to slow down, breathe deeper and begin to narrow down your focus, engaging the limbic part of your brain and connecting more with your third eye. You traverse into a more intuitive realm and in this way the Oracle Deck becomes an invaluable tool for assessment, self-growth and a perfect coaching tool that works in tandem with your own intuitive gifts to bring you more clarity. Working with an Oracle Deck typically can bring healing and lightning "aha" moments and it's a quick way to get yourself grounded and centered. My fifth book is the one you hold in your hands now. In addition to being an author, a certified Life Coach, women's group facilitator, oracular creator, artist, singer and Goddess advocate, I am a certified New Yorker living in Texas. I am a mother of three, married for over 15 years.

After hearing that introduction about who I am and what I do, it becomes clear, I am a *"manifestor."* It also is clear I work with Goddess energy, Feminine Archetypes and my specialty is supporting and empowering my clients through a more Feminist theology. Now some of you might have been thrown off by the term Goddess and women spirituality, and you might be unclear about just what exactly that means. Then perhaps, there are those of you who are very familiar with the term Goddess due to the wonderfully saturated usage of this term in recent years in our mainstream media & pop culture…Perhaps, it would be best to begin by first looking at our definition of Goddess and what is a Goddess woman.

According to the urban dictionary, Goddess is defined as, *"…a woman who is so beautiful, brilliant and wholesome that she is simply not like any other woman on earth and therefore possesses some sort of uncommon spiritual element that while it cannot be solidly defined, it is clearly present."* Pretty Cool, huh??? Another definition in our modern day dictionaries is, *"a woman of superior charm and excellence, a woman who is adored, especially for her beauty. Goddess is a woman whose boundless charm is greatly worshipped and adored; a woman of extraordinary power, grace and appeal."* In these two examples, it becomes pretty clear that Goddess is a term now often reserved to define a woman who *"has it going on."* A woman who appears to have herself together and who is admired and believed to have super woman qualities and celestial gifts is considered a Goddess. So no matter what your race, class, age, status or religious affiliation, you as a woman, can easily be elevated and considered a Goddess if we go by our modern day dictionary definition. The term Goddess becomes more palpable when we view it from this perspective and we also begin to see the value and relevance for a modern woman's life. Of course, what contemporary woman doesn't want to be seen as a Goddess? Who doesn't want to feel Goddess-like? **See, "She," Goddess, is not some lofty, up in the sky, ideal. "She" is here, ever present among us, within us, across the mirror in our reflection, across the numerous faces of our gender. This is where we begin to unearth her & embrace her.**

"So what is the connection between, saying yes to Goddess and revamping myself and my life?" you might be asking. Why is it so important for us as women to embrace the Goddess?

The exploration and adoption of Woman affirming spirituality and Goddess identity, opens a woman up to her authentic value and gifts. It frees her up to explore them further with greater urgency, fulfillment and a laser like sense of purpose as she walks the earth... When a woman embraces her inner Goddess and begins to walk this path....

- She heals long standing known and unknown wounds.
- She unveils layers of truth that had been previously hidden from her.
- She uncovers another aspect to herself that perhaps she hid even from her own psyche.
- She begins to see herself as a valuable component to the overall wellbeing and growth of her gender, as a collective whole. She's not alone and does not accept isolation as truth.
- She surrenders complacency, discovers her unique voice, maybe even her own ROAR.
- She welcomes a palpable strength and invites a different quality to her existence.
- She acquires sight for all kinds of oppression and injustices towards her gender.
- She no longer allows herself to be devalued, degraded, silenced or oppressed.

- She walks upon this earth fully owning her right to be here, embracing and owning her space.
- She recognizes, accepts and develops a conscious relationship with her physical body, knowing it can be a powerful tool of magick.
- She exist taking up her rightful space upon the earth and is no longer plagued by the subconsciously fed falsities of inferiority and unworthiness.

It is my belief that women are better served with a Feminist Theology/Thealogy and that a woman who embraces the Goddess, more specifically, the Goddess within herself, is a force to be reckoned with.

*"Imagine a Woman who names her own Gods.*
*A woman who imagines the Divine in her image and likeness,*
*who designs a personal Spirituality*
*to inform her daily life..."* **Patricia Lynn Reilly**

A woman, who identifies herself as Goddess and associates herself and her ancestral lineage with that of the Divine Feminine, is a powerful *manifestor*.... She becomes an even greater asset to herself, to society as a whole and to her loved ones. She becomes an unstoppable force that is, consciously, plugged into this matrilineal power; a source that has its sovereign roots in ancient times.

After so many years of personally walking the path of the Goddess and working with women, from all walks of life, to support them in their respective journey, I have been privy to many observations that confirm for me, the necessity and value for us as women, to embrace the Goddess. Perhaps due to our societal indoctrination, as women we tend to, unconsciously, do a lot of self –sacrificing and more often than not, prioritize other's needs above our own. This often can lead to self-neglect, physical ailments and overwhelming stress levels. Women may sometimes find themselves chronically depressed, confused, complacent and inundated with self-doubt - far removed from their authentic powerful, Goddess-self. It is my observation that women often do not prioritize themselves as much as they should and while this may stem from many different reasons, one prominent cause is often related to self-worth and self-esteem. Sometimes this questionable self-worth issue, for women, is subconsciously tied into the exposure to, long standing patriarchal societal messages. We also tend to endlessly seek validation and worth from people who would rather keep us small, silenced and oppressed. When we unearth and embrace Goddess tenets we find self-expression, self-compassion, autonomy and self-love, as we begin to view ourselves as embodiment of the Divine Feminine. It can also sometimes come as a great shock, when we, as women, find ourselves before a professional female life coach or amidst women only circles and there...discover a fountain of strength and support never experienced before. Putting aside the learned patriarchal tenets and practices of cut throat competition, envy, sabotaging and back stabbing of our sisters, we enter a realm of camaraderie, co-creation and collaboration; which begins to heal deep seated wounds of our gender. In coaching we also exam our

tolerations levels to gain deeper insight about selves. My observation is that, as women, we tend to tolerate too much that is not in alignment with our highest good.
- Bad relationships where we are not fully honored
- Friendships that are superficial and non-supportive
- Families that try to encapsulate us and trap us in the past, blocking our future growth
- People that violate our boundaries
- Handing over our power
- Letting others define who we are, where we're going & what we can do
- Undervaluing ourselves and our gifts
- Neglecting our physical & spiritual being - a.k.a. our unique radar
- Unexplainably complacent or confused about our life purpose
- Settling; for fear of drawing in too much attention or causing too much trouble

In our present day society, where patriarchal tenets are exalted and God is mainly viewed as masculine, there are a number of damaging belief structures that infiltrate our subconscious minds, globally and tragically, weakening us as potentially powerful Goddess women. It is imperative that we think higher of ourselves and that we **unearth, embrace and fully employ the Goddess within.**

Saying Yes, to Goddess!!! We need Goddess and with her; we awaken, we heal, we discover our value and strength as women and we embrace our worthiness, self-compassion and self-love. Consequently we also change our interaction and view of other women as a direct result of this work. With Goddess you remember and you take up all of your gifts and plug into this reservoir of deep support from the universe and the immortal Sacred Feminine.

**In reviewing the message here and the three ways to unearth, embrace and employ Goddess to revamp yourself and your life we see that....**

1. You **unearth** Goddess by learning more about the various faces of the sacred Feminine and her existence in myths, historical books and ancient writings. My books, in particular, can help you start this process but you can also call out to the Universe, in a prayer or meditation, to help you learn more about the Goddess and bring opportunities to expand your knowledge of her existence.

2. Once you begin this process, you will automatically and quite intuitively, begin to identify yourself with her energy and the many tangible/ palpable archetypes. You will find yourself **embracing** the Goddess, and most importantly, embrace the reflection of Goddess within yourself and women all around you.

3. Finally, **employing** the Goddess to revamp yourself and your life is simply a matter of anchoring your new identity with the Divine Feminine. Once you begin to identify with the Goddess you elevate your self-esteem and sense of self-worth and this positively colors every aspect of your life. Yes, you will inevitably revamp yourself and your life as a result of discovering Goddess; it is only to be expected in this type of transformational work. You will have the energy and the clarity to pursue your goals and the courage to live from your heart. With an identity anchored in the Goddess, your perspective shifts and your life has a chance to be revamped fully as you envision it.

***

## **CONNECTING TO GODDESS MEDITATION**

    I invite you to find a comfortable spot to sit or lay down upon. Make yourself comfortable and relax. If sitting in your chair is your only option, that's fine too. Our auric bodies are flexible and we can achieve relaxation first and foremost with our minds. So, I invite you now to close your eyes, relax your mind and breathe. We are going to begin this journey first with our breath. So, let's take a slow, deep breath in and exhale. I will be counting from 1 through 4 and while you listen to my voice count, I invite you to breathe in and breathe out rhythmically. With each inhalation go deeper into relaxation, 1-2-3-4 breathe out and with each exhalation release all tension from your body. 1-2-3-4 and breathe in, deeper... expanding your lungs with each inhalation, 1-2-3-4. And now breathe out, exhaling any stress or concerns, 1-2-3-4. Breathe in, 1-2-3-4, and breathe out, 1-2-3-4. Breathe in 1-2-3-4, with each inhalation feel your lungs expand ever deeper and with each exhalation, 1-2-3-4 release any concerns from your day... Continue to breathe in and out in this manner, falling deeper and deeper into trance. Follow my voice now as it safely leads you deeper and deeper into trance. 1-2-3-4 breathe in and out. (pause) Remember that you are safe throughout this journey and that you are in full control of the pace of this trance. Go as far as you feel comfortable to go. Breathe in and out. (pause)

    Today we will journey to the Goddess. Her name alone conjures up vivid, bright images of ancient times from long ago. Of helmet wearing, fierce warriors and primal dancers, gyrating their hips upon corpses with piercing flicking tongues, of tunic wearing maidens running wild and free with stags and hare in the wilderness, of massive pregnant bellies continuously birthing new life. Yes... the term Goddess brings forth all kinds of images of strong, beautiful, wise, fertile, frightful, inviting, powerful, nurturing, intriguing, hypnotic, unstoppable sacred beings- all of them appearing like you and me, as women. We might remember them from our history books and old myths from long ago but their appearance is as alive and as tangible as you and I now. They are the many faces of the Sacred Feminine, our ancestresses of long ago, and they live on today.

She of over Ten-Thousand names, seen and represented in a myriad of sacred images found scattered across the globe, throughout history. Present in a myriad of ancient cultures, the Sacred Feminine, the Goddess, whose infinite existence cannot be denied, whose pulsating veins still runs through **our** blood, **we honor you today.**

Palpably felt in our auric fields, Goddess who beckons us to look ever deeper into our own reflection, welcome here now. *Goddess, who shows glimpses of herself revealed in thy sister's gaze, welcome here now. (pause)

In your mind's eye, look around you now, see the ocean. See the ocean as it appears magickally before you now and watch the waves flow hypnotically, in and out. Breathe in these ocean waves as they hypnotically go in and out. (pause) Welcome the Goddess. She who rises from the emblematic sacred yoni, delighting in the effervescent white, sea foam greens of the Cypriot ocean. See her rising now clearly into our view. (pause)  Golden as the sun, come, oh joyful one... I hear you in these ocean waves and all of creation climactically sighs in your presence. *"**You hear yourself say, be near me now, Goddess and teach me thy gifts. Initiate me into your sacred mysteries from this day forth that I may know your ways as mine own.  Into your bosom I will rest now, protected and guided in your embrace."** Ocean Goddess Aphrodite agrees and bids you adieu.

Walk on the shore in your mind's eye and in the distance see before you a dark cave. Boldly enter this cave and be still to listen to the whispers of those from long ago (pause). Sweet young maiden, now darksome queen appears. She who tends to souls, with pomegranate stained lips, beholder of light in dark shadowy spaces, I know you Goddess, *"**You hear yourself say to her, be near me now, Goddess and teach me thy gifts. Initiate me into your sacred mysteries from this day forth that I may know your ways as mine own. Into your bosom I will rest now, protected and guided in your embrace."** Earth Maiden Goddess Persephone agrees and bids you adieu.

Hear now the screeching sounds in the distant breeze approaching ever louder and the strong flapping wings above your head. The Nocturnal one is soaring, delighting in her boundless freedom. She lays down beneath for no one and reminds you of your sovereign strength. Though she screeches and hoots like an owl, her primal language is understood.  Call upon her with respect as you hear yourself say, *"**Be near me now, Goddess and teach me thy gifts. Initiate me into your sacred mysteries from this day forth that I may know your ways as mine own. Into your bosom I will rest now, protected and guided in your embrace."** Winged Goddess Lilith agrees and bids you adieu.

Hear the distant Tahitian drumming; the Bora Bora chants sung in offerings to her erupting flames. She is revered in these ancient volcanoes, her molten lava answering to her name. Passionate awakener from mounds and folds of the deepest of sacred caverns, I hear you calling and to you I say, * "**Be near me now, Goddess and teach me thy** gifts. **Initiate me into your sacred mysteries from this day forth that I may know your ways as mine own. Into your bosom I will rest now, protected and guided in your embrace."** Flame Lava Goddess Pele agrees and bids you adieu.

In your mind's eye see her. She who swirls and twirls a hypnotic dance, with her fertile round hips, invoking tribal beats from across the Nigerian river. Welcome her, she whose mocha skin drips in honey and sweet nectar & pearls. Welcome her, she who is seductively inviting you into her rhythmic, swaying dance. Goddess is welcomed now as you hear yourself say, *"**Be near me now, Goddess and teach me thy gifts. Initiate me into your sacred mysteries from this day forth that I may know your ways as mine own. Into your bosom I will rest now, protected and guided in your embrace."** Goddess/Orisha Oshun agrees and bids you adieu.

**"Goddesses of over 10,000 names surrounding me now in layers of protection and love, allowing me to see thy sacred faces, allowing me to get to know them, one by one, I call on you from infinite realms be here now....."** (*) **"Be near me now, Goddess and teach me thy gifts. Initiate me into your sacred mysteries from this day forth that I may know your ways as mine own. Into your bosom I will rest now, protected and guided in your embrace. Goddess, I welcome you now."**

Feel as one of the Goddesses steps forward and comes before you now, as she places a crown upon your head. Take a moment to speak with her personally of anything that concerns you and listen closely to her response and any additional messages. (pause) Now prepare to bid her a final adieu with sincere gratitude. Take a brief moment now to reconnect with your physical body and survey how you are feeling. This journey is coming to an end and you are asked to prepare to follow my voice as it will lead you back to this time and space. Make note of your breath and with each inhalation draw closer to me. Follow my voice now as it leads you back. Remember how we began this journey and breathe in and out. (pause) Continue to breathe in and out while drawing closer to my voice. I will count from seven to one backwards, you are invited to follow my voice and by the count of one, return to this room- back to this time and space, safely and with ease. *7- 6- 5 breathe in and exhale, 4-3 breathe as this journey draws to an end. 2-1. Return to a waking state of consciousness. Welcome! When you are ready, open your eyes and gently stretch your body if you need to. Feel free to notate and document any significant messages, thoughts or images that came through for you in this meditation. Allow a few minutes to ground now. Welcome and Blessed be. )o(

*The meditation helps us, embrace the Goddess. Next we learn to employ Goddess in our personal lives....*

# *How to Employ Goddess To Revamp your Life*

One of the best ways to exemplify the process of **employing** Goddess is perhaps by sharing my own personal experience on how I employ or work with Goddess.

How many of you have a role model or someone you emulate or look up to or depend on, as your ultimate source of support and guidance? I want you to think for a moment and reflect on how vastly different your life would be without that source... Consider the impact of their valued presence in your life for a moment.... For me, my source has been Goddess. Now, I do have many other sources and people I also rely upon for support and guidance, but for me, the more I learn about Goddess & Women spirituality, the more positively supported I feel. I have found a restorative reservoir of support and guidance in Goddess spirituality and I am intuitively led to employ and work with this powerful energy on a regular basis for positive results in revamping myself and my life.

*********************

- *When I need to connect with the cathartic powers of Change and Transformation, I call on Goddess and She appears to me as the Yoruban Goddess/Orisha, Oya.*
- *When I need to connect with the energy of Self-compassion, I call on the Goddess and She appears to me as the Buddhist Goddess, Kwan Yin or Mother Mary.*
- *When I need to connect with my inner Healer, I call on Goddess and She appears to me as the Celtic Goddess, Brigit and sometime as Greek Goddess, Hestia.*
- *When I need to connect with my tomboy, inner maiden (especially if I am working-out or engaging in outdoor sports) I call on the Goddess and She appears to me as the Greek maiden Huntress, Artemis.*
- *When I need to connect with my own powers of creativity, I call on the Goddess and She appears to me as the Hindu Goddess Saraswati & sometime as the Mayan Goddess Ix Chel.*
- *When I need to connect with the Passionate, Insatiable one, I call on Goddess and She will appear to me as the Polynesian Goddess, Pele.*
- *When I need to connect with the energy of abundance and pleasure, I call on Goddess and She appears to me as the Voodoo Loa, Erzulie Freda.*
- *When I need to connect with the attributes of Steadfastness, I call on the Goddess and She appears to me as the Welsh Goddess, Rhiannon.*
- *When I need to connect with the Cerebral Wise one (the Strategist) I call on Goddess and She appears to me as the Athenian Greek Goddess, Athena.*
- *When I need to connect with the Primal One and the fierce Fighter, who delights in combat and showing off her strengths, I call on Goddess and She appears to me as the Hindu Goddess, Durga and sometimes as Kali.*
- *When I need to connect with the energy of Forgiveness, I call on Goddess and She appears to me as the Native American Goddess, Selu or Iyatikou.*

- When I need to connect with my Shadows and dark subconscious issues, I call on the Goddess and She appears to me as The Queen of the underworld, Persephone or the Wise, sacred Crone, Hekate.
- When I need to connect with my own Beauty and shake up my powers of attraction, I call on the Goddess and She appears to me as the Cypriot Goddess, Aphrodite and sometimes as the Egyptian Goddess, Hathor.
- When I need to connect with my inner Bitch or the one who will not be demeaned or oppressed/subordinated, I call on Goddess and She appears to me as the Sumerian Goddess, Lilith.
- When I need to connect with the nurturing one, I call on the Goddess and she appears to me as a mother Goddess like Corn Mother (a Goddess of the Americas) or Greek Goddess of the Harvest, Demeter or the Canaanite Goddess, Asherah.
- When I need to connect with my inner Spark and need help coming out of my shell to boldly shine my own light, I call on Goddess and she appear to me as the Sun Goddess, Amaterasu.
- When I need to connect with my powers of fecundity, fertility and proliferation, I call on the Goddess and she appears to me as Our Earth Mother Goddess, Gaia.

These are just some examples of how the ancient Goddesses of long ago are still relevant to us as modern day women and, how I have personally worked with and **employed Goddess energy** to revamp myself and my life. I hope it serves as a good, starting point example for those who are seeking to really upgrade their lives with her immortal omnipotent energy. So how can she help you? In what capacity can she be employed in your life right now? Be mindful that the Sacred Feminine is known as the Goddess of over Ten-thousand names for a reason. The presence of the Goddess exists in a multitude of cultures and her infinite names and attributes are as numerous as the stars. What I have personally found is that when a Goddess wants to make herself known to you, due to developing circumstances in your life, she will strongly assert herself. And this assertion might happen at first in a subtle way (with dreams, coincidences, books and images coming through) and then it can become more persistent and obvious, if you have not yet gained consciousness of her. Embracing and working with the Goddess in this way can result in some powerful shifts, finding yourself fully supported, revamped and able to beautifully transform your life.

*"Human connections are deeply nurtured
in the field of shared story...."* Jean Houston

## **SOME GODDESSES TO GET TO KNOW**

### AINE
Irish Red Mare, Solar and Lunar Goddess, Aine, is the fiery enchantress who inspires the writer and the songstress. She is a Fierce Protectress of Women, especially those who have been mistreated, abused, molested or raped by men. Oath and vow guardian, she awakens in you a call to action, where action is needed. Defend yourself and unearth the confidence to utilize your own gifts of enchantment. She imbues the pursuit of your goals with her fiery energy and you are destined to succeed. Aine connects us with the energy of Fire, in her Solar aspect, although she was later similarly connected to the moon. At the Summer Solstice, we hone in on the various wonderful gifts of the element of fire and how to best utilize it in our lives, channeling it into the manifestation of cherished goals and with Aine's fiery solar energy we are blessed.

### AMATERASU
Japanese Goddess of the Sun; of truth and light, the mirror. She asks you to bring clarity and order into your life. Amidst turbulence and disruptive chaos, she calls you to breathe, regroup and reconnect to your authentic self. Look into the mirror and do not fear your own reflection staring back at you. It will reveal truths that perhaps, you have avoided seeing. She is the mirror and a personification of truth. She will awaken your own self-worth -a vital component for all magick. Pause for a moment, retreat, if necessary in order to regroup and unearth your Divine Light. Do not let situations or other people dim your brilliance. Amaterasu reminds you of your own gifts and your divine light. Stop hiding and shine your light, you are a powerful being!!!

### APHRODITE
Greek Goddess of love, beauty and attraction. Sweet, curvaceous watery Queen, she brings you the power of beauty and attraction and most importantly, the unwavering power of self-love. You say you want a new lover but are you the honey and light, love so often seeks to meld and attach itself with? She is the embodiment of attraction and love, in its many guises. From a gentle stirring, to an all-consuming passion, her Venusian gifts spread into so many different areas in our lives. Even in the passion we might feel towards our goal's fruition, creative projects and its unfolding sacred processes. Here she helps you cultivate your own powers of attraction, to attract whatever your heart truly desires. She invites you to acknowledge your own beauty and your powers of attraction, for these are her domain. Who or what do you ensnare in your life at this time? Where can you cultivate further, your Aphrosinian powers of love and attraction?

### ARADIA
Etruscan Maiden Goddess, she is the Magick woman, the Strega, bringing the gifts of sorcery. She comes into your life at this moment to awaken your inner Goddess and liberate your inner, sovereign priestess. She avails herself to whatever we may need help with and becomes a great source of empowerment and freedom of hopelessness. She is the embodiment of magick; a great teacher and guide. She reminds us that nature is our ally (within us and all around) to protect and heal us; to lend us their infinite wisdom. Her energy comes to offer the opportunity for occult knowledge, lineage, and ancient

respected traditions of the Craft. With Aradia, we acquire the empowering practice of magick and the gift of the priestess. It is time to connect with the powers of the moon, and the strength of the night. How do you empower yourself with your spiritual allies, magick and occult knowledge? How do we reverently employ magick and the sacredness of nature to propel ourselves forward?

## ARTEMIS

Greek Maiden Huntress, she is the Goddess of our untamable, wild inner child. As spring begins to make itself known, the energy of the wild maiden begins to awaken upon the earth with it. Soon enough you will feel that energy swirling around, making its way to you. Artemis arrives to remind you of your effervescent youth, your inner maiden, running care free, and the power intrinsic in youth's fearlessness. She is the Divine huntress, whose archery skills and keen focus are unmatched. She comes to awaken you to the gifts of friendships, supportive sisterhood, and to remind you of the power inherent in your gender, when it partners with other like-minded beings. She stirs your heart to a special connection to the beloved creatures that inhabit the forest. A liberated, wild force is driving within and it brings new hope and the pursuit of new goals with tenacity. The Huntress awakens in you the gift of a Maiden's will and energy. The archer's supreme, intense focus begins to take hold. What do you put your powerful will, mind and focus on, now? What do you aim for? What will you "will" to be into existence?

## ASHERAH

Asherah is the embodiment of the mother archetype and reflects our beauty, fertility, sovereignty and staying power as women. She is the grounded energy of the fertile earth and reflects the beauty found in nature. She is the Canaanite Goddess of the Tree and will ask you to embrace the distinct sacred aspect of Trees, as admirable reflections of your womanhood.

## ATHENA

Greek Goddess of wisdom, skills, war-craft and intelligence. She is the embodiment of a strong mind, tempered heart and fierce leadership. She inspires greatness in all your undertakings and blesses all hand crafted projects. She is the teacher and awakens in you a drive for excellence and competence. If magick is to be defined as, changing consciousness at will, then indeed aligning our mind with our will makes perfect sense, and Athena would be a great catalyst for this procedure. All things we wish to bring to fruition must first begin with a thought, an initial vision, a plan, and the engagement of the mind, this is Athena's realm. She comes into your life now to teach you that wishes and goals are best met, first and foremost in our initial imagining and strategizing. She beckons you to tap into the power of your mind; plan, strategize, organize to achieve your goals, for it can be much stronger than sheer brute force.

## BABA YAGA

She is the archetype of the old, wise crone. She is the Slavic hag and Dark Goddess, who frightens our inner child with her distinctly, gruesome appearance. Her bony hunchback body, her wild silver hair and long warty nose and her shrieking cackles are a frightening depiction of our worst nightmare. She is not someone we typically want to encounter, not the way patriarchy has defined her but she is a force to be reckoned with. Baba Yaga is the crone, a most imperative, crucial invaluable aspect of the Goddess. She is meant to dare you to take a daunting step towards growth and transformation, by initially first confronting her nightmarish appearance. Typically at around Samhain, Baba Yaga inaugurates the Dark season, when all appears barren and everything prepares itself for death. Everything at this time settles and enters into the deep, dark earth to compost itself. The sun wanes and the hours of night are long, treacherous and cold. She represents that which is frightening and unknown, as the start of the winter months so often brings a tangible fear of what the weather may become, will our harvest last throughout the next four months and will we confront death and survive. All that we fear but must confront is represented in the hag and she comes into our realm to challenge and build up our courage.

## BAUBO

Our immortal friend is found in the cackling, supremely bawdy, ancient Goddess, Baubo. She arrives, like an old dear playmate, bubbling with jubilee and radiating with laughter and naughty jokes. Just when you started to feel the pull of sadness and stress caving in on you, she comes with warmth, jokes, encouragement and sincere friendship. She lightens your load at this pivotal time of the year and reminds you of your most precious weapon against feelings of defeat, sadness and depression. It is within you, your gender, your labyrinths and inner caverns, where cathartic treasures are to be found, and Baubo has no inhibitions about revealing this to you. Have you ever looked at yourself, really looked at yourself and marveled with laughter? Do you take pleasure in your being and body? Have you ever heard the funny stories of an old friend echoing in your ears after a long, hard stressful day? This is Baubo's gift to you. She awakens you to the transformative powers of laughter. While intensely pursuing your goals, anticipating challenges and overriding obstacles, take the time to laugh; lighten up and allow the cathartic power of friendship and joy an honored place in your life.

## BLODEUWEDD

Blodeuwedd is the awakener of our dark shadowy places, our taboos and subconsciousness. She is the Welsh Flower Goddess of exceptional beauty and allure. She knows all too well the two realms of night and day, of shadow and wakefulness. She is the encased beautiful flower who becomes the free flying, night owl. She is the one who reflect the dichotomy our gender so often is subjected to; that of living in two realms. She reveals the sins of patriarchy and our gender's need to be awake and alert as the owl, in a world that would rather contain us as simply beautiful, voiceless flowers. She is both the shadow or secrets and the awakener to our inner power.

## BRIGIT

Celtic Goddess of the forge; she is the healer, the matriarchal nurturer and the "creatrix." Deep in the dark belly of the earth's womb, magick is awakening slowly, unseen by the naked eye but unquestionably forthcoming. All things are born from the hidden, in this deep dark, moist abyss and it is embodied by the Goddess. At Imbolc, things are manifesting themselves quietly underneath the harsh, solid frozen earth. Hearth fires are quite prominent at Imbolc, a reminder we are in the presence of the Divine. Brigit is the Goddess who thaws and warms our winter heart with inspirations to create and express ourselves. She, who also through her bright flames, is able to transform us inside and out, is our beloved matriarch. She offers us the healing gifts found in both fire and water and beckons you to approach her at the sacred well with ribbons of supplications. Brigit enters your life now, asking what needs to burn to ashes, and like the Phoenix, be transmutated so that healing may come. She brings self –transformations, sacred initiations and the willingness to begin "the Journey." What will be transformed in you, now? What do you initiate and dedicate yourself to unearthing now?

## CORN MOTHER

She is the nurturing sacrificial iconic Corn Goddess, embraced by the myriads of indigenous tribes, across the Americas and abroad. Corn Mother shed her blood so that her people would strive onward and not extinct. She, who willingly sacrificed her very own truncated body so that her people would never hunger again, is the supreme being of compassion. Despite the unappreciative nature of her greedy children and her community, she understood her role and obligation in the larger scheme of life and thus, she awakens the sacrificial Mother within every one of us. She calls to mind your core, your heart-chakra and asks you, *"How do you nurture your heart?"* Step back, if you will, and consider for a moment what sacrifices are required of you at this time of the year? What is in your heart now, that requires sacrifice for the greater good of all? What symbolizes your sacred blood and where is it being required to pour forth and serve a greater good in the Universe? Consider your initial goals at the start of the New Year, have you abandoned them, altered their conception or achieved them? Or is there something else required of you to proceed onward? With the change of season, how can you adjust to change and manifest balance? Are initial plans working or do they need to be re-assessed, self-forgiven, released and moved into a different direction now?

## DANTOR

Dantor is the spirit of the revolutionist who incites our courage to stand for what is right and just. She is the Voodoo Loa Mother, who defends her offspring at all cost. She is the fierce, machete/dagger wielding energy of the Dark Goddess. Protectress and defender of women and children, she will go into battle when the only way to be emancipated is to finally fight back. When wars need to be fought she incites the heart with strength and when we must face our abusers and oppressors, she equips us with the courage. She is a love Goddess like her sister Erzulie Freda but her energy has a ferocious passion that will bring about monumental changes.

## DEMETER

Greek Goddess of the grain, she is the benevolent Harvest Mother who supports, protects and nourishes her children. She comes into your life at this time to inaugurate the Mother within. She awakens in you a connection to all things that need nurturance and protection, including yourself. Like the immortal Goddess, who would not let the grain grow until her daughter's return, where are you being asked to put your foot down? Where are you being called to fully care for your needs and not compromise your dignity? Where will you utilize your own bargaining power? And where will you need to make some initial sacrifices to attain your goals? As the wheel turns, this Goddess asks, where in your life are you being called to be the Mother? It is a time of assessments and preparedness for letting go. The Harvest season supports this endeavor of deep consideration and taking stock of what you have done thus far, and what else will need to be done to reach your goals. The change of season is upon us once more, with autumn, and this time of the year, we are required to let go of many things, including summer. Demeter invites us to consider our role as nurturing mother to our creative pursuits and take this brief pause in our journey to reflect, assess and review.

## DURGA

Multi-armed, Hindu Goddess, Durga, is the ferocious tiger. She is the fierce warrior maiden but also the protectress guardian Mother. She is Goddess, embodying supreme strength and power. When presented with demons and threats to her world, she fights and she delights in that combat. She takes great pleasure in the actual blood spewing battle and is guaranteed victory. With her numerous arms there is nothing she cannot tackle and her wielding arms are so reminiscent and symbolic of our gender's numerous roles and obligations. Durga is anger manifested and employed into action. She was born from the collective powerful emotion of anger that stemmed from the Gods. This anger is not held within to self-destruct your soul, no; she uses that anger as a vehicle of action for her victory, while defeating those who are trying to destroy her. She is the embodiment of sovereign autonomy and awakens us to our great strength when facing adversity and the seemingly unsurmountable.

## ERZULIE

Voodoo Loa of love, beauty, refinement and abundance, she is the embodiment of romance and those delightful luxuries of life. She, who demands nothing but the best, invites you now to hold the same standard for your own life. She awakens in you a desire to pursue prosperity, abundance and all that is juicy and good for you; including the right type of love. What are some of life's luxuries that you are willing to manifest at this time? Is your "Love" bringing you true fulfillment? Are you approaching life from a place of lack or from the rich fertile realm of abundance and appreciation? Are you imbuing the pursuit of your goals with love? She enters your life at this time to awaken a desire for the finer things in life and calls you to treat yourself with reverence and love.

## GAIA

Primordial fertile Earth Goddess who is the essence of fertility, proliferation and the powers of creation. Life is full of wonderment and all around us, there are examples of her fertile creative gifts. It is her very nature to proliferate and multiply her sacred creations and she invites you to do the same. It is encouraging and inspiring to know that her primordial gifts are vibrantly within us as well, for her blood courses through every single one of her creations and that includes her earth children- humanity. There is much that we can create in the spirit of the Goddesses of abundance and propagation. She comes into your life at this time and asks you, "How do you create prosperity and enjoy small and big luxuries in life?" At this stage in our Goddess journey, the sacred wheel of the year supports our endeavor to multiply and tap into our own powers of fertility; whether they are used for creativity, prosperity, ideas or actual birthing of children. She awakens in you a desire to multiply and manifest your gifts on the earthly planes. How close are you to achieving your most cherished wish? Have any flowers bloomed and come to fruition on your unique vine, from the seeds reverently placed within her sacred womb back at Imbolc? She invites you to enjoy the birthing process and tap into the sacred energy of the fertile season and the earth.

## HATHOR

The Beloved Egyptian Goddess of Pleasure and Love, she is the bringer of beauty, joy and sensual gifts. She is the highly venerated Bovinian Goddess that awakens us to our physical body and the importance of pleasure in our life. Whatever you do in life, make sure it brings you joy and gratification. As spring turns into summer, all upon this earth appears fertile, colorful and brightly adorned. When it seems as if the vibrant earth is a vision of great delight to all of our senses and we are in a state of titillation and arousal, the Celestial Bovine becomes the ideal Goddess to call upon. Her message to you is to seek joy, harmony and pleasure. She exalts the transformational magick of music, dance, sex and physical adornments. Amidst the doldrums of our obligations and the unavoidable mundane, seek to know and honor the highly cathartic power of ecstasy. She beckons you to delight in all the beauty that is surrounding you from within and from without, across the earth. Seek to know and explore the power of ecstasy!

"*For all acts of love and pleasure are my rituals...*" Doreen Valiente, -The Charge of the Goddess.

## HEKATE

Ancient, immortal Goddess of the Threshold, she rules the night, death, sorcery, witchcraft and the sacred portals that lead to the underworld. She is the venerated archetype of the wise crone. Hekate brings a plate offering with our lineage and ancestry and the importance of our spiritual connection. She is the night wandered and facilitates travels through all the realms. She is the guide through all of life's various thresholds and portal of transformations. At Samhain/Hallowmas/ Halloween, it is a dark time of year, when day light wanes, while the dark of night gains power and mysteries are unfolding for us. There is much wisdom to unearth in our ancestry and in our past-lives and Hekate guides us through this realm to attain knowledge and our ancestral connections. As the nights grow longer and the earth seems to slow down, it is time to do, as the critters of the land, and go deep within, for some soul searching. Ask yourself, "Have I been on the right track?" "Is this the right path for me?" "Does my work and ultimate life goal, fit who I am, who I am becoming, and my life's greater purpose?" "Are these goals meant to be reached by me at this point and in this lifetime?" Hekate arrives to help you connect to spirit allies and your sacred ancestors for guidance. She awakens in you other realms, other sources for support and other ways of knowing. She awakens you to your sacred role as an ancestress and your intrinsic part of your family's lineage. Ancestresses that you are already...what will you leave behind for your beloved one? What legacies will you leave for them? This is the time to look closely at who we share this realm with, honor our Spiritual family, and the sacredness of the cycles of life and death.

## HESTIA

Greek Goddess of the Hearth and one of the beloved twelve Olympians, Hestia is the immortal Maiden Goddess. She is the embodiment of our hearth fires, the flames of our spirit and the core of our very being. She directs your attention to the highly esteemed core of our personhood; our heart and our spirit. Hestia comes to remind you to honor that part of yourself that is in tuned with the Feminine Divine. She arrives with the gifts of old, venerated traditions and honored family customs. At this time of the year we are also awakened to the spirit of Gratitude and the great significance of our own Hearth and

Home; which vibrates with its very own unique essence and life force. Home is more than just where we sleep. Consider for a moment, the beauty and value of your own abode at this juncture, what does it reflect? Consider your relationship with this place, the land, and the many ways it feeds, protects and nurtures you. We give thanks for the spirit of home and hearth with Hestia. If you are in the market for a new apartment or home, reflect on what will your next home look like. What will be of utmost importance to you in a home then? As we approach the end of the calendar year, she comes quietly and serenely to inaugurate a time to give thanks for what we've manifested thus far and our respective journey. She invites you to pause and give thanks for what you've created up to this very pivotal moment in time. The Goddess arrives and we are thus opened with Gratitude for life and all the many blessings (big and small) and the place we call home is one of great significance. It is here where we may start familial traditions, continue old ones and honor the spirit of gratitude for its existence. With Hestia, it is time to show reverence to your familial and spiritual traditions, the place you call home, and honor your journey thus far, while also giving thanks to all those who have added the invaluable, loving, diverse, golden threads of your strong familial tapestry.

## HINA
Hina is the primordial Polynesian rainbow Goddess, who makes the ancient Moon her home. She comes into your life to remind you of the sacredness and necessity of sanctuaries. She arrives at this point in your life to ask you, *"Do you have a personal space that nourishes and heals you and keeps you protected?"* In life, among chaos and moments of stress, we all need to identify where is home.... *where is our safe haven? Where can we retreat to regain ourselves?* Physical vacations are common and act as our temporary escape and retreat, but, what if we have available to us, a mental and spiritual place to retreat to, whenever situations require an escape? The question she now presents to you is, *"Are you able to keep your sense of self and retreat as needed, to your sanctuary? When confronted with toxic situations or people and negative relationships, are you able to find a sacred space within, to guard and recharge yourself?* While pursuing your goals and crafting the magickal life of a Goddess wommin, you must also have in place, your home, your sacred temple. As demands in life increase and as projects and work become demanding, it becomes necessary to have these astral sanctuaries in place for our own protection and wellbeing. *Are you able to manifest safety, serenity and peace of mind?* She enters your life at this time and beckons you to erect your core spiritual home and unearth a place of peace. With the Goddess Hina you are invited to create your personal sanctuary.

## IX CHEL
Ancient Mayan Lunar Goddess, Ix Chel rules over the waters, the moon and our gender's emotions. With Ix Chel we begin to open ourselves up to the gifts of our gender, reflected in her watery realm and the sacred Moon. This Mayan Goddess has a story to tell and it echoes the story of so many women throughout "Herstory". She awakens this connection to the Great Mother Divine and reminds you of your own fertile, luminescent gifts. No matter, if you are a spicy-wild maiden, nurturing mother or a wise old crone, all of these archetypes reside within you and all are sacred reflections of Creatrix-Goddess. Water is the healer and has much to teach us about going with the flow and honoring all that is Feminine. *In your efforts to achieve your goals, are you leaving some room for flexibility? Are you feeling parched and dry in some areas of your life or are you overly saturated?* Ix Chel enters your life now to connect you with balance and the healing

power of water and the moon. What personal message is the element of water conveying to you now regarding your life journey?

## LILITH

The Sumerian Goddess of liberation, Lilith, is a most fascinating, yet controversial Goddess. She enters your life in a most distinctly irrefutable fashion and her influence is probably one of the most impactful on a women's life. She is the Dark Goddess that rises from the depths of our subconscious and provokes you into your own powers. When the Goddess Lilith asserts herself in your life you will feel the depths of her rage and intolerance for women's suppression and inequality. She is the adamant voice that will not be victimized, oppressed nor engage in patriarchal rules. Lilith is autonomy and freedom and she will not succumb to societal pressures, no matter what names are flung at her. You can call her demon, bitch, cunt, dyke, witch, monster, whatever... but she WILL remain whole and authentically true to herself, for she will not lay herself down, beneath anyone. She will not subordinate herself for man's pathetic, sick ideologies and she soars in flight with her autonomous woman power intact throughout the ages because of it. She is brazen pleasure seeker, whole unto herself and epitomizes woman's sexual liberation and a powerful representation of Feminism.

## MA'AT

The highly esteemed, Egyptian Goddess of Truth, Ma'at is cosmic law. She is the Divine being we expect to greet, in the golden hall of the Afterlife, where the Celestial Scales are presented before us. These sacred scales weigh our heart against Ma'at's ostrich feather, which determines our fate in the afterlife. Ma'at is an ancient, highly venerated Egyptian Deity that some believe existed before time itself. She is the personification of truth and the power of final judgment. She beckons you today to take an honest look at your whole life now. It is time for some serious assessment of your soul, your heart, and the choices you are making in this lifetime. She lays down the invitation to closely inspect your heart to unearth what weights it down now and offers you the cathartic gift of an unburdened soul.

## MAMAN BRIGITTE

The Voodoo Loa Maman Brigitte is the gatekeeper, threshold guardian and beloved Ghede Mother of Bones and the dead. In the darkness of the unknown, on the threshold of life and death, we must all eventually pass through these realms; here she makes herself known to us. At Samhain/Halloween and the days surrounding this holiday, our focus is mainly on all things (popularly considered) scary, creepy and deathly. At this time of the year, when nature itself appears to be morphing and surrendering to death, Maman Brigitte arrives with a rather unusual sass, lightheartedness and humor about death. She reminds us, it is not a finality but a transition and one that should be approached with love, not fear or trepidation. *"What are you afraid of, death is simply a transition and if you are free of this fear, there is very little else to be afraid of in life...."* *"After all, there is no death, only transformations, my little ones..."* She draws near and the hairs on the back of your neck are felt rising. In her bawdy style, she jokes and dances for you, while daring you to enter her realm of cemeteries. We begin to consider our very own mortality and the content of our lifetime now. Amidst longer nights and the barrenness of the earth, it appears as if the earth is preparing for its own death, as it, along with animals of the land, embark on its hibernation. It is here where we begin to reflect on our own cycles of death and rebirth and yet it is not as frightening as some may have you think. She comes to remind you that your time here on earth is very limited, unlike your infinite spirit. And your life's purpose must be met within those physical time restraints. She arrives as a wake- up call, announcing death's unpredictability, as never too far away. Whether young or old, she awaits to reclaim your sacred bones when that time does come. *Will you be ready to relinquish your bones to her, upon your death? Will you be ready to surrender all that you've known in this physical life to enter the next stage in your development, with a Mother who will lovingly and humorously guide you into the next phase? Are you living your life mindful of the expiration of your flesh and the infinity of your spirit? How are your goals and actions reflected of this monumental realization?* Maman Brigitte is the crone that prepares you for death and transitions, whether metaphorically or in actuality. Her energy however, is not one of doom and gloom but rather celebratory.

## NIKE
Nike is the Greek Goddess of Victory. The laurel wreathed Goddess of Triumph, rewards generously for works accomplished, this is her sweet domain. She anxiously awaits your success and stirs within you a healthy dose of competition and ambition. Our laurel wreath is awaiting and she stirs in you a desire for her presence –a desire for success. At New Years we have the gift of beginnings. *Do we enter it victoriously; projecting a sense of ordained achievement? Or have we already failed before we have even begun?* At this point, the Goddess Nike invites you to celebrate the small and large accomplishments in your life, knowing that this mere acknowledgement will positively influence future ones. With Nike, we celebrate the small and monumental victories and ambitiously project that victorious energy into our future goals.

## NU-KUA
Nu-Kua is the ancient Chinese Goddess of creation and order. She is attributed for creating the human race out of little clay figurines. It is so empowering to our gender to learn of this rather unique cosmology and naturally, as the Goddess who created humanity, she is highly revered. Her gifts to us are similar to Gaia's as one can surmise, and thus Nu-Kua awakens us to our own gifts of creation. Nu-Kua is a powerful sovereign Goddess that is deemed as the Mother of humanity and her presence awakens our own maternal gifts. She was also known as humanities' saviouress whose ingenious quick thinking helped save the earth from a cataclysmic disaster. She represents the strength to dive into chaos and make order and peace out of Global disasters. Calamitous events do not need to destroy us but rather can give us an opportunity to display strength and great powers to formulate order and peace; this is yet another one of her messages to us.

## OYA
The Yoruban Orisha, Oya is the fierce Goddess of storms, thunder, winds and soul-transformations. In her presence, drastic change is inevitable and life will never look the same. She is the fierce flagellation of a whipping tornado, the rumbling desolation of an

earthquake, the electric omnipotent thunderstorm and the power to unexpectedly crumble your neatly existing structures, called life. She is the Goddess of Drastic Change. Are you ready to surrender to her will and let things go? It is only in this severing of the old and outworn, that we get to allow a new life force to take root, grow and manifest - healthier and stronger than before. This is how our most cherished wish comes to fruition. She comes like the intense windstorms and tornadoes, to sweep that which does not serve you well anymore. She comes to sweep away, with her long rainbow colored skirt, that which impedes your progress. She awakens in you the courage and strength to welcome change. Things may need to be surrendered, shattered, and fall apart, before greater things can come to fruition. Trust in the power of severing the old and rebuilding anew and with great reverence approach the ferocious Dark Goddess for her protection.

## PELE

Pele is one of the most well-known Goddesses in our modern times. She is the ancient Polynesian Volcanic Goddess, still very much venerated today in Hawaii. Her energy is palpable to us as women, when we are deeply connected to our rage, anger and sexual appetite. The volcanic, uncontrollable, erupting, passionate Goddess awakens us to great strength, willpower, desires and insatiable energy. She is the energy of a gnawing feeling within, those initial rumblings inside right before the spewing, eruption of hot lava. She is the embodiment of our orgasms. She awakens passion deep within and a relentlessness to pursue that which your heart desires. She inaugurates a type of boiling fire energy sweltering from deep within that needs to be approached with great awareness and reverence. She beckons you to give credence to your feelings, validate them, and give them strength. Pele demands that we give volume to our voice. *"Speak out, roar it out,"* she says. Like the rumbling of her volcanoes, she awakens in you the ability to acknowledge the sacred cathartic emotion of passion but also anger. Pele invites you at this time to banish complacency and get real with your true voice. Then let it be heard! Like the rumbling of her Volcanoes and the spewing of her scorching lavas, don't hold your true emotions inside, let them out... let it all out and let your passionate voice be heard. Pele's message to us is that our voice needs to be heard and our feelings expressed.

## PERSEPHONE

The Greek Maiden Goddess, Persephone is the daughter of the Goddess Demeter. She is the one who directs the flowers and the corn fields to blossom and grow and gives light to a most auspiciously dark realm. Persephone is she who is Queen, Wife, Daughter, and Mother. She embodies all of these archetypes at once and she is every woman on the face of this earth. Our gender is constantly required to wear a multitude of hats and roles, sometimes even conflicting ones. Yet we never falter in our ability to comply and execute them flawlessly. Persephone enters your life to offer you balance and compassion for your own self and the multitude of offices you hold. At this time, she also wants to direct your attention to your origins and a dear woman, who has paved the way for your existence- your very own human, birth mother. Pele's message is, "I am daughter but I am so much more." It's important to cultivate right relationship with our mother. We may have differences, but we also share many similarities with the woman who birthed us into existence. Consider what kind of Mother would complement your own personal journey in life? Consider, if you aren't a mother yet, what would make this role most challenging, to you and your offspring? New roles emerge bringing new responsibilities and through it all, we seek balance. Persephone's story exemplifies this best, as she was forced to move into contrasting realms and still maintain her identities. Walking in multiple worlds and in a multitude of different roles, while we pursue our most cherished wish is quite the challenge but the Goddess Persephone reflects an example we can anchor our faith in. She comes into your life to inaugurate an awareness of the necessity of balance, as we walk in various roles, pursing our life's mission.

## RHIANNON
The Welsh Mare Goddess, Rhiannon, is a symbol of steadfastness and forgiveness. Her story is one that classically depicts the struggles of woman as maiden, as bride and then as sacrificial mother, who mysteriously loses her child and a part of herself in the process. She teaches us the importance and cathartic powers, of releasing the painful suffocating chains of the past and allowing forgiveness to heal our hearts when tragedy has ensued. She exemplifies for us how to persevere despite tragedies and represents the strength and unwavering faith in the face of adversity, prejudices and injustices. When we feel unsupported and marginalized by our community or are being accused of some horrific act, we can find comfort in the messages the Mare Goddess presents to us.

## SARASWATI
Venerated as one of the first matriarchal deities mentioned in the ancient sacred text of the Rig Veda, Saraswati is the beloved Hindu Goddess of Wisdom and Sound. She is the Goddess of sacred learning and was embodied as the once fertile Saraswati River.
She awakens in us our powers creativity, higher learning and the value of our voices. Do not think you are immune to her gifts as the swirling power of creativity has numerous guises to reveal itself. The written word, scriptures and sacred sound are her gifts to us as well and she blesses the writer, the teacher the songstress and the artist. When Saraswati appears in our lives we have the ability to create various works of wonder - big and small, they are all of equal value to the Divine. Saraswati asks you, "What are you creating? What artistic projects are you working on? Ask yourself, "How is my unique soul transmitting through my hands and voice? Do I have the spirit of creativity? The Hindu Goddess arrives in your life at this time to awaken artistic offerings of the self to the Great Divine.

## SIF
The beautiful Norse Goddess, Sif, is the embodiment of the Autumnal Harvest. Sif is the sacrificial one, who chooses to act considering the bigger picture and her community. She is less concern with the individual and chooses to align herself with the overall good of the clan. Sif is the one who seeks to formulate peace and harmony among her tribe and will often offer herself up in sacrifice for the peace and greater good of all. She willing surrenders parts of herself for the protection and sustenance of her tribe. With her, we are made aware of our role within our community and the sacrifices sometimes required of us for peace, harmony and prosperity. Her beautiful blonde tresses, which resemble the wheat in a Harvest, is cut, pruned, and sacrificed, and this very act blesses the clan with a number of additional, invaluable gifts. Sif is the golden Harvest that must be sacrificed and pruned in order for greater prosperity to eventually ensue and bless the community at large.

## SKADI

Skadi is the Norse Giantess Goddess, who fiercely defends what she believes to be right. She is part of the ancient early tribe of Norse Gods. As the Snowshoe Maiden Goddess she is an archer, connected to the wilderness and the snowcapped mountaintops and she is known for her strength and her physicality. She awakens the Amazon woman within you and offers the gift of physical wellbeing, strength and perspective. How vastly different our challenges appear when we see them through the eyes of the Giantess, up high on the mountaintops? How vastly altered you would feel, to walk and act in the armored body of a Giantess, like the Norse Goddess, Skadi. Skadi's energy is proud and strong reminiscent of the Greek Maiden Goddess, Artemis. When she enters your realm you will feel her inviting you to honor your body and tapping into your inner and outer strengths. Unearth your birthrights for physical wellbeing and tap into your righteousness and positive convictions. Know that you can manifest powerful changes now and the Giantess Amazon lives in every woman.

## SRI LAKSHMI

The Hindu Goddess of Prosperity, Beauty and Love has garnered quite the reputation throughout the years and as one can surmise, she has a myriad of devout worshippers. The beautiful, Sri Lakshmi, is often depicted in gold, bejeweled from head to toe, accompanied by the elephant God, Ganesh. She represents our feminine beauty, fecundity and prosperity. She enters our realm appropriately at the time of the first Harvest to make us aware of our many riches and our potential to maintain and manifest even more. She is the abundant golden Harvest itself with her great beauty and palpable ripeness and she beckons you to embrace, with gratitude, the gifts of abundance, love and beauty.

## UZUME

The Japanese Goddess of merriment, Uzume, is often closely connected with the Sun Goddess, Amaterasu; much the same way as the Goddess Baubo is forever immortalized with the Greek Grain Goddess, Demeter. She is boldness and merriment all contained and reflected in the physical body and she introduces us to the powerful art form of the Burlesque. Uzume exemplifies for us the power and magick, found in our beautiful physical body and the gift of dance. She also awakens us to ecstatic trancing and the value of shamanistic practices. Uzume's silliness and buoyant laughter helped eradicate darkness on the earth and return the Sun Goddess to her rightful place in the heavens. She is thus, the cathartic power of laughter, ecstasy and the joys found in our physical body.

# MONTHLY GIFTS FROM THE GODDESS
## "She" of over Ten Thousand Names...

### DECEMBER — WINTER SOLSTICE

**Rhiannon:** Welsh, mare Goddess of the moon. Connection to Horse medicine. Awakener of steadfastness, sacrifices, forgiveness, survival, trusting in justice, truth.

**Amaterasu:** Benevolent Japanese Sun Goddess. Bringer of truth and honor, bringing us out of hiding and reflecting her sacred mirror. Awakener of our value, self-worth and brilliant inner light.

**Athena:** Greek Goddess of Wisdom. Enhances our intellect & creative skills. Awakens fearlessness in the battle and inspires us to embrace the powers of our mind. Helps us strategize and see clearly the best solution to challenges.

### JANUARY — NEW CALENDAR YEAR

**Nu-Kua:** Ancient Chinese Goddess of Creation. Mother of Humanity, Gifts of creation, peace and order, amidst chaos, The Saviouress and Creatrix archetype.

**Nike:** Greek Goddess of Victory, whose wings guarantees our success. She inspires the charioteer's drive and ambition. In her embrace we are already victorious.

**Skadi:** Norse Jotunheim Giantess, who inspires us into action and fuels our convictions. Awakener of courage & the Maiden archetype. She teaches us to honor our physique and stand in our truth.

### FEBRUARY — IMBOLC

**Durga:** Hindu Goddess of War and Transformation. Known as the Wild One, she awakens our inner strength and empowers woman to stand their ground and fight for what they desire. She is the spirit of the warrior and the archetype of the Saviouress and the autonomous woman.

**Brigit**: Celtic Matriarchal Goddess of Healing. The transformer and inspirer, she encourages us to use our hands, our voice & creativity to birth new miracles, forged from the fires of our souls.

**Oya:** Powerful thundering Orisha of transformation. She awakens strength for battle and incites courage. She serves as a reminder of our debt to our ancestry & those who paved the way for us.

### MARCH — OSTARA/SPRING

**Uzume:** Japanese Goddess of Merriment. She is the Maiden Goddess of Spring. Awakener to the power of our sensual, physical body & teacher of ecstatic dancing. She reminds us to eradicate darkness & confusion with joy and laughter. She brings in the energy of spring.

**Pele:** The Polynesian Volcanic Goddess of passion. She stirs and awakens great passions. She encourages us to value, embrace and express all of our emotions and pursue our heart's desire.

**Artemis:** Greek Maiden Huntress, Goddess of the Moon & the wilderness. She breathes into our soul, autonomy, empowerment, feminism and the love of animals. She is the awakener of Sisterhood and connects us to our lunar lineage. Our primal selves are born with her energy.

### APRIL — EASTER

**Asherah:** The Canaanite Matriarchal Goddess of Fertility. She is the Sovereign Mother archetype and awakens our powers of fecundity, protection & creation. She connects us to the gifts of the earth and our linage to the sacred trees.

**Aphrodite:** Cypriot Goddess of Love, Beauty and Attraction. She is the teacher of luxury, attraction and love. She brings Love, in all its many guises; most importantly, self-love. She awakens our powers of beauty and the ability to attract what we most desire into our lives.

**Hathor:** Ancient Egyptian Goddess of Love and Pleasure. She is the awakener of all the many splendors that brings delight to our senses; beauty, sensuality, dancing, music, art, love-making, merriment, wine, cosmetics, physical adornments and gemstones. She brings pleasure and joy.

## MAY                                                                                                      BELTANE

**Blodeuwedd:** Welsh Flower Goddess of Awakenings. She is the Goddess of shadows, beauty, passions, betrayals, and love. She awakens us to taboos, our hidden dark subconscious and awakens us to massive transformations. She brings the gifts of Owl medicine.

**Ix Chel:** The Mayan Goddess of the Moon. She connects us to the ebb and flow of life; the powers of water and our gender's strong connection to the Moon. In her realm we are awaken to the protective Mother archetype. The gifts of fertility and creativity are inspired in her lunar light.

**Baubo:** The Greek Goddess of Laughter. She brings with her the gifts of true friendship and the therapeutic powers of a good, hearty belly laugh. She points down below to our sacred yoni and invites us into its beautiful cathartic labyrinth. She is the liberator of depression.

## JUNE                                                                                              LITHA/SUMMER

**Lilith:** The Nocturnal Sumerian Goddess of Liberation. She is the autonomous, freedom lover. Considered the first feminist, she inspires freedom, retribution, anger, pleasure and sexual dominance. She won't tolerate oppression and will demand that you prioritize yourself.

**Saraswati:** The Hindu Matriarchal Goddess of Knowledge. She awakens spiritual connection to the Divine and your inherited creative gifts. She inspires the love and search for knowledge, the written word and the value of your voice. She is the awakener of Divine Knowledge.

**Aine:** Celtic Goddess of Enchantment. She awakens our creative gifts and writing abilities. She teaches us the art of an Enchantress, encouraging us to fight to protect children and ourselves.

## JULY                                                                                          USA-INDEPENDENCE

**Dantor/Black Madonna:** Beloved African Loa and Saint of Protection. She is the revolutionist, Dagger Queen, Protective Mother, Fierce Defender of Children and Woman, Courage awakener.

**Erzulie Freda:** Goddess and Voodoo Loa of Love, Luxury and Beauty. She will support our pursuit for the greater things in life. She is the awakener of sensuality, appreciation for romantic gestures, flirtations, beauty, feminine charm and abundance.

**Gaia:** Primordial Greek Goddess of the Earth, she is the awakener to our gifts of fecundity and creation. She inspires our ability to flourish and connects us to the fiercely protective nature of the Mother. She is a reminder of our infinite lineage & the sacred roots connecting us to one another.

## AUGUST                                                                                                   LAMMAS

**Sif:** Norse Harvest Goddess of Sacrifice. She is the peace-maker and the negotiator within the tribe. She alerts us to the importance of sacrifices for the greater good of all and invites you to embrace your family and your harvest.

**Demeter:** Greek Matriarchal Goddess of the Grain. She supports you in your role as nurturer and devoted mother. She teaches us the gift of fierce negotiation when most needed. And inspires us to honor the cycles of life and the changes each season brings.

**Persephone:** Greek Maiden Goddess of spring and the Queen of the Underworld. She models for us how to live and survive in two opposing worlds. She strengthens us to accept that sometimes, life must be lived within certain confinements but always in perfect balance. She is a teacher for priestesses who walk through multiple realms and for women balancing various, challenging roles.

## SEPTEMBER                                                                                    AUTUMN/MABON

**Sri Lakshmi:** The Hindu Goddess of Wealth & Beauty. She awakens in us our sovereign gifts, the powers of our gender, as women and attracts; abundance, prosperity, creativity, beauty and much success. We attain our heart's desire and connect to the archetype of the wife, mother and Queen.

**Selu, Corn Mother:** She is the Matriarchal, Sacrificial Goddess of Native American tribes. She teaches us the power of compassion, nurturance and sacrifice. Within her sacred corn we learn the importance of our legacy & the value of what we leave behind to future generations. We learn forgiveness, living life in proper balance; finding inner nourishment for both, our body and soul.

**Aradia:** The Etruscan Goddess of Magick & Sorcery. She is teacher of the Ancient-Craft; Stregheria tradition and the mysteries of life. She offers us the tools of protection from our oppressors and elevates our spiritual knowledge and experiences. We delve into the spiritual realm and develop our intuition further with her blessings. She is a most welcomed guide those on the Priestess path.

## OCTOBER                                                                                              SAMHAIN

**Baba Yaga:** The Russian Slavic Goddess of Fright. Our primordial wise Grandmother and the archetype of the wise Crone, she challenges us to confront our deepest fears. We journey through dark terrains & foreboding forests to unearth our true courage. Known as the Hag, the Dark Goddess encourage you to embrace and scrutinize what you consider ugly and revolting. There is beauty in all things and there is nothing to fear with her as your guide.

**Hekate:** The Greek Goddess of the Crossroads and Patron Goddess of witches, she is our teacher and guide of the Mystical arts and helps us to connect to our departed loved ones and our sacred ancestry. Divine protectress, she holds the sacred lantern for us, so that we may navigate through the darkest of realms with her insight and divine light.

**Grand Maman Brigitte:** Goddess & Voodoo Loa of the Cemetery. Devoted mother of the dead and keeper of the bones, she takes us to the very edge and teaches us to honor the sacred threshold of life and death. She connects us to our ancestry & reminds us to honor our sacred bones.

## NOVEMBER                                                                                 GRATITUDE DAY (USA)

**Ma'at:** The Egyptian Goddess of Justice and Truth, with Ma'at we embrace a life lived with integrity, honor and truth. We are in tuned with our heart and are mindful of our respective journey and the judgment of the afterlife. She awakens the power of heart-centered living.

**Hina:** Polynesian Goddess of the Moon. She is our sanctuary & spiritual safe-haven. She awakens our need to retreat & recharge within her cathartic lunar light. We are allowed to repose, regenerate heal, realign and connect with the Divine. She teaches us the value of finding our sacred space.

**Hestia:** Greek Maiden Goddess of the Hearth. Teacher of traditions and rites, she awakens the value of our home, connects us to our lineage, inspires us to tend to our spiritual growth. Our temples & consecrated spaces are born out of her hearth fires and she imparts to us the sacredness.

# 12. ALLIES IN MAGICK

*"We are connected to all women in the past, present and future. We are the trees, waters and the land of Mother Earth. Awaken daughters and remember who you are. Bring your gifts into the world..."* Katherine Krueger

## ANCESTORS & GUIDES

*"When we know about our ancestors, when we sense them as living
And as supporting us, then we feel connected to the genetic life-stream, and
we draw strength and nourishment from this...." Phillip Carr-Gomm*

## ANCESTORS & GUIDES

At the risk of intruding personal family space and a very subjective issue, I wanted to briefly introduce the subject of our deceased loved ones. After all, we are exploring different ways to enhance our powers of manifestation and revamp our lives; and connecting with our ancestors is a time honored tradition that can positively influence our respective journeys.

Almost all early tribes and indigenous people honored their elders, including their ancestors in the afterlife. Their deep reverence and connection to their ancestry almost equipped them with greater strength, knowledge, support and guidance. They felt their ancestors' wisdom and consistent protective shield and it's not surprising they would later become almost deified. What is remembered lives onward and for many, our ancestors indeed remained with us throughout the years. Today, this type of ancestral worship still exists in numerous traditions that maintain their roots in ancient practices. And to a lesser extent we unconsciously continue this tradition when we remember to light a candle on an anniversary, a birthday or a special date surrounding their death. Even our mainstream macabre holiday of Halloween, encourages us to commemorate our deceased loved ones. For many cultures and spiritual traditions, our ancestors are the only remaining evidence of the divine.

In our fast paced, contemporary world, and with the rise of technology, our close connections and interactions are getting somewhat lost. I can certainly attest to this. We spend more time on our android phones or laptops, than we do chatting eye to eye, physically connecting to our friends and family. And unlike other eras, where knowing and being a part of your tribe assured your survival, we are living in a time when that has changed drastically. Today our ancestors and bloodlines are not always known to us and if they are, we might lack a direct physical and personal experience with them in this lifetime. However, that doesn't mean we have to remain in this darkened, complacent state. We can reach out to establish a connection with our ancestors and we can rebuild bridges to mend our relationships with them; whether they are in physical or spiritual form.

Establishing a connection with your ancestors can prove to be invaluable in your spiritual life, as they become, if you let them, your spirit guides. One of the ways our ancestors live on is through the tales we tell and hear of them, so a first step might be simple inquiry. Ask around the existing members of your family for memorable stories and insight into your ancestors. Begin to dig around and gather documents, old letters and photos of your deceased family members to piece together who they were and still are in spirit. When you feel called, you might even create an altar or a special box or shrine in their honor. Sometimes you might find yourself intuitively reaching for things to add to it, to honor your ancestors and this may begin the spiritual interaction between you two. It can promise to lead you to begin conversations and prayers to your beloved ancestors, as well as, inquiries and dialogue between all parties. Like any relationship, your investment or lack thereof, will determine the scope of its value.

When your ancestors become your spirit guides you gain the most powerful allies and teachers on your side. Their additional guardian eyes carry you through all of life's shadowy realms and spiritual journeys. Their wisdom and nurturance becomes more palpable in your dreams, in your prayers and moments of deep meditation and eventually, in your mundane interactions. When you establish a consistent spiritual practice of ancestral honoring; including them in your world and conversing with them regularly, they show up. They become our steadfast consultants and oracle, and their trustworthy guidance is relied upon when making important decisions in our lives. Much like in ancient times, their voices and invaluable wisdom is given the proper platform to be heard and honored. Connecting with your ancestors as your spirit guides, requires simply your respect and desire, and yet it can have a most impactful influence, not just on your spiritual path, but upon the course of your whole life.

# ARCHANGELS

"Make yourself familiar with the angels, and behold them frequently in Spirit; for, without being seen, they are present with you" *St. Francis of Sales*

# ARCHANGELS

Among your numerous allies, you can add a special group of Spiritual beings known as Archangels. Although angels can be found in various traditions, the Archangels are typically connected with Abrahamic religions; Judaism, Islam and Christianity. They are known as messengers of the Divine; helpers and interceptors between humanity and God.

The word Archangel means Chief angel. "*Arche,*"comes from the Greek word meaning, ruler and "*angelos*" means messenger. According to Christian traditions there were Nine Orders of Angels; Seraphims, Cherubim, Thrones, Dominations, Principalities, Powers, Virtues, Archangels and Angels. Some traditions only recognize Michael as the sole Archangel, then there are other Religious traditions that only recognize; Michael, Gabriel and Raphael as the only legitimized archangels. Consequently, these three angels mentioned have been canonized by the church and are often also invoked as Saints. However, it must be noted that, traditionally there are believed to be Seven Archangels. The four exalted archangels are typically; Michael, Gabriel, Raphael, Uriel and these are the ones I have included in this chapter. There does not seem to be a consensus when it comes to the remaining three angels. Some believe they could be; Chamuel, Jophiel, Zadkiel, but this also varies depending on the spiritual tradition. There are those that believe you do not need a religious affiliation to work with Archangels because they are their own entity, meant to be helpers and messengers for humanity to connect with the Divine.

## **ARCHANGELS**
## **MICHAEL –AIR- EAST**

Archangel Michael is also known as *"Mik'ail," "Sabbathiel,"* and *"Beshter."* His color is crimson red, when he appears before you. Yet, he is sometimes purported to bring blue or purple flashing lights to announce his presence. He is popularly shown holding a large threatening sword in his left hand and the justice scales in his right hands. You will also find him in popular depictions standing over a demon, ready to strike down with his sword. Archangel Michael is the one we call upon when we need to sever ties with a situation or a toxic person. When we are facing the seemingly unsurmountable, whether it is a terminal illness, a demanding job or an abusive spouse, it is Archangel Michael that can be called upon to intervene and remedy the situation. He is the angel of protection, truth and integrity. We call on him when we need courage, strength, confidence and self-determination. Interestingly enough, he is also linked with being able to fix mechanical or electrical problems. Archangel Michael is highly venerated, deeply beloved and called upon by many, from various religion faiths. His name translates as, *"He who was like god," "like unto God," and "He who is like the Divine."*

According to early scriptures, Archangel Michael was the first angel created by the Abrahamic God and thus, he is considered the leader of all the archangels in this religion. Light workers across the globe consider him, their beloved angel and patron saint. In 1950, Archangel Michael was canonized as Saint Michael, the patron of "police officers" because of his direct connection with those, brave individuals, who are in the role of service, to help and rescue humanity. He is known to carry the celestial, flaming sword and his mission is to rid the world of negative entities and all toxins in the universe formed by fears. He is reputed to be able to cut through etheric cords, help us find our true calling and protect those who are under physical, emotional or psychic attacks.

## RAPHAEL- EARTH-NORTH

Archangel Raphael was also known by the name, Labbiel and in the Muslim tradition, he is known as one of the four important angels named, Israfil. His name is interpreted as, *"Medicine of God," "The Healing Power of God," "The Divine has Healed,"* and *"God Heals."* In the Hebrew language the first part of his name, *"Rapha"* means Healer. It quickly becomes apparent that Archangel Raphael is closely linked with the power to heal. Raphael, as the Healer of the earth, was in charge of restoring and cleaning the earth when it was defiled by the sins of fallen angels. He is often depicted either standing on top of a large fish or holding a fish. He is also depicted blowing a musical horn. According to Islamic scriptures, Raphael (along with Michael and Gabriel) is believed to have accompanied Mohamed to Mecca. Archangel Raphael is said to be responsible for signaling the coming of Judgment day, by blowing a horn. This has forever linked him with the virtue of truth. His presence is detected by his brilliant green light of healing and he is considered one of the three most important Archangels mentioned in early scriptures. Although his name is not seen in the New Testament, unlike Archangel Michael and Gabriel, his presence is alluded to in the Gospel of John, (John 5:1-4) when the pool of Bethesda is mentioned. He is mentioned in the book Tobit in relation to the story of Sarah. Sarah had seven different husbands perish, upon the first night of matrimony with her. Tobias would be husband number eight and he feared his own death but the Archangel Raphael accompanied him on his first night of marriage to Sarah and helped him escape the curse of death.

Archangel Raphael is the patron for; healers, physicians, nurses, therapist, surgeons, the blind and travelers. He oversees all types of healing; physical, emotional, mental, and spiritual. Raphael tends to all healing and this includes animals. He helps humanity heal from past wounds and is always available to help remove negative entities from your life. He is known to assist Archangel Michael, exorcise, discarnate entities. He is known to have a very sweet, gentle disposition; chanting and conversing with mortals, with ease. He has even garnered a reputation for having a slight comedic side to him. His gentleness will help you recover lost items, including lost pets. He is also known to help those grieving for a lost loved one and those struggling with cravings and addictions.

In 1969, the Roman Catholic Church changed Saint Raphael's feast day and combined it with Saint Michael's day. September 29th became the feast day for Archangel Michael, Gabriel, and Raphael. All Archangels are celebrated on this day and even the Church of England acknowledges, September 29th as the feast of Archangels, including Archangel Raphael.

## GABRIEL- WATER- WEST

Archangel Gabriel is also named as; Abruel, Jibril Jiburili, and Serafili. Her name means, *"Strength of the God," "The Divine is my Strength,"* and *"God is my Strength."* Although angels are typically depicted as androgynous, Gabriel is one of the only few depicted as unquestionably female. She is known as the Divine messenger and immediately, I can't help but connect her with other celestial messengers like the Gods, Hermes & Mercury. Her presence is known by her celestial green light and she is the angel that strongly inspires you to take action. She is patron to artist, writers, speakers and all who are in the role of communication. Because she is known as the Divine messenger, she is connected with all forms of divine communication, unblocking our third eye and facilitating channelings and all spiritual interaction. She is connected with the element of water and all mysteries are resolved with her energy.

Interesting to note, she is one of the four Archangel named in the ancient Hebrew tradition and both she and Archangel Michael are considered the two most powerful, highest ranking angels, for the Judeo-Christian and Islamic religious faith. When called upon, she helps parents attain children; whether through biological means or through adoption. She can also be called upon to assist with residential moves and any drastic life changes. If you are empathic and easily absorb other people's negative energy, call upon Archangel Gabriel to help you cleanse and disconnect from other people's toxic energy. She will help you clear and purify your physical, emotional and spiritual body. She is also reputed to help you with your life purpose and spiritual vision. With Archangel Gabriel we are motivated to conquer fears, procrastination and move forward with ease.

## URIEL-FIRE-SOUTH

His name means, *"God is light," "God's light,"* and *"Fire of God."* Archangel Uriel is deemed as one of the wisest angels that can offer assistance of an intellectual manner to humanity. Uriel brings us the gift of alchemy, powers of manifestation, spiritual understanding and mystical knowledge. Archangel Uriel was one of the angels mentioned in Christian documents of the eighth century, when Pope Zachary removed the seven Archangels from the church's rank acknowledgment. The Pope, at this time, was strangely disturbed by the unusual rise in angel worship and fearing dissention from his flock made some changes. Archangel Uriel appeared to be so popular, at this time, that it concerned Pope Zachary.

We call upon Archangel Uriel to illuminate situations, shift our perspective and bring us deeper understanding. Archangel Uriel can offer you predictions, prophetic dreams and interestingly enough, warnings of impending natural disasters. When faced with floods, tornadoes, hurricanes, fires or devastating earth changes, Uriel can help avert the disaster or bring healing in the aftermath. Uriel brings knowledge and warnings, like in the biblical story of the prophet Ezra, who was alerted of the coming Messiah. With Archangel Uriel we attain help with oracular or divinatory interpretations and we are able to expand our understanding of spiritual matters.

# FAERIE MAGICK

*"Faeries are invisible and
Inaudible, like Angels, but their magick
Sparkles in Nature..."* Lynn Holland

# FAERIES AND ELEMENTALS

Fey/Fairy/Faeries are recognized as a race of magickal beings throughout European myths and folklores. They were not deemed as humans but rather a cross between divine angels and human beings. They are a form of spirit, often described metaphysically as, supernatural or preternatural. They were believed to one day ascend and evolve to deva status but while on earth, they are meant to assist humans. They are also responsible for guarding certain places amidst nature. Legend reveals that faeries actually went into hiding when the humans began to greedily encroach upon their home. Studying the etymology of the word fairy, we learn its origins are connected with the French. The word fairy derives from Middle English word, "faierie," which originates from the old French word faerie, meaning; land, realm enchantment of the legendary people of folklore and romance known as fee/faie. Faie or Fay means, land where fairies dwell. In Latin, "fata" means, one that personified the Fates. Hence, it means a guardian, or spirit. In Italy the word is fata. In Portuguese, the word is fada and in Spanish, it is hada. All of these words mean the same thing; a guardian or a spirit. The word faie, thus becomes known in modern English as fay; a spirit or guardian.

## EARTH FAERIES — GNOMES

Known among the various types of Earth Faeries are; Pixies, Leprechauns, Brownies, Gnomes, the Green Man, Bali Boggs and Boggart, to name just a few. There are also mountain fairies and they are known as Goblins, Dwarfs and Trolls. Earth Faeries help to maintain the physical structure of the earth. They live in trees, under the earth, in caves and in gardens. They appear close to the ground, short, plump and round, in human-like form. They can be found in different shades of browns and shades of dark forest green, colors that allow them to camouflage themselves with nature. They are industrious; always working on intricate projects and are very creative and talented. They are known as blacksmiths, passing on their valuable traditions to their offspring, and they are excellent with their hands. Their hands, by the way, are a bit rough from always working with them, within the earth's rich soil. They hold such deep wisdom when you look into their sparkling eyes and study the moss covered tiny wrinkles upon their skin. They are keepers of ancient wisdom and the knowledge of all rocks, minerals and gemstones within the earth. They know the secrets of crystals and where gold and silver can be found. They are very wealthy and never go hungry. They appear to me to always have a berry or something to nibble on. In my mind's eye, I see they are great collectors of material things and always have the right tools for any occasion. Interesting to make note, they are also very cautious about who they share their knowledge with, not that they are stingy, just that they don't want to be taken for granted. If you call on them expect to negotiate and know that they can also help you find deals when you go out shopping. Some of them might have whiskers, horns or tails or and other animal physical traits, as there is a strong correlation between earth faeries and the animal kingdom. Our senses, like our sense of smell and touch, might be particularly heightened when they are nearby.

They are beholders of the secrets of the earth and some, are even caretakers of the bones laid to rest.

## AIR FAERIES                                                                 SYLPHS

Some Air Faeries are known as Sylphs or Sylphid, Ariel, Light Elves, Vila and Sylvestres, to name just a few. They bring the gift of creativity, inspiration, imagination, mental stimulation and enhanced visions. They are winged creatures, slender and child-like; appearing like dragonflies. Their absolute freedom is very important to them. The saddest thing in the world is to see one caged, unable to spread its wings to fly. It delights in its fluttering wings and the air's supportive rapture when it's in flight. They are like the young maiden; very active, autonomous and smart. You might even find one wearing spectacles upon her eyes, like a Sherlock Holmes, inspecting something or another. Vision and clear sight is her domain. Ask them to help you see when you are in the dark and they will illuminate your path, with new, greater vision. They fly to and from with ease and swiftness. They move with such lightning speed that sometimes, it's hard to discern their physical form. Makes you wonder, do they have a physical form or are they simply the ferocious wind? Air faeries are light and sometimes transparent in appearance; vaporous, resembling those white feathery clouds in the sky. We usually can catch sight of them above or near our heads and their love of birds will frequently find them interacting with them. You might confuse one for a butterfly or a dragonfly. Their distinct faery wings can be found in numerous shades but more commonly are linked to the colors of white, yellow or blues. Their appearance brings a cool breeze across the flesh, an elevated shift in our energy and a sense of new hope.

## WATER FAERIES                                                               UNDINE

Water faieries are recognized as the Undines, Mermaids, Selkies, Kelpies, Leanan Sidhe and Melusines. The etymology of the word, Undine, can be traced to the Latin language. Unda, means, "wave" in Latin, a reference to water movement. Undines are seen as spirits of the water. Water Faeries are known to lure you to the edge of the water simply to have companionship and if you're not careful, you might easily find yourself within the water, submerged by her hypnotic beauty. They are known to communicate to humans through water, in dreams and haunting melodies. Water faieries are considered exquisitely beautiful and graceful, with long flowing hair. Their bodies' are curvaceous, loose and inviting. They appear so seductive, as if the maiden has just awakened to her sexual powers. They flow to us in all bodies of water; lakes, rivers, springs, oceans, pools, waterfalls, fountains, even in our own tears and heartfelt emotions. They sing incessantly of love, passion, sensuality and pleasure. They have the most beautiful, harmonious voices that can enchant the pants off of you. If they are not singing, they are humming and either way, they will enchant you. They almost demand your admiration and unwavering respect. Water faeries love it when they hear you playing music, dancing or singing to yourself. They will quietly join you in almost any heartfelt expression. They can weep very easily or climactically sigh and laugh when moved to. They are very empathetic, compassionate and easily moved to help your cause. They move slowly, deliberately, with all the time in the world. In my mind's eye, water faeries appear to stretch like taffy when they walk towards you and their constant lilt matches their bodies' gently sway, back and forth.

## FIRE FAERIES                                                                    SALAMANDERS

Drakes and Salamanders are two of the best known Fire Faeries. I view these faeries as particularly jumpy and impulsive. Their physical movement is choppy and quirky. You might find them with short spunky hair in shades of red, yellow, black or orange. They can be tall and clumsy and in different shapes; some are slender and some of medium weight. In my mind's eye, they have dominant freckles across their faces and their eyes have the ability to glow like burning coal. Their skin may feel warm to the touch, if you are ever so lucky to touch one. And when they are nearby, you will feel the shift in warmer temperature. They can take on the form of human beings, but much like so many other faeries, they can shape-shift easily into animals and objects. They consume fire and live within our hearth flames. They love to play with your pillar candles. Stare closely at the flicker of a candle's flame and you will begin to see the subtle shape of her form. They speak in strange, hissing whispers, with the occasional, unexpected outburst and screeches. While they are very passionate, they are also known to anger easily. Call on them when you are seeking vengeance or help with a judicial issue. Fire faeries are fiercely protective, most especially of women and children. They have unusual strength and power and have an affinity to the sun.

# THE ELEMENTS
*"Earth my Body, Water my Blood, Air my Breath and Fire my Spirit..."*

*"The Air we breathe, the Water we drink, and the Land we inhabit, are not only critical elements in the quality of life we enjoy, they are a reflection of the majesty of our Creator/Creatress...." Rick Perry*

# ELEMENTALS

## THE ELEMENT OF AIR

The element of air is related to the ethers, to things that are beyond our physical grasp. It rules over the mind and our initial thoughts and ideas. It is our curiosities and inquiries and daydreams that take us to new heights. It starts to strategize and imagine the world. It taps into its vision and begins the journey. Air is the realm of eyesight, vision, awareness, clarity. It invites us to look around and make assessments. Air is the place of conception, of initiations…where "The Fool" begins his explorations. Air is the lightness of a feather and the inaudible whispers of the nocturnal winds. It is the gentle breeze that caresses your skin or the fiercely powerful wind that catapults you into flight. It is intellect, communicative and can cut through illusions. It has foresight, wisdom and expanded vision. It has owl eyes and Athena's sword; unrestricted with its itinerary, it is a vehicle for Spirit to come through.

## THE ELEMENT OF FIRE

This is the realm of the alchemist and the blacksmith. Fire is where we take our ideas and turn them into creative works of art. This is the realm that beholds our creative fires, our drive and ambition. It is the place of magick and transmutation. Here is the friction and spark caused by the aggressive rubbing of two opposing objects. Here is the birth of the diamond, the newborn and our most cherished dreams. This is the realm that propels us to move forward and commit one hundred percent. This is our hearth fires and the core of our home. This is the magick of the oven and the magick of our nurturing wombs. Here is where we fiercely protect and fight for justice and change. This is the place where we delve into our passions, pleasure, anger and frustrations. Fire is heat from our blood and our sexual organs. Fire is contained in our muscles and our yoni. It is the heat born from the energy of drive and necessity. This is the realm of the athlete and the bubbling nerves before we engage in something important that we truly desire. Fire is the realm of the pulsating heart, of the determined runner approaching the finish line.

## THE ELEMENT OF WATER

The element of water relates to the realm of emotions and healing. It is cascading waterfalls and unexpected drizzles on a hot sunny day. It is where we feel and where we are in tuned with how others feel. Here is compassion and infinite flowing tears. Here is ecstasy and the ebb and flow of our gender's sacred womb waters. Here is Her Lunar influence and the pool from her ecstatic juices. Here is her thirst quenching rain and the sweat that pours forth, from her dance of reverence. Here, in the realm of water, we splash and swim to the mermaid's songs. We dive deep and submerse our soul and rise to embrace our emotional waves that foam to the surface of her crystalline ceilings.

## THE ELEMENT OF EARTH

The element of earth is associated with our planet earth and our physical bodies. It is where we exalt our flesh and bones and the actual soil that supports and holds our weight upon the earth. This is the realm of riches, minerals and manifestations. Where we see our seeds fully manifested and where we can behold tangible things that are of great value to us. Earth is the realm of transformations; regenerative and nurturing. Here is where our senses are alive and where we delight in our fruits of labor. Here is where we celebrate the harvest and relish each morsel that passes through our lips. Here is where we can connect to our primal energy and embrace our form, our bones our fertile capacity. Here is where we see ourselves as living embodiment of the pulsating earth itself. Here is our magick of transformation and growth.

## ELEMENTS

Below is a list of attributes associated with each quarter. It is only a short list of suggested images you can use, when calling the energy of an element into your ritual work.

| EAST<br>AIR | SOUTH<br>FIRE | WEST<br>WATER | NORTH<br>EARTH |
|---|---|---|---|
| Sword/Athame | Wand | Chalice | Pentacle |
| Feather | Candle | Water | Soil |
| Bells/Chimes | Hearth | Emotions | Plants |
| Birds | Lions | Swans | Snakes |
| Eagles | Dragons | Fishes | Rocks |
| Breath | Rubbing Hands | Body Fluids | Flowers |
| Panting | Heart | Tears | Animals |
| Fairies | Blood | Orgasms | Fertility |
| Intellect | Desire | Moist Kiss | Touch |
| Clouds/Sky | Underworld | Rain Forest | Earth |
| Airplanes | Forge | Harmony | Physical |
| Kites | Cauldron | Liquids | Regeneration |
| Gentle Breezes | Passion | Rain Mist | Mountains |
| Tornadoes | Obsession | Depth | Transformation |
| Twisters | Ambition | Ebb & Flow | Embrace |
| Conceptions | Cravings | Dew | Growth |
| Beginnings | Volatile | Menstrual | Change |
| Ideas | Consumption | Wine | Food |
| Inspiration | Persistence | Balance | Manifestation |
| Blue/White | Red/Orange | Turquoise/Blue-green | Brown/Black |
| Knights Armor | Volcanoes | Singing | Human Flesh |
| Clarity | Tenacity | Music | Solidity |
| Nike | Brigit | Mermaids | Trolls |
| Athena | Hestia | Yemaya | Demeter |
| Aradia | Pele | Aphrodite | Artemis |
| Hina | Amaterasu | Saraswati | Maia |
| Cool Air | Sun | Rain | Baubo |
| Libra | Aries | Pisces | Taurus |
| Aquarius | Leo | Cancer | Virgo |
| Gemini | Sagittarius | Scorpio | Capricorn |
| Incenses | Body Heat | Blood | Strength |
| Sylphs | Salamanders | Undines | Gnomes |
| Air | Flames | Seashells | Salt |
| Mind | Sensuality/Sex | Emotions | Herbs |

# 13. NATURAL MAGICK

## **NATURAL MAGICK**

What is Natural Magick? As you proceed here, you will find that more will be discussed on this particular subject throughout book, especially in the chapters of *Sex Magick* and *Our Oracle Body*, but for now I simply wish to embark on the initial inquiries of what is considered Natural Magick.

Magick, our spirituality and our powers of manifestation can be explored by numerous venues, as the premise of this book will reveal, but one of the simplest and probably the oldest form of magick can be found in our very own natural bodies. Our sacred body, which encompasses glimpses of the Divine and a symbol of her Creatrix life force, here is one aspect of magick so often overlooked. Yet, magick is also in the uncultivated wild nature; by the sea, in the forest, in the crops, and fields of our harvest, in our hearth fires and yes... our bodies. There is potency in our physical body, yet so often we fail to see and value it, opting instead to crown our spirituality as the sole authority in magick making, but it is an incomplete premise. Our physical body can become our ally and one of our first teachers in the art of magick and transformation. It requires no special education nor in depth training. It simply requires our astute attention, openness and committed connection.
In trance, I explored deeper the meaning of natural magick....

## **A CHANNELING/TRANSMISSION**

*What is this natural magick you speak of?*
*Our form of natural magick needs no hierarchy, nor explanation; it just is.... It is following your primal instincts. It is getting low to the ground, to mother earth, to breathe in her pungent, aromatic scents upon the land... It is getting your mangled tresses soaked in a climactic thunderous rainstorm as you dance her into your exaltations. It is spiraling in cackling ecstasies and joy, as her essence trickles upon your hungry skin. It is your hands and feet blackened by her dark moist, fertile soil....*
*Uumm... yes....*

*It is connecting to our four legged friends and infinite teachers who share breath on this earth and it is walking paths with them.... It is listening to the winds, whether gentle or fierce, quietly detecting her breeze to let it whisper its sweet wisdom to you.*

*It is crouching down... down, down to our deep inner soul roots, to listen intently and connect to the messages from our twisting and turning dancing guts; recognizing its oracular gifts. Yes, our lovely branches reaching quite high, garners much love and guidance from above but it is deep in our roots, traveling through these trunks that we survive through incarnations and incarnations... Here, we nurture with gratitude and listen to our sacred roots.*

*Natural Magick....it is listening.....listening.....with far more than our ears. It is listening with the receptors on our flesh and the million eyes upon our crown. Ancient ears attuned, listening in the void, listening, as silence speaks her esoteric language that only a few have dared to acknowledge, let alone comprehend...*

*It is walking, not away, but towards dark shadows, when sometimes you fear it's a revelatory light..... And it is welcoming strange sensations, like elevated hairs upon the back of the neck, for they announce more than our physical eyes can see... It is recognizing that all around us.... There ... there exist magick, natural magick!!!!*

*Everything is alive, vibrating, humming, singing, speaking its sacred whispers...seeking its counterpart, to appreciate its sound, wisdom, warning and messages.... Natural magick.... it is running towards veiled portals to unearth altered realms of our subconscious... It is opening... Opening....*
*Opening.....being the chalice that invites union and co-mingling of spirit....*

*This is Natural Magick... It needs no validation, no school or certification. It needs no approval of what's right or wrong; it relies on its inner wisdom and judge...and feeds from the multitude of infinite Devas and our ancestral guides as support. It yearns to be heard, valued and embraced from the inside out... It needs nothing yet it needs and relies on everything.... Everything all around you....everything that is within you....*
*It does not separate itself by species or gender or race or planet or by any of the other claim... It knows that in the end, **that is**... if there really **was** an end, for we are continual Spirals.... It knows that our true authentic form is formless... vapors..... breath upon breath.... Because breath upon breath we are made, **continually** made, breath upon breath.*
*And so.....*

*Natural magick is attuning ourselves to everything, but most importantly putting ourselves in that equation of attunement. Connecting and forming a bond with yourself, your inner core, your spirit, realizing that this bond... this connection will never lead you astray.... It will only bring you back to you...in the spiral... back to your true strength, back to your true essence which is love, back to your true power....which is your DNA make up, which is love. This is natural magick. It exists, breathes and strives within you and recognizes itself as inseparable from nature and the Universe at large.*
*In Lakesh....*

# II. HOLIDAYS & SABBATS

# EIGHT WICCAN SABBATS

| Theme | Sabbat | Suggested Deity |
|---|---|---|
| **December 20-21st**<br>Rebirth | Solstice/Winter | Amaterasu, Rhiannon, Hina, Hestia, Kwan Yin |
| **February 2nd**<br>Initiations | Imbolc | Brigit, Oya, Durga, Sekhmet, Pele, Nu Kua |
| **March 20-21st**<br>Growth | Ostara/Spring | Artemis, Skadhi, Eostre, Persephone/Kore, Uzume |
| **May 1st**<br>Pleasure | Beltane | Aphrodite, Lilith, Freya, Ix Chel, Shakti, Asherah, Blooduewedd |
| **June 20-21st**<br>Sun, Vitality | Midsummer/Litha | Gaia, Erzulie Freda, Oshun, Saraswati, Hathor, Bast |
| **August 1st**<br>Gratitude, 1st Harvest | Lammas | Corn Mother, Lakshmi, Hambodia, Gaia, Demeter |
| **September 20-21st**<br>Sacrifice, 2nd Harvest | Fall/Mabon | Demeter, Selu, Isis, Inanna |
| **October 31st**<br>Death, | Samhain | Hekate, Baba Yaga, Ma'at, Maman Brigitte, Ereshgigal, Cerridwen, Sheila-Na-Gig |

## SOLSTICE/ WINTER-DECEMBER

# WINTER SOLSTICE  December 20-23

The Winter Solstice is the Wiccan sabbat that celebrates the slow, gentle return of the sun's power. It comes on the heels of Yule and the Christian Christmas holiday, which has retained a lot of Pagan influence obscured and veiled over the years. It is at this point that the sun begins its steady climb to its zenith, which will be experienced fully by summer. We celebrate the birth of the sun and while the sun in some cultures might be considered masculine, here we will honor her, as the Feminine powerful source of warm light she is so often believed to be in various other cultures; like Celtic, Welsh and Japanese Shintoism. This is the shortest day and the longest night of the year and to our ancestors, surviving this night amidst community was significant.

Winter Solstice and Yule are steeped with the influence of numerous ancient cultures and traditions. In the Germanic language the word Yule or "Jul" means, "Wheel," an embraced ancient view of the sun. Many believed this was originally a Norse holiday that commemorated the birth of the Sun and growing light. Often, it was celebrated with communal bonfires, gifts and storytelling.

For the Romans this was the time to celebrate the weeklong Saturnalia festival, a holiday in which everything was allowed to be topsy-turvy and awkward. Men would dress as women, clothing attire would be worn inside out and parades of such silliness were held out on the streets for all to enjoy.

The commemoration of Winter Solstice, some believe however, began in Britain long before Christianity infiltrated its Christ birth theory. For the Druids this was a holiday that commemorates life amidst the darkness, stillness and death of winter. It was celebrated with a battle between the Holly king and Oak king, which was often role played by members in the community. The Oak, as their sacred tree, always attained victory at this time of the year and later, the burning of a yule log became a longstanding ritual tradition, believed to banish evil and bring light and blessings for the New Year. Another symbol of life, the venerated Mistletoe, was also cut from the Oak tree and often presented as sacred gifts to the community at large.

At this time of the year, the days will slowly, quite subtly, get longer and it appears as if the sun now will slowly increase in power. We observe the longest night of the year on this sabbat and celebrate hope, rebirth and the anticipated return of light to our wintry dark realm.

# IMBOLC-FEBRUARY

## IMBOLC/CANDLEMAS February 2nd

According to some scholarly text, the Gaelic word "*Imbolg*" means, "*in the belly*", and it is a reference to the Earth's belly, holding the promise of spring. Calves and lambs typically were born at this time in Ireland. Ewes would also lactate and this was often understood as a sign of hope, the impending end of winter, and the return of spring. In some literature the word Imbolc itself was believed to be a reference to the lactation of ewes. It becomes apparent that the word, throughout early folklore, had various meanings but it was most heavily associated with the Mother; gestation, birthing, holding, lactation and newborns.

This is typically one of the coldest months of the year in some parts of the world and the weather can be fiercely brutal, almost deathly, as our ancestors also faced a dwindling pantry nearing the end of winter. Amidst the wretched cold however, we begin to witness subtle signs that change is inevitable. In the U.S.A., we search for the groundhog to gives us the hopeful sign of an early spring. In Ireland, a snake slithering out of her hole, coming down from the mountaintops, was the much anticipated sign of the Celtic Goddess Brigit and spring's much welcomed arrival. In ancient time, the snake was seen as the maiden Goddess herself, returning to Earth to announce spring's advent. At this time, you may hear larks and other birds begin to make their presence known with their songs. The Earth, in some places, begins to thaw after the glacial cold months but the biggest indicator of the seasonal change is the growing strength of the sun, as we begin to experience longer days and shorter nights.

The sabbat of Candlemass (*mass of the candles*), also celebrated at this time, was a Christianized name for the feast of candles. Candles and fire were traditionally seen as tools of purification, not surprising this sabbat became a feast of purification for all, including the church. It was also traditionally the time when candles were blessed and re-dedicated in most churches, a tradition still practiced today. Also, the Virgin Mary, one of many venerated iconic images of the Feminine Divine and representative of the importance of the Mother (life and light giver) at this time, was honored with candle light ceremonies and ecclesiastical processions. Naturally for many Pagans, the element of fire and the sacred rites of purifications and re-dedication to the craft becomes a beloved, common theme at this time of year.

## OSTARA/SPRING-MARCH

# SPRING/VERNAL EQUINOX/ OSTARA March 20-23rd

Day and night are equal and balanced at this pivotal time of the year and in some parts of the world we are greeted with a thawed, moist soil, that is ripe and ready to receive our hopes; our seeds. There is much anticipation for our first seedlings to sprout and form their first teeny buds of blossoming flowers. This Wiccan sabbat, believed to be named after the Saxon fertility Goddess, *Eostre/Ostara*, celebrates the arrival of spring.

For the Romans, at one point in history, this was actually considered the first month and the start of the New Year, as there was clearly a distinctive, undeniable feeling of newness upon the earth. Astrologically, the sun enters the first sign of the zodiac, Aries, and thus, this time of year was easily accepted as the start of the New Year.

On this sabbat, most of our ancestors commemorated the survival of the harsh cold weather and winter's bleak darkness. It was and still remains a time to rejoice in the promise of fruition and the arrival of gentler weather. Many of our spring traditions are steeped in ancient Pagan folklores and this time of the year is very much associated with the earth's potential and promised fertility. It is also reflective of our own potentiality and fecundity as we too unearth within us, great hope at this time of year.

Animals of the land, that best represent and mirror these fertile, frolicsome attributes of the season, were also venerated and continue to hold our adoration at this time of the year. The rabbit, best known for its fecundity and often very visible among the land at this time, was such a powerful symbol of spring that it continues to be exalted, even among Christians and their Easter holiday of resurrection. After the long, dark cold winter, animals begin to reappear upon the land that we share and it is as if everyone awakens from slumber. Among indigenous cultures, the rabbit and hare are acknowledged as an appropriate symbol of spring. The Full Moon of this month was aptly named, Hare Moon.

For most Dianic Wiccans, it is the frolicking maiden who is venerated at this time of the year, as she is daughter, returning to her beloved earth mother from the oppressive underworld and the darkness of winter. She surrenders Persephone, the Queen of the underworld and returns to the mother, as the Maiden Goddess, Kore.

Eggs have always been considered a symbol of conception, motherhood and the Goddess. As a common tradition for both Pagan and Non-Pagans alike, eggs are often painted, decorated and used in numerous fertility rites, due to their strong connection, again, not only to fertility but also to the tenet of rebirth. The Wheel of the Year turns once more and the Earth is now ready to receive our seeds. This is the time of planting; whether it is literal planting of your actual garden of herbs and flowers, or the planting of your new hopes and dreams. This is the most ideal time for your New Year's resolutions, not January, as nature itself will support the birth of new visions and goals. Though the weather, in some parts of the world, might seem unpredictable and "clingy" to the last days of winter, we place our seeds upon the earth and the auric field now. We continue exuberantly on our journey, with renewed hope and the energy of the Maiden.

# BELTANE-MAY

## BELTANE  April 31st -May 1st

Known as a Celtic Fire festival because of its connection to the heat and growing height of the sun's power, Beltane is the sabbat we celebrate this month. Beltane/Beltaine is also known as Mayday, and also celebrated as *Walpurgisnacht* (*the night before, on the eve of April 30th*). It is one of three most important fertility sabbats. Believed to be named after the Celtic healing Fire God, *Bel/ Belus or Belenos*, it is also considered one of the four major Wiccan holy days. The name of this sabbat is reputed to be a Gaelic word, translated as simply, the month of May. This is a time to celebrate the fertility of the Earth, as everything appears to be vibrantly colorful, exponentially growing, and the penetrating verdant hues surrounding us appear to be multiplying within itself.

All around us are signs that spring has indeed, finally, arrived and the dark, cold winter weather of the last few months, thankfully, seems like a distant memory. The month of May brings colorful flowers of all kinds; blooming and blessing our senses. Trees are no longer bare, but full and lush. Bright colors and sweet scents saturate the landscape and awaken our inner maiden. Animals, and even humans in various ways, are bringing forth their newly created offspring. The green lush grass has replaced the white blanket of snow and inspires us to relish in the warmth of the season with some frolicking. We celebrate the fruitfulness of the Earth now and our own frivolities. Traditionally at this time, lovers would make vows and betroth one another. However, this was not seen as a good time to actually jump the broom and marry, but rather a time for pleasure and enjoyment. Marriages and contracts of that sort were best done the following month, in June to receive the Blessings of the Goddess Juno.

For most Pagans this is a highly celebratory, sexualize sabbat with many illustrative symbols suggesting its prominence, at this time of the year. The traditional spiral dancing around the phallic maypole, the stomping of the earth with our bare feet and the colorful ribbons adorning our tresses and our bodies, are all reflective of what we are experiencing through nature's own offering. The Maiden is awakened and coming into her own true self. For Dianic Wiccans she is now a young lady experiencing her first menarche and sexual awakening.

Merriment and the various expressions of fertility can manifest itself in our lives now and this is the predominant theme of this sabbat. We celebrate our own fruitfulness and our ability to procreate, by jumping the broom, leaping the late night bonfires, spiraling with the swirling ecstasy of sun's heighten power and entangling ourselves with the colorful ribbons that hold each of our desires. Beltane is a celebration of the earth's awakening and the arrival of the Maiden.

# LITHA/SUMMER-JUNE

# SUMMER SOLSTICE/LITHA June 20-23

Summer Solstice is considered one of the four lesser sabbats of the Wiccan year. Litha or Midsummer, as it is sometimes called, marks the longest day of the year and contrast the Winter Solstice. As the name, Midsummer, implies, we are at the pivotal center of our calendar year at this point. This is the sabbat celebration of the official arrival of summer and the height of the sun's power. It is a holiday celebrated by many from various cultures, since ancient times, as it marks another pivotal moment when day and night are balancing one another.

In some parts of the world the summer heat is strongest now and we might be spending a lot of time outdoors enjoying our long sunny days. Undeniably, the arrival of summer highlights the power of the sun at its zenith, but for those who are in tuned with the Earth's natural cycles, you can sense that this sabbat actually marks the eventual decline of the sun's power. On this day, much like the Winter Solstice, the honored Sun, holds our attention, with an awareness that soon it will slowly begin its descent towards autumn. It won't be experienced immediately and it's hard to imagine when we're in the midst of heat waves, but already in the cosmos, the change has indeed commenced here. At this point the Summer Solstice really inaugurates the sun's height and very slow decline in power.

The darkness will soon take over the light. Our days will, quite subtly, grow shorter and our nights will slowly begin to grow longer, but these changes will go on imperceptibly until we reach our next sabbat celebration. For now, this is the time to relish and enjoy the summer days and be mindful that the Wheel of the Year continues to go forward and brings subtle changes in the atmosphere. We find ourselves standing in the middle of our calendar year; reflecting on what has passed and what will come to be. Day and Night stand in perfect balance, giving us an opportunity to re-create balance in our own personal lives.

Many ancient Litha/Midsummer Rites involved elaborate processions, communal bonfires, and donning crowns and floral head wreaths. This was also the ideal time for hand-fastings and marriage ceremonies, a tradition that continues to influence our modern world. Many elect this month to marry and June, typically sees an increase in wedding ceremonies.

You are encouraged to celebrate, for the Wheel of the Year has turned once more and for most Dianic Wiccans, the Maiden has reached the maturity of womanhood. It is at this time that the Goddess communes and merges with her lover. As the Earth appears fertile, loving and ripe, we too, at this time, can exemplify these attributes in our own lives. We celebrate the Sun's height now, our own fertile juiciness and observe the turning of the sacred wheel.

# LAMMAS-AUGUST

# LAMMAS July 31-August 1st

Lammas is an important agricultural sabbat that commemorates the first fruits and the first grains. Here on the first day of August, we arrive at the sabbat of gratitude. This is essentially embraced as our Thanksgiving holiday. Known also as the Celtic holiday of Lughnasadh; Lammas is one of the four major Wiccan holy days. It was named by the Druids, after the Sun God, Lugh, and its celebration was well documented in various cultures, in ancient times. Although many of us might not be exposed to agrarian living, today many Pagans and Neo-Pagans alike, still commemorate this holy day as the sabbat of the first Harvest and our official day of Gratitude.

Traditionally, the day of Lammas, was the day that church offerings were made, with baked breads, prepared from the grains of the first harvest. Thus, it became known among the church as Loaf mass day, abbreviated and known to medieval Christians as, Lammas. This is the sabbat that celebrates the sacredness of the Grain and reflects the initial sense of gratitude, for those first fruits. We have something to celebrate now and give our initial thanks, as we also anticipate what the next harvest may bring. We celebrate the gifts of this first harvest and naturally make our offerings to the Gods, in sincere gratitude, as our ancestors have done since ancient times.

Although amidst sweltering heat, it feels as if August is the height of the oppressive summer heat wave and the sun's unquestionable power, it actually marks the noticeable descent of the sun and unlike the Summer Solstice, this change becomes more apparent at this time of the year. What began at the Equinox, is now visibly and indisputably felt, as we begin to experience the days becoming shorter and the nights slowly beginning to grow longer. The evening breezes might begin to feel slightly cooler by the end of the month in some parts of the world. The trees, flowers and the grass take on a slightly different hue. By the end of the month, we are saying goodbye to our summer vacations, the season of play, frolicking and fertility and we begin to set our sights on new projects, and new school years. We bid farewell to the Maiden and we approach the period of harvest and hard labor. We take a step forward and stand on the threshold of a new season. Autumn looms ahead and begins to beckon us to slowly turn inward.

The Maiden is now a Wombmyn, ripening, pregnant and pouring forth of her first bounty. Her seeds are now producing tangible proof of her great agricultural powers and we take this time to inspect our own lives and give thanks for the first initial manifestations of our hopes and dreams via her bounty and first fruits.

## MABON/ FALL-SEPTEMBER

## AUTUNMNAL EQUINOX/ FALL/MABON September 20-23

This is the celebration of the Autumnal Equinox, when we stand in perfect balance between night and day. It is also the sabbat of the Second Harvest and a time of much anticipated hard work, as we prepare for the inevitable dark season. Traditionally, for Pagans, this can be a time of more gratitude but it is really a time of labor and assessment. This is the time to reap what we've sown, evaluate our progress, save and prepare ourselves for the anticipated fallow challenges of the dark season.

Mabon was known as Harvest Height and Harvest Home but there is some controversy over the term Mabon for this sabbat. It appears to be a fairly new term created in the 1970's, attributed to Aidan Kelly, and not related to any documented, ancient Celtic tradition. The name might have some connection to characters from Arthurian Welsh mythology, as their God of the Harvest is known as "Mabon ap Modron". His name translates as the divine son of the Mother. According to the Mabinogion, as an infant, Mabon, was kidnapped from his mother for three days and found himself in the underworld (Annwfn) where immortal youth was bestowed upon him, as well as the blood that intoxicates. He later would become well known as the Green Man and also linked to Apollo, the Greek Sun God. It is a tale reminiscent of Persephone's descent into the underworld and yet, another example of how our ancestors viewed this sacrificial time of year. The Autumnal Equinox has indeed been observed since ancient times and most practicing Pagans include it as one of the revered eight sabbats.

It is a cross quarter holy day and a time to reflect on how balanced we are in our own lives, as day and night are suspended equally in the cosmos. We labor to secure our second harvest knowing that our work now will determine our survival during the dark season. The hopes that we held, back in December and January, were planted into seeds in February and March. By May and June we were thrilled to witness the very beginnings of our seeds taking shape. By July and August we had much to do and celebrate, as those initial blossoming revealed themselves. At the Second Harvest, we begin to take stock & engage in the work before us; gathering the grapes, the apples, the wheat and corn and various other grains plucked and harvested now before the first frost arrives. Our land (internally and externally) is now beginning to prepare for the changes winter brings. Inclement weather and blistering storms in some parts of the world are inevitable after these next few weeks.

The theme of Sacrifice is very much imbued in this sabbat, as the Grain Goddess Demeter must sacrifice her daughter, Kore and surrender her to Hades, in the underworld at this time. Nothing will grow amidst the Mother's sorrow and nothing will grow when the flowering Maiden takes her fertile light away from the earth and buries it deeply, with her, in the underworld. Traditionally, this was the time our ancestors gathered their food, stock and supplies, filling their pantries before the harsh winter months. Animals and the herd were also prepared to move inward. As the sun appears to be dying and the Earth will soon lie still, barren, fruitless and nothing will grow. It behooves us to also prepare ourselves physically, mentally and emotionally for the inevitable changes the new season will bring. Remember, the maiden Kore, has now left us and her role, as maiden, to take on the role of dark Queen of the underworld, Persephone; Hade's wife. She takes with her the fertile gifts of the corn and in her sad mother; the fertile green earth is suspended. We give thanks for our bounty and the fruition of our hopes and dreams, as we also prepare ourselves for the sacrifices this time may bring. We gather ourselves, take inventory of our work, our failures and successes and look ahead in preparation. We commemorate the second Harvest and prepare for the impending dark season.

# SAMHAIN-OCTOBER

# SAMHAIN/ HALLOWEEN October 31- November 1st

One of the most venerated holidays for both Pagans and non-Pagans alike, this Celtic, ancient sabbat has even infiltrated Christianity with its proselytization of honoring the dead. For most Pagans, our Wiccan year has come to an end and we come to the season of deep introspection. Samhain marks the end of our solar year and the beginning of another and thus, like all thresholds, there is magick to be found within the veil of this transition. It is considered one of the most important major holy days for most Pagans. A time to reflect on issues of life and death, Samhain is a time to visit with our ancestors and consult our inner shamans. We call on the Mistress of the Cemetery, the Dark Mother or the Crone, the Goddesses of Sorcery and Magick. The Maiden has left our land to join her consort, Hades, in the underworld and she, as Queen of this realm, now inaugurated the season of Darkness. It is also considered the season of the venerated Crone, for "She" is no longer frolicsome maiden, nor juicy bountiful Mother, but rather the introspective, dark wise one.

Samhain means *"Summer's End"* and has its inception far back in ancient times, as the Druid's New year. Documented and celebrated in various cultures, there was a common belief that the spirits of old would come out to play on this day and they were believed to be visibly walking, among the living. For this reason, scary costumes of zombies, skeletals and Jack o Lanterns carved in scary faces, became a tradition, to confuse and trick malevolent spirits; at least this is one of the more common folklores. Thus, it is believed that this is the time when the veil between the worlds is the thinnest. Our world of the living and the realm of the spirit and the dead, blurs for this night, according to Pagan beliefs, allowing for deep reconnections to our loved ones who have passed on.

A sabbat that clearly honors the sacredness of thresholds, Samhain celebrates the darkness and the unknown, and these are the prominent themes of the month. Our ancestors, at this time of year, did not know what kind of harsh challenges the month would bring. They did not know what they would face in the coming winter months, adding to the ambivalent, agonizing mystery of the season. Daylight hours were short, resulting in many long hours of darkness and this too added to the eeriness so often associated with this time of year. It is a month that typically reflects shadows and uncertainties. Samhain conveys a most noticeable threshold, as it is the gateway to the approaching dark winter.

There are numerous ways this special day is celebrated among various cultures. One belief they share in common is that it has become a night when we traditionally honor those who have died; reconnect with lost loved ones and acknowledge the spirit realm. Naturally, it is a most powerful night for divination, oracular and spiritual workings and, for most Earth based religions, it is indeed a holy day; revered and celebrated, not as scary (as the mainstream media so often enjoys portraying it) but as one of the most sacred of nights of the year....

# III. SOUND TOOLS OF MAGICK

*"Sound will become the medicine of the future...."* Edward Cayce

# THE MAGICK OF SOUND

*In the beginning was the word...* In almost every early form of civilization there is a strongly held belief that our words have power and that sound, tones and music, are a direct reflection of the Divine. From the earliest of shamans, wizards, stregas, witches, priestesses & priest, teachers and orators; our spoken words carry the weight of gold. Yet, it is not just our words spoken from our lips that hold such effable power but sound, by its very nature, and its vibrational component.

In the Egyptian Book of the Coming Forth by Light, it states, "... I am the eternal...I am that which created the word.... I am the word...." In Hindu cosmology the Universe is created, destroyed and re-created, in an eternally repetitive series of cycles. It is in the sacred text of the Rig Veda, however, that we get a glimpse into how important sound is, as it destroyed the chaos to give birth to our Universe. The Vedas describes the origins of the universe, revealing that in the beginning was Brahman, with whom was the word, and the word is Brahman. Brahma is the Creator (the male principle of creation) and it is his Sacred Feminine counterpart, the matriarchal Goddess, Saraswati, who utters the sacred "Om" or "Aum," thus giving birth and formation to the initial chaotic, formless Universe.

## **The Power of the Word**

Christian scriptures also reflect a similar tenet about the omnipotent power of sound and its relationship to the birth of the Universe. Below is a quote, as found in these Biblical versions; *"American Standard Version," "American King James Version"* and *"King James 2000 Bible."*

>*John 1:1 "In the beginning was the Word,*
>*and the Word was with God,*
>*and the Word was God...."*

Words explain our inner thoughts, our inner mind and knowledge. Since the earliest of ages, our words are valued as expressions of our thoughts, shared with others through varying means; more specifically through our voice. The son of God, according to most Christian tenets, was sent to earth to reveal the mind of God, the father, to the world. There is a clear indication in this text, as in many other ancient texts from various cultures, that the word predates form. And before anything came to be, there was the word and the word itself was Divine. All things are born from our thought and words are sacred as a vibratory expression of these thoughts. Word is deemed as God/Goddess, the Divine, and all things exist first and foremost through its omnipotence.

>*John 1:14 "The word became flesh and*
>*made his dwelling among us.*
>*We have seen his Glory, the Glory of the one and only son,*
>*who came from the father full of grace and truth..."*

For the Greeks, "word" is known as "logos" and "word" here, is translated to mean, reason. One could infer that Logos or Word is not a reference to a single word but rather a collection of them or the expression of thoughts and reason. According to Greek Platonism and its student, Philo, Logos was God's son; a deified personification of the word. He was deemed as another God in the heavens and it is directly through him that the world was created. The Universe as a harmonious world in which chaos (another God) was banished and sent away, came into formation, to birth order through the gift of the word, Logos. Logos removed the irrational, bringing a harmonious world through his sacred existence. According to this mythology, Logos was born of the mother "Wisdom" and it is through the word, Logos, that great leaders are believed to eventually learn Gods' expectation of them. The value of our words is clearly exemplified in these examples of early cosmologies. Christianity would later synchronize this son of God, Logos, with the story of the Christ. For most Christians, Jesus would then be seen as the human personification of the God, Logos.

*"The energy of intention is carried on the frequencies of sound..."*
*"Sound is a carrier wave of consciousness..." says Steven Halpern.*

In Norse mythologies, our word, in our vows and oaths, were of exceedingly great substance and value. It was all you needed to seal a deal or a fate, as few dared to betray the Cosmos with a broken, unfulfilled oath. Even in our modern times, our words, in an oath or a vow, like those taken in nuptials and numerous judicial court hearings, has enormous weight and validity. Your agreement to, *"speak the truth and nothing but the truth, so help you God..."* is enough to allow you to sit by the judge, at the witness stand, in a court of law. On inauguration day, every four years, our American President places one hand on a Holy book and raises the other, as he takes the Oath of Office. Those seeking American citizenship make verbal oaths before the proper authorities and pledge allegiance to their country, all with their spoken word. There are numerous other examples of how, even in our modern times, our words create powerful bonds and sets into motion new established realities. Without artifacts or superfluous effects, we need only our voice to make a powerful oath and vow. And this stems from our deeply suppressed ancient knowledge of the primordial laws of the Universe. No one knows the power of word better than the priestesses, shamans, witches, conjurers and magician. As the spoken invocation is the powerful catalyst that initiates the change and the magick, for that which we most desire to see manifested. If you still don't believe in the power of our spoken word, just study a professional established actor. Witness an actor's transformation, as they take on new personas and express this metamorphosis through the power of the word to create new, believable realities.

The shaman, with only her voice, casts out the demons, the priestess calls forth the presence of the Goddess, with her will and word, and the magician says, it is so and, it is... Our word is everything! It is simultaneously rooted in the Divine and yet, it is in fact Divine. Some, in our modern world, have forgotten this commanding truth and as a result, have lost an element of their power and their voice. As students of magick and seekers of valuable esoteric wisdom and gifts, this is probably one of the most important Metaphysical tenets to embrace.

Never make a promise you cannot keep. If you do make an oath or a vow, be 100% committed to it. Recognize that every time we tell a lie, fail to follow through on our word, or deviate from our truth, we make a destructive tear to the fiber of our authentic true power. Tap into your voice and courageously speak your truth as often as you can, it will strengthen the efficacy of your voice. Consider your words with much love and forethought when crafting ritual invocations to the Divine and realize that your spell works are highly influenced by your voice and chosen words. Words are the foundations of spell workings and we begin the manifestation process through our own unique voice. You will find no greater foundation to your Spiritual work than the realization that our words, not only carry strong vibrational frequencies, but are one of the most potent tools of magick we naturally behold. Our Words are Divine! Embrace them as powerful living entities that, when in perfect alignment to your soul, can enhance your powers of manifestation.

*"All physical matters are composed of vibration..." Dr. Max Planck*

# **THE POWER OF SOUND FREQUENCIES**

Numerous beliefs, discoveries and theories have been developed over the years regarding music and vibrational frequencies. The earliest of traditions, like Hinduism, often amalgamated science, religion, spirituality and music, a practice that is not so often embraced by Western culture. Yet one of the earliest theorists, Pythagoras of Samos (c.570BC - c 495BC) introduced compelling concepts about music, science, philosophy and religion, that would later be the foundation for further contemporary studies.

Pythagoras of Samos (c.570BC - c 495BC) was an Ionian Greek philosopher, mathematician, mystic, scientist, teacher, religious and brotherhood founder, to name just a few of his titles. He is attributed for creating and documenting numerous, pertinent theories, related to music and mathematic equations; in particular the study of space and distance between tones and the discovery of chords and octaves. He discovered that a pitch could change vibration and tone when a string was stretched or stopped and clasped, at varying intervals. He noted the repetition of tone, at different special points, presumably at an octave distance. Many of our upheld theories on Metaphysics are attributed to him. He was believed to probably be the first scientist to really utilize Music as a form of medicine, to heal the physical body and elevate the soul. Interesting to note, the two primary musical instruments he used for healing purposes were the flute and the lyre and he documented most of his findings, which gives us a glimpse into early theories on sound, religion and science. He defined music as the perfect union of opposing or contrary things and strongly believed that music, with its harmonious nature, could impose order out of chaotic systems. Early cosmology asserts that our planetary spheres, rose up to the heavens, originating first from the earth. The spheres ascended on a presumed celestial ladder and each sphere corresponded to a different note on the grand musical scale, these beliefs were later expanded upon by Johannes Kepler.

German Mathematician, Astronomer and Astrologer, Johannes Kepler (1571-1630) would later take these initial theories and findings of Pythagoras and expound on them in brilliant way. In 1612 he published, *"Harmonices Mundi"* one of numerous scientific publications attributed to him, where he expounded upon Pythagoran theories and proved that sound/harmony prevailed in the Universe; more specifically our Solar System. Kepler believed that harmony permeated every space in the Universe. He believed every planet in our solar system emitted a vibrational tone which varied depending on surrounding circumstances in the galaxy. It was later, in 1852, when German physicist, Winfried Schumann (1888-1874), introduced us to the scientific premise that the earth emits vibrational frequencies and this became known as the *"Schumann Resonance."* This idea would not be fully confirmed until much later in the early 1960's. The concept that the earth emits a tone and that many objects in our solar system are vibrating at varying levels to produce sounds, is quite fascinating and relevant to the study of magick; especially, when we know frequencies and vibrations exist in all living matters.

In 1905, Einstein introduced us to *"The Law of Vibration,"* which states that nothing is ever at rest. Everything moves and is in a constant state of vibration. Vibrating energy is also known as frequencies and it expands our understanding of Universal laws. A sad or low feeling state of being will emit lower, slower vibrations, while a state of joy and bliss; will produce a faster and higher vibration. These are compelling theories to apply in our own personal lives when we are studying magick and the art of effecting transformative changes.

According to established scientific studies, frequencies of vibrating energy can be perceived by colors and sounds; pertinent information for the student of magick. Just consider how there are seven colors in a rainbow and seven notes in the musical scale and there are seven main chakras on our body. Let us not forget, in the beginning of the study of astronomy, only seven planets were recognized in the heavens and all of these components interplay and correspond to one another. This observation can be of great value when learning about spirituality and healing modalities.

In recent years astronomy and scientific studies have revealed that the frequency of the earth itself is actually 7.83Hz. The hertz (Hz) is the most common unit of measurement for a frequency. It is considered one vibrational cycle per second, therefore something that is vibrating at 700hz, means that there are 700 cycles of vibration that are occurring every single second. Some have even referred to the 7.83Hz as a magick number that reflect the vibrational frequency of the Goddess Gaia, known as our Mother earth's frequency. For those following Hinduism traditions, this 7.83Hz frequency emits the sound of Creation. It is the sacred "Om" or "Aum" from which all of creation was born.

Now, I am well aware that I am attempting to touch upon a vast, multifaceted subject here that far exceeds the initial premise of this book and it is much too complex to be covered fully in just a few pages, but the knowledge and usage of vibrational frequencies is invaluable to us. The power of sounds and the acknowledgement of our vibrational Universe is the one thing I wish to convey to the student of magick here, for it can prove to be invaluable as a tool of magick. If we accept that we are vibrating beings and that everything around us is vibrating at different levels, it's easy to see how we can utilize this theory to improve our wellbeing and explore the use of music and vibratory sounds to effect desired changes in our lives. Whether those changes involve changing the energy of a room or influencing the actions of another or changing our own mood and levels of health; the positive potential are endless. It is really for you to decide how to best use this information in your own personal Spiritual journey. In our esoteric studies, as we endeavor to learn varying ways to enhance our powers of manifestation... music, vibrational energies and the potential for healing found in the use of frequencies, are all yet more positive, compelling tools to explore and tap into.

*"'Sound tools are instruments of compassion because they gently nudged the listener into a memory of wholeness and wellness..." Diane Mandle*

**While channeling, this poetic message came through for me....**

## MUSIC'S GIFT AND POWER

The power of music can lull the beast,
and awaken the most reticent, slumbering soul.
It has the power to unite a nation, break it free,
or launch the next victorious campaign or show.
It can move you to heart-breaking tears one minute,
and the next - make you feel invincible.
It has the power to dictate atmosphere,
and emotions attached to it.
It places itself under our feet,
like a magick carpet to serve our deepest needs,
and speaks the ancient language of patterns; chords and melodies.
It reaches far deep into our archaic soul,
if we allow it, just a smidge,
to speak its Divine message
and bring us into states of bliss.
Its magick is in its ability;
to shift us in and out of energetic fields,
restore atoms and cellular paths,
and face what we truly feel.
It reaches the pinnacle of our heart and soul,
and speaks beyond the borders we create,
to rescue us from the numbness,
of an ordinary fate....

# SOUND HEALING MEDICINE

As Spiritual practitioners and students of magick, it's important to understand that vibration, which is expressed in sound, creates the perfect state for deep meditation and thus, can help us attain much wisdom, peace and creativity. It becomes an additional tool of transformation for us to engage in as we endeavor to enhance our powers of manifestation.

In recent years there has been a resurgence of holistic medicine and alternative lifestyles that has inspired a new generation to critically examine our traditional Western medicine practices. Perhaps with the rise of technology and the birth of this super matrix, information highway, the era of knowledge is right at our fingertips, begging to be explored. We appear to be opening ourselves up to the abundance of vastly different information; cultures, religions and spiritual practices. More than ever before, our world does not appear so vastly large and distant, but rather makes everything appear within tangible reach. We are considering all aspects of a person's life, as contributory to a holistic wellness and we are seriously looking at all forms of healing modalities to enhance our life's journey.

Modern medicine now appears to be retrieving some of its knowledge from the wisdom of long ago, for in ancient times, sound and vibration's curative qualities were not disregarded. We are coming to the realization that the power of sound and vibration is able to heal numerous illnesses; spiritual and emotional maladies, and even more astonishing, physical illnesses. Sound-healing is being explored and it's becoming wildly accepted in the mainstream medical industry. Holistic doctors, who have been proponents of varying Eastern healing modalities, are helping to bring awareness to the Medical industry, of all the varying energy medicines available to restore wellness and heal pain, depression, cancer, physical, mental and emotional disorders.

Vibrations and sound are a kind of energy medicine that is now being seriously promoted for their curative physiognomies. In the 1930s, with the discovery of ultrasounds and its Medical properties, scientist began to reconnect with the ancient powers of sound and vibration. Today, with the rise of more medical and scientific research entering new fields of studies, it is becoming clear we are unearthing more experimental tools that bring much needed new forms of therapy. Many, more than ever, are exploring Sound and Energy-healing with great enthusiasm and renewed hope that it will lead to further progress and advancement to medical research.

Healing is the process of becoming whole, freeing ourselves from grief, evil, pain and troubles, to restore ourselves to good, sound health. Healing is a process not a destination but a verb. It is a movement from disharmony to harmony and it requires us to connect to our vibrational energy with that of the Universe, because the Universe has infinite, restorative energy for us. The very science of grounding is based on the belief that when our physical bodies, which are also vibrating with its own vibrational energy, plugs itself into the earth's natural vibrational frequency, we are attuning ourselves to the cathartic vibration of the Universe. This can also happen when we are near or submersed in a body of water. It simply requires of us to slow down, direct our energy and focus on these elements, to connect and interlace our sacred energies.

There's a commonly accepted belief in Hinduism, that every cell in our body creates a sound. In the study of Chakras, where we learn that we behold pivotal points on our body, we also learn that there are corresponding energy fields that are directly connected to musical tones. *(Chakras are explored further in chapter VI.)*
For example,

> Our **Heart 4th Chakra** resonates with the tone of F or Fsharp.
> *A singing bowl in this key would facilitate our connection to deep emotions and it would bring healing in this area of the body.*
>
> Our **Throat 5th Chakras** resonates with the tone of G or Gsharp.
> *Singing bowls in this key would help heal our throat maladies and help facilitate healing in the area of communication, speaking our truth and being heard.*
>
> **Brow 6th Chakra or the Third Eye** resonates with the tone of A or Bflat.
> *A singing bowl in this key would facilitate healing with our sight and intuitive gifts.*
>
> **Crown 7th Chakra** resonates with the tone of B.
> *A singing bowl in this key would facilitate healing in the area of your body, around the head, brain and the cerebral cortex.*
>
> **Solar Plexus or 3rd Chakra** resonates with the tone of E or Eflat.
> *A singing bowl in this key would facilitate healing in this area of our body and bring healing to our digestive system.*
>
> **Sacral 2nd Chakra** resonates with the tone of D or Csharp.
> *A singing bowl in this key would facilitate healing related to fear, pleasure and helps heal our womb & the lower abdomen region of the body.*
>
> **Root 1st Chakra** resonates with the tone of C.
> *A singing bowl in this key would facilitate healing related to our sexual organs and the region at the base of our spines.*

Vibrations and sound opens the closed channels of our chakras and thus, it is a powerful tool for healing, rebalancing and awakening our body's power centers. There is also a belief that nerve bundles in our spine (Kundalini region) transmit vibrational sensory data to the brain stem and limbic system. This limbic system is our emotional processing center and every part of our body or bodies, as the study of Chakras reminds us, can receive healing vibrations, if we choose to direct our focus to this region.

> *If we accept that sound is vibration and we know that vibration touches every part of our physical being, then we understand that sound is heard not only through our ears but through every cell in our bodies....*

Sound can heal disparities on every level and it can play a positive role in the treatment of virtually any medical disorder, according to Dr. Mitchell Gaynor, director of medical oncology and integrative medicine at the Cornell cancer prevention center in New York City. One reason sound and vibrational therapy can effectively heal on a physical level is its innate ability to infiltrate our boundaries and transforms us, via our emotional and spiritual levels. It goes beyond our physical form, where disease and illness may reveal itself, to reach and tackle the depth and roots, which can only be found and healed via our spiritual core.

For most ancient religions there is a belief that all matter is energy; vibrating at different rates of speed. Indigenous cultures practice animism, the belief that all things, whether animated or inanimate, radiate a life force or a frequency or energy. Everything is vibration! This tenet on vibration goes hand in hand with the belief that nothing ever dies, it can only be transformed. If everything is vibrating energy, and energy cannot be destroyed but only transformed, then our Western medicine approach to the healing process must changes.

By altering the rate of vibration, most matter can thus be transformed and probably healed and restored. When something is broken, we want it to be whole and sound, because being "sound" is the equivalent of being whole and healthy. When something doesn't feel right within us, we might say; *"this doesn't resonate with me,"* for our intuition and inner compass reads and interprets sounds, vibrations and resonances. Being of sound mind…that is, whole and harmonious, is a valued asset in our ever evolving society. These are all reflections of how our semantics reveal our veneration of sound, whether consciously or unconsciously.

Since the earliest of times vibration, resonance and sound have played an important part in our Metaphysical, Scientific and Philosophical views of the world. All these terms, point to the connection between sound healing, harmony and wholeness, and their compatible journey for humanity's evolution.

# SINGING BOWLS

# THE POWER OF SINGING BOWLS

Hinduism, Buddhism Shamanism and many other Spiritual traditions recognize the important spiritual element of sound. Quite early, even before the sophisticated evolution of science, many indigenous cultures were already exploring and experimenting with the sacredness and healing powers of vibration and sound. And it is through the ancient culture of Tibet that we can begin to examine one of the most popular and beloved instruments of Spiritual enlightenment, the Singing Bowl.

Singing Bowls are also known as Tibetan Bowls, Himalayan Bowls, bells and Suzu gongs. It should be noted that they come to us from many different traditions, not just Tibet, but also Nepal and Bhutan. Singing bowls are a type of handcrafted and hammered metal bowls that are struck at the edge of the rim, usually with a padded mallet, to create a piercing, multi-layered, bell-like tone. Each bowl is assigned a different note from the musical scale and usually corresponds to a specific body point or chakra. By rubbing either your finger or a wood or leather mallet, around and across the edge of this metal bowl, you create a tone that will emanate beautiful harmonic overtones. As you keep encircling the rim of your metal bowl, the vibrations and overtones produced will appear to almost sing to you; filling the room, easily lulling you into a trance. Some call the tones hauntingly beautiful, enchanting and almost familiar; as if your soul knows these tones from another era or realm of long, long ago. Because it is reputed to easily put one in a Zen-like trance state, it is often used for meditation and spiritual practices. They are quite remarkable and depending on their size, quality and specific creation, they can be utilized to produce all sorts of beautiful sounds and healing vibrations.

The Himalayan bowls or singing bowls vibrate at the frequency of the Universe known as the sacred "Om" or "Aum." For some traditions like Hinduism, this is the sacred sound that created the Universe. Thus, it is believed the consistent use of singing bowls can bring us back to our natural state of being, back to who we are at the core and bring us back to Source. For Shamans and Spiritual practitioners, singing bowls remind us of our true nature and return us to a blissful state of being. These bowls are known to shift energy, expand our consciousness, and are connected with our body centers; also known as our chakras. It is a long standing belief that the tones from singing bowls can open us up and heal, not only our chakras, but can heal us physically, spiritually and emotionally.

Much controversy and mystery surrounds the use and history of Tibetan singing bowls. Some believe they were hand forged by Monks in monasteries, where proper alchemical formulas, secret ancient rites and sacred mantras were chanted continually over them, as they were being created. Further research however, might stir even more question and intrigue regarding their existence.

While modern Tibetan bowls are now being created out of, mostly, copper, tin and iron metals, ancient Tibetan bowls were alleged to be comprised of seven different metals. These seven metals corresponded to the seven planets that were the only known planets in our Solar System, at the time. Seven, as we have already learned, is a powerful number; as it relates to our seven chakras, seven colors in the rainbow, seven musical notes, seven planets etc…etc… The first metal used, Gold, represented the Sun. The next metal, Silver, represented the Moon. Mercury represented the planet Mercury and Copper represented the planet Venus. The use of the metal, Iron, represented the planet Mars, Tin represented the planet Jupiter and Lead represented the planet Saturn. It would be hard to imagine these bowls being used for food today, especially if they contained lead and mercury, but indeed modern Tibetans, and quite possibly ancient ones as well, incorporated the use of these bowls in their spiritual and mundane lives, as dishes and water offering bowls.

The history, creation and usage of Tibetan singing bowls appear to be shrouded in secrecy and mystery. In modern day Nepal and Tibet, not many people will admit to the use of singing bowls, let alone admit to owning one, but step a little closer, into the privacy of their homes and you might find singing bowls scattered around their homes and kitchens, unbeknownst to them, being utilized for cooking or simply as dishes. It is a modern day practice that perhaps had its beginnings a long time ago, when invading armies, forced natives to hide and conceal their ancient spiritual traditions. We must not forget the volatile, dangerous and vulnerable situation the natives of this land have found themselves in, since the invasion and occupation of Communist China, in the 1950s. It should come as no surprise that many would be protective and secretive of their ancient traditions, especially when the risk of speaking might lead to complete eradication of one's family. Tibetans are known for their peaceful disposition and indeed guard fiercely, what's left of their heritage from Western appropriation.

We don't readily find much tangible proof or documentation of singing bowls being used in Buddhist rituals or monasteries, but there's no question of their value and usage. Some have even claimed that any remaining sacred scriptures and documentations are probably well guarded and hidden away in the numerous caves and unscathed Himalayan Mountains.

Singing bowls can be traced back to 7th century A.D. and more likely came to Tibet by way of the Trade route involving Mongolia, India and China. Researchers believe the Singing Bowl was mainly a Shamanistic ritual tool attributed to the traveling Mongolian Shamans. Because its early usage was mainly connected to Shamanism, some believed Buddhist tried to separate themselves from any association with this tool; however, it is clear the Singing Bowl was indeed used by Buddhist, though today we don't know to what extent, due to the lack of scriptural evidence. It is important to note, however, that the birth of Buddhism was very much influenced by Mongolian Shamanism and Hinduism, as well as China. As a matter of fact, early on in the inception of Buddhism there were two known braches; one of them was "*Bon*," which was much more Shamanistic in its approach to rituals.

Nowadays Native Tibetans and young modern day monks are at a loss for words when it comes to details and historical information about the usage of singing bowls. The military invasion of Communist China sadly changed the landscape of the peaceful,

Tibetan people; their culture, rich spirituality and religion. They have sadly been silenced, controlled and oppressed. When trying to garner information about singing bowls, most Tibetan are either oblivious about the heritage of the use of singing bowls or are just not talking. Then there are those who are rightly very protective and guarded about sharing this kind of information. Older monks, who remember a time before the Communist invasion, have a different view on singing bowls and can scarcely remember a time when they were indeed used.

In an eye-awakening article I read, an Elder monk, possibly in his late seventies, recalled the early usage and profound wisdom of the Singing Bowl in relation to Buddhism. He recounted a time when the Singing bowl was solely a relic from India, passed down to the Buddha, himself. There is a belief among older Buddhist monks that the sound of the Tibetan bowl emits Buddhist teachings and esoteric knowledge. Thus, the Tibetan bowl becomes an instrument that channels the wisdom from the Buddha, and passes it down to us through these unique harmonics.

### *Everything that gives sound, gives a teaching...*

Singing bowls are believed to reveal the sound of Dharma, the sound of the void, the sound of enlightenment. It is a powerful tool of transformation to help humanity become more like Buddha. It attunes us directly to the ancestral teachings of the Buddha and helps us receive transmissions, channelings and teachings from our Ascended Masters. There is a belief that every person receives their own unique teachings from these singing bowls and their spiraling overtones. They are part of our ascension and personal spiritual evolution. There is much positive hopefulness, when we realize the Singing bowl's sound and tradition has crossed over to reach the Western world now. It is believed to be bringing enlightenment to the heart of all, regardless of whether they are Buddhist or not and it is clear our human race is on the path of evolution. The significance of Singing Bowls to us is connected to their unquestionable spiritual heritage.

> **Our intention is powered by**
> **the healing energy of sound and this is**
> **the very key component to improving,**
> **not only our health but our whole lives.**

Today Tibetan bowl are used in various Spiritual traditions and by numerous Holistic practitioners. They can be found in yoga studios, meditation retreats, sound healing & music therapy session. They can also be found in religious and spiritual practices, temples and a plethora of different ways, including, just simple personal enjoyment.

> **Intention consist of using your focus, thoughts feelings and visualizations,**
> **to attract whatever is desired, such as enhancing oneself.**
> **The energy of intention is carried on the frequency of sound.**

# **AFFIRMATIONS**

An affirmation is a positive statement made to ourselves in the affirmative, to help us anchor, visualize and manifest our heart's desire on the physical plane. It is a simple tool to enhance our powers of manifestation, implemented by writing or by daily speaking and affirming our vision, as already manifested.

Affirmations are best created, not from a place of lack, but rather from a place of exaltation and gratitude for that which has already transpired. When we choose our words for an affirmation we select words or phrases that are saturated in positive energy and inspire the very best from us. Before beginning the process, it is suggested to prepare your space and your mind. Using relaxation techniques in preparation, will allow you to dig deeper into your subconscious mind to find just the right words to create your personal, empowering, unique affirmation.

It is most effective when we commit to writing or stating our positive affirmation on a consistent schedule. Scientist claim a new habit requires at least 21days for your physiological system to begin to accept it as reality, thus, most affirmations should be consistently practiced for at least three weeks. Oftentimes, the start of a new affirmation can be powerfully coordinated with a particular moon phase, holiday, sabbat, or anniversary or any other particularly special day of your choosing. And, sometimes people will rely on oracle cards, tarot and other visual tools as yet another effective way to help with daily affirmations.

The most important thing for its effectiveness is to remember to practice saying or writing your affirmations consistently and unequivocally committing to embracing your wish as already in the realm of reality; manifested.

# EXAMPLES OF AFFIRMATION TO INSPIRE YOU

**LOVE:**
I love and honor myself
It is my birthright to be happy, loved and prosperous
I only attract that which is in my highest good
The love that I seek is right here already
I am surrounded by the most loving trustworthy people
What I seek, I find first within me
I am a good friend therefore I attract good friends
I only allow people that affirm my existence in a positive light
I am love, infinite and boundless, I transcend
I only invite compatible positive people in my life
I am a magnet for trustworthy, loving people in my life
I am more than enough

**SUCCESS:**
I thrive and succeed even in the midst of competition
I am a magnet for all good things
I am present and committed to the now
My past mistakes do not dictate my future
I am open to new possibilities
I have more than enough energy to get it done

**WEALTH:**
Money flows with ease into my life
I have more than enough to pay my bills & live comfortably
I am a magnet for positive transformational energy
Money is coming to me effortlessly
From unexpected and expected sources, money flows into my life
All of my needs and desires are met quickly and with ease
I am a magnet for money in my currency
Wealth is my birth right
I am a prosperous being
Abundance reveals itself and it is in positive alignment with who I am.

**HEALTH:**
I attract pure health and wholeness everyday
I am grateful for the healthy healing, I know
I recognize myself with the ability to regenerate and heal
My body craves only the healthiest foods for me
I am capable and ready to heal my body
I will treat my body to foods that support me well, in this lifetime
I love and respect my physical body and welcome its healing
I always choose options that are best for my health
I am surrounded by those who support and encourage my healthy lifestyle
My body and Spirit remembers how to restore itself well
The reality I choose to experience now is one of joy, love, abundance and wellbeing.

*Now it's your turn to create your very own personal affirmation which you will commit to repeating consistently.*

# MANTRAS

In our exploration of sound tools, there is yet another helpful magick-making component we can explore now, and it is the subject of **mantras.** The subject of mantras is quite extensive and merits its own specialized books on the vast subject but I'd like to begin discussing its value here.

The Hindu word, Mantra, is a Sanskrit word meaning, "sacred utterance" or "mystical/celestial sounds." When examining the word, we see the first part of the word, *"man"* denotes, *"of the mind"* and the second half of the word, *"tra"* in Sanskrit means, *"a tool or instrument."* One can thus deduce that the word mantra literally means, "Instrument of the Mind." It is erroneous to think mantras only exist in Hinduism, for we see many examples of mantras in numerous cultures. Like chants, they are found in other spiritual traditions. We can see this in the Hawaiian, love and forgiveness mantra called, "Ho'oponopono,"and also in some short prayers to the Virgin Mary, in Christianity.

It's important to note that mantras appear to even predate language. In the sacred ancient text of the Rig Veda, it is the primordial, sacred sound of "Om," from which the Universe is born. "Om" is the shortest and most complete sacred mantra one can utter. Mantras are chants and sounds imbued with sacred energy and their consistent repetition can help to elevate and shift our consciousness. They are used both as a meditative tool and in conjunction with other spiritual traditions. They help lift our spirits, shift our energy centers and raise our consciousness. They are a universally embraced powerful tool to attune our minds to the Divine and we can incorporate them into our Metaphysical, manifestation practices.

For some spiritual traditions the mantras themselves are considered as deities and thus, receive the same omnipotent reverence when uttered. There are devotees that believe that mantras should be specifically given to you, by a guru, or through divine intervention. Their most potent value to us comes from saying the sounds of the words, visually seeing the mantra and repeating them consistently, while allowing them to vibrate through your physical body, up to your buzzing crown chakra. A specific mantra can be repeatedly stated 108 times per day or 54 times, twice a day, and as you engage in this consistent practice you will feel the distinct positive effects to your overall wellbeing. You will feel yourself enter a transcendental, euphoric Zen state by the time you are done with your mantra and you will detect the shift in your energy. Arriving at this tranquil, more positive state of mind through the chanting of mantras, you are now more open and receptive to the creation of magick and for the student of Metaphysics this is important to note.

There are many books and websites available to us now, with a plethora of information regarding this vast topic. "Healing Mantras" by Thomas Ashley-Farrand is a rich, resource on mantras and the author is a leading expert on mantras and their usage. For the purpose of our subject at hand, I have included Hindu & Tibetan Mantras that I have personally found helpful in my own spiritual studies. In the chapter of Visual Tools (chapter V) you will also find additional Hindu mantras that correlate specifically to the seven days of the week, along with their numeric square illustrations.

# MANTRAS

## MANTRAS AND CHANTS FOR THE HINDU GODDESS OF SOUND, SARASWATI

**1. Lokah Samastah Sukhino Bhavantu....**
**Meaning:** May everyone, everywhere be happy, May the whole world be joyous!

**2. Om, Eim Saraswatyei, Swaha -----From the Rig-Veda**
**Meaning:** Om and salutations to that Feminine energy (Saraswati) which informs all artistic scholastic endeavors and for which "Eim" is the seed!

**3. Ambitambe, Naditambe, Devitambe Saraswati...**
**Meaning:** The best of Mothers, best of Rivers, best of Goddesses, Oh Saraswati.

**4. Saraswati saaram vaati iti**
**Meaning**: she who flows towards the absolute is Saraswati *according* to the Veda's Pada Paathat

**5. A Prayer to Goddess Saraswati** (*Saraswati Vandana Mantra*)
Yaa Kundendu tushaara haaradhavalaa
Yaa shubhravastraavritha
Yaa veenavara dandamanditakara,
Yaa shwetha padmaasana
Yaa brahmaachyutha shankara prabhutibhir Devaisadaa Vanditha
Saa Maam Paatu Saraswatee Bhagavatee Nihshesha jaadyaapahaa

**Meaning:** "May Goddess Saraswati, Who is fair like the jasmine -colored moon and whose pure white garland is like frosty dew drops; who is adorned in radiant White attire, on whose beautiful arm rest the veena and whose throne is a white Lotus, Who is surrounded and respected by the Gods, protect me. May you fully remove; lethargy sluggishness and ignorance..."

## 6. GAYATRI MANTRA
OM Bhur-Bhurvah- Svah
Tat savitur varenyam
Bhargo devasva dhimahi
Dhiyo yo nah pracodayat

**Meaning:** "We meditate on the glory of the Creator; Who has created the Universe; Who is worthy of Worship, Who is the embodiment of Knowledge and Light; Who is the remover of all Sin and Ignorance; May She Enlighten our Intellect."

# ADDITIONAL HELPFUL MANTRAS

1. Om Vaj ra Sattwa Hung — To Remove negativity
2. Om Chandra Meeli, Soorya Meeli, Kuru Kuru Swaha… — Evil Eye Remover
3. Om Shar avana Bhavaya Namaha — Attracting positivity and all good things
4. Om Thiru Neela Kantam — For Karmic Resolution
5. Om Hraum Mitraya Namaha — To attract True Friendship
6. Om BhasKaraya Namaha — Brilliance intelligence awakener
7. Om Gum Ganapatayei Namaha — Obstacle Remover calling Ganesh
8. Om Shrim Maha Lakshmiyei Swaha — To invoke Feminine Divine of Abundance
9. Om Shring Hring Kleeng Maha Lakshmi Namaha — To invoke Lakshmi prosperity Blessings
10. Om Shreem Kalikaye Namaha — Invoking She who is dark and powerful-Kali
11. Om Dum Durgayei, Namaha — Calling on the Feminine Divine essence -Durga
12. Om Kala Vide, Namaha — Om & salutation to the knower of the right time
13. Om Eim Saraswatiyei, Namaha — Invoking Saraswati Blessings
14. Om Mani Padme hum — Tibetan chant for peace & wellbeing
15. Om Aim Hreem, Kleem Chamundaye viche, Namaha — Kali's protection from the evil eye
16. Om Namah Shivaya — Peace, wellbeing & love mantra to Shiva
17. Om Shanti, Shanti, Shanti — To invoke Peace
18. Om Maakaral, Shivaya Namaha — Balances and removes negative Karma
19. Ong Namo Guru Dev Namo — To invoke the flow of Eternal Power, I bow to the Creative Wisdom & Divine teacher
20. Sat Nam — Truth is your identity: God's name is truth. Sat: means truth, Nam: means Identity

# PRAYER BEADS

## **PRAYER BEADS**

Prayers Beads, also known as Tibetan prayer beads or Mala beads, are a collection of beads held in the form of a long stringed necklace, or bracelet, which is used to keep track of our prayers, mantras and recitations. Used as spiritual tool of attunement, prayer beads are helpful to induce trance and relax the devotee. They help facilitate Zen-like states of consciousness and transcendence. They can be worn around your neck, waist or around your wrist, as a bracelet, or simply left to rest on your altar but their effectiveness comes from using them as a daily tool of meditation. In modern times they can be an excellent tool of Magick to be used with our mantras or daily positive affirmations. They are mainly used as a tool of concentrated, focused prayer, which allows the devotee to count effortlessly each prayer or mantra with each bead. Sometimes this very process alone can induce a state of trance and facilitate expansion of the subconscious.

Prayer beads exist throughout numerous traditions like; Hinduism, Buddhism, Christianity, Islam, Sikhism and many other cultures, to name just a few. In Hinduism and Buddhism, prayer beads are known as Japa Mala or Mala beads. Traditionally they are made of 108 beads or 27 beads which would be counted four times to complete one mantra cycle and they contain a large center bead, known as the guru bead. In Sikhism, the mala prayer beads also contain 108 beads. In Islam, they use prayer beads known as *Misbaha* or *Tasbih* or *Tasbeeh*. These Islamic prayers beads comprise of 99 or 33 beads. In Greece, they use something similar to a prayer bead but there, it is known as the worry beads, also known as the "*Komboloi.*" The *Komboloi* has an odd number of beads, one more than a multitude of four and they are not linked with any religious connotation. In fact, it is a common sight to see a number of older Greek men, gathered in local "*Caffenios*" *(coffee shop)* swinging their beaded *Komboloi* back and forth, in an almost trance like state.

The rosary, which comes from the Latin word, *rosarium*, meaning a rose garden, is used in the Roman Catholic Church. It typically has 54 beads and an additional five. Interesting to note, the Eastern Orthodox Christians uses a rosary bead tool made up of a hundred knots on a rope, sometimes you might find them with 50 or 33 knots as well. This type of prayer bead necklace was known as a prayer rope and it appears reminiscent to a traditional witches' ladder, or knot spell, which is also a rope, maintaining wishes upon special knots. They also used a type of rosary called "*Chotki*" which was specifically made of knotted wool. In Japanese, they use the *Juzu*, which translates as Prayer beads. It is comprised of 108 beads and four larger head beads, which symbolize the four great Bodhisattvas; Jogyo, Muhengyo, Jyogyo, Anryugyo. The 108 beads are symbols of 108 earthly desires and there are specific details and traditions regarding their usage.

Let's examine the etymology of the words Mala and Beads. Mala in the ancient Hindu language of Sanskrit means a wreath or garland. The word for bead, in the Old

English language, was "bede." Used as a noun, "bede" means prayer, thus it becomes clear, Mala beads, are *a garland-like tool for prayer*.

The Earliest existence of mala beads can be traced back to the Hindu religion in India, where it would later naturally influence Tibetan culture and Buddhism. In some cultures, prayer beads are made of wood, clay, seeds, pebbles seashells, semi-precious gemstones like; carnelian, jade, onyx, quartz, agate, amethyst, amber, etc. As you can surmise, the unique characteristics of each gemstone used on your prayer bead necklace will influence the type of energy it will project and exude. Typically Japa Mala are made of woods like Tulasi, sandalwood, rosewood, walnut, ebony, wenge wood or from olive seed. Seeds from the Bodhi or Rudraksha tree, which is associated with the eye of Lord Shiva, are typically used for Japa mala beads in the Tibetan and Hindu tradition, but there are so many options available to us now when it comes to the creation of prayer beads. You are encouraged to connect with your intuition and select your prayer beads based on what feels right to you. Many nowadays handcraft their own personal prayer beads, feeling that they can customize them as they wish and imbue them with their own personal energy, making them that more powerful.

Typically, you chant or pray over your mala beads, one bead at a time and as time goes on, it's believed to enhance its potency and effectiveness each time you chant over it. It is recommended to choose one mantra prayer bead strand for each individual theme or issue you are focusing on. In other words, you might use your rose quartz or rosewood mala beads to recite your daily mantras for love and beauty to Lakshmi. Likewise you might be dealing with an illness, grief or a severe negative situation in your life and here, it's best to use a separate mala bead, dedicated to that specific purpose. You would then choose and dedicate that mala bead to be used for that specific situation, maybe opting for a mala bead made of dark ebony to chant Kali's mantras over it.

Across numerous cultures and throughout the ages, the practice of repetitively chanting and praying over a stringed beaded, necklace-like tool has been a source of healing and really, a form of magick. In our efforts to learn various techniques from different traditions that serve to expand our knowledge of Metaphysics and enhance our powers of manifestation, prayer beads are yet another easy tool to implement in our personal spiritual practice.

# EVOCATION: DRAWING DOWN THE MOON

A long-standing, documented tradition of priestesses, witches, shamans and so many other spiritual practitioners, involves, Drawing Down the Moon. It is an ancient rite that aligns our energy with that of the Goddess.

It is always a matter of preference which Full Moon to best utilize for this type of lunar rite. Traditionally, it would be done every month at special esbats and sabbat rituals; either as a solitary or within a coven. Devout priestesses would certainly see the benefit in consistently Drawing Down the Moon at every Full Moon but some also opt to do it at certain pivotal sabbats. Others may choose to use the Full Moon that most speaks to them personally; like a Full Moon in a water sign or one in an earth sign or maybe even the Full Moon closest to your birthdate. Clearly it is a matter of personal preference.

This traditional, ancient rite helps to align our energy with that of the Moon, which is one of the oldest, most sacred symbols of magick, wisdom, and the Divine. The Moon, viewed as Goddess herself in some cultures, has always been connected with women, water, psychic realm, our menses and our emotions, the esoteric and the Sacred Feminine.

To begin, choose a place, late at night, where you will not be disturbed, preferably in the wilderness or by a body of water. Those living in the city need not fret. Looking out the window or standing on a Fire escape in New York City has served me just fine in the past. The important thing is to stand under her lunar light and be in a place, and state of mind, where you can receive her light unobstructed.

Under the Full Moon, take yourself out to be right underneath her silver brilliant sphere and allow yourself to become a receptor; a sacred chalice to receive her divine light, for it is through her light that we draw her down. Spend some time gazing into her piercing light. Study her brilliant orb realizing that this is the same infinite light worshipped by our distant ancestors since the beginning of time. Be mindful of this moment in time and its sacredness. Continue to focus your sight upon the Moon, allowing yourself to fall into a subtle, slight trance. When you feel called, raise both of your arms up towards her light. Some, at this point, create a pyramid or triangle formation with their hands outstretched, raised towards Her. Feel her energy concentrated, like a laser, into this pyramid you've created with your hands and now speak. Declare an invocation, giving words to your inner most adoration and express yourself. Use your words of power; speak to her in structured prayer or free form. You may even wish to recite the *"Charge of the Goddess"* or you may have a prepared personal invocation that comes from your own heart and mind. You can also simply channel and see what natural come forth from your lips.

Under Her Silver Fullness, speak and then take this time to commune and co-mingle with her Lunar energy and when you feel ready, invite her energy into you. With your words, your vision, your will and desire, draw her down. In the cascading silence of the darken night, feel her palpable energy now swirling around you, beckoning you to open and receive her within. This pivotal moment may leave many of you in a euphoric state of ecstasy and it is for me, personally, one of the most powerful spiritual experiences.

Afterwards you have the option of lingering in this highly ecstatic state of being; maybe documenting it or using this as a stepping stone for other deep spiritual work like a ceremony, sex magick or divination. When you feel ready, be sure to eventually ground yourself and come back to your physical body. Do not drive or handle any dangerous machinery immediately after this experience, as you might have the loopy sensation of inebriation. Spiritual ecstasy has been known to affect the mind and body much like an intoxication; enjoy it but also be safe.

### The Charge of The Goddess
*I am the Beauty of the Green Earth,*
*And the White Moon among the stars,*
*And the Mysteries of the waters,*
*And the Desire found in Human hearts*
*Call unto your soul, Arise and come unto me,*
*For I am the Soul of Nature*
*that gives life to this Universe,*
*From me all things proceed and*
*Unto me all things shall return.*
*Before my face, Beloved of all,*
*Let thine inner most self*
*be enfolded in the rapture of the infinite.*
*Let my Worship be among the Heart that rejoices*
*For behold, all acts of love and pleasure are my rituals,*
*And therefore,*
*Let there be Beauty, Strength, Power and Compassion*
*Let there be Honor, Pride, Mirth and Reverence.*
*And you who thinks to seek me,*
*Know that your seeking and yearning*
*shall avail you not,*
*less you know the mystery,*
*For if that which you seek*
*you cannot find within yourself*
*you will never find without,*
*For behold,*
*I have been with you since the Beginning*
*And I am that which is attained,*
*At the end of desire.*

...Excerpt from the Charge of the Goddess by Doreen Valiente,
It has also been rewritten and modified by both Starhawk and Z. Budapest

# CHANNELING

When we invite the energy of a spirit, deity, devas, angels or non-physical being to speak through us, we open up to an extraordinary experience that brings us closer to a vast world of ancient wisdom and infinite esoteric knowledge. Channeling is the process in which a human individual is able to download, showcase and embody a nonphysical entity, or spiritual being. It is a process that gives voice to spirit helpers, guides and spiritual entities, from varying dimensions, time and place, that are eager to be a part of humanity's' evolution. The host or person, known as the channeler, allows themselves to be a vehicle for spiritual communication to unfold for the non-physical being. It is quite a phenomenon to witness as the channeler is observed metamorphosing, going through the process of surrenderment, as they take on the characteristics of the Spirit. Their physical body stance might change, their auric energy shifts and even their language, dialect and inflections, might also change, though, it's not always compulsory. Oftentimes, there is something deep in the gaze that drastically changes and alerts us to the presence of a spiritual visitor.

Today, with the rise in technology and the birth of *YouTube* on the internet, we have access to numerous gifted channelers from across the globe. In addition, we now also have access to black and white, documented recordings from many years ago, which allows us to excitedly bear witness to important pioneering channelers from the 1970s. Although, there have been a number of trail-blazing channelers throughout history, like, Edward Cayce (1877-1945) and Madame Blavatsky (1831-1891), most in earlier times were simply considered psychics and mediums. Channelings became a modern version of mediumship and its popularity appears to have resurged in the 1960s.

In the 1960s and 1970's, a woman by the name of Jane Roberts (May 8,1929-September 5,1984) and her husband Robert Butts opened their home to a small group of people to begin holding E.S.P. classes and channeling sessions with a non-physical being. Most of these sessions were documented and video recorded. Later on, books were published to share the phenomenon. Jane and Roberts were married for about nine years, living in Elmira, New York, when they started experiencing, what they believed to be strange, paranormal occurrences. In their community, they were known as writers and artist, respectively; well educated in poetry and history, but somehow, these paranormal phenomenons baffled the couple. In an effort to gain more understanding they consulted a *Ouija board* and this resulted in the introductory appearance of Seth. Seth introduced himself through the slender petite frame of Jane Roberts, as a non-physical being. The ability to channel and disseminate his spiritual messages came at such lightning speed for Jane that she surrendered the initial use of the Ouija board in preference to direct channelings from him. It was December 1963, when the couple had their first encounter with Seth. Three years later they documented and published their experience, in 1966, in

"*Seth Speaks.*" Later, in 1973 they would re-publish this phenomenon as the book, "*The Coming of Seth.*"

From Sept 1967 to July 1982, for 15 years, Jane and her husband held recorded channeling sessions in their home featuring Seth and many were witness to these weekly sessions. Seth always had much to say through Jane but his main message and Universal truth to humanity was similar to that of many other modern day channelers. It has been simplified below:

**1. *We are co-creators of our reality.***
**2. *Our power is in the now, in the present tense.***
**3. *We are not at the mercy of our subconscious mind.***
**4. *And we are gods, essentially, expressions of the Divine.***

Today we are blessed to have many well-known, gifted channelers similar to Jane Roberts like, Abraham through Esther Hicks, Ezekiel through Nancy Joy, and Bashar through Darryl Anka. We also know of Marianne Williamson, SolaraAnRa and Lee Harris, to name just a few of my favorites on the internet. Many that channel share their messages through various outlets, like videos, worldwide tours, televised events, workshops and special conferences. But by far the most popular way they deliver their divine channeled communication is now through book publications. Typically these books are almost entirely penned by their spirit companion, with much wisdom to aid humanity's ascension.

The premise of this book is to discover and explore spiritual practices and techniques that can enhance our own powers of manifestation and help us transform our lives. I offered this brief introduction to channeling because I strongly feel it is an invaluable spiritual practice that can contribute, not only to our personal spiritual growth but also to humanity's evolution. It can offer us, as students of magick, deep esoteric knowledge and ancient wisdom from long ago that might've been otherwise lost. While the person doing the channeling, might not always recall the exact details of the event, channeling can have an impactful, most positive experience to those who are privy to witness it. The positive influence is potent to those witnessing a channeled message, just as it is to those who are gifted with the ability to deliver a channeling.

# MEDITATION & TRANCE
## **CONNECTIONS THROUGH MEDITATIONS**

## **MEDITATIONS**

The value of trance meditation for those on a self-transformational, spiritual path cannot be underestimated. Throughout this book you may have already encountered some helpful meditation offerings; like the Tree Meditation and the Animal and Goddess Meditation offerings from previous chapters. Here, we will look at three common archetypes in a woman's life (the Maiden, the Mother and the Crone) and explore them separately through three very distinct meditation offerings.

Meditation is indisputably, yet another powerful tool of magick to help shift our consciousness and energy levels. It can help us clarify our goals and discover our true allies in order to achieve them. It allows us to travel through all types of inner realms, time and space, to unearth healing, courage and confront our needs and fears. It not only can help us relax and tap into other recesses of our psyche, but can awaken our creativity to help us visualize healing and goals attained. Meditations can be embarked upon and custom made, according to our own particular scenario and it is an unquestionably an invaluable tool for those on a spiritual path, regardless of your culture or tradition.

# **CONNECTING TO THE MOTHER IN THE BELLY-AN IMBOLC MEDITATION**

Frost is seen on the cold ground. The frozen land is under your feet and you feel the crisp piercing, frigid breeze upon your skin. From where you are, you study the long bare branches from a nearby tree and survey the vast frozen landscape before you. It seems like forever since you last saw a fertile green tree. Holding this bare cold branch in your hand, you recollect the last time you saw this tree full, with bright green leaves and an array of plump berries ornamenting its crown. It brings lively, bright images of last summer..... and last spring... and conjures up a vast collection of happy, memorable vignettes from your past. You come back to the tree, reflecting on how full they were then, in contrast to their barren, nakedness now and how cold and stark they appear...

The more you remember about last summer and last spring, the lighter you feel and the softer the ground beneath you appears to become....and suddenly you feel its subtle shift....warming, dissolving, its metamorphosis, awakening from long slumber... Beneath you, the Earth yawns and she softens to your weight. You slightly slump and then gently sink; first it is imperceptible, then it becomes more obvious; you are indeed sinking. You feel the heavy weight of your body upon the soles of your feet now, as you sink deeper and deeper into the earth.... Comfortably let yourself go deeper and deeper, as your legs relax into the ground that seemed impenetrable by frost, a few seconds before. Like a magnetic pull from the underside of this soil, it pulls you deeper, ever deeper still, until you are no longer above the ground, but rather underneath, submerged, deep within the earth. Your entire body now, nestled in her womb, surrounded by the deep dark rich soil of the Earth. Its profoundly dark hues of browns and black... Moist, warm, fertile soil, surrounding your body now. The air has changed and even your nose detects a different scent. Her womb cradles you now, holding you in a protective, warm embrace and here, deep in her cavern, you feel more charged and alive than ever before.

Adjusting to this new environment, you slow down your breathing and slow down the constant chatter of your mind to detect a golden silence. Soon this sweet silence is interrupted by a tiny inaudible sound.... (pause) You start to hear a thump... a consistent faint thump...."Her" heartbeat or your own? or maybe both- indistinguishable now. The sound seems to be coming from a glowing light further inside on your right. Surrounding this light, you discover the source of the thumping, it is water leaking. Trickling water, falling from above. Take this healing water and cup it inside your hand if you can. It is embryonic, uterine water from "Her" womb and it has the great power to heal. Place this water now, wherever you need healing most, on your body..... (Pause)

The glowing light becomes a strong, bright flame now, after having blessed yourself with "Her" waters. It is quite beautiful, with its orange, red and yellow hues. As you trance, deeply studying the quivering flames, you detect an inaudible murmur. The faint tone of someone's voice can be heard and it appears to be coming from this glowing light. Scry into the flames and look deeply at the shapes and images appearing before you. Listen carefully to discern what language is being spoken - for it does not initially sound like a language you are versed in. Listen now, with your whole heart and body, to translate and interpret the flame's message to you. (pause)

> *"Mine are the flames that bring healing, creativity and*
> *great transformation. How will you best utilize my sacred fires?* (pause)
> *What do you place in my forge of transformation?*
> *And when the snow has melted and the Earth is reborn anew,*
> *what will my fires help you manifest?"* (pause)

Consider carefully your response and take this time now to share with her, your goals and heart's desire…. (pause)

From the flames, out appears the form of a woman with scarlet, long red hair. She has lovingly heard your every word and now protrusively steps out of the flame. She places her warm hand upon yours and takes you on a journey through a labyrinth. The labyrinth appears to be ascending as you walk further upwards, further up it takes you, with her leading the way. Slowly you walk through the deep dark soil, passing by crystals, minerals and waterfalls. Like a spiral upward you continue now on this journey, and the familiar uterine warmth, felt down below, now begins to feel dry and cool. (pause) Upward you continue to walk this spiral, upward with her guidance…. (pause) The air is feeling very cold now and "She" stops momentarily to turn to you. Deeply gazing into your eyes, **the Mother** has one last message for you. Listen carefully (pause), then thank her and respectfully bid her adieu.

You reach a passage way and "She" now opens the door and invites you to walk through. You hear her say;

> *"For now this is the end of our journey and we must part, but*
> *you may call on me when you thirst for my healing waters or*
> *when Fire medicine is needed to create, heal and transform.*
> *Come during these sacred transitional moments in your life,*
> *when you find yourself at a threshold before embarking on change.*
> *Come during those pivotal, seasonal moments,*
> *as the Wheel of the Year turns once more.*
> *Come when you crave and seek to*
> *rest in the womb and belly of your Ancient Mother.*
> *Until we merry meet again, I bid you farewell,*
> *with peace, wellbeing, fires of creativity and love. Blessed Be…."* (pause)

Seven steps lead you upward back to where we started. Follow the sound of my voice as we return to our body and this room and this time and place…. We begin and you are called now to return. **Seven**…. Breathe and exhale, **Six**… follow my voice and return to this space, **Five**… breathe in deeply and exhale… **Four**… return here to the now. **Three**, take a deep breath in, hold and now let it all out. **Two**, return to this room and to the sound of my voice, continue breathing… **One**….. When you are ready, open your eyes and please, feel free to document any messages given to you during this meditation.

\*\*\***This particular meditation is found in**
"Gathering for Goddess, a Complete Manual for
Priestessing Women's Circles,"
By; B. Melusine Mihaltses
ISBN#978-0-9851384-4-8
Publisher: Feminine Divine Works, Texas, U.S.A

# **MEDITATION FOR THE MAIDEN**

I invite you now to find a comfortable spot to sit or lay down. Let your head rests comfortably on your neck and feel your shoulders gently drop their weight and relax. Take a deep breath and exhale. With your next inhalation feel your lungs expand and open up like a Lotus flower. Now exhale and with this exhalation release any tension or stress that you may have been carrying. Relax and let your body sink deeper. Let go and release any tension. Take another deep breath now and notice how it shifts something within you, notice how each breath regenerates you. (pause) Exhale once more, releasing with this breath, anything that is burdening you at this moment. (pause)

Summer is approaching and with its noticeable awakened warm breeze brings a strong shift in our energy. The warmer season brings forth the tangible recognizable seedlings, the ones that perhaps had been planted in her dark womb at Imbolc and Spring or perhaps you simply held these seeds quietly in your hands, in your heart while making a wish. Breathe and with this breath acknowledge that the universe is providing a new atmosphere, a fertile landscape for you to confidently plant yourself in. Breathe in this new air and sense what is trying to breakthrough and be reborn. Recognize that you are entering a new phase in life and sit with this new liberating insight. (pause) We are in the season of the Maiden; the liberated one, the exuberant one, the bold courageous one, the fierce young one who has little concerns, the unstoppable soul, the sprinter into action, the colorful one, the one who delights in her senses. The Maiden, as you now will take a brief moment to define her...(pause, take this moment to define her for yourself.) In Goddess myths and Women Spirituality, she is Artemis, Kore also known as Persephone, she is Athena, Shakti, Aradia, Skadhi and so many more deities that were considered, Virginal and whole unto themselves.

Take a long deep, slow breath and see if an image appears to you of the Goddess, the Goddess as Maiden. See if you yourself can unearth yourself, your own reflection in this image. Take a moment to notice every detail of the image that appears to you now. What does "She" look like, what is "She" wearing? What is "She" doing? What is "She" fully engaged in? What is she committed to right at this moment? (pause) When you have a clear picture of her in your mind's eye, see if you can recognize yourself or an aspect of yourself, in your youth, in this image. Be patient, open, compassionate and welcoming to the vision presenting itself to you at this moment. Breathe and continue to observe this image of yourself as the maiden. Remember to continue to breathe throughout this journey and with your next breath allow yourself to come face to face with your inner maiden. (pause)

Take this moment to gaze into her eyes and match your breath with hers, synchronizing with each other's rhythm now. With your mind's eye continue to breathe together while gazing into each other's eyes and breathe. (pause) Recognize her unquestionable natural beauty and sense the energy coming from her body.

Life's journey, stressors and obligations have taken you far away from her. With each year you got older, played the role of the responsible adult, while she slipped farther and farther into the back of your subconscious. You've strayed so far away from her that you almost forgot that she even existed but she does exist and she is right before your very eyes at this moment. (pause)

Your life has provided numerous opportunities to attain much wisdom and many unique experiences that have helped shape, who you are as a woman right now but before you stands a young maiden who does not have the benefit or limitation of this knowledge. She knows no limitations nor paralyzing fears or failures. She has yet to experience life as you have and only knows the exuberant pulse and energy of HOPE. And she holds herself before you, as an empty chalice ready to be filled. What will you fill this chalice with? What will you tell her that will positively impact the rest of her life? How will you empower her, your inner Maiden? Continue to gaze in her eyes, YOUR eyes, as the Maiden and speak with her from your heart. Share some of the wisdom and knowledge you've acquired as a woman that you wish you could've known as a maiden. Speak to your inner maiden with love and compassion and vow to maintain, protect, love and value her. (pause) Speak to your inner Maiden now... (pause)

Now listen... listen and let her speak to you as well, for she will have much to say to you and possibly even seek insight about the choices you've made or are making in your life now. Be still and quiet for a moment and allow her Maiden wisdom to come through, for she has something of great value to say to you as well. (pause) Befriend your inner maiden and invite the positive aspects of her energy into your life right now. Consider where her fierce, yet open energy can be best employed in your life and together allow for a cathartic, much overdue, dialogue to take place. (pause)

Finally, ask your inner maiden if she is happy and if she's not, what would make her happy now...? (pause) Take a deep breath and absorb her answer... then promise her that you will take her happiness and her well-being into consideration as you go through your adult life. (pause)

Breathe and with this next exhalation thank her and bid her adieu. With your eyes still shut closed, slowly bring yourself back to this room, back to where this journey began. Breathe and connect with your body with this next inhalation. Feel your chest expanding and contracting, feel your shoulders and the weight of your head upon them. Bring your attention to your feet, your toes, hands and fingers. You are in your body now. Make note of my voice and listen as it slowly brings you back to this time and space. I will count backwards from 5 to 1 to bring this meditation and our journey to a gentle close. Five*** four*** three*** two**** one.....

Welcome! Gently stretch your body now or place the palms of hands flat on the floor to further help with grounding, if necessary. When you are ready, open your eyes and join us back in the circle. If you have a pen and paper at hand take this time to document any images or messages that came through for you in this meditation. This is a perfect time to write a promise to yourself, to that inner maiden. Write a positive affirmation to yourself that can become a mantra for yourself. This mantra will be one that perhaps other Sisters can appreciate hearing as well...

## CRONE MEDITATION FOR THE DARK SEASON

Find a comfortable spot to sit or lie down in. In this journey, we begin as always with our sacred breath. Take a deep audible breath now and slowly exhale. Counting from 1 to 3 silently, take another deep breath and once more exhale (pause). With this next inhalation breathe in the crisp, cool, autumn breeze and its hues of orange, yellows and browns. Breathe and exhale; one, two three. Breathe in the seasonal changes visibly all around you now. One, two three, breathe in the sounds of autumn; like the crunchiness heard from each footstep upon the dry, fallen, autumnal leaves. Breathe in the scents of autumn; like the popular scents of pumpkin pies, hot mocha, clove and cinnamon…or the distinct smell of fire wood burning at the hearth. Breathe in the cool sharp, autumnal breeze as it grazes your flesh, sometimes piercing right through your cloak to reach your bare skin, raising the hairs on your neck. Breathe in the changes that the fall brings. As you exhale, release that which no longer serves you in this new colder period. We are departing from summer's energy and entering the dark season. Take a moment to give thanks for these past few months and allow yourself now to shed the vestige you held, from summer and previous months. Breathe in the stillness and introspection that autumn demand of you now. With your exhalation, release that which no longer serves you, as we commence this journey towards the dark season…. towards the Crone.

In the spring, upon the Vernal Equinox, we met her bright youthful, fertile and green. We met her smiling, childlike, so spritely and buoyant and full of wonderment. We met her full of hope and optimism, wrapped in her curiosity and her naïveté. She came to us in the young unopened blossoms that were just awaiting their grand entrance upon the garden of life.

Then summer came, and we met her in her royal regalia, of colorful gems and uninhibited growing blossoms… We met her sky-clad in fields of poppy seeds delighting in all that tantalized and heightened her pleasure sensors. We met her in her fertile prime, some would say and in her bright, breathtaking full moons. We met her in her lush, fertile green earth. In the garden of colorful blossoms now open and undeniably in bloom, begging our sweet admiration, she was there. In her brilliance and her plump juicy fruits and in the sweet dripping nectars of her bounty, we met her and delighted in her…

Then we came to autumn and here we met her amidst the abundant harvest, surrounded by the golden wheat, the towering lush stalks of corn, in the overflowing heavy, hanging grapes of the vines. We met her, in all her glory and in the generous harvest that begs to be picked, gathered and communally collected to be enjoyed among family and friends. We celebrated her bountiful gifts in community, among our cherished tribe. We met her and relished in her cornucopia. We met her in her golden regalia, oozing with her powers of nurturance and fruition and there, we joined the celebrations of all she manifested. We connect now to all of her….

Breathe and with each inhalation and exhalation we draw her ever closer. We draw her closer now, only she no longer wears the sprightliness green of the maiden, and she no longer exudes the juicy ripeness of summer, and her plump, nurturing overflowing Harvest robes have been dropped and swallowed whole now by the dark earth. She comes to us, no longer as the maiden, nor the mother, nor solely as the Harvest Queen. Today, in this meditation, we greet her in yet another important manifestation of the Goddess. We greet her as the Wise Elder, the Crone. (pause)

We greet her as the holder of our memories and experiences. We greet her as the cauldron of wisdom, as the stillness of night, as the unsuspecting shadow that can slowly slither and drape your very being. We meet her as the infinite guardian and protectress of wommin and as the spider's web, connecting all the important points in our soul's journey. We meet now the Old One, the Grandmother, the Wise One- the Crone.

We meet her and embrace, her deceptively, fragile bones that hold strongly our memories of all that was; spiraling between the now and different incarnations…. We meet her while gazing into her deep dark, (pool-like) owl eyes that hold a transcendent archive of past imageries and future visions. We meet her in her hues of black, grey, white and silver and greet she, who has already cast away her physical body to bring more prominence and value to spirit, and the wisdom of her many experiences. She is all knowing! We meet her with her silver, moon-spun head of gossamer threads, flowing wild and free and her equally wild and liberated cackles to alert you of her Divine presence. Yes, today we meet her and reach out between the veils to place our hands upon her long thin, bony fingers. We meet her bone to bone, eye to eye… She who's gaze begins to scry into our soul, like an ancient oracle. She whose silence might initially make us feel uncomfortable yet, only through her silent dark portals can we receive her most potent, spiritual messages. We meet her and hold her hauntingly, deep gaze, that seems to expose all of our hidden fears.

*Breath to breath, bone to bone, we meet her eye to eye, she who now begins to reveal the resemblance of a familiar soul. She who becomes a mirror of what we can chose to connect with now, if we wish to comprehend the effable. (pause) We draw her closer with each inhalation, we draw the Crone from within forgotten tiny crevices in our own psyche…Take this time to speak personally with your inner Crone. Be still and silent to detect her whispers and let her wisdom permeate your soul at this moment… (pause) Place your hand upon her heart and let her transfer to you the gifts and skills necessary to face your darkest fears. (pause) She who has been through so many personal battles and has witnessed the plight of many, who's inner and outer battle scars only reveals a fraction of all she has endured. The Crone has lived many lives and traveled many realms and knows the road you are on now…. (pause) She holds the map to your soul's labyrinth… Take a deep breath, exhale… take this moment to meet the crone in this journey. Present to her your fears or concerns and allow her to present the gifts needed to sojourn the dark season. (pause)

*Time has passed and in your gaze, fixed upon the Crone, you notice her long bony arms, begin to reach down towards her root chakra and you see her place her wrinkly hands within her Yoni and she pulls out a gift for you. **This represents the element of **Earth,** what personal gift does she pull out from this realm, for you now? (pause) What does she present to you? (pause)

After placing the earth's gift in your hands, you notice the Crone now stretching out her arms, as if to reach for the sky, but instead she reaches for her cranium, a symbol of the element of Air. From her head the Crone pulls out a gift for you. **This represents the element of **Air,** what personal gift does she pull out from this realm, for you now? (pause) What does she present to you? (pause)

Breathe in and notice now that the Crone places her hands upon her chest. Within her heart, there is the symbol of her great fires, she pulls out a gift most especially for you now. **This represents the element of **Fire,** what personal gift does she pull out from this realm, for you now? (pause) What does she present to you? (pause)

While looking down, admiring your three gifts now, you hear the sound of her lips being licked repetitively. You look up to find the Crone licking her lips and she places her hands to her throat chakra, then to her mouth. And from this watery realm you watch as she pulls out a gift from her mouth, especially for you. **This represents the element of **Water,** what personal gift does she pull out from this realm, for you now? (pause) What does she present to you? (pause)

Before we come to the end of this journey, contemplate on the Crone's image and the four gifts given to you. Take this time now to thank her for your personal gifts. (pause) Share any final words with each other and listen carefully to her whispers. (pause) With your final words having been shared now, make note of her final counsel to you. Share your reverence, respect and gratitude for her presence here today and now with your gifts in hand, lovingly bid her adieu. (pause) In your mind's eye, turn around and see a special tree lined pathway. Begin to walk towards the tree lined pathway and with each footstep feel the earth beneath you, supporting the weight of your feet, guiding you as you pass by the towering red wood trees and their dark brown bark and almost bare branches.

Feel the air around you now getting colder and colder, making you quicken your pace faster than before, as you walk through this labyrinth now quickly to return. Quicken your pace as you begin to spy a dim light. Continue to walk, towards that tiny dim light as it begins to get brighter and brighter. Follow this light as it slowly brings you back to this room, back to this time and space. Follow this light as it transforms into the brilliant rising sun and the light of a new day. The sun is beginning to rise now, night has ended and our journey has come to an end. Make note of my voice now as it leads you back to this room. I will count from 7 to 1 backwards and you will continue to journey deeper back to this room, back into your body, back to this time and space. As I count from 7 to 1, we end our Crone journey now. Continue to breathe in and exhale; 7, 6, 5, breathe, 4, 3 exhale 2, 1. With your inhalation now, return... Welcome back!

You are invited to stretch out your arms wide open, place the palms of your hands upon the ground if you feel called to shed and ground any excess energy. Take this moment now to document any important messages from this journey. With pen and paper nearby document how the Crone appeared to you and any special messages she might've had for you. List the four gifts imparted to you by the crone. In the next few days be prepared to note any insight that has been revealed to you as a result of this Crone meditation. Blessed Be )O(

# IV. TASTE YOUR WORDS, INVOCATIONS & SPELLS

*"Your own words are the bricks and mortar of the dreams you want to realize, your words are the greatest power you have. The words you choose and their use, establish the life you experience..."* Sonya Choquette.

In this chapter we will explore unique examples of invocations, prose and spells. This is a collection of one of a kind spells & invocations I personally created for the purpose of this book. I have many more beautiful examples in my book, **"Goddess Grimoire Journal, a Collection of Simple Prose and Spells."** Here, you may customize your own spells, using these invocations or be inspired to craft your very own personal ones.

## **ONE**

## INVOKING **PASSIONATE** LOVE

Scrying into the Crystal's spark,
Rainbows and foils
Opening my heart...

Infinite desires,
From disconnected cords,
Leaving me hungry,
In this lifetime, for more.

I am worthy of Rapturous love,
Of Passionate union,
And the gifts
from the Dove,

Of affection and fidelity,
Of connection and authenticity.
Of heart spinning euphoria,
And love vision manifesting.

Of deep inner knowing
That my heart is valued and safe
Of passionate fires burning
At the start of a simple embrace.

And two souls knowing,
Recognizing their fate,
That their journey is together
As true Soul-mates...

Awaken now the lifeless soul,
Restoring faith of long ago,
Awaken magnet, to draw to me,
The vision of love, I now seek

From atmospheric haze,
I now conjure you,
Let this flame from heart to wick
Make our union now come true.

Bound Round it will be,
These things or better, So Mote it be!!!

# LOVE & ENCHANTMENT

## GLAMOUR

Let me drink of your nectar,
Hold enchantment as my gift,
Let me wear your special girdle,
So that Glamour, I can enlist,

Let the power of the Strega,
Cast itself about my glow,
And the power of attraction,
Shine on me from head to toe,

I exude mystere and grace
Fit, toned body,
And an Angel's face,

Beauty, good health,
And youth I'll retain,
Discretion my ally,
As I safely play
These love games....

**A CALL TO TRUE LOVE**
Find me, Love
Break through all blocks
See yourself with me
Opening all cage locks.

Nothing can stand now
To keep us apart,
Twin Flames uniting,
We are works of Art.

We are lovers uniting
Finding our Bliss,
In each other's arms,
In each other's kiss.

Finding pleasure
in one another
Delighting in mutual, O's
Climaxing to ecstasy,
In gratitude, we are known.

I magnetize you,
And you magnetize me.
We attract one another,
Because we are each other's dream

You wished for me,
And I wished for you,
Here I am,
Hold me,
Feel how much I want you.

Long have we waited
To unite like this,
Find me, My Love,
Let's manifest true bliss.

Pluck me from this tower,
Rescue me from neglect,
Roads are now open
With this spell, YOU manifest.

## **SEX MAGICK**
Aphrodite, Lilith,
Erzulie & Hathor,
Venus , Isis…
Come through these doors.
> Dance in gyration,
> Slithering round my hips,
> Scents of intoxication,
> Wetting my lips.

Enter this Circle,
Enter my domain,
Here I invite you,
As I moan out your name.
> Pleasure, Beauty
> Awakener, ARISE,
> Within me, around me,
> With each Moonrise.

I am the daughter
Of the Mysteres of life,
Swimming in juices
From Climactic sighs.
> I am the Flower
> That opens its bloom,
> I am the Flesh Petal
> That welcomes the dew.

I am the Fibers
Of longevity's threads,
Weaved around cauldrons
From ancestral bloodshed.
> Herein in this dance,
> I call out to you,
> Pulling the syrup nectar,
> From our sacred womb

Round and round
I stir this pot,
What was ice cold,
Now turns red Hot.
> Rise the Fires
> Of Kundalini flames,
> Rise in me now,
> In thy Goddess name.

## **FERTILITY WORK**

Blessed Mothers, I call to you
Gaia, Hambodia and Selu...

Feed me, Nurturers,
In your embrace,
Fertile gifts,
I now awake.

In my womb, I invoke thee,
Here I await all thy seeds.

Firmly planted,
In your blood,
Welcomed here,
With all my love...

Fertile, Ripe, I ooze with thee,
Tapping into your energy.

Swirling potions,
Our body knows,
In her cauldron,
All will grow.

Swirl the magick
Of her time,
It transcends
And brings what's mine.

I awake to your embrace
Blessed that now, I see your face.

Healed and charged,
Ripe to be,
Sacred Mothers,
I give thanks to thee.

Now I hold
Your gifts and seed
This spell is done,
So Mote it Be!!!!

# TWO

**BLESSINGS**

## **FAMILY BLESSINGS**

I gather these flames,
Creating a Hearth,
To invoke a Blessing,
For those near my Heart.

Beloved tribe members,
Children and Elders,
I spark our protection,
Through these sacred embers.

And call upon our wellness,
Our union and peace…
I call upon longevity,
As prosperity increase.

I light the way for vision,
For guidance, through these flames,
Let light erase all darkness,
Let all discord now wane.

As flame flickers their dance,
Let warmth rise in our soul,
Let love, peace and harmony,
Surround our very Household

And with these sacred herbs,
I cast upon our land,
I send a Blessing of Wellness,
To our beloved Clan…

So Mote it be!!!!

## **PROTECTION FOR CHILDREN**

This spool of protection
Of Mama bear strength,
This thread I unearth
From all my ancestresses.

I gather in this rite,
And tap into its skill,
To cast a shield of armor
By my word and will.

To cloak my beloved children,
And keep them, ever safe
And guard their wellbeing,
If ever I am away.

To endear our ancestors
And benevolent spirit guides,
Plead, that my children
Have your protection and loving eyes.

To guide them in their journey,
That they may ever be Blessed,
That generations of Mama Bears,
Guard them in their nest.

Guide them and shield them,
Walk by their side,
Let them be safe and blessed
By your infinite watchful eyes.

Bound round, this wish,
For the greater good,
Protect my children, As I say it,
Let it be understood…

So mote it be!!!!

## ANCESTRAL MOON HONORING

Gaze upon her Silver Orb,
Feel the tug,
that begs for more.

Pools appear, before my eyes
Mirrors, aimed
To break all lies.

See Her there, She is me,
Grandmother Moon,
Infinitely,

Lifting veils for me to see,
Past, Future
And where they meet

Threads that fuse,
And bind us through
Love remains,
In this old stew,

Sharing tales of all that was
Lives now merging
Stirring a buzz.

Lineage honored,
Blood embraced,
In her light,
I see your face.

Thank you Mothers, of all tribes
In my heart
Are thy shrines.

Gaze upon her Silver Orb,
I'm remembering
All once more

Light the flame to honor thee,
Hail to you,
And all (our) Ancestry…

## **ANCESTRAL HONORING**

## **OUR BELOVED FAMILIES & PETS**

# ANIMALS & FAMILIAR WORKS

## TOTEM TRANCE CONNECTION
Come Owl, come Snake,
Come Wolf or Tiger's Clan,
Come Spirit in this time and space
Come as I go into Trance,

Let's journey to find one another,
Partnered through the veil,
Let me see the face of my familiar,
Now that we've erected, this magick trail.

Let this candle light the way,
For our journey to commence,
Long have I waited to see,
The guides I've often sensed.

Tenderly I'll embrace you,
Journey with the herd,
Give myself, in Gratitude,
Hear your every word.

Join me, Divine one,
Join me in this space,
Hear me, ancient creature
Gently Come,
Show your face....

# THREE

**ENERGY, WELLBEING and BODYWORK**

## MAIDEN ENERGY CALL

Beloved Atlanta,
Dearest Amazon Systers,
And Artemis I call you too.
In need of your spark,
To eradicate the dark,
And shine on me your Hare Moon.

Come, lend me your blessings
Found in the green,
Of forest and mountains and grass.
In trance I travel to your realm,
Led gently by immortal hands.

I find great strength in my systers,
Who travel all time and space,
Support me in my endeavors,
Engage me in this inner race.

From the depths of my soul I feel you
Surging wild from within,
From these feet that have now join you,
In the Astral Temple den.

Your essential omnipotence
And your energy of life,
Olympian vitality,
Taking me to great heights.

Coursing thru my blood.
Pulsating all through me.
From my blessed crown chakra
To the toes of my feet,

Let me feel you vibrating.
With this magick, fueling me.
These things or better,
As I sing,
So mote it be!!

## **RESTORING GOOD HEALTH**

I call upon the vibrant Sun,
The light of Venus
To get things done.

To heal malignancy
And restore all Health,
To help reverse,
The cards I 've been dealt,

To wane and dissolve,
What illness lurks,
Restore my Health
And smooth the hurt,

I bathe in green,
And rising smoke
And charge this poppet
With my soul cloak

I raise it to,
The Mother Moon,
And let Her rays
Melt all hopeless gloom,

Restore my faith
That I am healed,
Let my words spin
Good Fortune's Wheel.

I see myself restored, energized,
Releasing illness
That are no longer mine.

An it harm none
For the greater good,
These things or Better
As all is understood
This spell bound round
And it shall be
Reclaim good health now!!!!
So Mote it Be!!!

# FOUR

## PROTECTION & REVERSALS

## SENDING IT BACK
Waning Moon I call,
Draw closer to this work
And place thy shield
Around this space
To guarantee that I stay safe

A wrong's been done
That needs remedy
I cast this spell
To help bring relief

To soothe away
All ill intent
Reverse the wrong
That has been sent

With waning Moon
Dissolve this wrong
Let things get smoothed out
Before too long

What turned to salt
Let now turn sweet
Return the malice
and let it cease.

I draw upon my circle of light
Benevolent spirits
Who guard by my side.

Deflecting darts
With the light of my soul
That ill intent
Weakens its hold

Three times three,
Mirrors up to deflect,
Three times three,
I send back any hex

Three times three,
As I circle around,
Three times three
This spell bound round.

It is done, done done....
So mote it be!

## **BANISHMENT**
Into this black candle before me,
I banish and contain all maladies,
With waning moon and melted wax,
<u>Loa/Goddess</u> tend to what I ask.

Herein lies the pain of solitude,
Illness,
Inertia,
A mind that's confused,

Stricken with all kinds of needs,
Plagued with senseless poverty,
Let this wick absorb these things,
So that new life may now begin.

Joys and money,
Energy and health,
Courage to embrace,
My transformative self.

Able to turn all wrongs into right,
Banish the obstacles,
That have plagued my sight,

And by the light of this burning flame,
I burn and banish these things I name;
      I banish_____
      I banish_____(repeat)

## **POPPET WORK**

Maladies that plague me,
Cease to be,
Exit from my body,
Illness and disease.

Lose their strength,
Now weakening,
Spirit of good health
Retrieved and stirring.

Fainting with the waning moon,
All disease and plaguing wounds,
I release you herein,
And say my goodbyes,
Let good health now,
Be by my side.

With this poppet of herb and blue,
I am reborn, healthy
And spiritually renewed...

>By powers of **Air-**
>I blow you away and release you
>
>By powers of **Fire –**
>I burn you maladies out of existence
>
>By powers of **Water –**
>I drown you and wash you away
>
>By powers of **Earth –**
>I bury you, illness, like a corpse, bury to your end
>
>By powers of **Air –**
>I fumigate you now, renewed, to good health.

And by all the elemental forces that exist
By the powers of magick and the ancestors, I enlist.
By the Fae and the spirit of immortal ones,
And by my will and word,
It is now completely done!!!!

**ENDINGS**

## **HONORING ENDINGS**

Journeys commenced
On Labyrinth's path,
Joy of what was,
That now has past.

Grateful hearts
For lessons learned,
Spider now mends,
As The Wheel turns.

Silken threads,
Trampled upon,
Severing ties,
That once were strong.

Peacefully relinquishing
What can no longer be,
Spider I call you
To help heal me...

Fuse and make whole
The shattered bits,
Honor the endings
And all that has split.

Release with intent
For all is meant to be,
In Sacred trust, this ending is done
As I say, So Mote it be!!!!

**SPELL FOR CLEARING & FORGIVENESS**
I forgive, I release,
Sever ties that swallowed me,
Let the past be far removed,
So that all within me is smooth.

Lightly ease all doubt and pain,
As the moon each day now wanes,
Feel my heart grow wings to fly,
I transcend this moment in time.

No experience will label me,
Those who hurt me, I release,
From my anger and my pain,
I rise with new eyes
To meet each new day.

Give my soul
A chance to breathe,
A chance to love,
A chance to be...
I am more than these past tales,
I will rise,
Where yesterday I failed.
I rewrite the book of my life,
Liberated from the hurt,
I fly..fly.. fly...

# FIVE

**JOURNEYS**

## **TRAVEL WISH**

I close my eyes
And take a breath
By Air I travel
And find my rest.

Envision Sun rays,
Caressing my skin
And distant lands
Where I fit in

By Fire I travel
On those Sun rays
And cast this spell
By these sacred flames

By Earth I ground
This wish to soar
Fulfilling travel wishes
Deep in my core.

By Oceans in goblets
Inviting me to play,
This spell I cast now
Takes me to desired plains

Bound round this wish
An it harm none
I travel with ease
And seize the fun!

So mote it be!!!

## ASTRAL TRAVELS

Each breath I take,
Leads me to you,
Down in the spiral
I leap right through.

Astral traveling,
Past this realm,
Surrendering bones,
I once held.

Enter through breath,
Enter through intent,
Let My Journey,
Now commence.

Stiff as a Board,
Light as a Feather,
Traveling now
I ascend better

Repeating the phrase,
I enter this trance,
Stiff as a board,
Light, is my dance!!!!

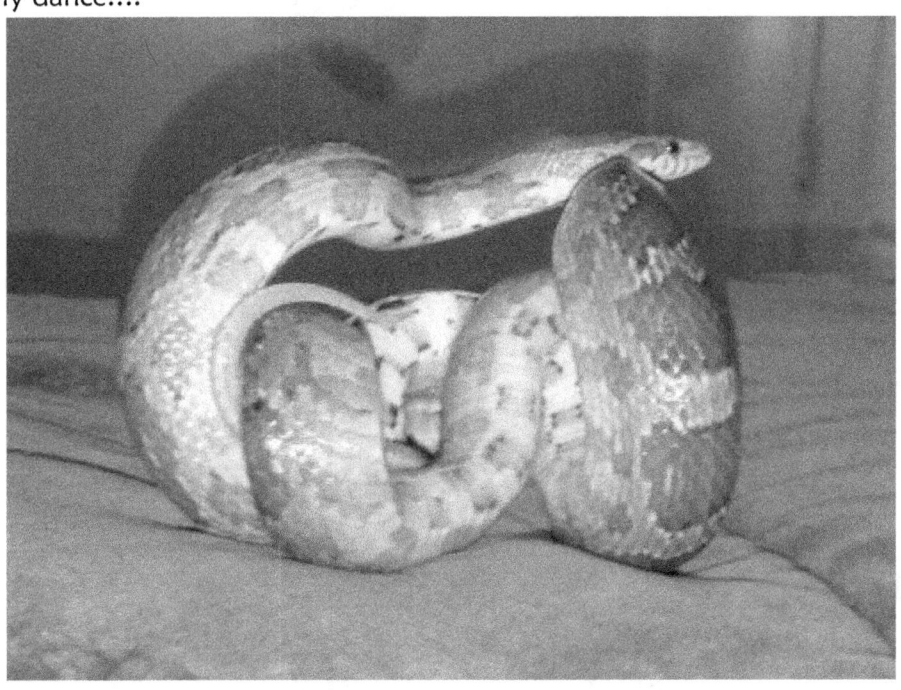

# SHAMANIC ANIMAL MAGICK

# SHAMAN ANIMAL MAGICK

Stillness, Quickening,
Silver Rays of insight,
Deep in the Shaman's Cavern
I arrive to be student of the night.

Opening to Her Wisdom,
Like the pedals of the Crimson rose,
Listening for Her primal essence,
Entering her sacred throne.

Quenching all stale thirst,
As she peels layers of truth,
The sacred animal holding Her Medicine
Is invited right through....

I welcome this Medicine,
I welcome this Guide,
I walk ever deeper into
The shadowy crevices of my mind.

I am led to expand,
All parts that were hidden,
My primal friend supporting,
Removing what sickens....

The rattling continues,
As we journey now further,
My primal friend cloaks me,
As I take on its essence.

And with its eyes, I have sight,
And the gifts of its tribe,
Unraveling the blocks
That were once hidden inside.

I journey ever deeper,
Now as you,
I wear your skin and energy
Your medicine has come through

Sitting still now, breathing gratitude,
Seeing what is revealed,
Oh Sacred Being of Mother,
In our journey together, I am healed....

## **SIX**

## **PROSPERITY**

**ABUNDANCE- GRAIN MOTHER HARVEST INVOCATION**

Remove the obstacles
That keep us from our Bounty
Remove the blocks
That keep us from our fruits
Ancient Sacrificial Mother,
Compassionate Goddess of Forgiveness
Herein this Rite we honor you!

Lead us through your realm
Of Birth and Transformation.
Teach us thy ways of Regeneration
And Self-Resurrections

You whose fertile grains
Feeds a Rainbow Nation
Thy Love's lesson burst,
Opening hearts for soul elevation.

I honor you Beloved Mother,
Who feeds me with thy wisdom,
Guide me as I enter
The darkness and I listen…

Sweet Devoted Mother,
Let me not in Soul-Hunger be.
Herein, the Sabbat is kept
And we honor you… )0( So Mote it be…..

# PROSPERITY & SUCCESS -INVITING GOOD FORTUNE

In surplus I am blessed
And sing my gratitude,
Good fortune is flowing,
In extraordinary multitude.

And I am exalting
Both large and tiny gifts,
For all are reflections
Of my deepest wish.

Prosperity is here,
Prosperity I manifest,
In this spell; I see it,
And thus.....I am Blessed!

In candles of green,
Surrounded in coins,
The currency doubles,
As word and will joins.

The incense smoke rises,
To dance upon my wish,
And wraps its long limbs,
To let the magick begin.

With soft gaze, I focus,
On Soul-Collages made,
And draw upon the visions I see,
As I invoke and play.

Come Gaia, Come Hambodia,
Come Lakshmi and Nike,
Come Grain Goddess and Empresses
And Priestesses with Blessings.

Come dance around this fire,
Of desire in my heart,
And celebrate the good fortune
That this night will now spark!

I welcome Her bejeweled,
Extend my open hands,
Our magick is now done,
Let all be as we planned.
*So mote it be!!!*

**CAREER BLESSINGS**

243

## EMPLOYMENT
## LUCK WITH JOB SEARCH

Gift to impress,
Eloquent and respect,
Let me enchant
My future bosses.

Amicable interview,
Rapport with results,
A job offered, more money
And great perks in bulks.

I am the "One" who gets this job,
Success and more money,
And Help from the Gods.

Competent I am,
Worthy of this,
My ideal job,
And employment bliss.

Offers now come
And utilize my skills,
I manifest employment,
By word and will.

This spell bound round,
And it shall be
To cause no harm,
On no one, nor me
These things or better -

So mote it be!!

# SEVEN

## STUDIES

## STUDIOUS BLESSINGS

Wisdom Goddess,
Born of the Crown,
I invoke you, Athena,
Where knowledge is found.

I call forth your Blessings,
As I study and research,
Like the owl by your side
By you, let me be perched.

To absorb all your Blessings,
And radiate in your light,
To expand my understanding,
And gain greater insight.

To grow smarter each day,
And excel with my goals,
To attain what I seek
And walk confidently & bold.

This Skull candle I offer,
And breathe unto it your name,
To awaken your blessings,
As I kindle its flame.

With consecrated oil,
And the rising scented smoke,
I send this petition to you,
With great ambition and hope.

Oh Grey eyed, Athena,
Be near me, Wise One,
In thy infinite, sacred name,
This spell is now done!!!!

So mote it be!!!

**CREATIVITY**

## CREATRIX AWAKENING

In Gaia's embrace,
Rooted in her womb,
I swim in her waters,
Of Creatrix boon.
> I coax my inner child,
> To come out and play,
> Uncensored and fearless,
> Inspired by Lunar rays.

She taps into Gaia,
And her proliferation gifts,
And multiplies her blessings,
As she twirls, in her creative mist.
> She links to sweet Mama,
> And brings remembrance to me,
> That I too behold,
> Her sacred energy.

Fearless I create,
Rightly I behold,
Let lose my expression
And let it take hold.
> Through canvas or words,
> Through dance or any form,
> I dive into her realm,
> And let the Artist be born.

Aspecting the vessel,
The sacred conduit of Her work,
I invoke her Blessings,
As I dive & soul search
> To create and unleash,
> Heal and to speak,
> Through forms I sculpt now
> With the blessings of her crown.

And now it is so…
I dive into seeds,
That grow in abundance,
With the nurturance I feed.
> This spell bound round
> And it shall be,
> These things or better
> I awaken **Creativity**…

**So Mote it Be!!!!**

## PSYCHIC DEVELOPMENT

Cast the circle,
Quiet the mind,
Call the Elements,
From where they reside...

Dig deep within,
Unearthing my flame,
Reflecting on journeys,
As they expand us to change.

Here do I stand,
Beneath her piercing light,
Casting the net,
For further insight.

Moon that serves
Her wisdom's flight,
Come and bring,
Thy Eagle's sight.

Come pour forth,
Thy Nectar's kiss,
Psychic growth,
I now enlist...

Here through skulls,
And eager hearts,
An open chalice,
Awaits the start.

Moon rites to call,
My intuitive side,
Third eye now opens,
As the incense smoke rise.

Sovereign hues,
Purples and blues,
I light these flames
That call on you.

Stir and awaken,
The eyes to see,
Grant me my gifts,
So mote it be!!!

# V. VISUAL TOOLS OF MAGICK

# TALISMANS & AMULETS

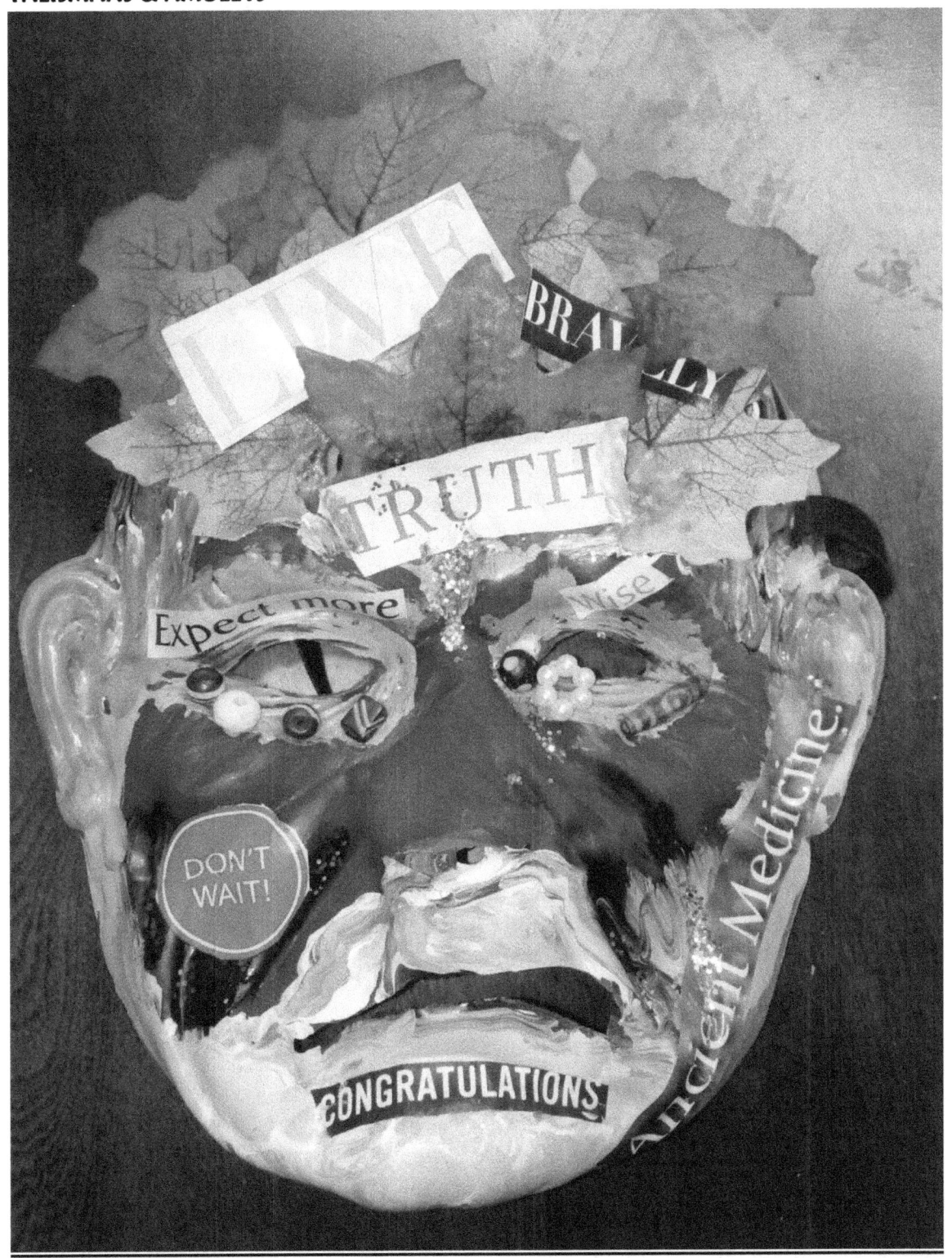

# TALISMANS & AMULETS

As has been mentioned before, the goal of this book has been to introduce a number of Metaphysical tools, techniques and ancient spiritual practices from various traditions from across the globe, to help us revamp our lives and learn how to enhance our own powers of manifestation. In this chapter we are going to be looking at visual, tangible tools, that we can use in our own lives to manifest magick and effect a desired change.

Two of the oldest tools introduced to us by a number of different indigenous cultures, that have survived to this day, are the use of talismans and amulets. These are terms that are probably familiar to most of us, due to their cross-cultural usage throughout the years but their significance and value might've been overlooked in today's fast-paced technological world.

The use of talisman and amulets can be perceived as probably one of the earliest forms of personal magick making. When we consider that early man might have, quite organically, reached for natural elements in his/her environment to comfort, heal, protect and find inner strength, it makes perfect sense. It should come as no surprise that when early man felt vulnerable, scared or threatened they would have naturally looked to their habitat and those creatures they shared that space with, to unearth a proper remedy. Stones, herbs, bones, feathers, animal skin and other natural objects found in nature have always availed itself to humanity with the promise of its natural magick and curative potency.

An indigenous warrior might have progressively studied the mammoth strength of a Grizzly Bear in his environment and finding himself in need of such powerful strength, to fight rival tribes in the battlefield, would come to the conclusion that carrying a small piece of that Grizzly bear might imbue him with the Bear's strength. Here, human's earliest amulet or talisman is conceived, as a tooth, a piece of fur, a bone or a bear's claw, which would become the object in nature that provides man with a needed gift. The same can be assumed about our feather friends who we share space with. If early man observed birds, like the majestic eagle, soaring and flying high up into the stratosphere; reaching the unimaginable heavens, and they desired this gift in their own personal lives, it would come as no surprise that its feathers would be coveted. Again, the eagle's feather would've been viewed as a perfect talisman or amulet for those seeking to embody the eagle's gift or protection. It is clear to see how the feathers of an eagle would have been desired and viewed as a potent tool of magick for those seeking wisdom and insight. For indigenous cultures, the eagle is indeed revered as a sacred spirit of extraordinary eyesight and great powers of flight. Anyone needing or wishing to attune themselves to these attributes would certainly seek to create a talisman from eagle feathers. Not surprising, the earliest form of amulets and talisman would be found in the elaborate regalia and head dresses of early indigenous tribes. Also of importance is the fact that protective amulets and powerful talisman made of bones, feathers and many other found objects in nature would've been ideal for those living off the land with dire stringent economics.

No…the option to shop at the local wizard store for an amulet or talisman was just not available back then, the way it is strangely available for us today, but I digress.

Since the earliest of times, it is clear, amulets and talisman have existed and were highly prized and used by numerous early, indigenous cultures. Their use today, however, is no longer limited to indigenous cultures or early man. A book about magick and personal transformation could not dismiss the potency and effective use of talisman and amulets.

The word talisman comes from the Greek word,"*telesma,*" which means, "consecration ceremony." The word amulet comes from the Latin word, "*amuletum*" or "*amoletum*" which means amulet; a small trinket worn to protect against illness, evil, mischief and the evil-eye. Already in the etymology of these words we begin to get a glimpse into their importance for spiritual practitioners and students of magick.

While some modern day spiritual traditions do not differentiate between the two, others are very adamant about the distinct differences in these two forms of spiritual tools. Both talisman and an amulet are a type of tangible charm that is maintained near the body for most effective impact. However, there are some subtle differences between these two types of charms that we need to make note of here.

An amulet is usually an object found in its natural state, while a talisman is often man-made, manipulated and crafted. An amulet can be a gemstone, a crystal, a seashell or a piece of wood or resin. It needs no further manipulation. A talisman, on the other hand, might be a collection of any one of these objects, added to a pouch, purse or medicine-bag or fastened together in some manner. It can be fashioned and crafted into a pendant or a doll or really anything you can imagine. Some consider a talisman to be a form of an amulet.

The most notable difference between a talisman and an amulet can be seen in its usage. An amulet is considered a more passive form of magick, as it is often employed to deflect negativity, defend its wearer and provide protection. It is traditionally used as a form of protection against evil, illness, jealousy, negativity or the evil eye. It serves to deflect unwanted energy and its main purpose is to protect the wearer.

A talisman however, is considered a proactive tool of magick, as its purpose is usually to imbue the wearer with specific characteristics. It is usually crafted with a specific purpose in mind and with specified assigned attribute for its wearer. For example a talisman can be crafted to imbue the wearer with eloquence in speech or great physical strength or enhanced psychic abilities or the power to attract love, etc., etc… As you can see, creating a talisman offers us many more opportunities to personally and uniquely manifest what we truly desire with great precision. When creating a talisman we have a chance to get more specific about our needs and the attributes we desire to achieve our heart's desire. In this way, it is indeed a powerful tool of manifestation. While an amulet passively protects the wearer from danger, a talisman gives the wearer certain specified attributes, like strength, to combat the impending situation.

A talisman can be seen as an amplifier that gives power and specific characteristics to its wearer. A magic sword, an athame, a crafted pendant, or any jewelry, medicine bag, poppet or placket, a head circlet or a magic hat and a sacred ritual mask are all examples of a talisman but, there are many, many more examples. We are only limited by our imagination when it comes to the creation of a unique, personal talisman. A talisman therefore, is an object that is charged with personal power to attract a specific energy or power, to its wearer.

An amulet is a natural and potent protective object that serves to protect and deflect specific energy away from the wearer. It is typically a deflector of negative energy. A wood or stone crucifix, onion, garlic knots, runes, a bone, lucky coin or currency, four leaf clovers, a rabbit's foot, a pieces of amber resin and even a horseshoe are just some of the many embraced and known amulets throughout the ages. They need no further manipulation as they are considered lucky by their very nature. We simply connect with the object, to charge it with our request and energy, and the magick is done.

Both an amulet and a talisman can be charged and empowered by the Moon, the Sun, the four sacred Elements and or a specific deity, angel or spirit. An amulet, however, might be more often associated with the waning moon because it is an object that deflects and removes energy, which goes hand in hand with the energy of this moon phase. When we look more closely, at the differences between a talisman and an amulet it's hard to imagine which one came first for early man, but there is no question both types of charms have been consistently utilized throughout the ages. They are wonderful tool of magick that have remained popularly in use by various traditions and spiritual practices and they offer us a chance to add yet another tool to enhance our powers of manifestation.

## SIGILS & SYMBOLS

No one can dispute the great influence and power a symbol can have on our subconscious mind. We see the drawing of a heart shape and we immediately think of love; we see the symbol of a dollar sign and immediately think of prosperity and U.S.A. currency. We may see a triangle and immediately think about the ancient Egyptian pyramids, Masonic rites and esoteric spiritual practices. When we see a drawing of the scales we might immediately think of our judicial system. For Wiccans, we see a star, or a pentacle, and immediately think upon our faith, just as Christians immediately connect a cross or a fish, as a symbol of their faith. As we study more Metaphysical subjects and tenets, we will encounter a plethora of examples of symbols and the importance of sigils. In astrology for example, each of the planets and the twelve different zodiac signs have a specific corresponding symbol that we immediately recognize as representative of that sign. We look up at our numerous constellations adorning the night sky and gain greater understanding of the power and relevance of signs, symbols and sigils.

A sigil is a symbol created with intent for magickal purposes and ceremonies. In Medieval times, sigils recorded in ancient grimoires, were often associated with ceremonial High-magick. The Keys of the King of Solomon and its numerous esoteric seals have survived throughout the ages and are most popularly known and used by Occultist. Squares, Seals and Sigils were used to invoke spirits; in particular angels, devas, spiritual beings and elementals. Nowadays, we consider mandalas, yantras, kabalistic pentacles and seals, planetary squares, voodoo veves and some talismanic designs, as powerful forms of spiritual sigils.

The word Sigil comes from the Latin word, "*Sigillum*," meaning a seal. It is believed every human being has a personal sigil or symbolism, associated with their spiritual makeup and in time, it is up to the individual to discover what exactly that is. Sigils have been assimilated throughout the ages with numerous spiritual traditions. We see them being used in runes, oracle cards and tarot, Ouija boards and in various other tool of magick and spiritual enlightenment. At times their presence appears to hold the same venerated significance as the Divine. Today, sigil usage can be found in various traditions including those exploring Metaphysics, Wicca, Shamanism and the revival of ancient Ceremonial rites. We are encouraged to know that anyone can incorporate sigils into their own personal spiritual practice as they see fit.

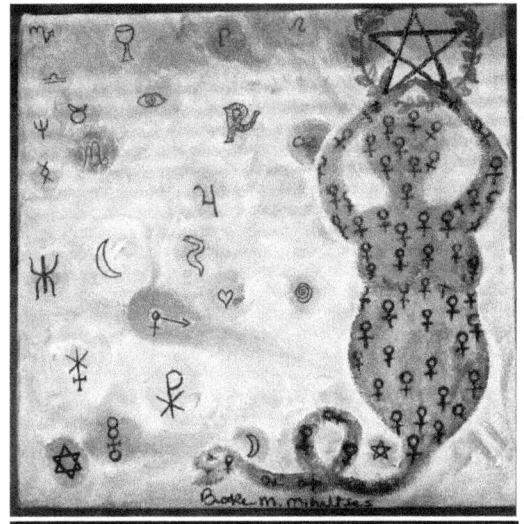

## VISION-BOARDS & SOUL-COLLAGES

## MANDALAS

# **Vision-Boards and Soul-Collages**

Vision-boards and soul-collages are also known as dream-boards and treasure mapping. They help us practice a freeform type of creative visualization that reflects our true soul's desire. A vision board is simply a tool to help us focus, clarify and unearth what is hidden within our subconscious. It helps us connect a face or a specific image or symbol to our deepest soul's longing. On this vision board we display what we want to be, what we want to do, what we want to have. We may also simply fall into a trance as we let our subconscious choose visually, the images that are personally speaking to our soul. It is clearly a very personal tool of expression and sometimes the very creative process of making a board can result in a very cathartic spiritual experience. With a vision board we declare our goals and dreams, which is typically the first step towards the motivation to take action to manifest them. Follower of the *"Law of Attraction"* teachings, advocate the use of vision boards as an effective tool to help us narrow in and focus on what our soul truly desires to manifest. *"Like attracts like,"* by focusing on the symbols upon your vision board, you can work to manifest these desires and bring them into conscious reality. Vision boards serve as a consistent reminder of what you truly desire and what you are dedicating yourself to, so that when life and personal situations; like the environment, family, friends and obligations, seem to cloud or overwhelm you and pull you into too many different directions, you are anchored and reminded of your authentic life purpose. We have a special, magickal tool, in our vision boards, which serves to bring us back to what is truly important in our personal lives.

It is already well established that our most precious goals cannot be successfully achieved without first engaging our sight and creative visualizing. Author, Shakti Gawain is the best teacher on this subject. Her book, *"Creative Visualization"* was groundbreaking in its promotion of using our minds and creative visualization to attain practically anything we desire. Numerous industries use vision boards to effectively campaign, express a business idea and communicate to associates in large and small corporations. Interior decorators and architects have always used vision boards in their presentations to their clients, as do many other businesses and entrepreneurs, salespeople and CEOs when conducting conferences. Its effectiveness as a business tool for powerful, persuasive communication and delivery of conscious and unconscious messages is undeniable. If it can work so effectively, for so many varying industries and organizations, why wouldn't we employ it in our own spiritual lives?

Vision boards help us get clear on what we truly desire thus, they become a powerful focus tool of manifestation. It enhances our ability to remain motivated on what personally matters most to us. It can help with daily positive affirmations, as you are able to incorporate words, positive images and phrases to gaze upon for daily inspiration. It serves as a visual of our unexpressed dreams and goals. By consistently creating vision boards, we delve deep to unearth our hidden, deepest desires and bring them up to the tangible surface. By giving these unformed, intangible ideas, fantasies and desires, palpable, concrete visual images, we begin the process of manifestation. These visual tools we create, thus, can become our source of motivation and inspiration and as we take the time to gaze upon them on a daily basis, it serves as a reminder of our goals. In creating a vision board for ourselves we are thus, moving our sometimes hidden desires from deeply buried parts of our psyche, to the forefront of our conscious reality.

**How to create a vision board?** It's quite simple really. We can create them within groups, as part of a group ritual or in private solitary rites, as part of our commitment to our own spirituality and personal transformation. In both instances; whether alone or in a group setting, you will gather a stack of magazines, scissors, glue bottles, and a sturdy cardboard or canvas, where you will later glue and display all your images.

I like to suggest setting the mood before you begin the work. We can set the mood in various ways. Personally, I love to include the scent of incense or smudge the area that I am working in, with sage and copal. You can use your personal preference for scents in this arena. On occasions, I might play soft music in the background, depending on the mood. The type of background music I select for my vision board crafting ritual will depend on the mood that I'm in. I will say, that the type of music that is heard in the background while you craft, can influence the experience of vision boarding on so many different exciting levels. For example, I will never forget the first time I used a tribal drumming track as background music for a vision boarding group ritual. I remember that experience being very energetic, thrilling and fast-paced, as we collectively exchanged this exuberant highly charged energy in the room. We gathered and chose images to cut out very quickly, happily and uncensored. I remember how maiden-like, bouncy and energetic I felt myself and all those around me, as we crafted our vision boards. Indeed we were raising energy and were highly influenced by the fiery drumming in the background. Never underestimate the powerful influence the primal sound of drumming can have on us. That day, I watched as we quickly selected images from our torn up magazine collection and just as quickly, glued our images to our boards, with little time to question or censor ourselves and there was much palpable giddiness in the room. It was quite exciting and produced a collection of the most beautiful, revealing expressions of our souls. There are other times when I choose to use a more serene, tranquil music track, as the background music, and this can quickly induce a very soft deep trance, in which you can lose track of time and enter silent introspection. It almost always has a very watery feel and you can really delve deeply into your emotions. I have seen how impactful a slow, tranquil environment for vision boarding can be, especially for those who are coming from a hectic or chaotic emotional place. The images that you choose in this contrasting setting can be just as revealing. In both settings you give license to your subconscious and allow your heart to choose the most compelling images for your vision board.

Although it's not absolutely necessary to choose a theme before starting, it's highly recommended that you sort of have an idea of what it is that you want to manifest. Rest assure, your subconscious will lead you deeper into your initial quest. Initially you might want to just have a simple idea or a word or one theme that you'd like your vision board to represent. For example, if I have health concerns or if I am seeking to manifest something related to my wellness and fitness, I can begin this process with that theme in mind and then allow my subconscious to start choosing symbols and images that will support this original idea and then let it go. I will make it a point to not be rigid but to allow myself to see what else wants to come through by asking my subconscious; what does it want to express and reveal to me, through the creation of this vision board, in relation to the initial theme that I've chosen? The same thing can be done if your initial goal is to manifest love or a relationship. If we begin the process with that in mind, you might soon discover many symbols will come for you that are closely linked with that initial theme. It's always astounding, however, when someone begins the process with one theme in mind and then the subconscious begins to pull out other elements of the theme or something related to the primary goal. Witnessing how that initial idea might evolve and be transformed by our subconscious, through the act of creating a vision board is always compelling.

You may begin with the idea of wanting to create a vision board for a specific job or a career and as you begin to collect images you might find yourself being drawn to images related to love and relationships. Here this vision board might reveal that your initial expressed desire for a job or a career is being overshadowed by your need for love. Our subconscious, through our vision boards, can thus reveal what we cannot deny any longer.

Once you've gathered all the images and you've cut them out, the next step is to arrange them on your board in a way that is uniquely pleasing to you. This very process can awaken our artistic side. It's very exciting to see how all these varying images, phrases and words come together to create a very unique and personal self-expression of our subconscious mind. For me, it is indeed a very powerful form of magick, expressive art and a tool for awareness and personal transformation. This is why vision-boards are included in this book, which aims to introduce metaphysical tools and creative techniques to help us revamp our lives and enhance our powers of manifestation. Soul-collages and vison boards are yet another potent tool of magick for effective personal growth and positive change.

Once you glue all of your images and words on your board, I suggest spreading yet another layer of glue over the top of your work or you might even be inspired to spray a protective varnish over your finished vision board to preserve it. It is a matter of preference, but you may wish to only create vision boards based on the cycles of the moon, which can add yet another dimension to your creation. I tend to craft my vision boards during the New Moon and on some occasion, use the Full Moon. I've also heard of people ritualistically burning or burying their vision boards after attaining their goals at the Full Moon. This is, of course, a matter of personal preference and you can decide ahead of time.

Finally one of the most important magickal steps in creating your vision board will be to display it somewhere, where it will be seen by you. Here is where it will have the most positive impact on you. As your eyes take in the varying images on your vision board, on a daily basis, you will be reminded of your goals, positive affirmations and your life purpose, consistently. This is probably one of the most important aspects to creating your vision board because an extraordinarily beautiful masterpiece of a vision board is useless to you, if it is sitting, hidden away, in your closet, unseen by you. Your vision board becomes a powerful tool of manifestation only when it is viewed consistently and only when you allow it to be a gentle reminder of your true heart's desire.

A vision board takes our fantasies, which can be seen as our creative visualizations, and turn these dreams into visually, tangible things, that are no longer just in our heads as formless ideas but rather quite possibly within our grasp. It turns our seemingly far-fetched ideas into achievable goals.

By focusing on the symbols and images on your vision board, you can work to manifest your goals and bring them into conscious reality. There is no right or wrong way to create your vision board and this is the beauty of this type of magick, for indeed, it is your own personal magick, wrapped and intertwined in your soul's expression and artistic creation of a vision board.

# **MANDALAS**

Mandalas are literally defined as the *"essence of having," "containing," "circle-circumference," "completion."* These are all various translations of the Sanskrit word, mandala. A mandala, in my opinion, is a revealing artistic chart, design or map of our inner journey. Crafted in a free flowing trance like state, it can unearth where our spiritual, emotional and present state of mind is and possibly where it yearns to go.

Throughout the ages mandalas, can be found utilized by numerous cultures from Hinduism, Buddhism, to Christianity. You can find these designs on the architectural floors of grand entrances to significant places of worship, majestic stained glass windows of churches, and the outer décor of secular monumental architecture. Of course, we see them in numerous illustrations found in both secular and sacred books of the past. If you look carefully, you will find all sorts of mandalas reflected amidst nature herself; think of seashells, flowers, tree groves, caves, rocks and crystals.

The images of a mandala have traditionally been utilize to establish sacred space, as is evident in the many ways we sometimes find them being used on the floor entrances of significant historical monuments, but they are also used as a form of concentrated focus and an effective form of meditation. In some cultures like the Navajo Indian tribe and for Tibetans, mandalas are created through sand paintings and released in sacred rituals that reinforce the teachings of impermanence.

A mandala and a yantra are similar, with the latter being more geometrical in design. The two terms are sometimes used interchangeably. However, yantras are often described as being a living, tangible representation of the Goddess/Gods and as a tool to invoke the respective deity. Mandalas are often crafted in a circular fashion, with a repetitive motif and powerful symbols that communicate with the subconscious mind, taking it on a journey that eventually leads one to the awe transformative, holistic center, like a personal labyrinth. One must also note that the colors and patterns combine within a mandala, evoke a different plane of reality that transcends time and space and thus, they are perfect to incorporate in our rituals to the Divine.

The world renown psychoanalyst, psychiatrist, Carl Jung described Mandalas as the ideal world represented and depicted within this circular imagery. He believed mandalas functioned to help a person with integration of the scattered parts of themselves. It was his belief that humans became disintegrated when their internal realities did not match those exterior ones created by outside influences such as; families, friends, and environment. He often encouraged his clients to tap into their unconsciousness by creating free flowing mandalas, as this was a successful method to unearth hidden parts of the self. Dreams, active imagining and creation of mandalas were just some of the various methods he advocated to connect with the forgotten pieces of ourselves. Lodged deep in our subconscious mind were aspects that a mandala could shed light upon. Jung believed Mandalas were Universal Archetypes that revealed our personal inner journey and self-development. *(Pg 14 "Mandalas and Meditations" by Cassandra Lorius.)*

Crafted alone, mandalas can bring about an intimate moment of deep self-reflection, but mandalas can also be a powerful tool of magick when done in rituals and created in sacred space alone or among a group or coven. Every person present lends their energy to its creation and that can be quite an amazing, magickal experience. Engaging our senses in the process can add many powerful layers to our mandalas as well. Humming, together, creating a cone of power, while we work out our design, can be an effective way to incorporate sound, as is playing soft music in the background to engage our auditory senses. Scented oils and the smoke of scented incense can tap into our sense of smell and if we are encouraged to engage our body in movements, as we paint our mandalas, we awaken our kinesthetic contribution to our work. Of course, our sense of sight is engaged most with the surrounding altar décor and the various colors and patterns utilize in the creation of our unique mandala. Whether you are creating a mandala in a supportive group setting or on your own, as a process of self-assessment and transformation; mandalas will prove to be an additional helpful tool of magick to explore deeper.

# YANTRAS, SQUARES & PLANETARY TABLETS

Yantra is the equivalent of the Buddhist Mandala related more to Hindu and Yogic traditions. It is a Spiritual visual tool made of geometrical shapes and patterns. It speaks of the external, visual view of the Divine; in comparison to mantras, which reflects the internal and consciousness of the Divine. Yantras are a visual tool for meditation and also reflect humanities' manifestation process and evolution. It typically contains at the center of these various geometric patterns and shapes, a black point, known as a *bindu*; which symbolizes unity, origins and the principle of manifestation.

Looking closely at the Sanskrit word of Yantra, "Yan" in Sanskrit means to behold and support the essence. The second part of the word, "*tra*" is connected to the Sanskrit word, "*trana.*" "*Trana*" in Sanskrit refers to liberation. Yantras are thus known as a potent tool of integration and also helps to facilitate altered states of consciousness to gain greater spiritual wisdom. Focusing on a yantra during meditation can enhance ones' spiritual practice but also the process of designing and drawing one can help shift energy and our own consciousness. The very act of creating a yantra requires much focus and precise concentration, which can help the individual with transcendence and gain esoteric knowledge. Some Yantras are even used as powerful talismans; carved and drawn unto metal pendants and stones. Below is an example of a Kali Yantra.

**Numerical Yantras/squares**, also known as **Planetary Tablets,** are great cosmic conductors of energy; they consist of a series of important numerical symbol combinations, placed within a geometric square. They are traditionally made out of copper and are used as talismans. They can be used as a visual tool when we chant their corresponding mantras. Like Yantras, they can help hold our focus & intention. Below are the corresponding squares/tablets & mantras for the planets.

*(See Reference page 329 for additional Kabbalistic, Talismanic Planetary Squares....)*

## 1. NUMERICAL YANTRA; MOON SQUARE

| 7 | 2 | 9 |
|---|---|---|
| 8 | 6 | 4 |
| 3 | 10 | 5 |

**Moon Mantra**
OM CHANDRAYA NAMAHA    **Pronunciation:** [OM CHANDRAAYA NAMAHA]

## II. NUMERICAL YANTRA; SATURN SQUARE

| 12 | 13 | 8 |
|---|---|---|
| 7 | 11 | 15 |
| 14 | 9 | 10 |

**Saturn Mantra**
OM SHANEECHARAYA NAMAHA **Pronunciation:** [OM SHANEEECHARAAAAYA NAMAHA]

## III. NUMERICAL YANTRA; JUPITER SQUARE

| 10 | 5 | 12 |
|---|---|---|
| 11 | 9 | 7 |
| 6 | 13 | 8 |

**Jupiter Mantra**
OM GURAVE NAMAHA    **Pronunciation:** [OM GUURAAAVEI NAMAHA]

## IV. NUMERICAL YANTRA; MARS SQUARE

| 8 | 3 | 10 |
|---|---|---|
| 9 | 7 | 5 |
| 4 | 11 | 6 |

**Mars Mantra**
OM ANKARAKAYA NAMAHA    **Pronunciation:** [OM ANGKARAAHAAYA NAMAHA]

## V. NUMERICAL YANTRA; SUN SQUARE

| 6 | 1 | 8 |
|---|---|---|
| 7 | 5 | 3 |
| 2 | 9 | 4 |

**Sun Mantra**
OM GHRINIH SURAYA NAMAHA or OM SURYA NAMAHA
**Pronunciation:** [OM GREENNNAI SURAAYAA NAMAHA]

## VI. NUMERICAL YANTRA; VENUS SQUARE

| 11 | 6 | 13 |
|---|---|---|
| 12 | 10 | 8 |
| 7 | 14 | 9 |

**Venus Mantra**
OM SHUKRAYA NAMAHA    **Pronunciation:** [OM SHUHKKKRAAYAA NAMAHA]

## VII. NUMERICAL YANTRA; MERCURY SQUARE

| 9 | 4 | 11 |
|---|---|---|
| 10 | 8 | 6 |
| 5 | 12 | 7 |

**Mercury Mantra**
OM BUDHAYA NAMAHA    **Pronunciation:** [OM BUDHAAYAA NAMAHA]

## Voodoo Veve

## Veve

In a voodoo ceremony the center holds the sacred pole that unifies the heavens and the earth and this sacred central pole arena is known as the, Um'phor, which powerfully influences the entire ceremony. It is around the Um'phor where we would typically recognize a drawing, an intricate magical diagram. This diagram is known as the Veve. It is usually found in the center of a Voodoo temple, created with ashes, coffee grounds, cornmeal, wheat flour or red brick dust. Because the veve is strategically created and placed in the center of a voodoo temple, one can only surmise its great importance in this spiritual tradition.

The veve is essentially used as a concentrated point of power; to attract the planetary influence and the energy of the loa, or spiritual forces. The veve acts as a portal for the blessings of the loa. Veves are used as a reliable tool to invoke the powers of spiritual forces and help open the gateway for one of the most important aspects in a voodoo ceremony, possession. The veve acts as a bridge between the physical world and the astral and it is only through the creation of this magical symbol, that the loa can come through. Our spiritual world and the physical, meet at the center of this important most auspicious diagram and it is the veve that helps facilitate the channeling for spirit.

Similar to Hindu Mandalas, yantras and Kabbalistic Metaphysical geometric seals, each Voodoo veve has a list of special attributes and characteristics that are associated with its respective loa. Fundamentally it is believed to behold the soul or spirit of the loa, as well as being a vehicle for the earthly manifestation of their powerful energy. It is important to note that traditionally, the veve is created and energized by the high priest or priestess. Most believe its power is dependent on the presiding voodoo priest or priestess because their belief in the veve gives it potency. Once it is uniquely created on the ground, water, that has been ritualistically prepared, is poured over it to awaken its power. There are also numerous sacrifices that are offered to it during the voodoo ceremony and this is the way its power is fueled and nurtured throughout, with food offerings.

Respectfully knowing the culture, spiritual traditions, and great importance associated with the veve makes it so much more hallowed. It is an invaluable Spiritual tradition used in Voodoo, similarly embraced by numerous other indigenous cultures. The plethora of designs and symbolism associated with the Veve are deemed as sacred and can also be considered beautiful works of art that are uniquely inspired according to the energy at hand. They are an important part of this tradition. While they are often created and amplified in their power by trained Voodoo Priest and Priestesses, for special Voodoo ceremonies, I have found them to be a powerfully effective visual tool of magick in my own personal spiritual practice. They are respectfully presented here in this book as yet another valid form of visual magick to be explored further by those seeking to transform their lives with metaphysical tools.

# DREAMS

It may sound strange to many people I share this information with, but I have always been able to acutely recall my dreams nightly. Since the time I was a very young girl I could awake every morning and loquaciously rattle off the plethora of images, stories and detail messages received nocturnally. By now I probably could've written an infinite series of encyclopedia-sized books, if I shared every one of my very detailed, prominent dreams from the last forty years or so. Some have led to extraordinary revelations, spiritual insights, divine messages, and are worth noting and some have simply remained documented in my personal collection of journals, for my eyes only. It is a most cherished gift passed down to me, possibly from my maternal side as my mother was the neighborhood dream interpreter. In our household dreams were something we excitedly shared with one another and relished, as we tried to discern their esoteric meanings. And thus, I learned from an early age to value my dreams and pay close attention to them. Throughout the years I have learned to walk through this realm, learn its language and benefit from its cathartic gifts. My spiritual life has been unquestionably greatly enriched because of this valuable element and I am indebted to the ancestral lineage that has passed it down onto me.

Below I share two recent prominent dreams as they were documented in my personal journals, in the hopes they might inspire you to value and make note of your own dreams. Given the subject of this book I thought these two particular dreams would be of interest but I must admit, there are a plethora of dreams I'd love to share and discuss but must restraint myself from doing at this time.

I have had many dreams where I was given direct answers to questions I presented to spirit before falling asleep and I have had divinatory and psychic dreams, as well as dreams related to karmic, past-life issues. I have had powerful visitations, in dreams, from spirits, deceased loved ones and beloved ancestors, and I have had recurrent dreams where important conversations have taken place.

In this chapter I simply want to encourage you to experiment and explore your nightly dreams and recognize them as another invaluable vehicle for spiritual growth. Honor your sleep time and nightly routines. Get into the habit of maintaining a dream journal and document any and all images that come to you through dreams. As time moves on, you will learn to appreciate this powerful spiritual tool and develop a nourishing relationship with your nocturnal, divine communicators. Create a dream sachet or dream placket to place under your pillow with corresponding herbs and stones that will welcome more dreams and facilitate recall and be open to anything that may come.

## **THE POWERFUL INITIATION DREAM**

*I could not talk.... I could not talk.... OMG!!!! I COULD NOT TALK... Imagine the horror for me, as a singer...as singer who sees the magick and value in her voice...yet, I could not talk.... I was made like a mute.... I felt the weight of my tongue and all the muscles inside my mouth felt weighted like lead, heavy as lard. All the muscles on my entire tongue felt like they were made of* metal and I wanted soooo much to form the words to speak but they would not form. I was wretched inside wondering why I was a mute, who did I offend in the heavens? All I could feel was the swollen heaviness of my ineffective tongue, just immovable, not able to utter a word, incapable of choreographing itself normally to form itself useful. I desperately searched in my mind for the whys. Was I being punished for something? Did I divulge spiritual information I was not supposed to speak of? Was Spirit trying to teach me a lesson, I thought? This can't be happening, there must be a reason? Why would there be such an awful restriction on my voice, why? This had to be a spiritual lesson of sorts, it just had to be? How can I, of all people, be rendered mute, how? Then...all the mysterious pieces of the puzzle started to unfold itself like magick and, as if the clouds in the sky parted, I was allowed to comprehend, as the dream continue onward....

 We were in a car, driving at night. I was assisting someone...it was like, I was her apprentice or something, or she was my work supervisor. It was clear I was working for her. We had to go where she was taking me, to some jobsite. It was very dark, clearly past midnight and we had to go into this peculiar house. The streets that made up this area seemed strange, really unusually dark. I saw the very noticeable, intricate iron-fence and gothic-like gates that greeted guest with much scrutiny and intimidation before they could even reach the actual house.

 Oh yes, I almost forgot. Before reaching the house, we had to find parking in the streets and I think I dropped my supervisor off at the house first and went on driving, in search of a parking spot on my own, though I was never really alone. I eventually found it and then had to walk a long way back to return to the house. Again, I was most perceptively aware of how strange and dark everything appeared and it felt foreign, like this was not America. The car was parked and I returned to the house, where I found her gathering with some other people. Charity was being offered, I think, because I felt all of a sudden like I didn't have enough for them. It was clear, the people in this house, needed so much more than I could possibly offer to them and I questioned how much I could give. It was then that I offered two young men, our Jet fuzzy warm blanket, but I made it clear that it was not fully available to them because it really belonged to my husband and I did not have the authority to give away something that did not belong to me. I instructed them that they could only touch and view it and appreciate it in this manner. Well, much to my surprise, the men were ever grateful and welcomed the borrowed gift. They were just happy, all too happy to be able to touch it, I think perhaps because it had the American football Jet logo. Then they wanted to take pictures of it to commemorate the special charitable moment. They expressed gratitude and it was okay that they could not keep it, even though, as poor as they were, they should have. They simply wanted to commemorate the night they touched it and have proof with the picture that they were in possession of this temporary gift from me. As I took the photo with the camera and witnessed others, also taking photographs here...here is the pivotal point. **Here is when it all started to spin and shift!!!!** As if someone had just put a "rufee" or drug in my drink, I felt my body spiraling at this moment, the room spinning faster and faster. I felt myself morphing and transmutating into the next realm.

 I found myself now walking the streets, the barren poor streets...no, this was clearly not the U.S.A. This place felt like a very impoverished country, it felt like Haiti after the earthquake or some other unknown land. In an instance, I felt eyes, so many eyes on me...policemen and citizens all studying me closely as I walked the street. But I am half Dominican, I thought, and I should feel right at home here, blending in with the locals... but I didn't. As I looked at myself at that moment, I realized I was bizarrely in a different body. It was a frail, skinny blonde, white woman's body. I was like the main character on "Sex in the City," Carry Bradshaw. I was in her Caucasian, woman's body. I realized then why I felt so out of place in a country I would normally blend in. I was skinny, frail, bony white and I felt myself walking down old cobblestone streets with my Manalo, six inch stiletto high heels and I could feel the eyes of others watching me with curiosity. I walked and reached the entrance of this place where I saw people gathering; old men and women, all gathering in the center, like a ceremony was about to begin & I just so happened to arrive right on time for it.

The gathering or event...was a rite. It was a voodoo ceremony taking place right there before me... I cautiously and respectfully entered the space, sensing something big and sacred in my midst and I saw what appeared to be a half circle starting to form itself. I saw many people but an old man with leathery dark skin and silver spun threads upon his head caught my eyes first. I tried to sit inconspicuously nearby, but the dark elderly man wisely stepped back, quietly adjusting himself within the circle, to widen it and visibly include me as part of it. With no words, he opened up and made the space for me to join in the circle and soon others joined in as well to create a full circle. I looked out, behind, all around me really, and saw the congregation, seated at a distant. They were like an audience, witnessing the rite. I saw my supervisor again (a teacher/guide) or family members there, they were the ones who were simply witnessing but were not part of the center ritual. They were in the pews seated beyond, like a witnessing congregation. I immediately felt they all made space for me and I humbly stepped into this sacred circle we were forming. As if the old man was saying I could not just sit nearby and be a spectator, he pulled me in; I belonged there! He said no words, but spoke intently with his eyes and his body made no question; I had to be included in the rite. He made the space for me to join in to be included into this special circle and that meant the world to me. The special rite with words and chanting began soon after....

I remember at one point, excusing myself for a moment so that I could go to the bathroom. My familiar matronly guide/Supervisor was sitting in the congregation and I heard her call out from a distance. While I was in the bathroom, she called out with questions to me when I was in there from behind the door. Quite bizarrely, she started asking me detailed ritual related questions, almost like an evaluator or assessor; testing me and my answers. "How do you serve the offering in the rite?" I heard her ask me. I finally found my voice and answered back, "you pour it directly...not scoop it and...." I continued with my answers in full detail for every ritual questioned asked, though I am not sure where I gathered all this information from. It was almost as if she was testing my knowledge of sacred rites; passing down esoteric knowledge and teaching me all at the same time. She was making sure I knew the difference between Santeria rites and Voodoo rites and revealing pertinent spiritual knowledge to me. Whatever it was, I was being tested and they were all satisfied with my answers.

In the bathroom I strangely had three stones in my hands; three pink stones that I strongly felt compelled to leave on a large sea shell, almost like an offering there. Then someone opened the door, and I came face to face now with my ol' friend, the supervisor again. Excitedly, I told her about my pink stones and how I wanted them to be an offering and...OMG... she was my mother... That woman felt very maternal, although I don't recall her face appearing like my mother, she was like my caretaker, my supervisor; very matriarchal, perhaps a maternal ancestress. It was clear she was my guide throughout this entire dream, appearing at different times as a teacher and non-intrusive witness, throughout the journey.

Then there was a part in the dream, towards the end, when I arrived at a gloriously white room where I saw my friend, my guide again, performing a rite. There was a young boy and she was doing something to him, a healing or some type of sacred ceremony. Throughout this ritual, she was talking to me, still mentoring me. She was instructing me even as she was performing this special rite. The boy within a few minutes began to vomit... yes vomit at full force, and I was reassured that this was a natural process and a good thing. It meant the ceremony was working and the boy was being released of the "stuff" or negativity. I watched as this was part of my mentoring and education. She was fulfilling her role indeed as my teacher, supervisor and spirit guide here. The other priestesses and priests in the room were amused by my sense of humor, as I later made a simple joke about the vomiting and the calling out of the "Juan." Towards the end...the crone, honored Elder and "Abuela" appeared. Oh, that sweet....sweet crone, the one I was initially intimidated by, for I intuited her greatness. She had so much power.... Well, I saw her there and she beckoned me to approach her on the lounging chaise of sorts and she pecked me on the cheek...yes. She kissed me, but not just an ordinary kiss; it was a tiny bite on my cheeks. I felt her teeny teeth sink into my blushing cheeks; it was little love bite. "There," she said... "You needed that...." Huh? I initially thought, and then I realized what she meant. I guess I needed that familiarity, that sweet peck/morsel bite on the cheek. You see, it was a family traditional kiss that she knew I would recognize and appreciate and thus, she said... that I needed that as confirmation, especially right before the dream ended. I started to morph back soon after that kiss. Before the dream ended I received this strange, final validation with that love bite and then I woke up.

When I looked at the clock it revealed, 8:08 am and I wondered the significance of that number. Slowly I started putting together the pieces to the dream. I was given the name Maman Brigitte... as I indeed woke up saying her name. I felt my mother or a mother like image but it could've been my great grandmother or a distant ancestress, clearly there were many ancestresses guiding me there. Whoever the main one was, she was my teacher and guide and she wanted me to have knowledge and succeed as a Priestess. She needed me to be educated and well informed on the proper process of rituals and ceremonial rites. I felt like I was an apprentice under her guidance and I also felt her great love. I belonged to her, to her lineage. And the whole dream was truly a journey from the beginning, in the car with her going to that house, to the end, walking into that ceremony. I was journeying the whole time in this dream. And wow, not being able to talk...well... isn't that Dantor...? Erzulie-Dantor is the mute whose tongue had been cut off. Omg, it was Dantor's presence because I felt that energy sharply. Then, there was that moment when I looked and saw myself embodying a bony, tiny frail, blondish, white woman. She felt like the cold bones of Maman Brigitte, within me, walking through the corridors of New Orleans's cobblestone streets. I even woke up saying the name Maman Brigitte but perhaps this was because, at the end, the granny elder, pecked my cheeks in a loving, grandmotherly kiss.She appeared like Maman with that energy.

OMG!!! And that old man who made the space for me in the circle, that had to be Papa Legba, portal opener, gatekeeper. He was old and his gaze revealed such an infinite, effable wisdom. He was the gatekeeper of that circle and it was through his grace that I was allowed to become part of the circle. My teacher/guide remained outside, sitting with the rest of the people, like a tribe, possibly our ancestral family, in the pews as the congregation, supporting....humm.

Admittedly, I have had an intense couple of days before this dream.... strange week really. I battled with some insomnia and it was in the early dawn hours when I finally did go to bed. The New Moon was just a few days earlier and I am sure that has affected my dreams. And any moment now, I can feel my unfertilized eggs ready to bust and bleed right out of me. I am sure this opens me up further to intuitive insights. Yesterday however, was a particularly emotional day for me... I received the spiritual call to listen to "A Change is Gonna Come," by Sam Cooke, so i proceeded to go on "YouTube" to hear all the numerous singers giving their own rendition of this powerful song. My heart fully received the spiritual message of this song and its lyrics. Who else would have even known to present me with this powerful form of communication? That is how my mother connects with me, through dreams, and through powerful songs. It would not be the first nor the last time my Ancestors and Spirit guides reach for me, from across the veil. Blessed be!

# **Winter Solstice 2012, an Excerpt From My Personal Journal**

It was the afternoon of the auspicious Solstice of 2012. I had already decided ahead of time that I was going to use this particularly powerful date to quietly connect within and meditate, especially after the tragedy of Newtown, Connecticut. Emotions were still very raw for many of us and it was easy to detect the introspective energy humming around this part of the globe. At this particular time, the kids were away in school, and my out-of-work husband was keeping busy in another part of the house. I had not slept very much the previous few weeks and I had just done several deep meditations. Needless to say my body and mind and spirit were already in a state of calmness and relaxed receptivity. On the couch as I heard one meditation coming to an end, I felt myself go deeper and deeper into a trance-like sleep and this is what I dreamt…

*******************

*We were in a small car, all of us… My husband was in the driver's seat and I guess two of my boys were in the back. Sitting in the front of the car was my oldest son, and my deceased mother. Oh yes, I was there too, right beside her. We were sort of squeezed together in the front of that tiny car seat. How we were all able to fit, I don't know, but we were all tightly squeezed in that passenger seat, smiling enjoying a song that was probably playing on the radio. My oldest son and I were smiling and singing; connecting the way we usually do in real life, when all of a sudden our eyes locked. He looked at my mother and then he looked at me. Then again, he looked at my mother, his grandmother and, without words, tried to get me to look at her as well. Then we both looked at each other with a kind of eerie-like, secret code understanding. We then both looked at my mother, who was quite contently quietly singing along with us. She was cheerfully humming the tune of the song. She was happily singing while sitting there in the car with us, appearing quite content. It must've been a rare thing for us to witness because it shocked the heck out of us, to see her in this euphoric state. Our mutual grin grew from ear to ear at this sight. And I'll never forget the look as my oldest son with his eyes spoke without words, "look mom, she's happy, she's actually singing with us, mama." I deeply gazed upon her form now, studying the "grenitas," the stray hairs upon her usual pulled back hair. I tenderly smoothed out her beautiful, distinct "grenitas," with the palms of my hands and gently cupped her beautiful face upon my hands, as I hugged her deeply with so much love, gratitude and compassion for her. I never felt so much love at that very moment. And I placed my hand tenderly with love over her head, dearly noting the size and shape of her beautiful cranium and her hair, which was in her usual bun. I placed my hands to cup one side of her face and on the other side; I tenderly placed my own cheek to rest upon her head with love; kissing my mother's head. It was a sweet tender moment. I still cry remembering!*

*Then all of a sudden my husband, who was in the driver's seat, presses the gas pedal really hard and we were now speeding on a highway in the wrong direction. Cars were coming towards us and there was a cliff, like those you see while driving throughout California. He was driving recklessly, really fast and this is where it happened…. Hold on to your hats… I felt the car go over the high cliff and while the car drove down, I felt my ascension. My body, my spirit had the sensation of lifting higher and higher. The car flew over the cliff going down and I felt myself go up, catching that weird butterfly sensation in the stomach, like the one you get when you ride an elevator or when you go on a roller coaster ride at the amusement park. It was then that I felt my* soul rise up with the car in that peculiar sensation. The car went over the rocky cliff and I saw it dive into the bluish ocean below.

I remember feeling my heart just stop, suspended in midair. You know, I don't typically like heights. Ask anyone who knows me, I abhor roller coasters but this felt like I was on a chaotic roller coaster ride that then, left me suspended, up in the air. The driver of that car disturbed the serene scene of one second to introduce the chaos of the next and I even remember saying to myself, " oh dear.. I don't like this..." It all happened so fast, I felt myself and my heart in physical form and then no more, and just as quickly, the car and everyone inside of it landed in the ocean, that is... everyone except for me. We (me in spirit and their father in physical form) started frantically searching for our kids to make sure they were safe. I saw my husband trying to account for every one of us, literally counting to make sure that everyone was safe. The kids were fine, thankfully, but as for me, they couldn't locate me. They kept searching for my body but they couldn't find me. I was standing right there, but they couldn't see me. I just was not visible to them any longer. Everyone was searching frantically but I was nowhere to be found. I didn't make it and they still had not realized this, when I did. I knew...I knew then, I was no longer in the flesh.

I watched as the rescue team started to search for my physical body in that wreckage... Within a few minutes, when I realized what had happened, I then saw my own vaporous form, despondently walking in a very lost, depressed way as I realized what had happened. I carried my slumped form, walking passed the wreckage, walking right passed all of my beloved children, in total surrenderment of what was and I left the scene. I started walking up, towards the large stairwell of a type of stadium. It felt like it was a stadium or a large auditorium and the stairs were going up. In a very melancholic way I walked the steps, going up, leaving my family and the chaotic scene behind. I kept walking up the steps and now I was passing by spectators, numerous people that were sitting in their seats, waiting for the show to begin. No one noticed me, it became clear I was not living in their realm any longer, I was in spirit form. In the ascension, while they had returned to their bodies, I had not.

I continued walking up and reached the top, which led me to an eerie vacant hallway, like that of a school or office building. I didn't quite know what to do with myself, so I decided to go to the bathroom. I felt so disoriented and was still processing the entire situation. Before me were two bathrooms and clearly there was a boy and a girl's bathroom but there was something strange in the language. I could not understand it, nor did I know how to read the signs for each bathroom. I couldn't discern which bathroom was the right one for me to go into because the language was archaic and foreign to me. So, I had to take a moment to breathe and connect with my intuition and at that very moment, I intuited which bathroom was the right one for me to go into. This appeared to be a spiritual practice session for living on that side of the veil; learning the language of my intuition and not relying on my eyesight any longer, was essential now.

When I came out of the bathroom I discovered that there was some sort of religious conference or convention and there were a whole bunch of tables set up. Every person was operating a table that had a religion that they wanted to share. Was this heaven... a conference with a plethora of religions being shared peacefully and lovingly? I walked around and saw one table packing up their material. I walked more and then approached a table where there was a man and a woman sharing their religion but as the man was speaking with me, he kept strangely interjecting a word over and over again in an illogical, most peculiar way. I immediately recognized this as a spiritual message trying to get to me. He would speak about his religion; haphazardly tossing the word, in between thoughts, questions and phrases and then in the middle of his sentence, blurt out the word, "cantifla." At first I thought how strange and then I realized the power and message in that word. See, that word would have only been said by my deceased father. The only *person I've really ever heard say that word was my dad in the living, but in this dream, although I didn't see him the way I saw my deceased mother, he was making himself known. I do believe my mother was standing near me as I was visiting this one table at this religious conference. It could've been someone else just as well.*

*I saw the image of a Hindu deity at this table and it inspire me to begin speaking to the woman and I heard myself saying, "well yes, I believe in the Goddess and the Feminine face of God and I believe we are inclusive, we follow, respect, believe in all religions and see the Goddess present in each and every one, I said proudly..." And I gazed at the Hindu image once again and I said, "yes... even in Hinduism we worship the numerous Feminine faces of the Goddess like; Kali, Durga, Lakshmi etc...," I said. I started to name all the (Hindu) Goddesses that I knew of and it was as if I was now representing the Goddess and Women Spirituality at this Celestial religious conference.*

*Then, I think it seems to have appeared like closing time, because people nearby were starting to pack up. Don't know how relevant time is in the afterlife, but it was clear that some presenters were starting to pack up their belongings and the food cart was also starting to pack up. At this point I suspected that my mother or whoever was with me now, was hungry and needed something to drink or eat. I assertively took it upon myself to go to the cart and grab a few things to eat, so that whoever was with me could get their nutritional needs met. As the food cart was being packed away, I grabbed a few things to eat and drink. Then all of a sudden, I noted music. Throughout this process, I could hear a faint song in the distance becoming more and more detectable. It was the song by Musik Soulchild, titled,* **"Love."**

*The song asserted itself ever so strongly, determined to catch my attention. Now this is a song I was never too familiar with, when it first came out, over 15+ years ago, this was before the invention of "Youtube." I quite frankly, never gave it much thought to seek or listen to and yet, here it was demanding my attention. This was a powerful message gifted to me in this dreams, through this song. When I woke up from this dream or was it a deep trance meditation, my android phone was nearby and so before being fully awake, I searched for the song on "Youtube" and immediately played it through my head phones. What transpired, I could have never predicted or choreographed. I was still very much in a deep trance like state, when I started to listen to the song. As I listened carefully to the words of this beautiful song, I understood, my whole soul understood... I knew within every cell in my body the gift that had been passed unto me and this, for me was my ascension on the Winter Solstice of 2012. Every fiber in my body knew and I could feel my deceased parents crowding my heart in that auspicious moment. What I felt next can only be describes as a profound level of euphoria and spiritual ecstasy....*

*My entire body started shaking uncontrollably and I felt the stream of tears pouring down my cheeks. I felt myself convulsing as tears just poured, poured down and now I was sobbing aloud. My sobs had become so powerfully audible that it reached my husband, who had been in another part of the house, listening to music, wearing his own set of headphones. He expressed concern for me but simply stood there as a witness to the phenomenon. To this day I am most impressed that he, with his limited knowledge of the occult and spiritual matters, was able to calmly witness me come out of this, as he has learned in the past to just witnessed me undergo monumental spiritual phenomenons. When pressed by him, I could not fully articulate what I was experiencing, nor why. I was still in limbo, not fully present and feeling very, very raw; like the tender oozing pink of an erupted scab... I could not be physically touched, for I didn't want to be reminded of my flesh; I wanted to stay in this ecstatic realm, ascended, high in spirit, if that makes any sense.... It was only days later when I realized, this was indeed my Winter Solstice Ascension and an unforgettable spiritual experience through yet another powerful dream from spirit.*

*"In sleep we become pure intuition,
out of that state of consciousness
we give birth to dreams,
a nightly channel of the Higher-Self;
a strata of the astral plane,
an aspect of our self as a pure channel of the Divine..." Unknown*

## **Dreams & Spiritual Communications**

Dreams are a powerful way for us to communicate with spirit(s). They afford us a chance to delve deeper into our subconscious minds and open up channels of communication with our spirit guides and our own inner psyche. For indigenous cultures, dreams hold an extraordinary amount of significance as they are viewed as omens, auguries and a direct phone line with the Divine.

The shamans hold a strong belief that dreamtime is the reality of life, while the world outside of us, that we so often tenaciously claim as reality, is really just an illusion. Numerous confirmations of this spiritual tenet have made themselves known to me in recent years, but none was more poignant than learning about the death of a beloved, comedic genius of my era, Robin Williams, in August 2014. I mourned his tragic suicide with the rest of the world in utter shock and one night, as a result, found myself journaling as I downloaded powerful messages from Spirit.

*Only in dreamtime are we able to let go; let go of emotional blocks, let go of man-created boundaries, let go of our physical forms and all the confinements attached to them. Only in dreams do we dive deeply into the pool of our true emotions and hidden subconscious, they have little chance of escaping this realm of truth. Only in dream time are we able to speak without mouths, see without eyes, enter our open hearts with acute spectacles to see deeply through dark portals. Only in dreams do we fly to great heights, travel to distant lands and mysterious realms by merely floating, letting go of the edge. Only in dreams, do we understand and are understood, as our unembellished, naked core is the channel of transmission. Only in dreams are we awaken to the illusion of time and boundaries and only in dreams do we get to temporarily return home...return to our true essence...return to where we have no other recourse but to embrace our authentic selves as the powerful spiritual beings we are.*

*The world that we call reality hides and disguises itself, over and over again, even from us, its very creator. So often our senses fail us in this realm we call reality. We think we see something, know something, hear something, but all is not how it appears. We think its concrete and this concrete is our so called reality, but in dreams, it reveals itself as vapor, its true form. Our state of mind creates realities that we claim are out there, out of our hands. Dreams reveal that they are more within our grasp than we realize and indeed we do co-create it all. We see what we want to see and sometimes, what we don't. Our senses paint pictures that are not based on truth but simple illusions and erroneous boundaries. Everything appears to be an illusion. The reality is in our creation, in our dreams, in our hearts, where we are not limited by self-imposed boxes, but are free.*

*How can one person experience a scenario as a tragedy and the next being experience the identical scenario as life-affirming? It is all first and foremost created in our mind. What makes one person, who, on the surface appears to have it all, give up on life and yet another person, who, on the surface, appears to have nothing, fight for life? The answer is found in the recesses of our individual minds, the creators of illusions, and our hearts, the announcer of our divine infinite truth.*

*In dreams we are fluid, open, renunciating our preconceived boundaries and rules about life and the way things ought to be. It is not so much our mind that dictates the realm of dreams, as it does so laboriously in our waking hours. Our hearts, our emotions, our spirit and our deep subconscious are the dominant rulers of the watery realm of dreams and they have quite a different language to express itself with. It is our spirit and our hearts that are in the driver's seat during nocturnal journeys. The shamans believe that this is true reality because everything else in our whole physical world(s) is created through our mind's interpretation. The outside world is created through our false presumptions and each mind creates according to its personal point of reference. In dreams, we tap into our gifts, true essence and our collective powers unchained.*

***"There are no facts only interpretations," according to Friedrich Nietzche.***
***"Life is only as the perceiver interprets it.***
***Everyone is seeing the world through different eyes,***
***creating their own interpretations and therefore, their own illusions.***
***We see things and interpret them according to our collective experiences***
***and thus, this is how we are creating worlds,***
***more specifically, this is how we create our reality..." B. Melusine Mihaltses***

*Dreams are yet another powerful tools of magick and spiritual communication, as we converse and receive guidance from our subconscious, our beloved ancestors, angels and our spirit guides. Dreams offer us a chance to really delve into our intuitive powers and psychic abilities. Dreams can also awaken us to our creative gifts and they can offer us solutions to pertinent complications in our lives. Some people astral travel in dreams and some can visit and be visited by spirits guides. There is no question; dreams can be used as a powerful tool of transformation and positive magick to help re-envision and revamp our lives on so many levels.*

## ORACLES & DIVINATION TOOLS

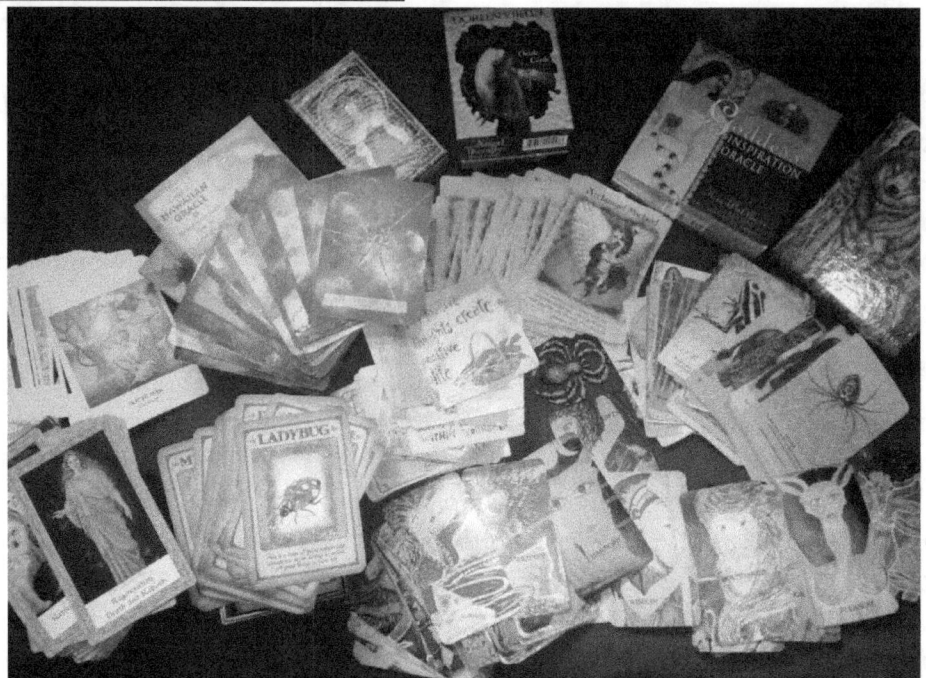

*Various Oracle Decks; Angel, Animals, Polynesian, Law of Attraction, Goddess Oracles, etc...*

Human beings since the beginning of time have sought various ways to connect with spirit and receive divine insight. Throughout history we have learned of the various methods used by our ancestors to communicate with the divine and receive celestial messages. We know of the oracle of Delphi, which originally belong to Gaia, the Goddess of the Earth and we know of the Oracle of Apollo, delivered by the Priestess, Pythia. Just as they were of great value to our ancestors in ancient times they continue to be of value to us in our modern world.

The word oracle comes from the Latin word, *"Oraculum"* and *"Orare,"* meaning to plead, pray, and speak, as an orator. Our modern definition of this word has a few varying subtle differences. An oracle, in ancient Greece, was believed to be a priestess or priest that could speak for the divine by becoming a channel for Celestial transmission to come through. An oracle then and now was also considered to be a shrine in which a deity could reveal hidden truths and divine knowledge. Oracles are thus, divine messages or an answer to a question, or an important decision that is delivered by Celestial means. It is a person giving wise authoritative advice or opinion, believed to be acting as a vehicle or messenger for the Divine.

In our modern day and age, we still value and consult oracles through various esoteric means. In this book we will be exploring the tarot but there are numerous, brilliant and effective oracle decks available to us. The publisher of this book has created an excellent 70 cards oracle deck titled, **"Feminine Divine Works Intuitive Oracle,"** available through http://www.femininedivineworks.com. There are also a plethora of angel oracle decks, made popular by Doreen Virtue, and various types of tarot, Ouija boards and other means to attain an oracle.

We will excitedly explore here one of the oldest and richest type of oracle; the Tarot. Many books have been written solely dedicated to the complex and multifaceted study of the Tarot. Here we will explore the simplified meaning of each card and encourage our readers to go even further in their tarot studies, including intuitive work with them, if they feel a calling to do so.

The tarot is an oracle deck consisting of 78 cards. It is divide into Major Arcana (22 cards, Journey of the Fool) and Minor Arcana (56 cards including Court cards). The Minor Arcana are divided into four categories that correspond to the four sacred elements; earth, air, fire and water. The Suit of Pentacles represents the Earth, the Suit of Cups represents Water, the Suit of Wands represents Fire and the Suit of Swords represents Air. The Court Cards for each category includes a Queen, a King, a Knight and a Page and this Court family is present for each of the sacred elements. The following is a simplified guide to facilitate the use of this traditional oracle and learn the meaning of each card in the tarot. There are a plethora of tarot spreads one can use for divination, however, in this chapter the tarot is introduced as a Visual tool of magick to be incorporated into our spell work and powers of manifestation.

### INCORPORATING TAROT IN SPELLS

The powerful images and attributes found on your oracle and tarot cards are perfect to be used in various ways. They can be effectively incorporated into your candle spells by surrounding your working candle with the images that best speak to you of your desired outcome. You may also include them in your herbal placket squares or personal medicine bag. You may even add the images to your vision boards or Soul-Collages. When you are trying to banish something you can select a tarot card as representative of that banishing element and then you can set it aflame, bury it or send it away by a body of water to banish it. The possibilities are endless and here is yet another Metaphysical tool that we can use to explore further our powers of manifestation. Let us now explore the meaning of the Tarot cards.

# TAROT
## THE MAJOR ARCANA

### 0. THE FOOL
The fool begins the journey into the unknown. He takes a risk that some may see as a foolish but he knows in his heart that the journey begins first and foremost with a risk. Traveling lightly with only his most treasured possessions, he commences his journey into the unknown, trusting the universe like an innocent child, believing that all will be well if he just takes one step at a time. This is the card of brand new beginnings, trust, bold new directions and risk taking.

### 1. THE MAGICIAN
The magician taps into the reservoir of her spiritual gifts and her infinitely strong willpower. There is strong motivation, courage, and skills too manifest your heart's desire. The magician unearths her great powers of manifestation.

### 2. THE HIGH PRIESTESS
The high priestess is the guardian and holder of the wisdom of the sacred feminine. She is the gift of intuition and psychic abilities. She knows that she must look at all situations with her intuitive third eye and trust in a higher power that is available to her when she allows herself to become the chalice of receptivity. All is not what it seems and she goes within to unearth sight, discernment and true clarity.

### 3. THE EMPRESS
The empress invites us into the fertile sacred womb of creation. She is the Goddess Demeter, the Goddess Gaia, the Goddess Hambodia. She is the embodiment of the nurturing, fertile Mother. Her gifts are those of fertility, fruitfulness, growth, abundance and creation. She announces a birth of some kind.

### 4. THE EMPEROR
The emperor is a symbol of the patriarch; male energy, the father figure. More importantly the emperor speaks to us about legacy and what we leave behind to our creations, our heirs. With the emperor we put form and structure to our initial idea. There is an authoritative, sometimes dogmatic energy but the emperor insist on getting things done the right way.

### 5. THE HIEROPHANT
The Hierophant is the card of tradition. He is also a spiritual counselor and advisor that come through the priest, the therapists, the shaman or the teacher. He invites us into his monasteries & sacred sanctuaries, built upon tried and true traditions.

## 6. THE LOVERS
The lovers often speak to us about a powerful significant relationship in the querent's life. This card is sometimes depicted with three individuals, in a Trinity/triangular form, representing the Celestial guidance and blessings upon partnerships. Important decisions involving relationships must be considered now.

## 7. THE CHARIOT
The chariot is about bringing into balance strong and powerful opposing desires. It can symbolize travels but oftentimes it represents ambition and great drive. Much careful skills need to be employed to steer our numerous passions into the right direction harmoniously. The chariot awakens our strong ambition and the skills to maneuver them in the best, balanced way.

## 8. STRENGTH
The strength card alerts us to an upcoming situation that will require us to tap into our great inner strength. She is the fierce Lioness; courageous and strong. She is the Goddess Sekhmet. Here we meet our inner Lioness and delve into our true strength.

## 9. THE HERMIT
The hermit invites us into the realm of solitude, the cave of the old wise crone, a place of divine isolation. There are times in life when we must secluded ourselves, remove ourselves from the chatter of day to day living and the sometimes noisy presence of others, in order to hear and connect with our inner guidance. This card speaks of the wisdom of the Elders; wisdom found in moments of isolation and deep introspection.

## 10. THE WHEEL OF FORTUNE
The most noticeable aspect of this card is the sacredness of the wheel and its perpetual movement. What comes up must come down and what was down will eventually come up. The wheel of fortune speaks of change; no matter what situation we may be facing, we can take comfort in knowing that the wheel is forever bringing change. Life is never at a standstill and we are reminded to learn to adapt, go with the flow and adjust to the inevitable change life often offers.

## 11. JUSTICE
The justice card speaks to us of karma. It can be seen as a card of retribution but it often connotes that the decision has been made based on the collective past. Sometimes it might also alert us to an unfinished lesson from our past that now reemerges for us to finally address and complete the lesson.

## 12. THE HANGED MAN
The hanged man is about sacrifices. It speaks to us about the sacrifices we willingly and happily do, in order to gain something greater or attain a higher ideal. It brings to mind

the shaman or spiritual disciple and who will fast from food and other mundane activities for days, in order to receive spiritual enlightenment. We can also see this explained in the pregnant mother who sacrifices her body for nine months in order to bring a new life into this world. This is the card of a willing sacrifice for something of greater value.

## 13. DEATH
The death card invites us into the realm of death, endings, letting go of what no longer exist and preparing for a rebirth of some kind. It is a card of transformation and regeneration. While you may feel ambivalent or hurt by this ending, we must honor the sacred cycle of life, death and rebirth. There is simultaneously an ending and a beginning.

## 14. TEMPERANCE
The temperance is card of compromise and integration. It invites us into the realm of moderation and balance. We're being asked to temper our emotions and strive to keep everything in perfect balance.

## 15. THE DEVIL
The devil card speaks of bondage and enslavement. Often it is a card that stirs confusion and fear, related to its numerous varying gory depictions, but upon closer inspection, it is an effective image that reminds us of our own powers of emancipation from those things we think have enslaved us. Our fears, our taboos, our addictions and our need to keep up with the Jones are just some of the things that (unconsciously and consciously) enslave us on a daily basis. The devil card serves to remind us to take a closer look at what we pledge our wholehearted allegiance to. What iron-clad chains are wrapped around our necks giving us pleasure but also suffocating the life out of us in our pursuit and devotion?

## 16. THE TOWER
The tower card alerts us of abrupt, sudden changes. It invites us into the realm of chaos and demolition. It is the edifices that can no longer sustain us because we have outgrown them or simply because life has something of greater value to offer us now. This abrupt change can be difficult and painful when we cling for life to something that has reached its expiration date and it's no longer of value to us. It can also denote structural changes within your physical home, long held belief structures and even in long standing partnership arrangements. Expect abrupt breakdowns and monumental changes.

## 17. THE STAR
The star card invites us into the realm of hope. Stars are generally seen as symbols of light, brilliance, clarity and positivity amidst a dark night sky. This card illuminates our capacity to stay positive and hopeful amidst darkness. It can also denote a rise in your popularity and reputation and it announces a positive outcome. Great insight appears.

## 18. THE MOON
The Moon is a nocturnal symbol of the Sacred Feminine. It represents our emotions, the ocean, our womb and the ever present life, pulsating, undetectably amidst the darkness. All is not what it seems. There are hidden undercurrents that our naked eye alone cannot discern but if we go within and commune with our own intuition, all will be revealed through our third eye. It is a card that reminds us to rely on our inner guidance system and allow the sacred silver rays of the Moon to be our reliable guiding light in moments of darkness and confusion. The Moon card reveals confusion and hidden forces that we can only begin to see when we call upon our intuition.

## 19. THE SUN
The sun card delivers one of the most optimistic, comforting messages for anyone who is in need of reassurance. It invites us into the realm of vitality, exuberance, enthusiasm and childlike energy. There is a guarantee of good health, wellbeing, success and achievement, and all things appear to be blessed in her solar presence. The sun card represents good fortune and auspicious blessings.

## 20. JUDGMENT
The judgment card invites us into the realm of spiritual awakening, culmination and reaping our reward. Often it denotes that a decision has been made and all deeds have been examined and assess.

## 21. THE WORLD
As the last card in the Tarot's major arcana, the world card denotes the successful completion of a cycle. It is a most auspicious card announcing success, achievement, prosperity and the full manifestation of your heart's desire. The world card represents harmony and celebrations for goals attained and achieved. The fool has reached the end of this exciting and yet, sometimes laborious journey. What began as a mere vision, a longing and foolish risk, has transformed the fool and has now led him to the riches of the world card. Completion and celebrations ensue with the world card.

# MINOR ARCANA IN TAROT

This is by far not a comprehensive examination of the meaning of each Tarot card in the Minor Arcana, there are numerous books out there, solely dedicated on the fascinating subject. This is however a helpful, simplified guide and my quick interpretation of each Minor Arcana card in the Tarot. It will prove to be very helpful for both the novice and experienced practitioner.

## EARTH: PENTACLE

**1 of Pentacles**
New Money, New Job
**2 of Pentacles**
Hustling, Juggling two things of Value, Two jobs
**3 of Pentacles**
Growth and much promise, Abundance
**4 of Pentacles**
Holding on tightly to Money, Status or Situation
**5 of Pentacles**
Loss of hope, poverty, in need of financial help
**6 of Pentacles**
Inheritance, Generosity received or given
**7 of Pentacles**
Choice between Old & New. Choosing To Stay or Start New Career Elsewhere
**8 of Pentacles**
Apprentice. Acquiring New Skills. Learning anew
**9 of Pentacles**
Money Card. Good Fortune Is Forthcoming
**10 of Pentacles**
Goal Achieved, Financial Blessings
**Page of Pentacles** Earthy industrious child or a messenger
**Knight of Pentacles** a hardworking young man, earth sign
**Queen of Pentacles** an Earth sign, wealthy woman
**King of Pentacles** an Earth sign, money man, a banker

## WATER: CUPS

**1of Cups**
New love, new emotions to explore
**2 of Cups**
Balanced Relationship, Harmony, a balanced partnership
**3 of Cups**
Growing Relationship, Fertile Ground for Love
**4 of Cups**
Gnawing feeling, Dissatisfaction
**5 of Cups**
Disappointment and Frustrations
**6 of Cups**
Nostalgia, Peace and Harmony, remembering
**7 of Cups**
Making decisions, Need to Examine Facts
**8 of Cups**
Surrendering, self-exploration, Solitude needed
**9 of Cups**
Attainment, Desires within Reach. Wish Card
**10 of Cups**
Love, Family Completion, Fulfillment of Dream
**Page of Cups** intuitive child, emotional issue, message

**Knight of Cups** a promising romantic young man, water sign
**Queen of Cups** a Water sign, an intuitive woman
**King of Cups** a Water sign, Romantic older man

## FIRE: WANDS

**1 of Wands**
New Ambition and Drive. Passion awakened
**2 of Wands**
Planning stages, waiting to hear news
**3 of Wands**
Exciting Growth and Positive Potential
**4 of Wands**
Something has already been Achieved, Celebrations and Gatherings
**5 of Wands**
Facing much opposition, fighting for your position
**6 of Wands**
Accolades, Recognition. Publishing Success
**7 of Wands**
Competition, Display, Proving yourself to others
**8 of Wands**
Travel card, Accelerated Success
**9 of Wands**
Challenged, overworked, a Final unexpected Obstacle to Face
**10 of Wands**
Overwhelmed, Overburdened, Taken on too much
**Page of Wands** an important message, ambitious child
**Knight of Wands** a fiery young man, or a residential move
**Queen of Wands** a Fire sign, regal woman who loves her home
**King of Wands** a Fire sign, ambitious older man with big plans

## AIR: SWORDS

**1 of Swords**
New Thought and Ideas, the Fighter is awakened
**2 of Swords**
Avoidance, not seeing, Blinded in ignorance, complacent
**3 of Swords**
Pain, Sorrow, Separation, Severing, Surgery, Divorce
**4 of Swords**
Rest, Retreat and Recuperate, Stillness
**5 of Swords**
A Battle, Facing other's Cruelty, subjected to abuse
**6 of Swords**
Invoking Peace, Water Journey, movement
**7 of Swords**
Politician, Tact and Diplomacy Required, careful of deception
**8 of Swords**
Paralysis, Trapped, Afraid To Make A Decision, hopelessness
**9 of Swords**
Nightmare, Mind Keeps Replaying the Worse Scenario
**10 of Swords**
Misfortune, Loss and sorrow, tough situation, The worse is over
**Page of Swords** gossip spreading, a messenger, smart child
**Knight of Swords** a fighting young man, verbally overpowering
**Queen of Swords** Air sign, autonomous cold woman, a widow
**King of Swords** an Air sign, dominating man

# VI. PHYSICAL TOOLS OF MAGICK OUR ORACLE BODY

## Our Oracle Body

Our body is a most valuable oracle, sadly ignored and underused by many. For those on a spiritual path connecting with our physical body becomes just as important as the connection we are building with our own spirituality and the spirit realm. How many times has a stomachache, a headache, an unshakeable gnawing feeling upon our flesh or a deep strange feeling in our gut, stopped us in our track? How often do you check in with yourself, and your body, to gain deeper insight into a stranger or a nebulous situation? These are examples of how our oracle body is consistently trying to have dialogue with us and when we become aware of this, it opens us up to deeper, more powerful and balanced levels of our psychic capabilities.

On another level, the priestess learns to channel and embody spirit, ecstatically dance a ritual into being, make magick and raise necessary energy, all through the powerful vehicle of her earthly body. Those on a spiritual path learn about esoteric spiritual matters quite early on, but also eventually reach a level of great appreciation for their physical, earthly body and how it can work in tandem to offer guidance, energy and enhance our spiritual work.

# **Yoga As A Tool Of Transformation**

Now to begin this subject I must say, I am well aware that the spiritual and scientific study of Yoga is far too ambitious to tackle comprehensively in a book of this nature. While there are numerous sources, books and Dvds on the market today, solely dedicated to the vastly detailed and complex study of Yoga, the subject is far greater than this book can elucidate on. However, its significant value to a student of magick and those seeking to transform their lives cannot be underestimated. Here we will look at Yoga as an important subject worthy of our exploration and indeed relevant to our course of study; that is, exploring the many different metaphysical tools available to us, in order to revamp our lives and enhance our powers of manifestation. In this sense, we've now traversed into the realm of our **sacred bodies** as oracles and as a potentially powerful tool of transformation.

The word "yoga" is a Sanskrit word meaning to *"yoke," "to unify."* More specifically, yoga refers to the union of the self; the ying and yang, male and female harmonization. It also refers to the union with the Supreme Being or the Divine. The internet dictionary defines yoga as: (dictionary.reference.com/browse/yoga?s=t)

*"A school of Hindu philosophy advocating and describing a course of physical and mental discipline for attaining liberation from the material world and union of the self with the supreme being or ultimate principle."*

Although in modern times yoga has become, not only a spiritual practice, but also a popular tool for flexibility and physical fitness, yoga first and foremost began as a tool of enlightenment. The practice of yoga has its roots in Hinduism thousands of years ago, some believe possibly 2.5 million years ago, during conceivably, the earliest stages of religion. There is still much controversy and debate regarding its origins but we do know it originated in India. Some attribute its birth to the Indus people, also known as Indus-Sarasvati civilization, which was believed to be one of the largest civilizations in early antiquity, named after the nurturing rivers that flowed in this region, in Northern India. Still others believed Yoga was invented by the warrior nomads, known as the Aryan, who invaded this region and took over the Indus civilization. Other, more modern research speculates that the Indus people and the Aryan (meaning Noble in Sanskrit) are actually both the same tribe, which simply were forced to become nomads when their river was drying up. As Yoga is believed to come to us from the Indus Valley, it is pre-Vedic, and it is mentioned in the ancient, revered scriptures of the *Rig Veda*, along with numerous other sacred texts, like the *Bhagavad Gita, Upanishad and the Mahabharata*. There are others that speculate that yoga's origins can be traced to the Aryan text of the time, and was first mentioned and documented around 400 B.C.E. in the *Katha Upanishad* text. Regardless of its veiled origins, its introduction to Western civilization has been unquestionably, instrumental and noteworthy.

Yoga has been embraced throughout the ages as an effective ancient practice which enhances both our mental and spiritual journey. In the late 1960s, with the rise in alternative religions, medicine, experimental lifestyles and spirituality, came a willingness and eagerness to explore other ways of being as well. There have been numerous, well-known Hindu gurus that are credited for helping spread the knowledge of yoga from India to the United States. Some believe the first introduction of Yoga to the Western world took place in 1893, at the Parliament of Religion, held in Chicago, U.S.A. It was Swami Vivekananda (swami means master) who first successfully garnered positive attention and financial support, to travel and spread the teaching and philosophy linked with the practice of Yoga. He wrote books and like many other gurus that followed, he helped promote the practice of Yoga by establishing schools, accepting students, authoring books and giving numerous talks and workshops. Swami Maharishi Mahesh and Swami Sivananda, a former Malaysian based physician, are also widely embraced gurus who helped spread the teachings and benefits of Yoga in the United States, as well as helped promote the lifestyle attached to Hindu spirituality. They traveled with their teachings, accepting devoted students who would also spread the word and established various branches of Yoga across the globe. Here in the western world we have seen an explosive rise in the interest over anything related to yoga and Hindu spirituality; especially in the last few years. The benefits of yoga can be easily recognized by many who are invested in their spiritual growth and journey.

There's no question that the practice of yoga has helped millions of practitioners shift consciousness, bring healing and transformation throughout the ages. It unifies our breath, body and mind through a series of distinct poses. It is important to note, there are numerous branches of yoga traditions; such as; Hatha Yoga, Bhakti, Raja, Jnana, Krija, Enochian, Ashtanga, Tantric and Kundalini yoga, etc…to name just a few here. And if you're seriously interested in the study of yoga, I'd highly encourage you to explore any one of these traditions that personally calls to you. While these traditions have varying motives and philosophies within their foundations, they share a common trait; the use of breath, energy, mind, heart and our bodies to form poses, better known as "Asanas," to help bring about a shift in our inner, personal world.

In Yoga we utilized our breath, mind and our bodies to create postures that open up our chakras and effect shifts in consciousness. It is something that we also aim for in the practice of magick and many other forms of spirituality. Being able to enter into altered states of consciousness and as a result, learning to transcend, manipulate energy and harness it for our spiritual growth, is a commonality between yoga and the practice of magick. In yoga, the goal is to control our Prana, that is, the energy of the Universe; which is viewed as the Ying and Yang, male and female polarities. The unification and harmony of opposing energies is a goal that is mutually shared in yoga and the study of magick and this is why it is an invaluable subject for us to explore deeper. The practice of yoga helps us cultivate discipline, concentration, patience and the exploration of our boundaries and timelessness. In yoga, you experiment with surrendering to deeper parts of your psyche and enhance the application of meditation and transcendence. The practice of Yoga heightens our ability to still the mind, trance and explore our subconscious. The practice of yoga complements the study of magick because they both share a mutual goal and that is to elevate our consciousness and learn to harness our willpower and the energy, to affect change within us and around us. Early trail blazers of the Neo-Pagan movement were big proponents and advocates of the use of yoga and immediately recognize its value when combined with esoteric, magickal studies.

Any medium that aims to bring us into union with our true nature, that is, with our spiritual core, is directly in harmony with the practice of magick. Yoga helps us to explore our subconscious mind through our breath and physical body; bringing awareness and deep healing on so many varying levels to our bodies, our spirit, our mind and our emotional state of being. It can help us tap into our inner strength and will-power and it is yet another tool to expand and elevate our consciousness.

# YOGA ASANAS

According to Swami Vishnudevananda, in his book *"The Complete Illustrated Book of Yoga,"* there are over 840,000 Yoga poses. Yoga is clearly a vast subject and obviously, we can't cover all the poses here but below I introduce some poses that you can begin to practice with much success. Keep in mind that Yoga poses (asanas) are a series of stretching exercises to increase circulation and help you relax, concentrate, breathe in the moment, connect to your spiritual and physical body initially and eventually transcended it.

**Padmasan** (Lotus pose) - Sitting on floor/mat, right leg folds at knee, placing it to rest over left thigh. Crossing legs now, left knee folds, placing it on the right thigh. You are sitting with knees bent, crossed before you. Hands are in a mudra or open over knees.

**Siddhasan** (adept's pose) -This pose is similar to the Lotus, but the heels rest near pubic bones, they do not rest crisscrossed over the thigh. Adept will use eyes to connect with center of forehead, looking towards the third eye.

**Pada Hasthasan** (Hand and Feet pose) -Stand erect, lift your arms over head and bend your body, falling forward to touch your toes with your hands. Feel your spine stretch slightly and bury your face, kissing your knees.

**Sirshasan** (Headstand) -Balancing entire weight of body, upside, on head or on interlocking hands, depending on which asana variation is chosen. It is essentially standing upside on your head.

**Trikonasan** (Triangle pose) -These are sideway bends. Stand erect, feet about 2-3 feet apart and bring one arms over your head to the side of your body, hold and feel the stretch. Then do the same with opposite arm, again raise it over your head, like a handing vine, passed your ears and stretch it over your torso, towards the side. Many variations from; twisting spine while one arm touches opposite leg, to bending your legs as you stretch sideways.

**Chakrasana** (Wheel pose) Lay flat on floor, facing sky and raise your torso off the ground. With your elevated body, straighten out your arms and bend your knees. Let your torso rest on your hands and feet, like a table. Another variation is to bring your hands towards your heels as your body makes the round shape of a wheel.

**Vrikshasana** (Tree pose) Stand tall and erect like a tree and balance on one leg as the other leg bends at the knee to rest towards inner thigh of opposite leg. Hands come up like branches.

**Vrishchikasan** (Scorpion pose) - Lying face down, chest facing ground, let your forearms support you on the ground. With palms down for support, bring up your legs. Legs are raised slowly up and over the head, coming up to a slight bend.

**Supta Vajrasan** (Kneeling pose) – Sitting on the ground with knees bent. Sitting essentially on your heels. Many variations, in which you let your upper torso lay flat on the ground, while knees are still folded. Another variation is to arch your back, bending your upper body so that the back of your head is touching ground, all while the knees are folded in a prayer position.

## Dance as a Tool of Manifestation

Now let's talk about the art form of dance, as a powerful tool of manifestation and a way to enhance our personal spiritual practice. Throughout history there are numerous documented accounts that reveal the great significance of dance in rituals and spiritual practices. Its usage dates back to the earliest of time & continues today in almost every culture.

For numerous indigenous cultures dance was, in and of itself, a sacred form of worship and was often utilize to bring about some type of a change. Native Americans today still practice Pow-Wows and traditional dances used for specific themes. "*Dances of the Sun*," dances to honor various totems, like the "*Hopi Snake Dance*" are just a few examples but there are also dances to celebrate births, victories, deaths and special rite of passages. Of course, who hasn't heard of a *Rain dance*, and its necessity to encourage the healing of parched dry land, with the thirst quenching rain.

For many cultures, a dance is used to symbolize, commemorate or manifest something of value. Just consider the tradition of the first dance between a father and daughter or the first dance between a husband and wife. We can also reflect on the tradition of Prom-night and the American traditions of *"hoe-downs"* & barn dances to see the correlation between modern day harvest dances and the ancient dances for fertility and harvest blessings. Our modern day ritual practices of going to a night club to dance in this darkened glitzy space and maybe, perchance encounter a new love, speaks to me of early mating dances that were practice in ancient times to attract love. And when we look at the spring tradition of dancing with colorful ribbons around the maypole, on the Sabbat of Beltane, we can't help but see and value the roots of its ancient tradition and purpose. Fertility dances, mating call dances, dances to assure a prosperous crop, dances to commemorate a special day or a rite of passage, dances to trance and leave our bodies, as well as dances to honor our chosen deities, have been a part of our cultural experience since the earliest of times.

Of special interest, is the use of dance in direct relation to the veneration of the Sacred Feminine. The Japanese Goddess of Merriment, Uzume, for example was known in ancient times as a shamanic deity who helped her worshippers reach ecstatic levels of consciousness. As a Goddess of Spring and Merriment there are special dances used in her traditional rituals, still practiced today in Shintoism, that are known as "Monkey Dances." In Bali, the Kecak cult incorporates a "Monkey Dance" as well, in some of their rituals. This also reminds me of the spiraling dance practiced in Sufism, to reach higher levels of enlightenment and transcendence. In the Hindu culture there are an impressive number of special dances used for a plethora of themes, including honoring the Divine. Most westerners are familiar with the fierce powerful Dark Goddess, Kali, who is often associated with the "Dance of Destruction."

In the ancient Roman and Greek culture there are a plethora of dances used, again, for specific reasons and to honor the Divine. These dances have thankfully been documented in numerous images, artworks and the writings of the time. However, one that struck me as fascinating is the "*Dance of the Bear*," performed by young Greek maidens. According to writings of the time, pubescent girls would dress in their short yellow tunics and mimic the distinctive movements of a bear, as they danced around in a circle formation. This dance honored and commemorated a special time in a young girl's life, when she would dedicate herself to the Greek maiden Huntress, the Goddess Artemis, who inspired their strength.

In modern day nuptial rites, we still see the presence of ancient dances passed down to us from a long, long time ago. One of the very first steps taken by a newly married couple in a Greek wedding is the *"Dance of Isaiah,"* and it takes place right there, upon the church altar. Though our eyes may miss this important aspect in a contemporary Greek wedding ceremony, it is important to note that indeed it is customarily considered, first & foremost a sacred dance, rooted in the old scriptures. At a pivotal point in the ceremony, the bride & groom are crowned and once this occurs the priests, holding their hands (creating a Trinity) takes them around the altar, singing hymns. All three bodies consciously go around the altar three times and by this very act, the priest is leading the newly crowned married couple to take their very first dance step as husband and wife. It is a very tender moment in a wedding ceremony and it is considered the precise point of union for the couple. Much later on, the celebrations and nuptial festivities continue on, with more traditional dances. Dances that celebrate the bride's arrival with all members of the family joining hand in hand, creating a circle. They dance around a circle, creating a spiral like dance, in her honor as the new bride.

The importance of dance in special rites for various cultures is evident throughout history. The Egyptian Goddess Hathor, in ancient times, was highly revered as a Goddess of intoxication and pleasure, music and dance. There are a number of documented dances practiced in ancient Egypt that were specifically done in sacred rites, in her honor. These sensual dances were done as a form of worship but also to embody the Goddess herself and to awaken within the worshipper her benevolent, divine attributes. If we take a closer look at the African culture and explore African based traditions like the tradition of Voodoo and Santeria, we will find a plethora of examples of how dance is a valuable part of spirituality and the ritual experience. Quite often it is really through dance that we are able to detect the presence of a spirit/deity/Loa in Voodoo ceremonies, as the Spirit or Loa takes possession of the physical body of whoever she chooses. When the possession takes place, spirit begins to manipulate and move the altered body; engaging it in a distinct dance that announces their full arrival into the sacred space.

It becomes clear that dance is an important part of all religious and spiritual traditions. Our bodies are the most effective vehicle for spiritual connection, attunement, enlightenment, ecstatic experience, growth and transformation. When we are on the path of spiritual growths and ascension, we begin to realize that our bodies really are the most powerful tool of magick we can behold. When we view our bodies with such a new vision, insight and reverence, we begin to value it and gain even deeper self-respect; we unearth a vastly new perspective on our body's positive influence to our powers of manifestation.

**You are encouraged now to experiment by creating a dance to exalt your inner Goddess!**

# SEX MAGICK

## SEX MAGICK

Across numerous cultures and traditions, sex magick has always held a special, albeit discreet, place in the study of esoteric magick and ritual arts. The practice of sex has indisputably been venerated and utilized as an important element in numerous ancient religious rites throughout history. Documented in several texts, images, cave paintings, and Egyptian papyrus, we cannot minimize the value and extent of its usage in ancient times. We see evidence of the use of sex magick in early Egyptian, Roman and Greek religious rites, as well as Hinduism, Tantra, Buddhism, Shamanism, Witchcraft, and Paganism, even in modern day Neo-Paganism, to name just a few. It is a valued form of magick that was embraced in ancient times and continues to be secretly practiced in many modern-day spiritual traditions, though, as one would expect, not openly talked about.

Sex magick literally means using your sexuality and erogenous body as a tool of magick and manifestation, but also as a form of worship and evocation. In ancient times, it was not surprising to have Temple Priestesses dedicated solely to this very powerful form of worship. Deities that were known to bless their worshippers with love and fertility attributes, like the Greek Goddess of Love, Aphrodite, had elaborate, well-known temples. These distinguished temples had designated Priestesses, whose job was to perform sex magick as a form of sacred offering and worship to the Goddess herself.

Since the earliest of times, sex and the climactic reach of an orgasm was/is universally recognized as a powerful, spiritual experience, closely akin to life, death and nirvana. The pleasurable transcendence moment of an orgasm was viewed as sacred and a gift from the Gods. It was not inconceivable to connect the experience of ecstatic sex with spiritual ecstasy, which often produced the same elevated levels of euphoria. Sex connects us to the primordial creative principal of life. By its very nature it connects humanity to three very significant components to our existence; it connects us to our human physical form, our spiritual and our primal aspects.

In many early spiritual traditions, sex was recognized as a portal for Divine communion, spiritual enlightenment and comingling of spiritual forces. All sexual orgasms begin with a tiny pivotal point of renunciation that feels like death and spiritual ascension before the completion of a climax.  In many other cultures but more specifically, France, an orgasm itself is sometimes called *"le petite mort"* (little death), for indeed there is an element of death, surrenderment and spiritual ascension within each climax.

Sex and all the fluids related to sexuality were closely linked with life force, creative energy, health, and fecundity. Blessing the land with the sacred act of sex and the pouring of our sexual essence unto our home soil was eventually viewed as a necessary ritualized act.  As sex magick was considered both, a sacred form of worship, and an offering to the Gods, it would not be surprising to see it being frequently employed in fertility and Harvest rites. As a form of sympathetic magick, the act of sex and the sacred fluids connected with arousal and fecundity would've been considered compulsory to a successful fertile harvest.  In Agrarian times, this form of magick was often used to petition the Gods and guarantee a prosperous crop. Whether in intimate partnership or in large group rituals, frolicking amidst the growing harvest was encouraged to assure a bountiful harvest upon the land. These beliefs and ancient rites continued throughout the ages, influencing new forms of worship and traditions that can still be recognized today. Just consider our traditional Beltane Wiccan sabbat celebrations and how one is encouraged to frolic upon the land and express love openly towards one another. The Maypole, a large phallic symbol, is venerated at the center of our joyful, ribbon-held spiral dancing. And at most Beltane celebrations there is indeed an ecstatic, sexual energy in the air.

Indigenous cultures and various forms of spiritual traditions believe that the pivotal point of climax creates such a powerful energetic field that this energy can be harnessed and used to heal and manifest your heart's desire. The orgasm is considered the pivotal moment when the gates of heaven open up. Aleister Crowley's famous declaration that, *"love is the law..."* and it alludes to sex magick and the power of uniting opposite forces; masculine and feminine, ying and yang, active and receptive, to harnessed our powers of manifestation. Much energy can indeed be raised during the act of sex and it is a perfect time to practice visualization, positive affirmations and become really focused on the pleasure senses, but also that which we wish to manifest. Typically, the very process of an orgasm can open up your chakras and invite a comingling of energies with your partner and the Divine.

For some, the practice of sex magick can be more spiritually potent than ceremonial magick. For one thing it can produce overpowering levels of ecstasy and physical pleasure and it requires no previous knowledge, eloquent invocations nor special hierarchical training. It uses your natural physical body and your inherited strong sexual impulse, which is akin to your creative life force.  During sexual arousal an enormous amount of energy can be channeled from our root chakra and genitalia, upward to travel all along the spine, to the top of our crown chakra. The study of Kundalini snake energy can be explored and utilized, when practicing sex magick, for greater wisdom in this realm.

The modern day principle for sex magick is really quite simple. It is believed that the drive, primal impulse and climactic energy so palpable during an orgasm, is a most powerful energy that can be harnessed and redirected for our intended purpose. In traditional magick we raise a certain amount of energy with the intention of applying it towards a desired result, vision, goal or personal manifestation. There is a plethora of ways to raise energy but once it is raised and tapped into we can then re-direct it with our intention and pour it into our desired outcome. For example, if you consciously begin the sexual experience with a particular goal in mind or something that you hope to manifest (it can be anything like a new job, good health or a better harvest) the premise is that you would have this clearly anchored in your mind's eye, and release it at the very point of a climax. Clearly this is a simple, natural, most potent, ancient form of magick that can be customized with your particular preferences.

Sex magick can be practiced alone, with a willing partner or it can also be practiced in groups. Whichever path you personally choose to take, please consider respectfully that this is an honored ancient tradition, not to be entered into lightly. It is not a license to start involving yourself or others, into life threatening, risky, degrading situations. Be conscious of what you are doing and have proper intentions and safety protocols in place before engaging in this form of magick. It should go without saying that in an era of sexually transmitted diseases and H.I.V/A.I.D.S. one should always take proper precaution, use common sense, and not take unnecessary risks. A word of warning should also be mentioned here; you should never be manipulated or cohorts into engaging in this kind of magick and neither should you manipulate anyone into this type of spiritual practice, especially without their knowledge or consent. This is clearly only for mature, consenting adults and only for the intended purpose, as agreed upon by the parties involved. I cannot stress enough the necessity for only consenting adults to engage in this type of tradition. It is also assume that the reader of this book has the maturity to choose and act according to their own free will and not surrender their rights or common sense to any author, including myself. That being said, I assume no responsibility for your actions and share this information with only the best of intention. There are some that would encourage practicing this type of magick on yourself, first and foremost, before ever involving others and I would have to agree; self-stimulation is the best way to begin exploring this realm, that is, if it's something you choose to explore.

To begin this form of magick, one should prepare the space and the physical body; understandably this preparation process can look very differently for each individual. Cleansing and preparing your physical body means, not only physically removing dirt and grime from your body with soap and water, but also entails psychically clearing yourself with consecrated salt water, oils, crystals, gemstone or a smudge wand. Again, you can use your intuition to deem what feels best. As with any sacred act or ritual, you may wish to create a special altar or have images and symbols that connote the sacredness of this event. You may have candles, flowers, scented oil and incense smoke in the consecrated space. You may also include symbols, sigils, photos or images that are relevant to your particular wish on display, to help facilitate the process of focusing your magick.  It is a matter of preference, but you may also wish to play soft music in the background; tribal drums, rock and roll, Gregorian chant, Celtic flutes, or any type of music that feels most appropriate to you, to set the mood.  At some point you may want to cast a circle in the traditional manner or simply visualize a protective shield encompassing you, the working ritual space and your partner.  If you are doing this with a partner you might want to take a moment to sit quietly, relax, gaze into each other's eyes and slowly breathe in and out together, to eventually synchronize your breathing. In a group setting situation it is important to establish trust and openness. You will need to establish consensus and set boundaries and rules that all involved are in agreement with, before anything can transpire.  In a group setting you would begin by holding hands and casting a sacred circle around the room first, as you do tantric breath work together. Doing synchronized breathing as a group and offering a trance meditation can also help establish a positive environment for all.

    As with any form of magick, we set an intention and have a clear picture in our mind's eye of this goal manifested.  We begin with this thought clearly anchored in our mind. You can create a positive affirmation or a simple word that you will repeat continually to help your subconscious mind connect to the intent of this sacred act.  As you are fully focused and engaged in the process, you are encouraged to send up energy from your genitals to your crown chakra.  Feel the energy rise in your Kundalini, as you repeat your chosen affirmation during the process. Your head or crown-chakra should feel like a chalice or a Lotus opening and receptive.  At the point of climax release your wish and see it fulfilled. Remember that our sexual fluids also have great power that can be used for several purposes. If your wish was connected to prosperity you may want to dab your sexual essence onto your wallet or currency. You can wipe some of it on an amulet or talisman to super charge them.  You can also bless your poppets, plackets or altar tools and if there are no sexually transmitted diseases, you may even use your sexual fluids to create an elixir or combine it with mead, wine or food.

    Today, in various spiritual traditions, Sex magick is still valued and discreetly practiced as a form of magick, evocation and potent form of worship.  It is still venerated as a powerful tool of manifestation that continues an honored, longstanding tradition established by our ancestor. As this book aims to explore different forms of techniques and spiritual practices that can help us personally revamp our lives and enhance our powers of manifestation, it only seems appropriate to include it here, especially in a chapter exploring our body's magick.  Not to mention the support for the obvious benefit and positive contribution a healthy sex life can have on our holistic wellbeing. Sex magick awakens us to the natural powers available to us through our physical bodies and it is yet another potentially wonderful tool of magick to explore.

# MUDRAS

Mudra is a Sanskrit word, meaning "seal." Mudras are sacred hand, fingers and body gestures that are used to affect the healthy flow of Prana- the breath and life force. Often used in conjunction with yogic breathing exercises and mantras, mudras can be used with meditation and chakra works, to harmonize Prana energy. There are numerous poses documented in various sources, but for our work here we will limit it to the few mentioned below.

## THE ELEMENTS & PLANETS REPRESENTED BY OUR FIVE FINGERS

Left hand gives and it represents the Moon. It relates to the feminine. Your Right hand receives and it represents the Sun, relates to the masculine. Each finger represents a planetary influence and elements. Below is a helpful chart with pertinent information regarding Mudra creations.

| **Thumb** | **Ruled by Fire** | **Mars** | **God self, positive ego** |
|---|---|---|---|
| **Index finger** | **Ruled by Air** | **Jupiter** | **Wisdom & expansion** |
| **Middle finger** | **Ruled by Spirit** | **Saturn** | **Devotion & patience** |
| **Ring finger** | **Ruled by Earth** | **Sun / Venus** | **Grace & Beauty** |
| **Little finger** | **Ruled by Water** | **Mercury** | **Communications** |

**Gyan Mudra,** is achieved by joining the tip of your index finger and your thumb, while holding up the other three fingers joined. This is believed to impart happiness, sharpens memory and intellectual development.

**Apaan Mudra,** is created by joining the tip of your middle and ring finger to the tip of your thumb, while holding the other remaining fingers straight. This is believed to reduce constipation and helps your body release waste.

**Prana Mudra,** is done by pressing the tip of your thumb with the tip of your pinky/little finger and your ring finger, while simultaneously holding the remaining fingers straight. This Mudra helps distribute life force energy throughout your body and is believed to help with your vision.

**Prithvi Mudra,** is achieved by joining the tip of your thumb with the tip of your ring finger, while holding the remaining finger straight. This Mudra is believed to impart happiness and a stronger body.

**Ling Mudra,** involves interlocking the fingers of both hands together and keeping the left thumb up while the right thumb encircles, around the left thumb. It is believed to produce heat in your body and help cure coughs and cold ailments.

**Mudra for Love,** bend and curl down ring finger and middle finger together towards the center of your palm, let thumb hold it there, extend all other fingers upward. Sit up straight and keep elbows up, breathe. Connect your thoughts to the feeling of love. Think of all the thing you love and raise positive energy as you expand this positive feeling and share it with the world.

**Divine Worship Mudra** place palms of our hands together, each fingertip touching uniting both hands, raise hands in front of your heart chakra. Breathe, relax and focus on your third eye.

**Yoni Mudra,** clasp hands together interlocking the fingers and then open slightly, allowing the tips of thumbs and index fingers of both respective hands to unite, pointing index outwardly, away from body, while the other fingers are weaved together. Let the tips of the thumbs and index fingers create diamond like shape. This mudra protects you.

# STONE WORKS, GEMSTONES AND CRYSTALS

Gemstones, and more specifically crystals, are known as vibrational amplifiers. They retain and disseminate important evolutionary knowledge of long ago and facilitate our own spiritual growth. Those that work with the sacred energy of the earth and are in the Holistic healing profession often use gemstones to help their clients in various ways. This chapter offers helpful information on the plethora of gemstones we can incorporate in our own personal spiritual practice.

# GEMSTONES

## 1. ROOT CHAKRA

**Bloodstone** is a type of opaque, green colored, quartz. It is known also as Heliotrope. It is dark green with tiny flecks of red, which symbolizes blood, hence the name. There are some gem folklores connecting it to the crucifixion and the blood that possibly splattered on the ground to create this stone. It is clear from this tale alone; the stone is highly linked with blood, vitality and life-force. Most gemstone literature asserts that Bloodstone is a known blood purifier and was believed to detoxify the spleen, liver and kidneys. It was also beneficial to other parts of the body like the heart and the reproductive system. Healers use it to remove energy blocks and treat different types of blood disorders. Bloodstone is best known for its gift of strength and increasing courage to its wearer. In ancient times it was believed to be a powerful, protective stone that removed all obstacles and kept its wearer safe, thus it could always be found on the breastplates of warriors before going into battle. In ancient Egypt, Bloodstone was used for tumors and abnormal growths and it was believed to bring blessings of auspicious strength. Soldier believed it could help stop bleeding and stimulate fearlessness, thus, it became known as, *"The Hero's Stone."* Bloodstone is a grounding stone that balances our root chakra, with an affinity to the element of earth. It is reputed to bring abundance and success to its wearer and was known to strengthen all relations. Today it can also be used to help build successful enterprises, invite more prosperity into our life, and help us conquer all fears of the unknown.

**Brecciated Jasper** is also a good stone to help with negative energy. Known as a stone to encourage creativity, it is also particularly effective to help in communications with animals. It is a stone that promotes good health and helps one recover from illnesses quicker. It is an excellent stone to explore issues related to our root chakra.

**Hematite** is a grey-silver colored, iron based stone. It is a magnetic stone used for numerous purposes. It helps to ground energy and can also be used to manifest and attract something towards you. It is known as a blood purifier and therefore used for healing. It helps to eliminate confusion, indecisiveness, that airy-spacy feeling and increases personal magnetism. It is best known as an effective stone for grounding oneself, especially after a deep trance and ritual work.

**Jet** is a gemstone believed to be first mined, as early as the 1500s. Much like many other ancient stones, it was used for numerous ceremonial tools and garments. In ancient times it was also used for rosary beads. Jet is a well-known healing stone, typically used to absorb and transmute negativity.

**Obsidian** is a highly revered stone used by Mayans and numerous other indigenous cultures as a warrior's stone, to empower ceremonial tools & garments. It is known to wards off negativity and blesses its wearer with strength and protection from negativity.

**Onyx** is known as a stone of protection, it is a Black opaque stone that transmutes negative energy. It is a stone that helps with our willpower, strength and discipline. It is best used for defensive magick and it is even reputed for lessening sexual desires. The planets Mars and Saturn rule over Onyx and it is connected with the element of earth and fire.

**Rainbow Obsidian** is a beautiful dark stone with hints of iridescent rainbow sparkles within its initial dark appearance. It is a highly protective stone to ward of negativity and guards the wearer. It deflects energy that is not in alignment with who you are and keeps you safe from psychic attacks.

**Red Coral** is known as the Garden of the Sea. It is a stone created naturally from the accumulated skeletal masses from the once living sea polyp organisms. We are focusing here on the red corals but they can be found in other hues. In ancient times there was a belief that our beloved red planet, Mars, was composed of red coral. Today it is an excellent stone to help us visualize and unearth our motivation and personal sense of direction. Red Coral symbolizes life and blood force energy and makes an excellent stone for our root chakra. It is reputed to cure sterility, lethargy and depression. It was believed to prevent illnesses and, if kept in the home, it protects the house from theft or lightning storms. Years ago it was worn around the neck to help with skin disorders and it was also given to malnutrition children to help them balance any nutritional deficiencies. The red coral was grounded up and made into a fine powder, then mixed and served in a liquid, like honey or milk. It was believed to stimulate the digestive system, heal and nourish blood cells and regenerate our body tissues. Red Coral incites potent passions, ambition and strong powerful emotions. Interestingly enough, the gemstone displays a lot of the attributes it shares with its planet of affiliation, Mars. It can encourage, within the wearer, anger, determination, stamina, independence and great strength. It facilitates the attainment and transfer of new knowledge and can bring honor, success and fame.

**Red Jasper** is a stone of endurance, courage and promotes authenticity. It helps absorb negative energy and lends protection to its wearer. It balances yin and yang energy and helps to re-energize the body. As a red gemstone it works best to stimulate our root chakra.

**Smokey Quartz** is a highly protective stone that transmutes negative energy; it is a crystal quartz that can be found in different shades of translucent brown and greys, possibly due to carbon, iron, titanium impurities or decaying radium within the crystal itself. Smokey Quartz is therefore a good stone for those exposed to radiation or chemotherapy treatment. Traditionally it was a stone used for scrying, crystal gazing and the psychic arts. Connected to the root chakra, it has the capacity to bring wisdom and financial success. It helps you balance and prioritize things in your life to reach your most cherished personal or career goals. It also encourages inner strength, stamina and courage.

It is considered a highly protective stone that acts as a physical and psychic shield. It enhances organizational skills and our receptiveness to acquire new knowledge. Placed around a workplace or home, it can foster cooperative feelings from the group and neutralize the energy. This grounding stone is linked with the astrological signs of Capricorn and Sagittarius and it is known to help with insomnia, hyperactivity, depression, stress, jealousy and anger. Smokey Quartz is used to cleanse auras and has the unique ability to connect us with prophetic sounds, including telepathic resonances. It is also reputed to connect one with the sacred reverberations of the Universe.

**Snowflake Obsidian** is a black gemstone with white flecks scattered upon it resembling the first snowfall on the ground. It is quite pretty and has the ability to connect us with information regarding our ancestors or past lives. It is a stone of perseverance and insight and facilitates connections to our spirit guides. It has an affinity with the element of earth.

## 2. SACRAL CHAKRA

**Carnelian** is an orange to red colored Agate (chalcedony) stone. It is a powerful, fiery stone that excites and helps one attain good health and vitality. It has an affinity with the Sun and the element of Fire and thus, it is a stone that inspires creativity. It is quite the motivating stone that helps stir ambition and the self-confidence to get things done. The gemstone, Carnelian, has long been associated with courage and it is believed warriors, in ancient times, would wear it upon their breastplates before going into battles to assure their success and bravery. It is a stone reputed to keep evil away. It is also alleged to strengthen the voice of the timid and weak. This stone is known to help the reproductive organs and therefore it is seen as the magick stone of fertility. It is an ideal stone for large families and groups settings because it helps stimulate a cooperative, joyful energy among groups. Known as the radiant stone to inspire and motivate its wearer, it can help manifest great creative achievements and financial success.

**Sunstone** is a dark to light orange colored stone that helps stimulate the sacral chakra. It is related to masculine energy and it is ruled by the sun. Naturally, it is affiliated with the element of fire and it is a wonderful stone to explore your sacral chakra. It emits warm energy and encourages good health and vitality. This stone helps the wearer tap into their ambition and also has a protective quality regarding health and safe pregnancies. It is an excellent stone to help you develop better leadership skills and unearth the courage to move forward. It is also reputed for igniting and balancing sexual desires.

## 3. SOLAR CHAKRA

**Amber** (resin), though it is not technically a gemstone, it is an amazing resin worth mentioning. It is a tree sap that has gathered and hardened naturally over the years, sometimes thousands and thousands of years, to create a beautiful resin. It can have many interesting inclusions in the stone; from herbs & flowers to various different insects, mummified, trapped naturally while forming itself. Its softness makes it an ideal stone for carvings and ornamentations but it is also burned as a sacred incense. There are many color variations; from translucent orange to honey or opaque yellow. It is ruled by the sun and the element of earth and fire. Amber emits warmth and a protective quality to its wearer. It is known to transmute negative energy into positive and it is one of the most beloved stones for priestesses, shamans and healers to work with.

**Citrine** is one of the best, all-around, beneficial gemstones you can work with. It can be found in different shades of translucent dark or light yellow. As you can imagine just by looking at it, it is closely linked with the Sun and the element of fire. It promotes confidence, joy, prosperity, accolades and helps attracts good friends. As a solar gemstone it exudes a positive warm energy that supports optimism, wellbeing, good fortune and inevitable success. Not surprising, it was also known as the lucky, "Merchant-stone," reputed to bring prosperity to businesses that kept citrine near their cash registers. It was also known as the, *"Stone of the Mind,"* and helps to promotes willpower, while clarifying and magnifying personal power and energy. Citrine helps relieve depression and heal digestive disorders. This makes it an ideal stone for healers working with the third chakra. It increases creativity and honesty and helps to eliminate fears of being judged by others, which is a personality trait most creative artist desire. Citrine is known to eliminate negativity but, unlike other stones, it does not absorb negativity from its surroundings, it simply transmutes it. This gives Citrine the very unique attribute of never needing to be energetically cleaned or cleared. It is able to regenerate and restore itself, autonomously. This is an interesting attribute that its wearer can explore further, as well.

**Orange Calcite** exists in abundance, for us to easily acquire nowadays. It is also fairly inexpensive. It is a highly energized stone traditionally used for mental clarity and to elevate one's general disposition. This sunny stone is well-known among healers due to its bright hue and its solar connection. It enhances trance meditation practices as well as astral projection and it is quite easy to work with. It is a cleansing stone, used to dissolve obstacles, fears, depression and health issues related to excessive mucus. As a calcite, related to calcium, many athletes affirm the benefits of using this stone for joints and bone health. It can also bring healing to our reproductive system, enhances creativity and balances our sexuality. It helps those trying to acquire more wisdom from research, reading material and it is known to help discouraged children fair better, with scholastic challenges. Orange Calcite is also reputed to help further develop our memory. Due to its powerful optimistic energy, it is a stone that eliminates phobias and emits joy and vitality.

**Tigers Eye** is a superb grounding gemstone of protection that enhances integrity, confidence, good fortune and strong will-power. It is a quartz stone, found in varying shades of light and dark brown. Sometimes referred to as, "Cats Eye," due to its appearance of a cat's pupil, it is reputed to help remove illusions, bring clarity and connect us with the proper use of power. It also has the ability to help us unearth, embrace and apply our hidden talents in a way that best serves our highest purpose.

Tiger's Eye is known to promote wealth, happy travels and enhance good luck. There is also a belief that Tiger's Eye can bring to you just the right kinds of helpful people, at just the right time, thus, it is a most auspicious gemstone to work with. It has an obvious affinity to the element of earth.

**Yellow Jade** is a yellow opaque colored gemstone with a positive solar energy. It promotes personal growth, vitality and an optimistic perspective. Healers work with its peaceful energy to build self-confidence, help with self-expression and promote balanced digestive system.

**Yellow Jasper** is a bright solar stone that benefits your endocrine glands. It is known as an emotional energizer. It gives you physical energy, which has a positive effect on our mental and emotional health. It is related to the third chakra, our Solar plexus, and helps us explore self-expression, while connecting us to our regenerative gifts. It also helps relieve stomach bloating and soothes digestive disorders.

## 4. HEART CHAKRA
**Amazonite** is a pretty green microline feldspar stone that promotes balance and peace. It is linked with the heart and throat chakra and it is known to soothe the mind. An excellent stone for those with nervous disorders and temperamental issues, it is a healing stone. It is also reputed to help with menstrual symptoms. There are some mysteries related to its name but some believe this gemstone is named after the Amazon River and the Amazons; warrior women that worshipped the Maiden Goddess of the Moon, Artemis. This stone is therefore often associated with balancing masculine and feminine energies and connecting with our true heart's calling.

**Aventurine** is a gentle, greenish colored quartz stone that promotes peace. Known as an emotional balancer, it transmutes negativity and soothes any hurt or emotional discomfort. It is intrinsically connected with opening and healing the heart chakra. It aligns the body, mind and spirit and facilitates the expression of love. Aventurine promotes wellbeing and helps with emotional and mental blocks. Used as a talisman for extra luck with lottery and gambling transactions, it is reputed to improve one's eyesight. It also has an affinity to the elements of water and earth.

**Kunzite** is a highly vibrational stone of love. It can be found in varying shades of pretty pinks and its color is attributed to the magnese and the high content of lithium. Lithium, is important to note, has been studied and used extensively for psychiatric disorders, which only adds to the healing quality of Kunzite. It is a gemstone that awakens the heart center and promotes self-tolerance and respect for others. Kunzite, in recent years, has also been embraced by the drug and alcohol addiction community, as a helpful stone to encourage personal sobriety. This pretty pink stone is known to help gently soothe away stress, anxiety and panic attacks. As a conduit for Universal love, it helps you face challenges with grace and ease. Regarding physical health, Kunzite is a wonderful stone that is known for balancing the thyroid glands, women's hormones and assisting with muscle and nerve conditions. It has the ability to stimulate the immune system to attain healing. Kunzite is a gentle stone that helps you face life's challenges, while emitting the cathartic, great powers of self-love.

**Peridot** is a beautiful olive to lime green stone that draws its color from the amount of iron it contains. It is esteemed throughout history by numerous different cultures. The Inca civilization used it for its ability to help clear the mind. Egyptian priests drank out of chalices bedecked in its brilliant jewel and it was believed to promote wealth and power to the wearer, as well as ward off nightmares and jealousy. It was sacred to the Egyptian Goddess, Isis, as well. Ancient soldiers wore peridot on their breastplates before going into battle. In Hawaii, this gemstone is believed to represent the tears of the highly venerated, Polynesian Volcanic Goddess, Pele. To the ancient Greeks, peridot was known as, "Midnight Emerald." And, interesting to note, Napoleon Bonaparte presented his love, Josephine, with a peridot ring as a symbol of his undying love. Peridot is a beautiful stone that emits high vibration of peace and love and endeavors to dispel negativity. Among its numerous purported attributes, it helps promote the balance of polar opposites in life, by integrating emotions and logic; body, mind and spirit. It is known to inspire higher levels of consciousness and dispel maladies and negativity. A beautiful grounding stone that represents the beauty of the earth and reminds us to bring balance into our lives; it is a much desired, benevolent gemstone. Its greenish hue reflects attributes of friendliness, love, healing, purity, simplicity and wellbeing. It is traditionally used for healing the heart, the spleen, lungs, liver and the digestive tract. Peridot is also related to the attainment of wisdom and knowledge, and the intricate learning process, for those who have difficulties with perseverance and concentration. It offers the power to stay keenly focused on learning and thus, it is perfect for those who are involved in the academic field. Peridot is connected with the heart chakra due to its deep lime green hue and it is known to help resolve relationship conflicts.

**Rhodonite** is a gemstone found in varying shades of pink with black vein-like patterns. It is a love gemstone that promotes generosity, compassion, altruism, peace and dispels confusion. It is even reputed in helping trauma victims. Rhodonite is connected with the elements of fire and earth, and the planet Mars. It is connected with auditory blessings as well. With the gemstone, rhodonite, we unearth our hidden talents and nurture our gifts.

**Rose Quartz** is probably one of the most well-known gemstones for issues related to our heart and our emotions. It is recognized as a gemstone that helps soothe and heal a broken heart. It is a pink quartz known as the gentle love stone, for its ability to console the heart, remove negativity and heal emotional wounds. It is known to return the wearer to Self-love and can also help attract positive, beneficial friendships. It is reputed for helping the actual heart, circulatory system and reproductive organs. It helps to shift and uplift vibrations and connects us with our true emotions. Rose Quartz has also been used as an elixir to reduce wrinkles on the skin and maintain a youthful appearance. When used in romantic spell workings, it is reputed to bring a higher soul-mate connection.

**Serpentine** is considered a new type of Jade. It is can be found in subtle varying shades of light and dark olive green. It is a gemstone of peace. As a heart-chakra gemstone, it helps with fidelity, peace, compassion, love and the realization of one's true potential. It emits a calming energy and supports positive experiences during trance meditations. Placed under the pillow, it can help with dreams but also, aid a woman's sexual climax. It is known to help nursing mothers produce more milk and can ease menstrual symptoms, thus making it a wonderful gemstone for women to explore further. It is ruled by the planet Saturn and the element of fire and it promotes resourcefulness, prosperity and the gift of attracting happy clients & customers for your business.

**Unakite** is a beautiful green and salmon colored stone, a variation of Jasper. It is a highly spiritual stone that helps to induce psychic visions. It is thus, a stone that can connect you to the gifts of the psychic third eye and also your heart chakra. It is a very protective gemstone ruled by the planets, Mars and Venus. Unakite also has an affinity to the elements of Fire and Water. It is known to dispel depression and negativity, and it helps one to unearth and process, the experiences from the past. It really helps you to integrate body, mind and spirit, and helps one find the spiritual roots of physical maladies. Unakite can help increase body weight and works as an excellent sleep aid. It is a known balancer of emotions and it is purported to help with addiction concerns as well.

## 5. THROAT CHAKRA
**Azurite** is very similar to Chrysocolla. It is a greenish-blue healing stone from the copper family. It has a long history of inspiring creativity and cultivating discipline. It emits feelings of peace, patience, compassion and it is known as a balancer of emotions. Azurite also helps with dreams and supports healing and throat chakra blessings.

**Chrysocolla** is a beautiful greenish-blue healing stone. It is a coppery gemstone, much like Azurite and Malachite; it will reflect tiny specks of copper within its make-up. It was believed to be, first mined in the legendary mines of King Solomon, in ancient Egypt. During this time it was also considered a special gemstone that imparted great wisdom. Chrysocolla is highly valued by Native Americans and numerous other cultures, across the ages. One story tells us that Cleopatra allegedly carried a piece of Chrysocolla with her, at all times, believing it was necessary to help her with creating innovative strategies, when dealing with opposing diplomatic relations. It is known as a highly creative stone that inspires new ideas and blesses ones throat chakra. The lovely, greenish-blue stone, therefore, becomes a desired gemstone for singers, public speakers and coaches, orators and teachers. It also helps one remain calm in the midst of a chaotic situation and

Chrysocolla is known to dispel nervousness; allowing one to remain neutral in the face of instability.

The name comes from the Greek word, which means gold (*chrysos*) and glue (*kola*). In ancient times, smiths used the greenish stone as a type of connecting glue with gold metal jewelry and thus, it attained its name. It has an affinity to Gemini and Taurus and the planets Venus and Mercury.

**Lapis Lazuli** is an exquisite, deep blue stone, with metal, gold-like brilliant flecks, better known as pyrite. Mined in Afghanistan, it is simply beautiful to behold the deep blue stone of Lapis Lazuli. As mentioned below, it can sometimes be wrongly confused with Sodalite, because they both have a similar appearance. Both however, are stones of wisdom, spirituality and enhanced mental capacity, due to their deep blue hue. They are both beloved stones of truth and blessed self-expression. For centuries, Lapis Lazuli has been a valued gemstone throughout numerous cultures. We only have to look at ancient Egyptian artifacts to see how often it was used in decorative and sacred object. In both Babylon and Egypt, the stone was well regarded. It was a beloved gemstone for the Egyptian Goddess of Love, Hathor and the Goddess of Truth and Justice, Ma'at. Egyptian priests were purported to have worn necklaces around their neck, with a replica figure of the Goddess Ma'at, sculpted out of Lapis Lazuli. And much like Malachite, Egyptians would ground up Lapis Lazuli into a fine powder and mix it to be used as an early form of cosmetics. In Israel, we find Lapis Lazuli among other stones, set upon the breastplates of priests and soldiers- it is clear this was a highly desired and respected gemstone. Its most notable characteristics are; its ability to stimulate the mind, promote clarity, spiritual purity and deep studious concentration. Known as the "*Stone of Enlightenment*," it boasts the ability to connect the wearer with higher levels of consciousness. It is a thought-amplifier that can facilitate self-knowledge and deeper levels of awareness. Lapis lazuli is reputed to support the throat, lungs and the nervous system. It can also help with reproductive issues and it's known to be a powerful healer to boost overall health and immune system. Like bloodstone, it shares the gift of being a blood purifier and it is an igniter of life force. It has an affinity to the element of water and the planet Venus.

**Malachite** is a stone that can be found in varying subtle shades of dark and light green. It is one of the ores of copper and can be found in combination with other stones like Azurite. It has a long history of being prized and used as a talisman to repel evil throughout the ages. In Italy, malachite is used to protect against the evil eye. For the Egyptians, malachite was sacred to the Goddess Hathor and used in numerous ceremonial tools of magick. It was also grounded up into a fine powder and converted into a cosmetic, to be used as eye makeup. Babies were protected from negative forces with this gemstone nearby, according to several cultural folktales. Malachite has an affinity with the planet Venus and the astrological sign of Scorpio. The elements of earth and water are aligned with Malachite. It is reputed to help with the reproductive organs, as well as help in fighting mental illnesses. Known as a stone of transformation, it can assist in vision quest and promote loyalty, love and good friendships. There is one important thing to keep in mind when working with the stone of malachite. Its very nature is one of amplification, and thus, it can amplify negativity, if the wearer tends to be negative or the space is entrenched in negativity. Happily, the opposite is true, when there is positive energy, this too, can be amplified by this beautiful green gemstone.

**Sodalite** is considered the gemstone of truth. It is reputed to open up the channels for honest communication. It protects and blesses the throat chakra as a vehicle for this expression of truth. It dispels negativity, illusions and deception and promotes logic, intellect and rational. It is considered especially good for writers and all expressive artists. Sodalite is also known as the, "*Stone of the Poet*," due to this particular attribute. It is named for its high sodium content and its Latin name is "*sodanu*m." The interpretation of its Latin name is, "*a cure for headache*," thus, we can only surmise, this is an excellent stone to use for chronic migraines. It also helps to overcome calcium deficiencies and it's reputed to prevent insomnia. Sodalite also promotes metabolic balance and healing to our thyroid glands and any throat maladies. It works favorably with both writers and athletes, as it stimulates stamina, self-esteem and self-trust. Sodalite is a beautiful, deep blue stone, often wrongly confused with lapis lazuli. It is however, more economical than Lapis Lazuli. The difference between these two, deep blue, stones is that Sodalite will sometimes have milky, white veining patterns and Lapis lazuli typically has subtle pyrite/copper/gold/ metal flecks; not to mention the price difference in these two gemstones. Sodalite helps you to have access to your subconscious and intuitive abilities. It is known to enhance mental performance, deepen intuitive gifts and expand our third eye, psychic gifts. Sodalite is ruled by the Moon and it has an affinity to the elements of water and air.

**Turquoise** is a beloved ancient gemstone for healers. It promotes love, friendship, good fortune, prosperity and wellbeing. It is a protective stone that dispels chaos and negativity. Cherished and used by numerous cultures, including Native American tribes, it is respected as a beautiful stone for self-realization. It is a highly intuitive gemstone, used by many in various ways. It awakens creativity and connects us to the element of the earth and the planet Venus and Neptune.

## 6. THIRD EYE CHAKRA
**Amethyst** is the well-known stone of Spiritual enlightenment and psychic awareness. It is a violet-purple colored quartz crystal, often used in metaphysical spiritual practices. Used to facilitate trance in meditations, it is also a companion stone for those practicing divination or oracle/tarot readings. Interesting to note, it is reputed to help lessen addictive habits and can help prevent hangovers. Amethyst opens your mental capacities and helps you attain clarity. When placed under your pillow it can also help with insomnia.

**Moonstone** is a milky white, sometimes peachy opalescent colored stone with an affinity to the Moon. It is therefore an emotionally balancing stone that heightens our psychic abilities and blesses women. In particular, Moonstone supports with fertility & menstrual symptoms. Moonstone is believed to promote calmness and peace to the overly emotional and helps facilitate communication with the subconscious mind. Our direction and sense of purpose is clearer with moonstone and we are ready to embark on new spiritual journeys. Moonstone is reputed to help the body eliminate toxins, improve the digestive system and can also be used to treat hair, eye and skin disorders. In India, moonstone is a highly regarded gemstone, connected with the Goddess. It emits a beautiful peaceful, harmonious energy and enhances our connection to the moon, as women. It stimulates our psychic tendencies and connects us to the value of all the precious cycles held in our lifetime.

**Sugalite** is a rare and fairly new discovered gemstone. It is found only in a few places in the world, like Australia, India, Italy, Japan, Wales and South Africa and it can be a pricey gemstone. In its most raw form, it resembles turquoise and thus, it initially became known as "*purple turquoise.*" Interesting to note, it shares similarities to Jasper and very often, a purple dyed jasper, is passed off as an authentic Sugalite stone, unbeknownst to the novice. It is a highly desirable gemstone for its powerful protective qualities and it high vibration. It is considered a love stone that emits a potent harmonious energy, connecting us to higher levels of consciousness. It dispels negativity and helps to bring balance to our significant partnerships. As a protective stone, it helps you to disconnect to those things, and people, that are not in alignment with your highest good. It can also help the wearer face drastic changes with grace and ease. Sugalite is known to dispel pain, gloom, despondency and hopelessness. And it helps shift your vibration to connect you to source. It protects the wearer from shock and trauma and helps with all types of transitions and transformations. Known as a stone of peace and harmony, it is purported to eliminate negative entities that may be causing trouble, in a home. With its intense beautiful, purple-violet hue, it is a gemstone known to enhance psychic and intuitive gifts and it is believed to help clarify our thoughts and balance emotions. This stone has an affinity to the benevolent planet, Jupiter and it is connected to the element of water. It can enrich your immune system, and, being a crown-chakra stone, it can support any mental challenges like; dyslexia or memory loss. It is truly a beautiful rare gemstone that helps to open up the channels of communication with our higher self. This stone is able to harmonize and bless our heart, crown and third-eye chakra, thus becoming a very desirable stone for most healers to work with.

## <u>7. CROWN CHAKRA</u>
**Clear Crystal Quartz** has been prized and used since the beginning of time by numerous cultures. Crystals have long been known for their ability to record, store and emit knowledge and energy, and thus, it is a perfect tool for spiritual healing (physical, mental and emotional healing as well). Because clear crystal quartz is alleged to have a similar

vibrational quality as humans, it is the ideal stone to work with for spiritual knowledge of our evolving species. It has the ability to transport and impart ancient esoteric knowledge to us, kinesthetically, and our understanding of the world is exponentially expanded by its very presence. It is an invaluable tool for spiritual growth and psychic development. The clear crystal quartz has the ability to amplify and transform our own energy. When we are feeling exhausted or scattered and confused, working with our crystal quartz can help bring us back to alignment and balance our energy. It is also a powerful tool to work with, when doing trance meditations. It allows one to connect with our higher consciousness and can facilitate channelings and communications with spirit guides. It can also be used in conjunction with our divination and oracular practices. As a purifier, we can transmute almost any negative energy with clear crystals. Clear crystal quartz, in particular, has the unique ability to amplify anything near it, more specifically; it can amplify and purify the attributes of nearby stones. Connected with the element of; air, fire, earth, and water and all the directions from; south, north, east and west, it can be used in conjunction with other stones when working with our chakras. It can also act as a substitute for any gemstone needed in chakra work. For those practicing magic and ritual spells, the use of clear crystal quartz is invaluable. It can enhance the potency of your herbs and spell works. We are able to cleanse, purify and psychically charge any item we wish, by simply pointing our crystal quartz to the object or by letting the object rest upon the clear crystal quartz. This can be anything; from a pendant, a special ring, a sachet or poppet, a wand or a candle, a piece of ribbon or head circlet, a piece of parchment paper or a writing pen etc… etc… Anything that you wish to clear, purify and psychically charged can be done with a clear crystal quartz on hand. It is important to note that clear quartz can help with chronic fatigue, arthritis, fibromyalgia, intestinal problems as well as a number of other ailments and disorders. It is reputed to give off physical and mental stamina and strength. Almost every culture throughout history has valued the clear crystal quartz. The ancient Greeks believed it was actually water from the heavens that was converted into **eternal ice** by the gods. The word crystal to the ancient Greeks was "*krystallos*" which means, ice. For the Australian aboriginals, crystals are closely linked to a substance called "*maban*," which they believe is where all wise shamans attain their magical powers. Native American tribes and the aborigines used clear crystals to invoke thunderstorms. It is one of the most common minerals found on the face of the earth and it can be found in all types of environments and all types of rocks; sedimentary metamorphic or Igneous. Although found in many areas of the world, it is still mainly attained through Africa, Brazil and the U.S.A.

**Charoite** is a beautiful, purple to violet, colored stone, with some indigo veining patterns adding to its beauty. It is a fairly new stone, alleged to be founded only in one region of the world; Siberia and Russia. It is a stone of high vibration, known to enhance one's psychic powers and opens up channels within the individual, to receive divine messages. It facilitates communications between spirit and our higher self. It balances our crown chakra and helps to ground and clear the energy of all chakras. This is why it is known as the "*soul-stone.*" Charoite is a very protective spiritual stone that dispels anger, negativity, fears and chaos. It can even help those struggling with migraines and obsessive-compulsive disorders. It is a stone with a high love frequency that helps promotes peace and harmony and supports those who are suffering with pain and major life transitions. If you feel like someone is draining your energy, this gemstone can intervene to help you better assess the situation and gain deeper rooted insight. It shields the wearer from psychic vampires and negativity, making it a perfect stone for naturally empathic individuals. It is a good gemstone to sleep with, under your pillow, to ensure deep sleep and prophetic dreams. It encourages lucid dreaming and helps to integrate both the head and the heart. Charoite has an affinity to the element of water and it is ruled by the planet of illusion and enlightenment, Neptune. It would come as no surprise then, that this prized gemstone is most connected with both the heart and crown chakra.

**Diamond** is known as one of the hardest substance in the world and is most sought after by the wedding industry. Its very nature absorbs and amplifies the thought of its user. It can also strengthen or weakened the attributes of any other gemstones nearby. Diamonds have also been used to help with detoxification.

**Labrodorite** is a beautiful iridescent gemstone, known to stimulate mental capacity. It is also reputed to relieve stress and anxiety and helps heal the digestive system. Known as the "*Temple of the Stars,*" it was traditionally used in the treatment of brain disorders.

**Selenite** is a very fragile gemstone that can easily be dissolved in water; therefore one must be very careful when handling this white stone. It is a very calming, peace generating stone that promotes reconciliation between lovers and emits a peaceful environment. It helps to inspire partnerships and form strong bonds of love. It is named after the Greek Goddess of the Moon, Selene, because of its specific moonlight glow quality. As a gemstone intricately connected with the moon, it is particularly beneficially for women to work with this stone. It stimulates fertility and increases the chances of motherhood. Selenite is reputed to unblock stagnant energy and allows one to see the inner truth. It promotes mental clarity and helps to improve communication skills. Selenite dispels fears and negativity and helps one see through lies and deception. It creates a peaceful atmosphere; conducive for trance meditation and it is considered a powerful psychic connector. It will help you connect with spirits and established a bond with your ancestors, angel guides, and loved ones. It can awaken you to your lineage and connection to past lives.

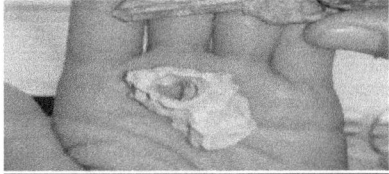

***Hag Stones are stones with a naturally formed hole clearly visible to the eye. They were viewed as portals and considered lucky. Often Hag stones are associated with magick and sorcery.

# CHAKRAS AND GEMSTONES

| NAME | LOCATION | COLOR | GODDESSES |
|---|---|---|---|
| **1st Chakra** | Base of Spine | Red/Brown/Blk | Kali/Pele/Gaia |

**MULADHARA/ROOT CHAKRA:** Fire Agate, Red Jasper, Onyx, Obsidian, Hematite, Garnet.

Security, physical existence, stability, the self, earth grounding, home, basic human needs, sexuality, it is considered the sex chakra for men.

| **2nd Chakra** | Yoni/Belly | Orange | Sheela-na-gig/Baubo |
|---|---|---|---|

**SAVADISTHANA/SACRAL CHAKRA:** Carnelian, Variegated Jasper, Tiger's Eye.

Sacral realm, sex chakra for women, womb, water realm, creative expression, self-worth, emotions, energy.

| **3rd Chakra** | Upper abdomen | Yellow | Amaterasu/Oshun |
|---|---|---|---|

**MANIPURA/NAVAL SOLAR PLEXUS CHAKRA:** Citrine, Yellow Topaz, Yellow Jasper, Peridot, Serpentine.

Ego, willpower, impulses, anger, personal Power, our strength, desire, Confidence, interactions with others, realm of fire,

| **4th Chakra** | Heart | Green/Pink | Aphrodite/Ix Chel |
|---|---|---|---|

**ANAHATA/HEART CHAKRA:** Kunzite, Morganite, Rose Quartz, Green Quartz, Howlite, moonstone, Aquamarine, Bloodstone.

Love, compassion, trust, relationships and community.

| **5th Chakra** | Throat | Blue | Saraswati/Hathor |
|---|---|---|---|

**VISUDDHA/THROAT CHAKRA:** Turquoise, Malachite, Chrysocolla, Lapis lazuli.

Speaking, Singing, eloquence of speech, speaking your truth, hearing and being heard, Creativity.

| **6th Chakra** | Third Eye | Purple/Indigo | Athena/Hekate |
|---|---|---|---|

**AJNA/THIRD EYE CHAKRA:** Sodalite, Lapis Lazuli, Amethyst.

Intuition and Psychic realm, Clarity and related to the Mind, Sight, Telepathy, Astral travels.

| **7th Chakra** | Crown/Head | White | Hestia/Kwan Yin |
|---|---|---|---|

**SAHASRARA/CROWN CHAKRA:** Quartz, Clear Crystals of various kinds, Single or double-terminated, rutilated crystal, Moonstone, Zircon.

Enlightenment, Ascension, Wisdom, Divine connection, integration, receiving Divine insight.

# ELEMENTAL WAYS TO CLEANSE AND CHARGE YOUR STONES

**EARTH:** Burying your gemstones and crystals in a bowl of salt or soil. You may use a potted Herbal plant like Sage or Rosemary and bury the gem inside the soil for a few days.

**WATER:** Running your gemstones and crystals in lukewarm water, then a cold water rise and sometimes using rose water.

**FIRE:** Using Solar rays, let your gemstones and crystals soak up the sun outdoors or by a windowsill. Let it soak up the strength of the mid-day Sun.

**AIR:** Smudging your gemstones and crystals with Copal and or a Sage Wand Bundle. Let the smoke of an incense swirl around your stones, as you hold it up into the swirling smoke.

**SPIRIT:** On the night of the Full Moon, let the light of the Moon permeate and fully charge your crystals and gemstones.

# CHAKRA MEDITATION

### 1st ROOT CHAKRA

We begin this Chakra healing meditation by first bringing our focus to our Root Chakra, located down below near our tail bone. Think upon where the Serpent neatly snugged is coiled up in your Kundalini region, the base of your spine. In your mind's eye now see a crimson red apple, an apple like the one we imagine Snow White received from the Old Crone in the famous, beloved Childhood fairy tale. Or better still; envision a red rose with all of its numerous veiny petals and the passion it often connotes. Notice this deep red color and now think upon our blood and how similar its color is to this apple and this crimson red rose.

Consider when we bleed; whether pricked by a needle, slashed by a kitchen knife or through the dark crimson blood of our monthly menstruation as women. See this pool of dark redness, lulling you back and forth into a trance, and allow your mind to delve into this deep red color. See this red now at the base of your spine, flowing back and forth like a Cabernet Sauvignon swishing in a contained large chalice... back and forth it swishes, reminding you of your vitality, reminding you of your life force... reminding you of your passion and your sacred womanhood. Life to death, death to rebirth.... Blood, crimson red blood.... this red is located in your Root chakra. It symbolizes life, the roots of your personal tree, the veins that transport vitality to your very being.  Open yourself up to its power at this moment. This is the gateway of the earth. It is the sacred gateway to your very birth and existence... Honor this Root Chakra now. (Pause)

### 2nd SACRAL CHAKRA

At this time I invite you to hold in the palm of your hands a tangerine... hold a bright ripe orange fruit, ready to be personally tasted by you. First however, before peeling it, notice the texture of this Orange in your hands. Notice its slight grainy skin and the vibrancy of its hue. Now, look down on the ground, by your feet, and see if you can spot the same hue on the fallen Autumnal leaves. Take a moment to trace with your mind's eye the many times the color orange asserts its presence in your life right now. What else do you see in this Orange hue and how does it make you feel? Continue to hold the Orange fruit, smell its spicy sweet scent and now begin to peel it. When it is peeled, hungrily place it in your mouth and taste it. Let its sweet tangy juices burst and dribble down the side of your lips, as you delight in its taste, and allow yourself to get sticky from its sweet nectar. It's okay if you get messy and it's okay to delight in its sweet taste. At this time you are being invited to tap into your aesthetic awareness, your pleasure markers and sensuality, which just might connect you to your sexuality; the realm of your Second Chakra. Bring this Orange hue, its juicy stickiness from its orgasmic spillage and its sweet scent, all to the sacred region above your genitalia. Spend a moment experiencing this vibrant hue of Orange through all of your senses while resting in your Sacral Chakra. Open yourself up to the gifts of a balanced Second Chakra as it invites you to explore your sensuality, your powers of fertility, the magick of your physical being and a balanced ego. Let it offer you its gift of optimism and creativity. It is the Gateway of the Moon, home of the self and home of your sweetness. Take a moment to honor the Sacral, Second chakra.

## 3rd **SOLAR PLEXUS**

As a child, when asked to color or paint a picture of our Sun, oftentimes we reached for the brightest Yellow crayon, or paint, to proceed to depict what we perceived to be the brightest star in our galaxy, the Sun. I invite you now to retrieve this picture you yourself might have created in your youth. Retrieve this image of the sun and allow yourself to even remember its warmth and piercing bright yellow light on a perfect summer's day. If you can, reflect on the cathartic powers of the bright yellow sun as you might have found yourself happily sunbathing on a beach or on a grassy fertile field. We are about to enter the Gateway of the Sun through our third chakra, our Solar Plexus. (Pause) Consider the joy and laughter the color yellow inspires you to feel. Contemplate for a moment, on the many positive attributes the Sun conjures in our memories; memories from our childhood, memories of running wild and free without many cares or concerns or fears. This yellow is a powerful confident hue and it spins like our very sun in your third chakra above your navel.

In your mind's eye see the Yellow Sun spinning vibrantly, awakening your self-confidence and exuding balance, strength and appropriate self-expression. See this solar yellow disk, spinning brightly above your navel area, under your chest. It is alive and this third chakra is a magnet for respect, confidence, popularity and positive recognition. Take a moment now to honor the Manipura, your known Third chakra, the Solar Plexus.

## 4th **HEART CHAKRA**

Bring your attention, if you will, to the middle of your chest. You may also wish to physically place your hands in this region. Feel the pulsation of your own heart now against the palm of your hands, beating in affirmation of your fertile existence. It is helping you transcend to the realm of emotions, this is Anahata. This is your heart Chakra…gateway to the winds. These gentle breezes stemming from this realm will carry you now to the season of spring. See yourself amidst a grove of bright green colored trees. As it is to be expected in the springtime, everything surrounding you takes on this bright, fertile green hue. The trees with their bulbous bushy green crowns, the tall blades of grass beneath your feet, the tiny leaves on a bouquet of roses, the various insects that cross your path at this time of year. They all share in this bright cathartic verdant hue, the color of your fourth Chakra. Let your eyes now wander, for a moment, as you spy numerous objects around you in this flourishing green hue. How does it make you feel? What emotions in your heart does it conjure up for you? Take this moment to see the vibrancy of this fertile green within your Heart chakra. This is the realm of unconditional love, altruism, empathy and great human compassion. As the green hue spins its doors of compassion wide open within you, see if you can detect how best to put this gift to good use in your own life. How different can your life be experienced with this chakra opened, healed and balanced? Can you offer your own self, the gift of compassion? Can you offer compassion to your perceived enemies? Take this calming moment to connect with your heart and honor your Fourth Chakra, the Anahata.

## 5th THROAT CHAKRA

Now I invite you to move your energy and focus from your heart to your throat region. This is Vishuddha (the Purifier) it is the Fifth Chakra also best known as your Throat Chakra. Spend a moment here still, quietly assessing the sensations you might be feeling in this region. Does it feel healthy, moist or dry and scratchy? Is it relaxed or tense and cut off? Take a moment to quietly assess and connect with your truth expressor. In subtle ways, if you listen closely, it will reveal to you its true present state. Have you been comfortable speaking your truth and expressing your authentic self? Are you being as imaginative and freely creative as can be? This is the Gateway of time and space and I invite you now to dig... yes dig a little deeper for your answers... (pause)

You are now invited to notice the blue of the infinite sky above your head and the turquoise blue of the infinite oceans, a blue that has been since the beginning of time. Let yourself journey in this trance by this turquoise blue, a blue symbolizing the infinite Universe. And now, catch a glimpse of a blue sphere as it forms on the top of the skin over your neck region. With your mind's eye, take your hand and gently press your larynx in this area. Feel your fingers, over this blue sphere; pierce gently right through your flesh to enter your throat region. You intuit there is something wedged, blocking your throat chakra and at this very moment it is imperative you pull it out. Gently feel your fingers explore, wiggling as they search around this sacred region of your throat. You detect a small smooth pebble, the obstacle in your trust and communications. Gently, try to extract this stone from your Throat Chakra now and take this moment to inspect it.

Herein this stone were all the thoughts that went unexpressed by you; all the doubts you brushed away, all that you suppressed in fear of being revealed, all the words you feared to speak, all the true emotions you kept securely locked to avoid the eyes of judgment, all the parts of you -frugally hidden away. This stone you have unearthed within may be tiny but its power to silence and sabotage has been great and today we end its reign.

Rub this discovered stone within your fingers now and watch as it pulverizes in the light of day. Let its fragments and debris fall and evaporate in the air. Breathe now and with each breath allow your throat chakra to heal itself as it mends the hole that once held the block, in this old stone. Breathe. Remember the blue of the infinite sky... they are within you here in this chakra. Remember the blue of the infinite waters.... They are within you here in this fifth chakra. Breathe and take this moment to honor Vishuddha, your sacred Throat Chakra.

## 6th PINEAL THIRD EYE CHAKRA

Bring your attention now to your Pineal gland, better known as your third eye. It is locate on your forehead between your brows. Known as Ajna, it is the realm of perception, intuition and wisdom. Here you will see with no eyes, hear with no ears, feel with no touch, journey to internal and external far off realms all through your sixth chakra. Take this moment to bring your attention to this special place now. (Pause) With your eyes closed try to bring your focus to the middle of your forehead by gently crossing your closed eyes to look into this direction, between your two eyebrows. In this region, carefully search for any sign of the color indigo. Search and continue to look deeply to discern quite subtly the glow of a purple, indigo color. See this indigo color spin in a circular motion ever so gently as it transforms before your eyes into an Amethyst crystal. Continue to look deeply into the Amethyst crystal as it becomes your third eye. Open this divine third eye, blink and open it wide to see what is before you.

Now, if you will, begin to reflect on the concept of gratitude. With your open third eye, see what you are most grateful for in your life…. and let your intuitive sight now gaze on the feeling of gratitude. This sixth chakra is known as the Gateway of liberation….the place of detachment, of Universal compassion, the realm of our interconnection awareness and the freedom found in a non-dualistic view of life. Here is where your true sight originates from. Here is where self-mastery and extrasensory gifts are born. Continue to gaze with your open third eye as the purple Amethyst crystal and allow yourself to absorb it and its intuitive attributes into your Ajna chakra. This amethyst is your third eye and it sees with an exceptional acuity, far better than any physical eye can see. Take a moment to receive its personal message to you. When you are ready, prepare to shut your precious third eye close and express gratitude for all that revealed itself here today through your sixth chakra. The Gateway of liberation has freed you from illusions. We take this moment now to honor our sixth chakra, honor its intuitive attributes and the immeasurable powers of our Third Eye.

## 7th CROWN CHAKRA

Journey now upwards and bring your attention to the top of your head, your Crown. Feel if you will, the weight upon your head, as it sits upon your relaxed neck and shoulders. Extend your awareness now to the space above your head and feel this space lightly vibrating overhead. Like a blossom, feel the top of your head now open… open, simply open in a state of receptivity. Allow your head to open like a multi petal lotus flower, becoming a sacred portal for Divine light and sacred union to take place. Here is where we are the chalice. Here is where we become one with source. Quietly observe your seventh chakra, welcoming this moment of transcendence…listening for the whispers emanating from the flecks of the streaming Divine light. You are the chalice, inviting the nectar of life.

In this trance you have journeyed through almost all of your chakras and now you have arrived at the Gateway of the Void, your Seventh chakra. This chakra is known as Sahasrara; meaning a thousand petalled. This is the realm of receptivity and union with source. Take this moment to honor this sacred realm, as you intuit the subtle vibrational energy. Inviting the light, begin to detect the sounds that birth our Universe. **Om….**Unearth the state of bliss and unity… **Om…** Connect to all things within and around you now. **Om...** Open your seventh chakra now and in this very special moment; honor yourself, honor your Crown, honor and weave the thread that connects you to this expansive Universal tapestry of humanity. Honor your part in the infinite, sacred circle of life.

Keep your Crown chakra open for a moment and welcome the Divine and Her message into this portal. When you are ready, gently close it and briefly go back and revisit all of your chakras to make sure they are now cleared, balanced and then closed. If it helps, see yourself zippering or buttoning close each one of your seven chakras, as we prepare to end this meditation. We will count slowly from seven to one backwards to help us in transition back to this room, this time and space. Please take a final, deep cleansing breath as we begin to count; **seven, six.** Breathe, **five, four,** and take one more energized breath, **three,** exhale and release. Follow my voice back to this space, **two and one.** Gently stretch out and place the palm of your hands flat on the earth to help you ground better and ease you back into this room and with both hands in prayer pose, welcome, Namaste!

## EMBODYING SPIRIT

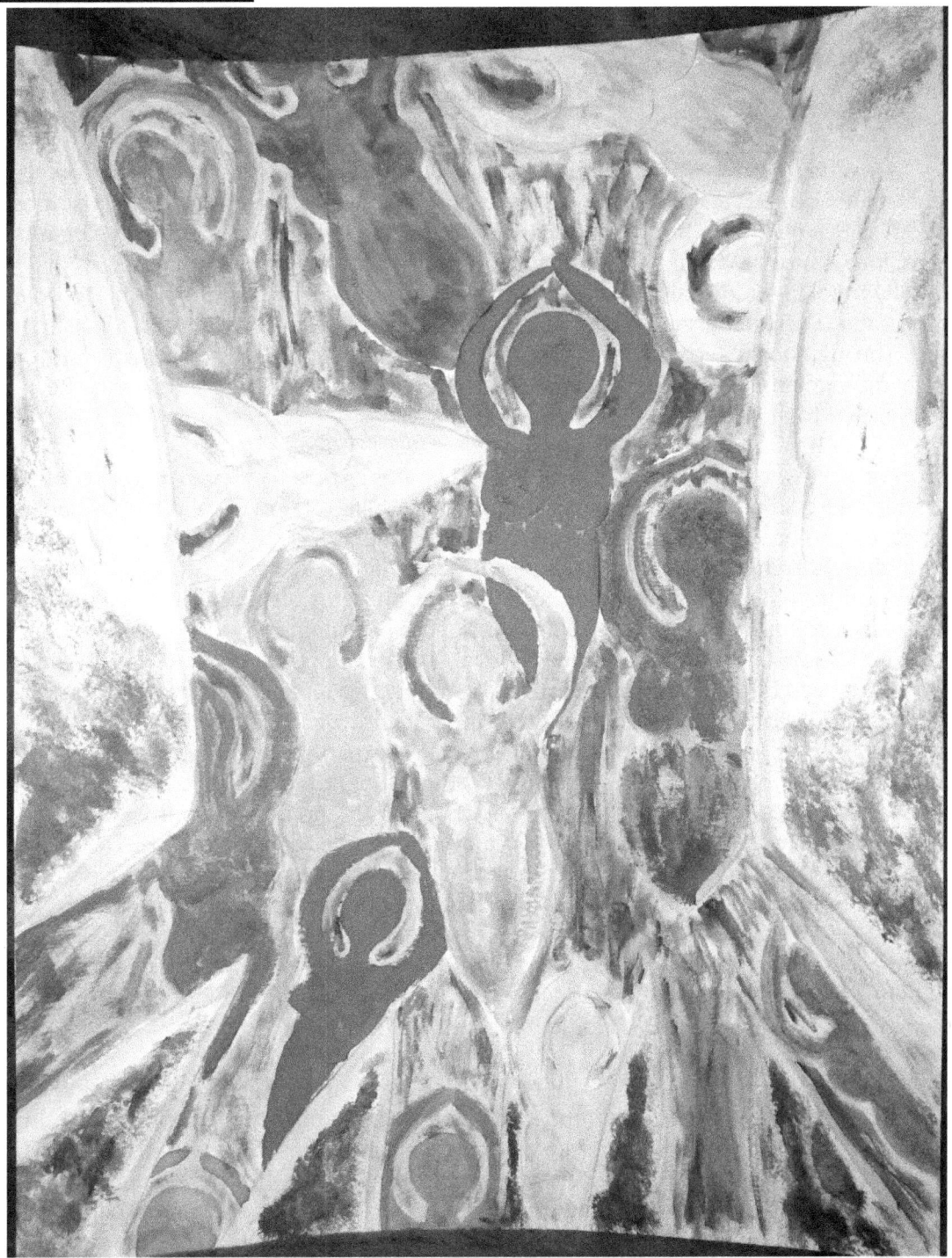

"*A Woman Shaman, like a spider spinning, must learn to lead from the womb...To move our attention from head to the belly; from the mind to the body...a woman must learn to read the signals and to trust them..*" Vicki Noble

*"I have worshipped woman as the living embodiment of the Spirit of service and sacrifice..." Mahatma Gandhi*

# EMBODYING SPIRIT
# PERSONAL THOUGHTS ON ASPECTING

Aspecting is often a term used to describe when a priestess opens herself up to channeling a Goddess, a Spirit or an attribute of the Divine. This very sacred act is done in an effort to truly embody the Goddess in physical form, and present her living, breathing essence, into a ritual. When a woman avails herself to the art of aspecting, she is essentially invoking and calling into herself the Goddess. She is allowing herself to be a vessel for that Divine energy to enter and manifest itself, for all to witness in a ritual setting. Through her speech, her gaze, the timbre of her voice, her inspired actions, her physical movements, via the body of the Priestess, the Goddess will essentially make herself known to all present.

For me, aspecting is the Goddess bringing me, her priestess, even closer to her and her divine energy. It can evolve quite naturally over the course of some time and with patience, as you become more absorbed in your Goddess studies. After spending some cerebral time learning about a particular Goddess, exploring her academically, it will come as no surprise that you will long to know her on a deeper level. It is quite natural for priestesses to aspire to intimately know the Sacred Feminine through our senses and our physical bodies. On a purely practical level, this strong need to connect with the Goddess can even become urgent if there is an impending lunar rite, sabbat or open ritual, which calls forth her sacred energy. In my pursuit to invoke her, I will spend time meditating on the specific deity; reciting her name as a mantra, writing poetry dedicated to her and reciting prose as offerings. In my own personal practice, I typically would set up a special altar for the Goddess that I am working with and on this altar incorporate things that would personally awaken her from within and endear her to me. Daily I would endeavor to visit this altar and call her into me. I commit to communicating with the Goddess, night and day, the way a lover slowly but surely bonds with her target of affection. Daily the bond grows stronger until eventually, the Divine feels ready to take me deeper into this spiritual labyrinth and bring me even closer to her. It is quite a palpable experience and one I begin to feel as a tug and pull, and then a surge; like that of being in the ebb and flow of "Her" amniotic waters.

Slowly I float to the back and she floats to the front and She is welcomed into me and I welcome this exchange. I surrender to this dance, trusting her, as she is entrusting me with her Divine essence. When I am aspecting, I can feel the Goddess through my very pores, I do not entirely disappear, but it feels as if I am in the background, the shadow, while She -Goddess -becomes the foreground. The Goddess therefore becomes a forward manifestation. I am still there, but She is the dominant one before me and in this position she becomes living, breathing borrowing my physical form, while at the same time, allowing me to touch her essence deeply and feel who she truly is, at the core.

Some strange phenomenons happen when I am aspecting and I am not always aware of all of them at the moment that they are happening, but I am enlightened by other's observations and by my own hands. For example; my art work and my journal writing will reveal the most obvious points of when I am naturally aspecting. My penmanship changes, the language that I customarily will use, changes to reflect the Divine's voice. My brush strokes and the subjects of my art pieces, change - reflecting her taste. Months later I might find myself studying one of my old canvases and come to the surprising realization that, "oh..., it wasn't genuinely me creating that , where did that come from?" or "how and why did I paint that??.." It might seem sort of Sybil-like, but it's the only way I can explain the concept of aspecting for the Goddess.

Another phenomenon as a result of natural aspecting involves my body more intimately. For example; sex, by other's account, might appear as if I've become more insatiable if I have been working with a Sex-Love Goddess like Aphrodite, Hathor or Pele. On the contrary, I can start to appear quite frigid and chaste, if I am working with a Virginal Goddess like Athena or Hestia. When working with Artemis, I had a great need to be in the company of many women; I called them my beloved sisters all fighting for the same cause. I had an aversion towards the male species, although they are quite normally the object of my affection. I also tend to be very defensive over my privacy, vigilant over women's rights, and extra protective of children, according to my journal writings. While aspecting Nike, I felt very competitive and became obsessed with lifting weights. Don't know if it was Nike or some kind of Amazonian Goddess, but my body became my sculpted temple, very competitively fit and well defined. Running like a charioteer became a passion as well. A while back, I would crochet obsessively, non-stop, for hours on end, it was a time when I was working with the Celtic Goddess, Brigit. All day long without any breaks, I was fanatical with my crocheting projects. I literally felt like my hands were possessed during that time and my photo portfolio now reflects the wonderful accomplishment manifested through Brigit's hands. I now I have a collection of knitwear and a whole large wardrobe completed via her crocheting influence. Thanks also to the Goddess Brigit, I took up jewelry making and connected to my inner bard; writing many poems then. When working with Saraswati, I had a similar obsession with artistic expression; singing, painting circular works, writing and drinking lots of herbal infusions. Working with Athena I felt the pressure of her plate against my chest and a strange obsession for all things steel, metal-like and this strong urgency to teach. I also felt very comfortable in the company of men. Judging from my writing, I appeared less emotional and more cerebral, interested in controlling situations. According to family and those I share a home with, Demeter softens me and it is clearly a departure from my normal self. With her I cook more, living in the kitchen and garden and feeding everyone that comes along my way, like a Greek matriarch. I even found myself mothering strangers and of course, animals. I'd find myself weepy and my writings revealed a softer, more compassionate, emotional side. These are just some examples and personal notes from my own experiences aspecting the Divine.

Typically, I will choose to live with the Goddess I am working with in preparation for a seasonal ceremony, for as long as she will have me. It could be a week, a month or just a few days but when I am ready to come back into my own, I am led to approach my home altar and with a small prepared ritual, I thank the Goddess and release the energy back, with reverence and gratitude. Sometimes, it may take me a few days or so, to get fully grounded and back into my body, but I do eventually return to my ol' self again.

In the midst of sacred rituals, if I am aspecting I can sometimes feel my tongue and the formation of my words change and I can hear the timber of my voice alter at times.

My stance and the way my body moves, also changes, as she make her presence known to the group, then delivers her message and moves me through the ritual, as she sees fit. All along, I surrender......surrender to her Divine energy. I am not an advocate of spontaneous aspecting, as I feel this can be very tricky and rather dangerous to a novice. In my humble opinion, I feel it's very important for a priestess to know how to shield, protect and ground herself and block an unwelcome aspecting from occurring. There is quite obviously an intimate dance and relationship that you are undergoing when you are aspecting and needless to say, a great deal of trust necessary from both, you and Spirit. After all, you are lending out your physical form while she is lending out her essence and immortal spirit. And this is to be done with utmost delicacy, reverence and wisdom. Ideally you should not allow forces or Deities, to enter your sphere without your specific invite or consent. It is rather intrusive and for me, almost a violation to my well-being. Covering your crown chakra and holding on to some type of anchor, like a talisman or a mantra repeated in your head, can help you stay grounded and avoid spontaneous aspecting; if that is something you tend to naturally do. As you will soon learn, some Deities are easier to tap into, while others are not and it's important to remember to approach this practice with much love and reverence. In my experience, some Goddesses do not want to be aspected or contained, while others take great pleasure and reward your devotion with their presence. For safety reasons and for my own well-being there are some Deities I just wouldn't recommend aspecting, but that is simply a matter of personal choice and others might feel differently.

The skills and the wisdom that results from aspecting have been personally monumental for me and unquestionably enlightening. It takes patience and great desire to commune with Spirits, deities and Divine energy in this way, but the rewards are well worth it and your spiritual journey and rituals will benefit greatly. Happy aspecting!!!!

# VII. LAW OF ATTRACTION

*"...Nothing splendid has ever been achieved except by those who dared believe that something inside of them was superior to circumstance..."* Bruce Barton

## Law of Attraction and a Few Final Words...

With movies & books like, *"The Secret,"* by Rhonda Byrne and the revival interest in authors of the 1900's *"New Thought Movement"* period like; Genevieve Behrend, Florence Scovel Shinn, and Elizabeth Towne, there is a renewed interest in Metaphysical principles. It appears everywhere you look someone seems to be speaking about or championing the *"Law of Attraction."* And with so many *"Law of Attraction"* workshops drawing audiences by the millions across the world, its popularity does not appear to be waning one bit. Our knowledge about Metaphysical ideologies and the "Law of Attraction" has increased in the last few years as more and more people are stepping into their own power and are embracing their spirituality and alternative lifestyles. The rising popularity of the "Law of Attraction" has some deeming it as a sort of cult, quickly infiltrating all kinds of demographics; from the rich to the poor, to numerous cultures in between. The Law of Attraction seems to appeal to so many who encounter it and with video sharing websites like, *"Youtube,"* it is becoming increasingly easier to learn more about it.

Now, much has already been said, about the Law of Attraction and there are numerous books dedicate exclusively to its tenets, but I wanted to explore and present it here, as yet another useful modern tool that can strengthen our very own powers of manifestation. Throughout reading this book you would've found many subtle references to its tenets; tenets that are extremely reminiscent of the many, compatibly found in various ancient spiritual traditions. So, what exactly is the Law of Attraction?

The Law of Attraction is an intention based process that encourages you to focus on your desire. The more you focus on what you desire the more the universe can help you give it form and manifest it into your physical reality. It encourages us to put more value in our emotional state of being and consider the creative, limbic portion of the brain, for this is the area that is active in our sleeping life. This is our feeling nature and it is the fuel for any form of manifestation, according to the Law of Attraction tenet.

The Law of Attraction dismisses the analytical mind and the part of your brain that is constantly trying to base future experiences on the negative past. It wants you to live in a state of possibilities and the "*what ifs.*" It wants you to abandon that rationale part in your brain that demands concrete evidence of eminent failure. In other words, if you've done something in the past and it caused you much pain and failure, you might not be so hopeful of a different outcome if tried again, so the emotions tied to this memory will almost always create a negative reality. However, this is not the way it has to be, according to Law of Attraction. We typically hold strongly the belief that if a certain situation changes or if we attain something new in our lives, it will make us feel happier and bring all the wonderful feelings we associate with the manifestation of this one thing. However, Law of Attraction contradicts this old modality. It advocates finding that uplifted, amplified happy state of being, first and foremost, in order to attain that which you seek. Being in a positive uplifted state of mind appears to be almost a prerequisite to attain your heart's desire, according to this tradition. With the Law of Attraction, much emphasis is placed on your emotional and mental state of being, and maintaining that positive high vibrational state of being to magnetize your heart's desire. Therefore, the obvious first goal would be to always feel good, as this will facilitate your powers of manifestation. Law of Attraction principles almost declare that we cannot attain our heart's desire if we are in a state of lack or any negative, disempowered, hopeless state of being. We are co-creators! We are *manifestators* and we do our best manifesting when we are in the right state of mind, connected to our higher vibrational powers, positively envisioning the outcome as we wish it to be, and anchored into our heart and vortex.

With the Law of Attraction, our very ideas become our beliefs, but our beliefs are not necessarily based on truth. Our beliefs are not entirely who we are and this is the struggle that most people have when trying to affect a change in their lives. We become so attached to our beliefs that they stifle any room for expansion and potential growth. These beliefs, both conscious and unconscious ones, tend to spread a vaporous hue all around our being, influencing our state of mind. Developing and tapping into the ability to shift our energy and vibration, is part of the magick necessary to learn to activate our powers of manifestation. This holds true whether you are a novice student of magick, an occultist, a Goddess priestess, a Wiccan or a disciple of Law of Attraction tenets.

Nature exudes high energy and high vibration naturally that can contribute to our own wellbeing and when we too connect with our natural environment, we tap into this infinite resource, fueling ourselves with energy. This is one easy way to elevate our vibration and shift our state of being. There are numerous other ways to elevate our state of being so that we are more receptive to our powers of manifestation and in this book we've explored many of these techniques; meditation, chanting, affirmations, dance, yoga, music, rituals, crafting etc... One of the vital ways the Law of Attraction encourages us to shift our state of being is through gratitude. When we are grateful, for even the appearance of the smallest of things, we create the fertile ground for the proliferation of more of those things we desire.

> ***Our minds and souls hold the indelible imprint***
> ***of our collective experiences***
> ***and some would argue these experiences***
> ***are not limited to this very lifetime***
> ***but reach far back into the recesses of time...*** B.Melusine Mihaltses

The basic tenet of the Law of Attraction is, "*like attracts like*" and if you are in a state of abundance, you can attract more abundance. Conversely, if you are in a state of "*lack*" you will remain in this needy state; that is, if you don't change your mind set. What we focus our attention on is exactly what we manifest according to Law of Attraction, but this is a common belief among many who practice Metaphysics and the spiritual arts.

Everything that life is offering you right now, whether love or conflict, poverty or success; is all merely a reflection of your point of attraction, according to the Law of Attraction principles. Life is mirroring what you are pointing your direction or energy to. It therefore behooves us to be mindful of what we are putting our focus on. It calls for us to be more responsible and conscientious about the power of our mind and what we choose to place our attention on. The Law of Attraction declares that if you remain focus on only the negative things in your life; complaining about all that is not going right in your world and all that you don't like, you will simply multiply this negative point and create an invitation for more of what you don't want. Conversely, if you train your mind to focus on the positive and with your mind's eye create the laser beam that only considers the manifestations of your dreams as reality, then it will be so. What we seek to manifest, must already be so, in our mind's eye. This indeed can challenge us to embrace our powers of co-creation and realize that we are at the center of all manifestations in our lives; whether good or bad. It is our job to simply prepare the way for our heart's desire to come to fruition, by already expecting it and acting as if it has. Placing our attention towards appreciation and holding a state of gratitude for what we already behold facilitates a rich, fertile ground for our powers of manifestation.

To our powerful minds and our infinite soul, which has a different interpretation of time, feelings related to a situation exist whether that situation is real or false. Consider how stressed and frazzled we get when we worry about something that has not even occurred in reality but has only occurred in our mind though worry. The process of passing a school exam, meeting your supervisor's expectations or even suspecting a cheating spouse, are just some examples of how we can worry ourselves sick over something that has not even occurred in physical reality but has already strongly influenced our internal reality due to our invested emotions. Thus, it behooves us to choose good feelings. It goes without saying that for many of us, it can be quite a challenge to retrain our mindset and adopt this belief, but it is one that is prevalent in almost all forms of magick and spiritual traditions. The power of sight, acute visualization and the gift of the focused mind are the most prudent gifts for a student of magick and a devout practitioner of Metaphysics.

*"We are what we think, all that we are, arises with our thoughts and with our thoughts, we make our world...." Buddha*

The Law of Attraction speaks of the "**vortex,**" the place where all of your most cherished dreams, your ideal life, and your heart's desire converge. Here is the realm where all of your dreams are manifested as you wish them to be. In the vortex you are swimming in ecstasy and pure joy, for your life is, as you have manifested it to be. It is the place where we ideally want to find ourselves in and remain, for an indefinite amount of time. However, our human nature will often create obstacles to keep us from even acknowledging the existence of such a beautiful place. The renowned spirit entity known as Abraham, channeled by Esther Hicks, speaks to us about the vortex but also about rampaging, during "Law of Attraction" workshops worldwide. **Rampaging** is the art of clarifying for yourself, whether verbally or through writing, what it is that you truly desire. The very act of rampaging will shift and expand your consciousness to help your mind create a different reality; one that will magnetize your powers of manifestation.

There are numerous modalities found in various spiritual traditions for attaining clarity on our life purpose and our true heart's desire. Throughout this book I have mentioned quite a few; like creating Soul-collages or Vision boards and tapping into the messages of your nocturnal dreams and exploring oracles. Rampaging, however, adds another dimension that can be of great help when seeking clarity and a shift in our perspective. In the Law of Attraction, when we rampage, we begin thinking of the **"what ifs"** *and* slowly move away from all the barricades and obstacles we naturally create. When we rampage, our obstacles, self-limiting beliefs and negative thoughts begin to slowly wane and lose their grip on us. When we enter this realm of the *"what ifs,"* we engage the part of our brain that is thinking about all the possibilities, we turn on the positive light switch of our hearts and turn down the negative one, in order to create a more hospitable environment where our deepest wishes can come true. We create a conducive, bountiful, magnetic environment where our dreams can take root to form and our visions are guaranteed to realize themselves.

Through rampaging we are drawn closer and closer to our vortex....and the vortex is the ideal world we have co-created with the Universe. We aspire to live in this blissful place known as the vortex; some might even call it, "the zone." I must make note of something very important however, because when you think about it, it's not an actual place, like a country or a fortress cathedral that you go to. The vortex exists in our mind. It is our own state of being. When we think about it, all the things that we want as human beings; wealth and abundance, health, love, a successful careers etc, etc..., all of these things, we presume are external. Upon closer inspection we will discover these are things found first and foremost internally, in our hearts. Indeed they really begin with an internal state of being. They are a reality that is first and foremost established in our mind, before they have a chance to be seen, tasted or felt and experienced in our physical realm.

Law of Attraction shares a glimpse into some very ancient esoteric tenets that have survived throughout the ages and have sustained themselves all these years. These spiritual principles seem to transform and metamorphosize themselves to infiltrate whatever vernacular our present world is using. Thus, the Law of Attraction, with its numerous catchy phrases and lingo, is still speaking to us about ancient esoteric and Metaphysical wisdom from long, long ago.

>  ***"...If that which you seek you cannot find within you, you will never find without..."* Charge of the Goddess.**

We manifest reality, first and foremost, in our hearts and mind, before it comes to fruition in our physical realm. For shamans and the indigenous cultures our sleep time is the reality, while our waking time is the illusion. Our reality lies internally in our mind, not outside of it or apart from it. And if we go even deeper, we will see that in truth, if we use our hearts as eyes and ears, we will see how our physical reality is subordinate to our vision and spiritual capacity. Our ancestors and teachers of long ago have taught us that we can see without eyes, smell and taste without our noses; we can speak without mouths, we feel, travel and experience life and its multitude of energies, with and without our physical bodies. These are the important consistent gifts given to us by our ancestors and our spiritual teachers from ancient times and they continue to be explored by us, today. From the Scientist, to the Gurus and Shamans, to the Alchemist, Ceremonial magician and Hereditary Witch these are the basic principles of magick & transformation that are prevalent and exploratory in almost all spiritual traditions. These are concepts that may be challenging to grasp while we are tenaciously holding onto the limitations and our physical realities but they are the foundation to our emancipation. They are the pivotal grounds and building blocks for, modern appearing traditions like, The Law of Attraction. Understanding them can open up a vastly different world than what we've been sold…That's right, sold, because we've been told so many self-limiting, corrupt illusory beliefs that are only meant to restrict, confine and keep us in states of ignorance, enslavement and disempowerment. "*The truth*" as they say, "*shall set you free,*" for once you know the truth of your being and your true nature, there are no boundaries, no self-limiting beliefs and no obstacles to keep you from your freedom to happiness. The truth is you behold the powers to manifest your reality as you wish it to be. You hold great powers! You are a Divine being, comprised of sacred energies from your foremothers and forefathers.

We explored various ways to expand our minds, shift our perspectives, raise and use energies, elevate and expand our consciousness here. And all of these practices can have a significant impact on our perceived reality. Herein is the power to transform and revamp your life. It is my hope that this book has at the very least cracked the door open to your true nature and your power, and that all the numerous exercises herein can assist your very own evolution as a spiritual being. There are so many different ways we can facilitate our own spiritual growth & expansion, and it is all contributory to our inherent powers of manifestation. I send you much love and blessings as you continue onward to explore your powers of manifestation and revamp your life to be everything your heart desires. Blessed be!!

*"No one has been granted the authority to tell me how my life should be lived. I answer only to myself and to Spirit..."* Jonathan Lockwood Huie

✼✼✼✼✼✼✼

# REFERENCES & RESOURCES
## *QUICK REVIEW OF FIRST CHAPTER* SPELL-CRAFTING MAGICK

1. **Visualization:** We begin by first fantasizing and envisioning the manifestation of our spell, with as much detail and clarity as possible. See it already coming to past. Celebrate it and imagine it has already come to fruition. This requires you to possibly sit still and ground at first; center yourself for the inception of this powerful work you are about to engage in. Connect with your third eye and become aware of what you are about to do. Some people opt to meditate at this time or simply be still and empty their minds of any negativity in preparation for the spell. Allow yourself to simply envision all coming to fruition.
2. Next we **connect with our Spiritual allies**. Open yourself up to their assistance and look out for signs of Spiritual Communications
3. **Making it Your Unique Spell**. Take the time to create your own unique hand-crafted incantation.
4. **Tool & Vehicle of Magick**: Chose your mode of magick and once you've decided, take this tool; clean and consecrate it. Whether that is a candle, a poppet, herbal placket, witch bottle, a knot cord, or a piece of paper etc…you are to clear, clean, consecrate and charge it by all the Elements in preparation for your spell.
5. **Timing is everything:** Next we decide what is the best day and planetary hour to actually execute your spell. What moon phase and what astrological sign is best for the kind of spell you're working on? It only takes a brief moment to research this information in your Farmer's almanac or on the internet but traditional Occultist find it is invaluable for successful spells.
6. **Show time:** At the appointed day and hour: begin by centering yourself, assure your privacy and that you won't be disturbed for a while. Relax and center yourself and begin to visualize your wish.
7. **Energy Creation:** Next begin to raise your energy. Select any of the numerous ways suggested to elevate your vibration and raise energy. The simplest method is with our hands, rubbing our two hands together but also through chanting, singing dancing, sex or mantra chanting. Simply chanting "Om" can be very effective. You can also raise energy by drumming and dancing, moving, singing and engaging the physical body into sweat and rapid heat beating. This can be a fun process but must be done with clear purpose and intention.
8. Pour this raised energy into your spell (your chosen vehicle of magick) and then, with vigor, speak your incantation with all of this intention and energy. Organically **channel this raised energy into your special Spell working**; whether it is a lit candle, a simple knot cord, a written note, yantra pattern or mandala creation or a vision/collage board. We now approach our spell, offering it our most positive intention and powerfully raised energy as a vehicle for this manifestation.
9. **Lastly, Release the Spell:** When it is done, trust and release it out unto the Universes. Trust that it's indeed done, as you **cap your spell with a karmic protective statement**. The end.
10. **Clean up** your space and put everything away. Set reminders for yourself if you will need to relight or rework your candle, such is the case with a knot candle, which is lit daily for seven days.

11. Finally, **let the magick take hold!** Do not jeopardize your hard work with excessive talk about it, over analyzing or obsessing over it. As the popular pagan chant goes, "*It is Done!!!.*" You have raised the energy, crafted the spell, released it towards the Universe and now you must trust that it is done. Allow the Universe a chance to show you the magick manifested. Visualize all, as complete and done according to your vision and move onwards now with trust. Our magick can reveal itself on a completely different time schedule than our human linear concept of time. Spells may take one full moon cycle to manifest or sometimes six, and if you haven't specified urgency in your work, it may even take a bit longer. Be patient, continue learning and continue practicing and enhancing your magick, Blessed Be!

# *KABBALISTIC, TALISMANIC PLANETARY SQUARES*

### The Table of Saturn

| | | |
|---|---|---|
| 4 | 9 | 2 |
| 3 | 5 | 7 |
| 8 | 1 | 6 |

### The Table of Jupiter

| | | | |
|---|---|---|---|
| 4 | 14 | 15 | 1 |
| 9 | 7 | 6 | 12 |
| 5 | 11 | 10 | 8 |
| 16 | 2 | 3 | 13 |

### The Table of Mars

| | | | | |
|---|---|---|---|---|
| 11 | 24 | 7 | 20 | 3 |
| 4 | 12 | 25 | 8 | 16 |
| 17 | 5 | 13 | 21 | 9 |
| 10 | 18 | 1 | 14 | 22 |
| 23 | 6 | 19 | 2 | 15 |

### The Table of the Sun

| | | | | | |
|---|---|---|---|---|---|
| 6 | 32 | 3 | 34 | 35 | 1 |
| 7 | 11 | 27 | 28 | 8 | 30 |
| 19 | 14 | 16 | 15 | 23 | 24 |
| 18 | 20 | 22 | 21 | 17 | 13 |
| 25 | 29 | 10 | 9 | 26 | 12 |
| 36 | 5 | 33 | 4 | 2 | 31 |

### The Table of Venus

| | | | | | | |
|---|---|---|---|---|---|---|
| 22 | 47 | 16 | 41 | 10 | 35 | 4 |
| 5 | 23 | 43 | 17 | 42 | 11 | 29 |
| 30 | 6 | 24 | 49 | 81 | 36 | 12 |
| 13 | 31 | 7 | 25 | 43 | 19 | 37 |
| 38 | 14 | 32 | 1 | 26 | 44 | 20 |
| 21 | 39 | 8 | 33 | 2 | 27 | 45 |
| 46 | 15 | 40 | 9 | 34 | 3 | 28 |

### The Table of the Moon

| | | | | | | | | |
|---|---|---|---|---|---|---|---|---|
| 37 | 78 | 29 | 70 | 94 | 62 | 13 | 54 | 5 |
| 6 | 38 | 79 | 30 | 71 | 22 | 63 | 14 | 46 |
| 47 | 7 | 39 | 80 | 31 | 72 | 23 | 55 | 15 |
| 16 | 48 | 8 | 40 | 81 | 32 | 64 | 24 | 56 |
| 57 | 17 | 49 | 9 | 41 | 73 | 33 | 65 | 25 |
| 26 | 58 | 18 | 50 | 1 | 42 | 74 | 34 | 66 |
| 67 | 27 | 59 | 10 | 51 | 2 | 43 | 75 | 35 |
| 36 | 68 | 19 | 60 | 11 | 52 | 3 | 44 | 76 |
| 77 | 28 | 69 | 20 | 61 | 12 | 53 | 4 | 45 |

### The Table of Mercury

| | | | | | | | |
|---|---|---|---|---|---|---|---|
| 8 | 58 | 59 | 5 | 4 | 62 | 63 | 1 |
| 49 | 15 | 14 | 52 | 53 | 11 | 10 | 56 |
| 41 | 23 | 22 | 44 | 48 | 19 | 18 | 45 |
| 32 | 34 | 38 | 29 | 25 | 35 | 39 | 28 |
| 40 | 26 | 27 | 37 | 36 | 30 | 31 | 33 |
| 17 | 47 | 46 | 20 | 21 | 43 | 42 | 24 |
| 9 | 55 | 54 | 12 | 13 | 51 | 50 | 16 |
| 64 | 2 | 3 | 61 | 60 | 6 | 7 | 57 |

# CHART OF PLANETARY HOURS

*from astrolabe.com but often attributed to Maria Kay Simms from her Book; "A Time for Magick" (Llewellyn 2001) also can be found in Charmaine Dey's, "The Magic Candle".*

| Sunday | Monday | Tuesday | Wednesday | Thursday | Friday | Saturday |
|---|---|---|---|---|---|---|
| 1. Sun | Moon | Mars | Mercury | Jupiter | Venus | Saturn |
| 2. Venus | Saturn | Sun | Moon | Mars | Mercury | Jupiter |
| 3. Mercury | Jupiter | Venus | Saturn | Sun | Moon | Mars |
| 4. Moon | Mars | Mercury | Jupiter | Venus | Saturn | Sun |
| 5. Saturn | Sun | Moon | Mars | Mercury | Jupiter | Venus |
| 6. Jupiter | Venus | Saturn | Sun | Moon | Mars | Mercury |
| 7. Mars | Mercury | Jupiter | Venus | Saturn | Sun | Moon |
| 8. Sun | Moon | Mars | Mercury | Jupiter | Venus | Saturn |
| 9. Venus | Saturn | Sun | Moon | Mars | Mercury | Jupiter |
| 10. Mercury | Jupiter | Venus | Saturn | Sun | Moon | Mars |
| 11. Moon | Mars | Mercury | Jupiter | Venus | Saturn | Sun |
| 12. Saturn | Sun | Moon | Mars | Mercury | Jupiter | Venus |

### *After Sunset/Hours of Night *

| Sunday | Monday | Tuesday | Wednesday | Thursday | Friday | Saturday |
|---|---|---|---|---|---|---|
| 1. Jupiter | Venus | Saturn | Sun | Moon | Mars | Mercury |
| 2. Mars | Mercury | Jupiter | Venus | Saturn | Sun | Moon |
| 3. Sun | Moon | Mars | Mercury | Jupiter | Venus | Saturn |
| 4. Venus | Saturn | Sun | Moon | Mars | Mercury | Jupiter |
| 5. Mercury | Jupiter | Venus | Saturn | Sun | Moon | Mars |
| 6. Moon | Mars | Mercury | Jupiter | Venus | Saturn | Sun |
| 7. Saturn | Sun | Moon | Mars | Mercury | Jupiter | Venus |
| 8. Jupiter | Venus | Saturn | Sun | Moon | Mars | Mercury |
| 9. Mars | Mercury | Jupiter | Venus | Saturn | Sun | Moon |
| 10. Sun | Moon | Mars | Mercury | Jupiter | Venus | Saturn |
| 11. Venus | Saturn | Sun | Moon | Mars | Mercury | Jupiter |
| 12. Mercury | Jupiter | Venus | Saturn | Sun | Moon | Mars |

# BIBLIOGRAPHY

### SPELL-CRAFTING MAGICK
Spells and How They Work,
By Janet Stewart Farrar
Phoenix Publishing, Inc, Washington

The Magic Candle, Facts and
Fundamentals of Ritual Candle-Burning,
By Charmaine Dey
Original Publication, New York

The Witch's Worksbook, by Ann Grammary
Pocket Book a Division of Simon and Schuster,
New York, New York

What Witches Do, a Modern Coven Revealed
by Stewart Farrar
Phoenix Publishing, Inc, Washington

The Witch's Worksbook, by Ann Grammary
Pocket Book a Division of Simon and Schuster,
New York, New York

### CANDLE MAGICK
The Magic Candle, Facts and
Fundamentals of Ritual Candle-Burning,
By Charmaine Dey
Original Publication, New York

Spells and How They Work,
By Janet Stewart Farrar
Phoenix Publishing, Inc, Washington

### COLOR MAGICK
The Metaphysical Handbook
By David Pond & Lucy Pond
Reflecting Pond Productions
Port Ludlow, WA
Copyright 1984
Third Printing edition, 1985

### NUMEROLOGY MAGICK
Numerology, the Romance in Your Name
By Dr. Juno Jordan
J. F. Rowny Press
Santa Barbara California
Copyright 1965
Third Addition 1982
DeVors & Company, Marina Del Rey California

### MOON MAGICK: ASTROLOGY
The Secret Lore of Magic, Books of the Sorcerers,
By Sayed Indries Shah
The Citadel Press, Inc, New York

### PLANETARY HOURS AND DAYS
Numbers and You, a Numerology Guided For Everyday Living
By Lloyd Strayhornth
Ballantine Books
New York City, New York
Copyright 1987 Sixth Edition Printing 1990

### HERB & FLOWER MAGICK, INCENSES, POPPETS & PLACKETS, OILS & AROMATHERAPY
Cunningham's Encyclopedia of Magick Herbs
By Scott Cunningham
Llewellyn Publications
St. Paul, Minnesota
Copyright 1985
22nd Edition Printing, 1997

Herbs for Magic And Ritual, A Beginners Guide
By Teresa Moorey
Hodder & Stoughton, A Member Of The Hodder Headline Group.
Great Britain London UK
Copyright 1996

### TREE MAGICK
Gathering for Goddess, a Complete Manual for Priestessing
Women's Circles. By B.Melusine Mihaltses –
ISBN #978-09851384-4-8

FeminineDivineWorks, Texas,U.S.A.

### ANIMAL MAGICK
Animal Magick, The Art Of Recognizing And
Working With Familiars, By D.J. Conway
2009 edition, copyrighted 1995
Llewellyn publications, a Division of
Llewellyn Worldwide, LTD.
Woodberry, Minnesota

Animal Messages, Seek Inspiration From
Your Animal Guides, Oracle Deck,
By Susie Green, copyright 2005
Cico Books, London New York

Messages From Your Animal Spirit Guides, Oracle Cards
Guide Book
Steven D. Farmer, Ph.D.
Copyrighted 2008
Hay House incorporated
Published and distributed in the United Kingdom

Power Animal Meditations, Shamanic Journeys With Your Spirit Allies
By Nicki Scully
Bear and Company,
Rochester Vermont copyright 1991

www.thunderbird sky.com slash dove totem
www. spirit-animals.com /dove
www.a-rainbow-of-spirituality.org/ostrich.html
www.healing.about. com/ od/animal-totems/tp/bird-meditation/ted andrews/ostrich
www.spirit-animals.com/tag/ostrich
www.ehow.com/info_8588658_meanings-ostrich-totem.html
www.native-american-totems.com/birth-/and totems raven
www.ravenscaw.weebly.com
www.spirit-animals.com/raven
www.shades-of-night.com/corax/totem.html
www.earthdna.word press.com/2012/04/11/black birds
www.linsdomain.com/totemspages/raven.html

www.dr.standley.com/articles/animals-totem/bats
www.shamanic journey.com/article/6080/b at-power animal
www.totem wisdom.com/b.a.t totem.html
www.wisdom of the animals.com/animal_totems/bat_animal
www.native american totems.com/animal-totem –medicine
www.what's-your-sign.com/animal-symbolism-bat
www.spirit lodged.yuku.com/topic/871
www.totemtalk.ning.com/group/b/forum/topics/bat
www.linsdomain.com/totems/pages/skunk.html

www. animal totem.com/store that html
www. healing that about.com/od/animal totem/ig
www.whats-your-sign.com/coyote oracles
www. shamanic journey.com buffalo
www.spirit lodged.yuku.com
www. cathy ginter.com/totem that html
-------
www.spirit animal.info/tiger-spirit-animal
www.angelfire.com/ma4/the lair/totem.html
www.healing that about.com/.../animal-totems-photo-gallery-tiger
www.wolfsmoon.tripod.com/white tiger totem.html
www.shamanic journey.com/article/6008/tiger-power animal
www.totem wisdom.com/tiger totem. html
www.wisdom of the animals.com/animal_totems_tiger
www.universeofsymbolism.com/tiger-symbolism
---------
www.linsdomain.com/totems/pages/skunk.html
www.totem wisdom.com/sky and totem.html
www.spiritlodged.yuku.com/topic/889
www.nativeamericananimal medicine.com
www.quasiskunk.org/skunk.  html
www.starstuffs.com/animal_totems/dictionaries_of animals skunk
www.native-american-totems.com/animal-totem-medicine-skunk
www.healing.healing.about.com/.../animal-totems-photo-gallerys-skunk

www.universe of symbolisms.com/tiger-symbolism
www.angelfire.com/ma 4/the lair/totem.html
www.totem wisdom.com
www.native bear spirit that com
www.spirit animal that info/-bear-spirit-animal
www.spirit-animal.info/-dear spirit-animal
www.native-american-totems
www.universe of symbolism/wolf.com
www.linsdomain.com/totems/pages/elephant that html
www.spirit-animals.com /elephant

www.wisdomofthe animals.com
www.mediamender.com
www.themagickmoon.com/elephant-animal-spirit
www.starstuffs. animal totems/dogs th
www.spiritanimal.com/snake
www spiritanimal.info/dragonfly-spirit-animal
www.animal totem/.com dragonfly.age tml th
www.universe of symbolism.com/symbolic-dragon fly
www.earthdna.wordpress.com/2012/03/23/dragonfly
www.drumworks shamanic healing.com/ peacock

workshops
www.astral matrix that work/peacock
www.morning start .net firms .com/owl totem.  html
www.mediamender.com/blogs/entry/animal-totem owl
www wisdom of the animals.com/animal_totems/dragonfly
www.spirit lodge.yuku.com//topic/988
www.totem wisdom.com/swan totem.html
www.cocreatingourreality.com/.../forum/topics swan medicine
www.linsdomain.com/totems/pages/swan.html
www.ascensionjourneysthatblogspot.com/2009/10/my-swantotem
www.totem talk.ning.com/groups/s/forum/topics/55 217
www.healing that about.com/.../-animal totems-photo-gallery/swan totem
www.native-american-totems.com/animal-totem-medicine-swan-totem
www.native-american-totems.com/emental-influence/ frogs
www.wisdom of the animals.com/animal_totems/frogs
www.shamanic journey.com/article/6059/frog-for work and among
www.totem wisdom.com/frogtotem.html
www.spiritlodged.yuku.com/ topic/ 984
www.native-american-totems.com/animal-totem-medicine-turtle
www.linsdomain.com/totems/pages/turtle.html
www.spiritlodge.yuku.com/topic/877
www.wisdomoftheanimals.com/animal_totems/turtle
www.spirit animal.info/turtle-spirit-animal
www.universe of symbolism.com/turtle-symbolism
www.spirit-animals.com/turtle
www.animal totem.com/turtle.html
www.native-american-totems.com/animal-totem-medicine-spider
www.spirit lodge.yuku.com/topic/ 892
www.windwhisperonline.com/.sample.html
www.spirit animal.info/spider-spirit-animal
www.linsdomain that com/totems/pages/tarantula.html
www.wisdom of the animals.com/animal_totems/spider
www.animal totem.com/spider.html
www.mrkay.org/projects/totems/spider.html
www.totem wisdom.com/spider totem.html

www.shamanic journey.com/article/6177/ladybug-power animal
www.totemwisdom.com/ladybugtotem.html
www.morningstar.netfirms.com/ladybird.html
www.healing.about.com/od/animal totem/insects/ladybug-totem
www.starstuff.com/animal_totem/dictionary/ladybugs

**GODDESS MAGICK**
A more comprehensive bibliography and reference guide can be found in; Gathering for Goddess, a Complete Manual for Priestessing Women's Circles. By B.Melusine Mihaltses -ISBN #978-09851384-4-8
Feminine Divine Works, Texas, U.S.A.

Living Goddess Spirituality, a Feminine Divine Priestessing Handbook, By B.Melusine Mihaltses
-ISBN #978-09851384-7-9
Feminine Divine Works, Texas, U.S.A.

Goddess Grimoire Journal, A Collection of Simple Prose and Spells  By B.Melusine Mihaltses
ISBN #978-0-9851384-3-1
Feminine Divine Works, Texas, U.S.A.

## ARCHANGELS, FAERIES AND ELEMENTALS
The Real World of Faeries
By Dora Van Gelder
The Theosophical Publishing House
Wheaton Illinois
India
London, England
Copyright 1977

Gathering for Goddess, a Complete Manual for Priestessing Women's Circles. By B.Melusine Mihaltses
-ISBN #978-09851384-4-8
Feminine Divine Works, Texas,U.S.A.

Living Goddess Spirituality, a Feminine Divine Priestessing Handbook, By B.Melusine Mihaltses
-ISBN #978-09851384-7-9
Feminine Divine Works, Texas, U.S.A.

http://www.Greatdreams.com/archangels.htm
www.catholic that org
www.angel focus.com

## HOLIDAYS & SABBATS
Gathering for Goddess, a Complete Manual for Priestessing Women's Circles. By B.Melusine Mihaltses
-ISBN #978-09851384-4-8
Feminine Divine Works, Texas, U.S.A.

## SOUND TOOLS
Vibrational Powers, Sound,
Healing, Singing Bowls,

*The Sacred Magic Of Abramelin The Mage, By MacGregors-Mathers (1949)*

## VISUAL TOOLS
## MANDALAS & YANTRAS
The Mandala Book: Patterns Of The Universe
By Lori Bailey Cunningham,
Sterling Publishing, New York, New York, 2010 Edition

## MANTRAS
Healing Mantras,
Using Sound Affirmations for Personal Power,
Creativity and Healing
By Thomas Ashley-Farrand
Ballantine Wellspring
The Ballantine Publishing Group
New York New York
Copyright 1999

Source: Mirabaihelperyoutube channel and http://Sanskrit mantra.com, LilaSakuraYoutube Channel,

Sarsawati; the Goddess of learning
By Stephen-Knapp.com and Riversaraswati,gsbkerala.com
Wikipedia.org..

## PRAYER BEADS
http://www.Mandalatrading.com/mala-beads
http://www.prayerbeadsworld.com
http://www.sunlotus.com/symbolism.html
http://www.shambhala.com/books/buddhism/tibetan.html
http://www.tibetanmalashop.com
http://www.destination.com/meaning _of_beads
http://www.prayerbeadsstore.com

## TALISMANS AND AMULETS
The Complete Book of Amulets And Talisman
By Migene Gonzalez-Wippler
Llewellyn Worldwide
Woodberry Minnesota
Copyright 1991
The 11$^{th}$ Printing 2009

http;//ezinearticles.com/?Talisman-and-Amulet,-Is-There-a-Difference?id=5307570

## ANCIENT OCCULT SOURCE
*Talismanic Magic/The Tables of Planets/Squares Is Attribute*
*Abbot Trithemius, Peter De Abano,  Cornelius Agrippa*
*Various Ancient Grimoires,*
*Clavicle/The Key Of Solomon, Son Of David, (Ba 2346-2348)*
*Secrets Of Albertus Magnus By Bishop Of Ratisbon*
*Fourth Book Of Occult Philosophy, Cornelius Agrippa, (Bm Slo.3850, Etc)*
*(Treatise)The Magus; The Celestial Intelligencer, By Francis Barrett (1801)*
*19$^{th}$ Cent French Occultist History Of Magic, By Eliphas Levi*

Mandala: Luminous Symbols for healing 10$^{th}$ Anniversary edition by Judith Cornell,
Squares and Planetary Tablets, Veve, Sigils & Symbols,
The Complete Book of Amulets And Talisman
By Migene Gonzalez-Wippler
Llewellyn Worldwide, Woodberry Minnesota
Copyright 1991, The 11$^{th}$ Printing 2009

## VISION BOARDS
http;//christinekane.com/how-to-make-a-vision-board/
http;//m.psychologytoday.com/blog/the-blame-game/201205/throw-away-your-vision-board-O
http;//minetteriordan.com/what-is-soulcollage/
http;//soul-paths.com/what-is-soulcollage/
Creative Visualization by Shakti Gawain

## TAROT- MAJOR ARCANA'S JOURNEY & MINOR ARCANA
Easy Tarot Guide by Marcia Marcino,
ACS Publications, SanDiego, CA, 1997 Eighth edition

Tarot Power, 22 Keys to Unlocking Magick, Spellcraft, and Meditation by Lexa Rosean,
Citadel Press. Kensington Publishing Corp.
New York, New York 2005 edition

Tarot Spells by Janina Renee,
Llewellyn Publications,
A Division of Llewellyn Worldwide, Ltd,
St. Paul, MN, 10th edition 1996

The Tarot,
Art, Mysticism, and Divination
By Sylvie Simon
Crescent Books, Distributed by Outlet Book Company,
New York, New York
Edition 1991

## PHYSICAL TOOLS AND OUR ORACLE BODY
Chakra Work Out,
Balancing Your Energy with Yoga and Meditation
By Maryhorsley
Sterling Publishing Co Incorporated
NYC In New York
Copyright 2007

The Crystal Handbook,
By Kevin Sullivan
An Armadillo Press Book
Signet/Penguin Group Publishing
New York New York
Copyright 1987

## MUDRA
Mudras; Yoga in Your Hands by Gertrud Hirschi.

Healing Mudras: Yoga for your Hands by Sabrina Mesko.
Power Mudras: Yoga hand Postures for Women by Sabrina Mesko.
Ballantine Wellspring Publishing, New York, New York,
First edition 2000

The Healing Power of Mudras by Rajendra Menen.
Yoga of Light-Meditations,
Mudras and Expressions of the Divine Feminine,
DVD, Featuring Sharron Rose

*Mudras; Yoga in Your Hands by Gertrud Hirschi.*

*Healing Mudras: Yoga for your Hands by Sabrina Mesko.
Power Mudras: Yoga hand Postures for Women by Sabrina Mesko.*

## YOGA
Maharishi-mahesh-th-promoter-of-transcendental meditation
www. swamij..com/history-yoga. htm
www. yoga learning center.com/articles/short_history
en. wikipedia.org/wiki/history_of_yoga
www.anahatayoga.info

Kundalini Yoga, The Flow of Eternal Power, A simple Guide to Yoga Awareness by Shakti Parwha Kaur Khalsa
Perigee Books, a Division of Penguin Putnan Inc,
New York, New York,
First edition 1996

The Complete Illustrated Book of Yoga,
by Swami Vishnudevananda,
Bell Publishing Company, Inc. New York, New York
First edition 1960

Yoga Journal. a Magazine periodical, published 9 times per year since 1975

Vegetarian Times, Eat Green, Live Well- a Magazine periodical

Learn How to Use Astanga Yoga & Meditation
by Jean Hall and Doriel Hall
Hermes House Publishing,an imorint of
Anness Publishing, ltd, London, UK
edition 2007

## SEX MAGICK
MODERN and sex magick; secrets of erotic spirituality by Donnell Michael Kraig

www.auntyflo.com/magic/sex/
www.ladymorgana.com

The Best of the Equinox, Sex Magick, Aleister Crowley (1875-1947), Weiser Books, San Francisco, CA, 2013 edition
The Book of the Law, Aleister Crowley (1875-1947), Weiser Books, San Francisco, CA, 2011 edition

## GEMSTONES & CRYSTALS
www. crystal-cure.com/gemstones3.html
www.old-earth.com/meaning-amber.html
www. gemstonebuzz.com/meaning/amber
www.astrobix.com/astroblog/post/charoite-gemstone.com
www.crystal vaults.com/crystal-encyclopedia/charoite
www. gemstoneadvisor lapis lazuli
www.crystalcure.com/suglite.html
www.pixiecrystals.com/summary.php/sugalite.com
www. gemstoneadvisor jasper
www. crystal-cure.com/jade-african.html

www.jademeaning.com
www.gemstonemeanings.us/jade-stone-meaning
www. gemstonegifts.com/smokey-quartz.com
www.blog.friendlycrystals.com/gemstone-meanings/smokeyquartz.com
www. gemstoneadvisor.com
www.fengshui.about.com
www. crystal-cure.com/kunzite.html
www.crystal-cure.com/gemstone-meanings.html
www.gemstonemeanings.us/pink-kunzite-meaning
www.gemstoneadvisor.com/gemstone-meaning
www. gemstonemeanings.us/peridot-stone-meaning
www.bloodstonemeaning.com
www.gemstone-dictionary.com/serpentine

Hay House Publishing, Carlsbad, CA,

The Essential Law of Attraction collection, by Esther and Jerry Hicks, The Teachings of Abraham,
Hay House Publishing, Carlsbad, CA, 2013 edition

Healing Crystals and Gemstones, From Amethyst to Zircon,
Dr. Flora Peschek-Bohmer, Gisela Schreiber
Konecky & Konecky, Old Saybrook, CT, 2002 edition

**CHANNELING EMBODYING SPIRIT**
Channeling into the new age-
that teachings of Shirley MacCLaine and other such gurus by Martin Gardner, Prometheus books, Amherst New York, 1988
Voices from beyond;-the age old mystery of channeling,
 in the fringes of reason by Ted Schulz, Harmony books New York New York, 1989

**LAW OF ATTRACTION & FINAL THOUGHT**
"The Game of Life and How To Play It" by Florence Scovel Shinn
"How To Live Life And Love It" by Genevieve Behrend
"Life Power and How To Use It" by Elizabeth Towne

Ask and it is Given by Esther and Jerry Hicks, The Teachings of Abraham, Hay House Publishing, Carlsbad, CA,

Getting into the Vortex: Guided Meditations Audio
by Esther and Jerry Hicks, The Teachings of Abraham

**B. Melusine Mihaltses** is a Certified life coach, a Published author, intuit artist, Priestess, writer and a Woman's group facilitator. She is also a classically trained singer, holding both a Bachelors and a Masters of Music in Vocal Pedagogy. From an early age she expressed and exemplified a passionate creative, artistic soul and her spirituality has always been steeped and deeply intertwined in her numerous creative expressions. She is a Goddess priestess, dedicated to the intense study of various goddesses from around the world and her commitment to understanding their positive influence on women is undeniable. As founder and priestess of, **Grove of that Feminine Divine**, one of the few all-women's Goddess group in Texas, she has been an active promoter of woman's empowerment and an advocate for women reclaiming their power and returning to their Goddess gifts. She Coaches her private clients weekly and monthly, she organizes beautiful gatherings in her home temple to encourage sisterhood, commemorate the changing seasons and honor various notable deities significant in every woman's journey. These celebratory gatherings are a testament of her love and devotion to her gender's empowerment and the immortal Sacred Feminine. Her first book, **"Gatherings for Goddess, a Complete Manual for Priestessing Women's Circles,"** holds her priestessing journey, invaluable lessons and precious experiences through-out the creation, nurturance and sustenance of this group. It is a treasure trove of insight for anyone heeding the call to promote community, wommin's Circles and Goddess Spirituality. In her other published books; **Goddess Grimoire Journal, a Collection of Simple Prose and Spells,"** and **"Living Goddess Spirituality, a Feminine Divine Priestessing Handbook,"** she continues to share her vast research on Goddess mythologies, her inspiring words, artistic creative expressions and her unique journey as a Priestess. They are available on Amazon, her FeminineDivineWorks Etsy page and you can also learn more about her books at http://femininedivineworks.wix.com/femininedivineworks.

As a Goddess Gathering Women's group Facilitator and a private life coach, she incorporates her training as a Certified Life Coach to help women. Her mission in life is to fully support and empower women to reshape their lives and reclaim their inherent gifts through a more Feminine exalting tradition found in Goddess Spirituality. You can learn more about her Life Coaching Practice at www.Goddessempowermentlifecoaching.com.

Growing up in New York City afforded her many opportunities for Spiritual growth and knowledge. She was exposed to numerous learning venues, women's circles and greater opportunities to further her occult studies. In these numerous wommin circles, B. Melusine unearth great magick, empowerment, healing, sisterhood and an ancient way of being that resonated deeply with her core beliefs. A student at The Source of Life and at the New York Open Center, she studied tarot with renowned psychic/tarot reader Patti Canova. She also participated in numerous seminars on spiritual matters, drumming circles and rituals. She participated in open Sabbat rituals held by thealogian Susan Marie Hellerer, DMIV, lectures by Margot Adler, author of *"Drawing Down the Moon"* and Phyllis Currott, author of *"Book of Shadows"* & *"Witch Crafting"* and HP of Temple of Ara. At the Learning Annex she took classes on traditional magick, tarot and participated in lectures and rituals held by Donna Limoge, co-author of *"Sexual Bewitchery and other Ancient Feminine Wiles."* She was part of a yearlong Pagan Grove study, at New York City's emblematic "Enchantments, Inc." and at the Zodiac Lounge, on the upper Westside, she was a member of The Zodiac Lounge Women's Circle, an all-female Goddess centered group led by High Priestess Jezibell. At "Crystal Quilt," in

Manhattan, N.Y.C. she participated in a weekly, all female circle, advocating the tradition of – "Wise-Woman Healing Ways" and it was facilitated by Robin Rose Bennett, a well-known Herbologist, student of Susun Weed, Green-Witch and author of *"Healing Magic; A Greenwitch's Guide Book."* It was in these early precious Wommin's circles, amongst some of the most amazing powerful teachers and sisters (*"all of us were hungry for wisdom, healing and knowledge,"* she remembers) that her life started to shift in ways she had not anticipated. These circles along with the numerous female centered Goddess literatures she was being exposed to like; Shekhinah Mountainwater, Z. Budapest, Marion Weinstein, Ffiona Morgan, Diane Stein, all sparked a greater interest in Women's spirituality. These early Goddess and wommin centered groups enriched her life greatly and in the presence of such great teachers, facilitators and priestesses, she was privileged to learn a great deal about how to formulate groups and circles that nurture Women's spirituality.

Mrs. Mihaltses also participated in several Goddess Gatherings sojourns; traveling to San Jose California, to attend the 2008 Goddess Gathering, where she finally met and was initiated by beloved founder of the Feminist Dianic Wiccan tradition, Z. Budapest. The following year, she traveled to Madison, Wisconsin to attend yet another important Dianic event.
This time B. Melusine partook of Dianic Author and songstress, Ruth Barrett's Daughter of Diana. She attended this annual Goddess Gathering and here, she continued to expand her ritual experiences and knowledge of Goddess and Women Spirituality.

In the autumn of 2013, B. Melusine Mihaltses was a presenter for Goddess Spirit Rising, 2013 International Goddess Conference, held in Malibu, California. Early summer of 2013, B. Melusine Mihaltses was the recipient of "The Shift Network Team Scholarship" for additional studies on Women Leadership and Spirituality. This scholarship was offered to her for participation and further course studies in the, *"Soulful Women Rising, Living your Soul's calling to Co-create a New World,"* taught by Devaa Haley Mitchell and Elayne Kalila Doughty, the founders of, "Inspiring Women Summit." With this training she intends to enhance her work as a Priestess and Life coach for women and hopes to be of greater service in her Spirituality community.

A native New Yorker, B. Melusine is mother of three, handfasted and married for over fourteen years and is now making her home in the south of Texas. Currently she is working on the release of her debut recording of original Pagan Goddess chants and her fifth book. Along with her published books, you can also find her unique creations, her special Oracle card creations and Intuit-Goddess-Art on canvases at, http://www.femininedivineworks.com and information on her Life Coaching services at http://www.Goddessempowermentlifecoaching.com.

**Author, B. Melusine Mihaltses,** C.L.C., M.M., B.M.

# FEMININE DIVINE WORKS
## COMPANY ORDER FORM
# FEMININE DIVINE WORKS

We are a Woman affirming, Goddess exalting company, dedicated to the Sacred Feminine and all works created with a Goddess, Feminist Wiccan message. We offer heart & hand-birthed creations that promote Goddess and Women Spirituality. Our mission is to support and awaken women to their own inner Goddess and empower them to embrace their inherent gifts through our numerous offerings.

*Dear friends,*

Thank you for your interest in our growing company and our various tools that facilitate spiritual growth. We have many more helpful products available for our wonderful patrons. Below we have provided an order form with some of our current offerings for sale. Please feel free to utilize this form to place orders or contact us; either by email, social networks, our blog or website, mailing address or Phone. Thank you again for your support, we look forward to being of service to you.

## ORDER FORM

1. Living Goddess Spirituality, retail $19.99 — $18.00 qty___ _____
2. Goddess Grimoire Journal, retail $16.99 — $15.00 qty___ _____
3. Gathering for Goddess Manual, retail $26.99 — $25.00 qty___ _____
4. Feminine Divine Works Intuitive Oracle Book retail $20.99 — $20.00 qty___ _____
5. Goddess Gathering T-Shirts (s, m, l) retail $15.99 — $11.00 qty___ _____
6. ****Original Artwork by the Author *(Please contact, price varies)*

7. Meditation Recordings by Author, retail $15.99 — $11.00 qty___ _____
8. Goddess Songs Music CD Recording, retail $15.99 — $11.00 qty___ _____
9. Feminine Divine Works Intuitive Oracle **70x CARD DECK** — $50.00 qty___ _____
   _____

SPECIAL COUPON CODES FOR DISCOUNTS — Code___ _____
20% discount for purchases of 3 or more items: — Disc___ _____
Shipping and Handling (3.95 per item): — qty___ _____

Shipping:_____

SHIPPING TO:
_____
_____ ORDER TOTAL:_____
Please enclose Payment and this Order form in an envelope.
PAYMENT ENCLOSED_____
ORDER STATUS:_____

**FEMININE DIVINE WORKS**
P.O. Box 114, Schertz, Texas 78154-0114
Femininedivineworks@gmail.com
Visit our WEBSITE at: http://www.Femininedivineworks.com

www.ingramcontent.com/pod-product-compliance
Lightning Source LLC
Chambersburg PA
CBHW082315230426
43667CB00034B/2738